T0260163

Artificial Intelligence for Renewable Energy and Climate Change

Scrivener Publishing
100 Cummings Center, Suite 541J
Beverly, MA 01915-6106

Publishers at Scrivener
Martin Scrivener (martin@scrivenerpublishing.com)
Phillip Carmical (pcarmical@scrivenerpublishing.com)

Artificial Intelligence for Renewable Energy and Climate Change

Edited by

Pandian Vasant
Gerhard-Wilhelm Weber
Joshua Thomas
José Antonio Marmolejo-Saucedo
and
Roman Rodriguez-Aguilar

Scrivener
Publishing

WILEY

This edition first published 2022 by John Wiley & Sons, Inc., 111 River Street, Hoboken, NJ 07030, USA and Scrivener Publishing LLC, 100 Cummings Center, Suite 541J, Beverly, MA 01915, USA
© 2022 Scrivener Publishing LLC
For more information about Scrivener publications please visit www.scrivenerpublishing.com.

Wiley Global Headquarters
111 River Street, Hoboken, NJ 07030, USA

For details of our global editorial offices, customer services, and more information about Wiley products visit us at www.wiley.com.

Limit of Liability/Disclaimer of Warranty
While the publisher and authors have used their best efforts in preparing this work, they make no representations or warranties with respect to the accuracy or completeness of the contents of this work and specifically disclaim all warranties, including without limitation any implied warranties of merchantability or fitness for a particular purpose. No warranty may be created or extended by sales representatives, written sales materials, or promotional statements for this work. The fact that an organization, website, or product is referred to in this work as a citation and/or potential source of further information does not mean that the publisher and authors endorse the information or services the organization, website, or product may provide or recommendations it may make. This work is sold with the understanding that the publisher is not engaged in rendering professional services. The advice and strategies contained herein may not be suitable for your situation. You should consult with a specialist where appropriate. Neither the publisher nor authors shall be liable for any loss of profit or any other commercial damages, including but not limited to special, incidental, consequential, or other damages. Further, readers should be aware that websites listed in this work may have changed or disappeared between when this work was written and when it is read.

Library of Congress Cataloging-in-Publication Data

ISBN 9781119768999

Cover images: Pixabay.com
Cover design by Russell Richardson

Set in size of 11pt and Minion Pro by Manila Typesetting Company, Makati, Philippines

Printed in the USA

10 9 8 7 6 5 4 3 2 1

Contents

Section II: Climate Change   171

Preface

Our novel book offer was accepted by *Scrivener Publishing* for its broadly appealing, meaningful and timely properties and its promise on a world-wide stage. Thereto, also its analytical and applied characteristics contributed. This compendium and handbook together with our inquiries on renewable energy, on generation and distribution, supply and use of power are remarkable incentives which could become scholarly resources that investigate the efficient usage of contemporary electrical resources and natural renewable sources. These ought to have a positive effect on sustainable development in our urban and rural regions, in sea and sky, hence, for agility and communication, mobility and collaboration, for peace inside and between our peoples and countries, and all of our living beings and everything in the world.

The dynamics of Renewable Energy and Climate Change, and Supply Chain Management (SCM) has transformed and accelerated over the years; paradigms shifted and new ones have emerged and been added to respond to those switching and changing accompanied by an increasing economic, ecologic and social concerns and pressures. In today's international and competitive environment, *Lean* and *Green* practices in economies are most important determinants to increase the performances. Corresponding production philosophies and techniques help companies to advance their performances in terms of diminishing lead times and costs of manufacturing, to improve delivery on time and quality, at the same time becoming more ecological by reducing material use and waste, and by recycling and reusing. Those lean and green activities enhance productivity, lower carbon footprint and improve consumer satisfaction, which in reverse makes firms competitive and sustainable.

In previous decades, interest and awareness about clean energy have exponentially grown, together with a steadily growing concern about our natural neighborhoods and habitats, and about our well-being and health, our resources and atmosphere, our spaces and times. This progress has also been due to a reduction in the cost of both installed capacity of converters and generated energy. Such successes stories were possible by advances in modern technologies for the converter production, enhancements in efficiency in use of energy incoming, optimization of converter operation and data analysis based on records during the system operations with the chances of production planning.

From our editorial sides, this handbook was hoped to become a most valuable reference book from 2021 onwards in the areas of modern renewable energy and climate change by the help of Operational Research (OR), Artificial Intelligence (AI), Creative Arts and Sciences. Given all the hard work from the authors' and our sides, the research and application project has become successful in gathering and integrating emerging findings and outcomes of the state-of-the-art and inventions about and electronic and electrical, energetic and informational, recoverable and renewable, creational and recreational sources and their swift and mobile usages with care and responsibility. Now, the thus given work and compendium of scientific investigation on questions of renewable power and energy supply for cities and rural areas is a remarkable scholarly treasure which discloses the efficient employment of those modern-times resources that have a helpful influence on sustainable development of our megalopolises and our countryside, hence on migratory movements into big cities and eventually on social peace in and among our peoples.

For this book's international orientation it has turned into a unique resource that outlines newest progress achieved around the globe in related domains of OR, AI, renewable power, electronical, informational and transformational technologies. It is on the way of becoming accepted and classical at a worldwide stage because of its comprehensive contents ensured by analytical, applied and life-friendly approaches towards the whole creation.

Artificial Intelligence for Renewable Energy and Climate Change, is a hand-picked collection of creative research on and with methods and applications of mathematics, machine and deep learning (ML and DL) in the realms of business and management, economics and finance, natural sciences and engineering. While featuring topics including data-hybridization, computational modeling, and artificial neural networks, this book is designed and suitable for engineers and IT experts, analysts and data scientists, engineers and investigators, academicians and philanthropes, policy makers and caretakers, experienced ones and the youth, for whoever seeks for contemporary research on Intelligent Optimization in emerging smart-technological, energetic, environmental and creative industries.

The rise in population and the concurrently growing consumption rate necessitates the evolution of clean energy systems to adopt current analytic and computational technologies such as big-data, IoTs and 5G technology to increase production at a faster and smoother scale. While existing technologies may help in energy processing, there is a need for studies that seek to understand how modern approaches like OR, AI, ML, DL, hybrid technologies and advancements in mathematics can aid to sustain clean energy and climate change processes while utilizing energy sources efficiently and productively.

This book on *Artificial Intelligence for Renewable Energy and Climate Change* is an essential publication that examines the benefits and barriers of implementing computational models to clean energy systems, global warming, climate change, and energy sources as well as how these models can produce more cost-effective and sustainable solutions. Featuring coverage on a wide range of topics such as classical and nature-inspired optimization and optimal control, hybrid and stochastic systems, this book is ideally designed for engineers, scientists, industrialist, academicians, researchers, computer and information technologists, sustainable developers, managers, environmentalists, government leaders, research officers, policy makers, business leaders and students. This book aims to become a delight for practitioners in the fields of sustainable and renewable energy sustainability and their outstanding impacts on how to face global warming and climate change.

Invited subjects of this compendium welcome but are not limited to the following:

- o *Artificial intelligence,*
- o *Machine intelligence, Deep intelligence,*
- o *Metaheuristic algorithms,*
- o *Hydropower, Renewable electricity, Solar PV, Bio power,*
- o *Geothermal power, Ocean power, Wind power,*
- o *Bio-gas, Hydrogen,*
- o *Global warming, Climate change,*
- o *Renewable energy,*
- o *Hybrid technology,*
- o *CO_2 minimization,*
- o *Evolutionary algorithms, Swarm intelligence,*
- o *Computational intelligence, Soft computing,*
- o *Operational research, Data mining, Hybrid optimization,*
- o *Bioenergy Recycling, Biofuel supply chains,*
- o *Energy management policy, Energy efficiency, Energy-saving technology,*
- o *Small hydropower plants, Thermal treatments,*

- *Remote sensing,*
- *Optimization theory and applications,*
- *Optimal control theory and applications,*
- *Stochastic optimal control theory and applications.*

This book is grouped into 2 parts, namely: *Section I* – Renewable Energy, and *Section II* - Climate Change.

Subsequently, we provide a short introduction of the fourteen chapters of this work.

In the first chapter *"Artificial Intelligence for Sustainability: Opportunities and Challenges"*, the author *Amany Alshawi* focuses on AI in the sustainable practices across the environmental sector and related industries. AI uses tools and methods such as ML effective monitoring and prediction. A main establishment is on AI opportunities and multiple multilevel systemic approaches to systems in designing new techniques while considering the psychological and sociological factors as well as the economic values.

The second chapter *"Recent Applications of Machine Learning In Solar Energy Prediction"*, authored by *N. Kapilan, R. P. Reddy* and *Vidhya P*, among the renewable energy sources addresses solar energy which is preferred as its potential is high. But there are few challenges due to variability and uncertainty with solar radiation which results in lower energy conversion, intermittent power supply. They discuss basic concepts of solar energy, energy conversion methods and different types of ML used in solar photovoltaic systems, ML algorithms, challenges and opportunities in solar energy production.

In the third chapter called *"Mathematical Analysis on Power Generation – Part I"*, the author *G. Udhaya Sankar* addresses Seebeck and Peltier effects which are used to generate current and heat in a thermocouple, respectively; current from heat and heat from current. It is possible to produce light from electricity and electricity from light. They are the basics for theory of photovoltaic theory. The author derives a formula providing a linear relationship between product of current with voltage and heat in a thermocouple.

The fourth chapter named *"Mathematical Analysis on Power Generation – Part II"*, authored by *G. Udhaya Sankar*, states that is no exact analytic formula which is applicable for conversion of voltage to temperature for thermocouple-temperature sensors, even though there are theories and equations for thermocouples. However, it is possible to get approximate localized as well as approximate globalized polynomial formulas.

The fifth chapter called as *"Sustainable Energy Materials"* by *G. Udhaya Sankar* refers to Co-Precipitation, Microwave assisted Solvothermal and Sol-Gel methods which are chosen for investigation of the Zn-CuO nanoparticles in energy harvesting. The synthesized nanoparticles are examined by different characterization. Energy harvesting applications depend on thermal conductivity, electrical conductivity, Seebeck coefficient, power factor, and figure of merit.

In the sixth chapter *"Optimization of Hybrid Wind and Solar Renewable Energy System by Iteration Method"*, the authors *Diriba Kajela Geleta* and *Mukhdeep Singh Manshahia* is concerned with integration of knowledge, techniques and methodologies from many complementary AI tools for solving complex problems. A combination of intelligent controllers with adaptiveness appears as most promising in practical implementation and control of electrical drives. The authors briefly describe different MPPT techniques with main focus on FL, ANN and Neuro fuzzy methods.

The seventh chapter named *"The Contribution of AI-Based Approaches in The Determination of CO_2 Emission Gas Amounts of Vehicles, Determination of CO_2 Emission Rates Yearly of Countries, Air Quality Measurement and Determination of Smart Electric Grids Stability"*, authored by *Mesut Togacar*, states that it is now possible to provide automatic control of systems which can harm the environment with AI-based technologies. Four datasets are used. He employs long short-term memory (LSTM), bidirectional LSTM, convolutional neural network (CNN), CNN-based LSTM model, and recurrent neural network (RNN).

In the eighth chapter called *"Performance Analysis and Effects of Dust & Temperature on Solar PV Module System By Using Multivariate Linear Regression Model"*, the authors *Sumit Sharma, Ashish Nayyar* and *Vivek Pandey* experimentally collected operating and electrical performance parameters of SPV array. The data were used for the calculation of the CUF, PR, and power conversion efficiency of the SPV systems. A multivariate linear regressions (MLR) model is established to estimate the system's output performance with the consideration of conversion efficiency as the dependent variable, and ambient temperature and dust exposure day as the independent variables.

In the ninth chapter *"Evaluation of In-House Compact Biogas Plant Thereby Testing Four Stroke Single Cylinder Diesel Engine"*, the authors *Pradeep Kumar Meena, Sumit Sharma, Amit Pal* and *Samsher* investigate the usefulness of wastages caused by metropolitans and cities to produce biogas. They perform a comprehensive analysis of compact biogas plant in terms of its temperature, pH value, and efficiency for different kinds of wastages such as kitchen waste, fruits waste, animal dung and sugar as a catalyst, in view to increase production efficiency of biogas. Furthermore, a 4-stroke single cylinder diesel engine is tested by using dual fuel.

In the tenth chapter called *"Low-Temperature Combustion Technologies for Emission Reduction in Diesel Engines"*, the authors *Amit Jhalania, Sumit Sharma, Pushpendra Kumar Sharma* and *Digambar Singh* state that Diesel engines are lean burn engines; hence CO and HC emissions do not occur in substantial amounts in diesel exhaust. Emissions of serious concern in compression ignition engines are particulate matter and nitrogen oxides because of elevated temperature conditions of the combustion zone. They critically review the literature on low-temperature combustion conditions using various conventional and alternative fuels.

The eleventh chapter called as *"Efficiency Optimization of Indoor Air Disinfection by Radiation Exposure for Poultry breeding Rational for Microclimate Systems Modernization for Livestock Premises"* by *Dovlatov Igor Mamedjarevich* and *Yurochka Sergey Sergeevich* state that in I, II and III climatic zones of Russia, where the winter temperature reaches -18°C and the average wind velocity makes up to 3.6 m/s, the majority of farmers use no means of forced ventilation in cowsheds because they are energy-consuming. Due to the gas composition, the cows' productivity and the milk quality fall. In the course of both theoretical and experimental researches on a dairy farm in Moscow region, diverse results were obtained.

The twelfth chapter named *"Improving the Efficiency of Photovoltaic Installations for Sustainable Development of the Urban Environment"*, authored by *Pavel Kuznetsov, Leonid Yuferev* and *Dmitry Voronin*, presents research carried out at existing solar power plants and laboratory renewable energy sources purposed to increase the energy efficiency of photovoltaic installations with parallel and mixed switching of photocells, operating under uneven illumination, parallel voltage arrays of photovoltaic modules due to voltage equalization. They see the creation of a methodology for parametric optimization of power plants operating from renewable energy sources that contribute to the sustainable development of the urban environment in the context of digital transformation as an extremely important area of further research.

The thirteenth chapter named *"Monitoring System Based Micro-Controller for Biogas Digester"*, authored by *Ahmed Abdelouareth* and *Mohamed Tamal*, report that telemetry provides an additional ability to the measurement system by taking advantage of the transmission of the measured values through the local network or the Internet. They propose to control the process by measuring the state parameters of an anaerobic- methane is generated by the fermentation of waste deposited in the reactor. The system is all open-source hardware and software.

In the fourteenth chapter *"Greenhouse Gas Statistics and Methods of Combating Climate Change"*, the author *Tatyana G. Krotova* informs that economic growth in China has caused an unexampled surge in carbon dioxide emissions. The author sets the task to find out the sources of environmental pollution entailing climate warming and simulates an econometric model to calculate the values of statistical indicators required for the level-down of environmental pollution.

We as the *editors* wish that the chosen fields and selected topics of this book represent a core selection of global investigations coping with upcoming and complicated, occasionally long-lasting challenges and needs of *Intelligent Optimization* and their domains in *Renewable Energy and Climate Change*, with approaches, techniques and results of Operational Research and Artificial Intelligence. We are very grateful to the publishing house of *Wiley - Scrivener Publishing* for the honor of hosting and featuring our compendium as a pioneering scientific enterprise. Special gratitude is extended to the Editors of the publishing house, and also to Editorial Managers and Staff for their continuous advice and guidance in each and every respect. We say thanks to all the authors for their diligent efforts and generous readiness to share their emerging insights, ideas and smartest inventions with our worldwide community. Now we really wish that the authors' investigations will catalyze, crystalize and initiate cooperation and fruitful progress on a worldwide and exquisite level, as a powerful service to humanity and our entire creation.

The *Guest Editors*:
Pandian Vasant
MERLIN Research Centre, Ton Duc Thang University, Vietnam
E-mail: pvasant@gmail.com

Gerhard-Wilhelm Weber
Poznań University of Technology, Poland
E-mail: gerhard-wilhelm.weber@put.poznan.pl

J. Joshua Thomas
UOW Malaysia; KDU Penang University College, Malaysia
E-mail: jjoshua@kdupg.edu.my

José Antonio Marmolejo-Saucedo
Facultad de IngenierÞa, Universidad Panamericana,
Ciudad de México, Mexico
E-mail: jmarmolejo@up.edu.mx

Roman Rodriguez-Aguilar
Facultad de IngenierÞa, Universidad Panamericana,
Ciudad de México, Mexico
E-mail: rrodrigueza@up.edu.mx

Section I
RENEWABLE ENERGY

Artificial Intelligence for Sustainability: Opportunities and Challenges

Amany Alshawi

Communication and Information Technology Research Institute, King Abdulaziz City for Science and Technology (kacst), Riyadh, Saudi Arabia

Abstract

This chapter focuses on Artificial Intelligence (AI) and its application in sustainable practices across the environmental sector and all related industries. AI uses tools and methods such as machine learning for effective monitoring and prediction. The AI shift from the traditional energy resources such as coal, natural gas and fossil fuel-derived energy to the more green, sustainable and less carbon emitting energy resource will be the highlight of this chapter. The study will focus on AI and how it will facilitate and foster environmental governance. It has been established that there will be challenges as well as opportunities for businesses as well as societies in the incorporation of AI for sustainability. The research will highlight the opportunities which AI has in the current scenarios and the challenges it needs to address. The main establishment will be the opportunities which AI is going to offer. It will further offer multiple multilevel systemic approaches to the systems in designing new techniques while considering the psychological and sociological factors as well as the economic values.

Keywords: Artificial intelligence, renewable energy, machine learning, sustainable, sustainability, carbon

1.1 Introduction

Artificial intelligence (AI) has been transforming the manner of business operations in the industrial sector. Its encouraging prospect has reached

Email: AALSHAWI@KACST.EDU.SA

Pandian Vasant, Gerhard-Wilhelm Weber, Joshua Thomas, José Antonio Marmolejo-Saucedo and Roman Rodriguez-Aguilar (eds.) Artificial Intelligence for Renewable Energy and Climate Change, (3–32) © 2022 Scrivener Publishing LLC

the point where it can solve major societal issues. One of the major issues is related to the sustainability of the environment and the natural resources. Dereliction of the natural atmosphere and climate change have been increasingly complicated concepts which need extensive research as well as innovative and groundbreaking solutions [1]. With the aim of catalyzing the revolutionary research and practical implementation of AI is bringing more environmental sustainability, it is well supported and claimed by researches that AI can provide sustenance to culturally motivated administrations as well as corporate practices in reducing the consumption and disruption of the natural resource and energy resources while carrying out day-to-day functions and other matters of human life [2].

The exact and meaningful significance of AI is not only related to the fact that it will enable society to reduce its consumption of energy, water, and land and create moderation in the intensity of usage. AI will further focus on how to facilitate and foster environmental governance. It has been established that there will be challenges as well as opportunities for businesses as well as societies in incorporation of AI in sustainability practices [3]. Some comprehensive challenges to note before going into the details are the excessive dependence on the previous data collected through the machine learning models as well as the lack of trust in the human behavioral reactions to AI-based intermediations. It came to light that the increase in cybersecurity risks has been one of the major issues increasing the adverse effects of AI applications on sustainability practices. The complications in analyzing the impacts of interventions posed by AI have further complicated the implementation of AI strategies in the sustainability practices across businesses [4].

While it has been established that there are many opportunities which AI is going to offer, it will further offer multiple multilevel systemic approaches to the systems in designing new techniques while considering the psychological and sociological factors as well as the economic values. The main aim of having long-term effects of AI-based solution in deriving sustainability as well as their immediate effects still poses questions over the opportunities that it offers [5].

1.2   History of AI for Sustainability and Smart Energy Practices

The history of AI for sustainability and smart energy practices has to be mentioned. AI-driven advancement has been happening for the last 50 years and has been an active part of the construction of experimental

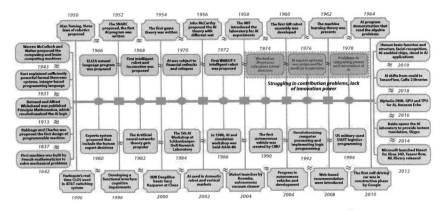

Figure 1.1 History of AI through time [7].

machines to conduct various types of intelligent performance in the energy and manufacturing industry [6]. The history of AI and its practicability in the world was explored by Alan Turing, who is seen as the pioneer of AI. He invented the imitation game, which was later termed the Alan Turning Test. A brief history of AI is shown in Figure 1.1.

AI suffered a bit of a cold period between 1975 and 1980. This also led to the reduction in the funding opportunities for all AI projects. The period 1990-2015 explored the usage of AI in the logistics planning in the US military as well as vertical markets, innovative and creative web designs, face recognition, and integrated online communication applications. Recently, AI has been taken to the next level by integrating it with sustainability practices [5].

1.3   Energy and Resources Scenarios on the Global Scale

The world has undergone a huge change in terms of energy resources, distribution, and usage. There has been a lot of pressure on companies to reduce their carbon emissions and devise proper ways to effectively and sustainably manage the power supply-demand balance in the energy sector. The main aim has been to make sure the shift is made from traditional energy resources such as coal, natural gas and fossil fuel-derived energy to the more green, sustainable and less carbon-emitting energy resource [8].

It has been clear that the world has been deriving most of its energy needs from the traditional energy resources such as coal, crude oil, fossils and natural gas, etc. The share of renewable energy resources in the usage of energy consumption at the global scale was only 17.48% in 2016.

The numbers have increased only slightly in the last four years. With the increase in global per capita income, the increased dependency on fossil fuels for energy usage, such as transportation, which lead to global warming and climate change, have raised more concerns [9].

The greenhouse gas (CO_2) emissions have increased as per the data collected by researchers; from 2015-2020, an average increase of 0.22% has been recorded. Global demand for the usage of the primary energy resources has increased by 2.3% since 2018. This has been supported by the fact that countries like China, USA and India are consuming 70% of the world's energy demand. The cumulative share of renewable energy is estimated to grow from 0.25% to about 45% by 2040. The recent development has not brought much encouragement, since energy crises over the globe have been increasing. Over 120 million people lost direct access to electricity in 2018-2019 [10].

By taking into consideration the vagueness linked to the future of technological advancements, it can be predicted that we will be witnessing much more progress as well as opportunities in the sector for bringing in more sustainability using AI-based solutions. The case of electrical access can be largely resolved by integrating solutions such as AI smart grid that will reduce energy costs and avoid sustained electricity blackouts by linking demand and supply for the countries struggling with an electric crisis [11]. In conclusion, despite the fact that AI will be facing a lot of challenges to be applied in the sustainability practices, it will have many opportunities to be applied across the globe, making it one of the tools for creating cheaper, trustworthy, clean and carbon-free energy resources.

1.4   Statistical Basis of AI in Sustainability Practices

1.4.1   General Statistics

In recent times many companies have been jumping on the bandwagon of implementing AI-based practices in their business solutions. One of the major statistical factors to consider in this case is the cost effectiveness in the energy and utilities sector. Figure 1.2 highlights the reduction in costs owing to AI-based strategies being employed in the industrial sectors [12].

Although there are numerous challenges which have been faced by enterprises in terms of maintaining cost margins and cutting spending, it is important to make sure that all applications offer security and trust in the business processes, variations in the commodity prices, transforming

	A. Projected market size (in $ billion)*	B. Operating expenses as a % of revenue** (in %)	C. Projected operating expenses for the sector (in $ billion) (A*B)
Oil and Gas	11,564.2	54%	6,243.5
Electricity utilities	2,840.4	53%	1,493.9
Water networks	181.9	60%	108.6
Electricity and gas utilities	1,471.1	55%	815.5
Energy services	705.2	54%	379.5

Figure 1.2 Cost savings expected from energy and utilities sector by integrating AI [13].

regulatory policies, and altering demand. Figure 1.3 below shows the energy and utilities organizations in countries implementing AI.

The statistical analysis of AI in recent times showcases many benefits which make it a very effective choice to be implemented in the business sector. The fact that it acts as a catalyst in employing automation and increasing the efficiency of the supply chain processes while bringing more sustainability is one of the major reasons behind its widespread usage. Many industrial sectors are still lagging behind in the wide-scale implementation of AI-based strategies, as is the case with the water utilities [14]. The deployment of automation services and their benefits are shown by Figure 1.4 below.

It has already been established that not all companies embark upon the journey of AI in bringing more sustainability. Companies need to effectively understand the AI initiative before trying it out. Companies have been dealing with a black box issue to a great degree in recent times in the implementation of the AI-based strategies [15].

Furthermore, deeper analysis showed that AI methods will offer environmental advantages much more than just the GHG emissions solutions. This will include the estimation of the environmental effects of the water quality, air pollution, deforestation and biodiversity. It has been established that AI is capable of analyzing satellite data and ground-based sensors data for effective monitoring of real-time forest situations. This allows it to provide early warnings related to the deforestation attempts. In prospect, it is expected to save 32 million hectares of forest from deforestation by 2030. Alongside that, AI-based sensors have been providing safer and accurate numbers for establishing air quality indexes in cities and populated areas to deal with air pollution. It has been estimated that this will save up to 150 million USD on the global scale by 2030. Add to this the significant impact of this achievement in reducing healthcare costs [16]. Figure 1.5 shows how utilizing AI for sustainability will increase GDPs, GHG, and net jobs around the world by 2030.

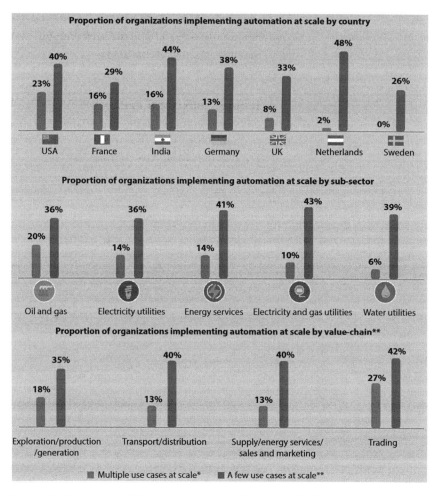

Figure 1.3 Energy and utilities organizations implementing AI [7].

1.4.2   Environmental Stress–Based Statistics

AI can provide sustenance to culturally motivated administrations as well as corporate practices in reducing the consumption and disruption of natural resources and energy consumption. Due to the growth and advancements in scientific analysis, data gathering and modelling has increased over the last few decades, allowing researchers to better evaluate and predict the effects of human growth and associated activities. The outcomes are worrisome, since the increase in the total human footprint is a clear indication of the fact that environmental stress has been rising. The major reasons behind the increase in environmental stress are as follows:

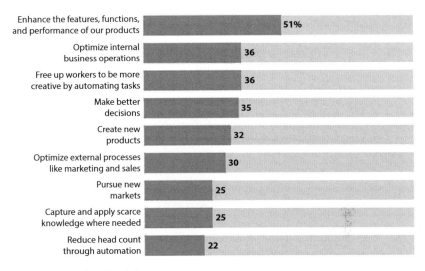

Figure 1.4 Benefits of AI [7].

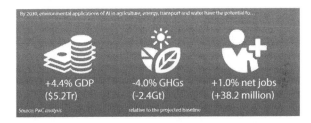

Figure 1.5 AI for sustainability globally until 2030 [17].

1.4.2.1   Climate Change

The increase in the levels of greenhouse gases is worrying scientists and environmental activists across the globe. The major reason behind that increase is attributed to the unsustainable practices carried out by all sectors and most specifically the industrial sector. The level has reached astounding numbers in comparison to previous years. If the recent Paris Agreement terms are taken into consideration, it is estimated that global average temperatures will rise by 3°C in 2100 in comparison to pre-industrial levels. This will be further accompanied by the 1.5C threshold which will be required to avoid the acutest effects of climate change in the future. The integration of AI-based practices will be a way to counter these issues in an effective manner [18].

1.4.2.2   Biodiversity

One of the other major issues which has increased environmental stress and highlighted the need for the persistent use of AI practices in a sustainable manner is the loss of biodiversity. The Earth has lost a lot in terms of biodiversity. The increased number of extinctions of various species has led to a decrease in populations. A sharp decline of 60% has been estimated since 1970. This is alarming since this will be impacting the overall cycle of life as well as sustainability.

1.4.2.3   Deforestation

Scientists have been worried about deforestation, which has been impacting sustainable practices in recent times. Recent deforestation rates have been decreasing. This has impacted the overall deforestation in the areas of the Amazon Basin. Deforestation has been reduced by 8% and is projected to further decrease, which will be accompanied by major regional rainfalls. This will further lead to the condition of a shift, which will form a "savannah state". This state will have more serious and wide-ranging effects on Earth's atmospheric practices. This will impact the overall biodiversity as well as the sustainability of Earth to a great degree [19].

1.4.2.4   Changes in Chemistry of Oceans

The changes and shifts in the chemistry of the oceans has been one of the other leading reasons for the increasing environmental stress levels. The changes in the chemistry of the oceans have produced the most drastic shift in possibly 300 million years. The subsequent acidification and mounting temperatures of the ocean will make an unparalleled impression on corals and fish stocks.

1.4.2.5   Nitrogen Cycle

The world has been dealing with the crisis of the nitrogen cycle in recent times to a great degree. The biggest and speediest influence on the nitrogen cycle has been seen in the last few decades in comparison to the last 2.5 billion years. This can be attributed to the increasing effect of the prevalent nitrogen and phosphate pollution which has been occurring due the usage of fertilizers into the crops and the dumping of chemicals in the seas by factories. The polluted water is used for consumption by sea life as well as for many human activities, which has impacted fish stocks and developed dead zones for sea life and ocean biodiversity in over 10% of the world's oceans. This is an alarming situation and needs to be tackled in the best manner possible. The use of AI for sustainable practices and predictions will help but it will face many challenges [20].

1.4.2.6   Water Crisis

The challenges faced by the global water cycle are unprecedented in recent times due to the actions carried out by the industrial sector. The lack of integration of sustainable practices and modern tools and technologies has been a major factor affecting these practices. The harsh impacts due to over-extraction and unrestrained pollution are the leading contributors to the water crisis on the global scale. AI technologies will be of great aid in this case since it is predicted that the global climate will suffer a further 40% shortfall in the amount of freshwater which will be required to aid the entire global economy in the coming decade. The statistics are alarming to a great degree and need solutions to be introduced at the earliest time.

1.4.2.7   Air Pollution

Industrial practices have been the major contributors to the rise in the levels of air pollutants, which have led to severe case of disease in humans. While over 91% of the world's population is accommodated in areas where the air is dangerous to breathe, as per the standards provided by the World Health Organization (WHO) in its air quality index, the concern is how this matter can be tackled in order to improve conditions for people to live. Human activities are the major contributors impacting Earth in a bad way, and this needs to be addressed. It is urgent that these issues be resolved as quickly as possible [7].

1.5   Major Challenges Faced by AI in Sustainability

1.5.1   Concentration of Wealth

AI has been facing a lot of challenges in recent times; for example, the concentration of wealth and power. Only a few companies are wealthy enough to implement AI on a very large scale; those are the ones who own the technology. The concentration of power and wealth is further limited to such companies and organizations, and the overall sustainability outcomes of the technology cannot be achieved by everyone [21].

In recent times, AI has been mostly limited to a number of large digital companies on the global scale, which include GAFAM24, Baidu, Alibaba, and Tencent. The major reason behind this concentration of power is that these companies have large chunks of propriety data that has led to the phenomenon of oligopoly. Although the sector has much a lower level of competition, it is facing jeopardy because the companies will not share the data with the society or even other companies in the same sector. The increase in price for sharing the data is also a cause of concern in achieving the outcomes of sustainability practices [22].

One major worry which is also a result of concentration of power and wealth is the fact that such organizations will have the capacity to offer high-quality AI services to other organizations using the data and propriety measures. In such cases, when AI is being incorporated as the service in the public sector, its property of being a black box is a major cause of concern for policy makers all over the world. The case of the Los Angeles Police Department announcing that it has been utilizing Amazon's face recognition app (Rekognition) in carrying out policy work raises concerns over bias. The easy manipulation of AI technologies by companies like Amazon raises a concern about whether AI technologies should be closed, shared or open [23].

1.5.2   Talent-Related and Business-Related Challenges of AI

Talent-based restrictions and resistance have been surfacing in AI-based interventions in recent times. The major reason is the lack of skilled and talented people, which makes it almost impossible for a company to implement AI-based practices for suitable actions. The employees also lack the motivation to learn about the technology and its wider implementations. More than 80% of employees seem to accept the idea of new methods while the rest show little or no interest. Although employee satisfaction has been raised by 78%, the decrease in the workforce by 70% is worrying employees about their job security [24]. Organizations have to come up with a proper design and more suitable skill and training strategies in order to accomplish their goals. This will allow them to engage the employees while bridging the gap resulting from lack of talent and skills. Automation of skills is one of the leading hindrances in the successful adoption of AI technologies in many companies [25].

Many companies have been struggling to identify suitable digital skills for their workforce in order to make sure that automation targets are achieved.

A centralized strategy will ensure that companies develop the workforce with the skills which are integral for effective functioning. Most companies at the top level have been employing a centralized or hybrid approach. The dedication of the top-level executives and leadership and the top-down approach in the organizational management focused on sponsoring the employees and their training will be fruitful for the future. AI implementation will only be successful if the automation groups are allowed to work in close collaboration with the team members of the entire business. This will allow the employees

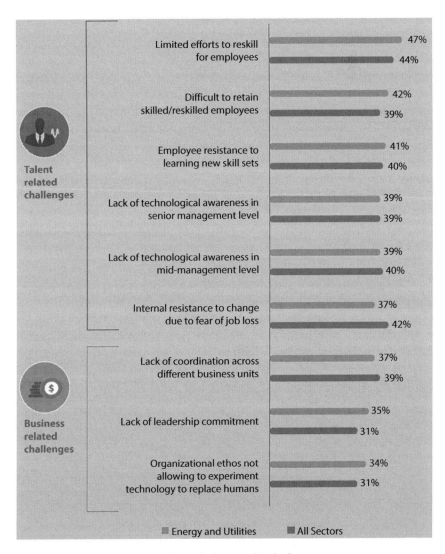

Figure 1.6 Talent- & Business-related challenges of AI [13].

to gain the skills and the momentum to move forward and make sure that AI adoption is very successful as well. Cultural issues and HR issues are the other business-related AI challenges which companies need to address in order to minimize the hindrances faced by the company in successful adoption of AI [13]. Figure 1.6 illustrates the talent and business challenges facing AI applications in sustainability.

1.5.3   Dependence on Machine Learning

One of the major challenges which AI has to face in terms of sustainable operations is the increased dependence on machine learning tools. Machine learning has been used on a wide scale for the development of AI-based practices in sustainability practices on the global scale for a long time. Machine learning is based on patterns and algorithms and it makes use of the linkage between collected data. Correlations are then used in making projections based on the learning practices and techniques. They have been analyzed by various research parties such as the Intergovernmental Panel on Climate Change (IPCC). This sector has been utilizing machine learning algorithms in an integrated manner. It was capable of projecting the probable future setups while enhancing the temperature from 1 °C to 6 °C on the level of the global average temperature [26]. Researchers such as Masson-Delmotte *et al.* have already come up with the idea that establishing standard datasets that utilize the added climate model mechanisms for elevated climate predictions will work wonders in the future for mankind. This is the advantage which can meet the challenges which the sector has been facing in recent times [27].

Buis proposed that the challenges are attributed to the fact that the existence of the past datasets will have inadequate value since past data are a reflection of the ages and climate cycles which existed prior to current human actions and resulted in Earth coming into the Anthropocene era. This development has been coupled with the human-produced climate crisis. Global warming has increased by over 30% as compared to the last three decades due to the higher indulgence in the industrial sector, usage of petroleum and other natural resources for energy as well as overpopulation of urban areas [19]. Human-related activities have been the major element making the entire process a lot more complicated, and this complication has been rolled down to the effective and successful incorporation of machine learning models on the wider scale. The challenge to address here is the increased cases of the unpredictability and the lack of evolution in the field to address the challenges at a better and advanced level. It is critical to implement a deterministic method in which prediction can be effectively and copiously performed, since it is hard to accurately quote the projected climate changes. The incorporation of the stochastic method will allow the intrinsic unpredictability with probabilities for diverse situations and will allow for the making of more theoretical subsequent models [28].

One of the other major issues related to machine learning which has been consistently concerning researchers in recent times is associated with the past datasets its relation to the variance-bias tradeoffs. Machine learning professionals are also favoring the models which are capable of generalizing new data and making use of data for effective prediction. But, since machine learning models are capable of variance by rigorously suiting models to previous data, this highlights the fact that it can easily predict the upcoming scenarios with a lack of accuracy, which is a bigger concern. It cannot provide or guarantee accuracy in predictions of future events of an increasingly robust climatic system [29].

In comparison to the above-mentioned crisis, if the machine learning practices and models are streamlined and are more elevated in terms of the bias, then they will be more than capable of performing adequately in regard to training and test data. Although variance-bias tradeoff is an unbreakable section of machine learning argument, the consequences and repercussions will be more highlighted and prominent in terms of its usage in sustainability solutions. While taking into consideration the climate crisis argument, it has been apparently clear that the robust socio-political aspects in the projections from these models will emerge in an alarming manner or will undermine the threat to a great degree. In each case mentioned above, machine learning versions and technical restrictions are attributed to other aspects such as political ideas or specific interest politicization which will further be interfering with the environmental governance. So, the suggestion here would be to make the wider considerations in the socio-technical prospects to productively create an effective control for the machine learning aspects. Although machine learning experts are working hard to make growth and impactful improvements in the tools and techniques, AI-based researchers will need to make sure that they divert their research to an emphasis on collaborations between machine learning techniques and models and decision makers in order to project events of the future in a sustainable manner [30].

1.5.4   Cybersecurity Risks

Cybersecurity risks have been mounting and have increased the challenges for researchers in order to implement AI on a bigger scale. The AI tools in the practices of environmental sustainability need the incorporation of data sets composed from a large number of researches. Increased cybersecurity and data management risks will lead to circumnavigate data sets and integration protocols. While many companies on the global scale have been using strategies to reduce cybersecurity risks, no effective solution has been found yet. Solutions must be chosen and incorporated carefully to deal with hackers who aim to gain access to the crucial information.

Companies like Google have used quantum computing, which is based on the influential supercomputers. Although it will help machine learning tools and enhance the processing speed, an increase in hacking speeds will result. So the increased and elevated cybersecurity threats will be an outcome of evolving AI-based sustainability strategies. Suitable cybersecurity risk management will need to more effectively develop functions and policies in order to make sure that the risks are mitigated at all levels.

1.5.5   Carbon Footprint of AI

There are many promises which AI-based practices have offered for the industrial sector. However, we cannot overlook the fact that sustainability practices and their applications have been increasing the carbon footprint. This is one of the major adverse effects and rebounds which AI has been causing for the global landscape. It has been found that a unit of an AI model has the capability to give out carbon dioxide similar to the lifespan of five cars. Since the model is very complex, the increase in the carbon footprint is considered a drastic effect despite using the same amount of energy resources. Many new software solutions are suggested to reduce the carbon footprint of AI models. Since AI is based on the high level of data usage, it contributes directly to more carbon footprint for the IT industry. The big data centers have a very high carbon emission rates, which will further impact the green ventures of the IT sector.

1.5.6   Issues in Performance Measurement

Policy-makers, governments, and citizens must demonstrate in a clear manner the effects of the intervention approaches in relation to developed targets including the nine Planetary Boundaries or the 17 Sustainable Development Goals. Determining the effects of AI activities effects has consistently been multifarious and often ineffective. For example, in the construction industry, professional decision-support instruments are frequently more erroneous, while theoretical models are unable to standardize to the real-time world. Calculating the positive and negative effects of AI impact on sustainability will be particularly problematic. The application of AI for effective sustainability needs a universal metric that fixes the technical and predictive performance tools while measuring the acceptance rate of these tools and AI-based activities in the target audiences. It must also consider the awareness of AI's technical restraints and the complication of climate issues [31].

1.6   Major Opportunities of AI in Sustainability

1.6.1   AI and Water-Related Hazards Management

AI applications play a major role in managing various environmental phenomena. One of the major issues is the water-related crisis which is considered a global challenge. Various countries have struggled with lack of water or even water abundance of some sort. Technologies such as AI will be very effective in utilizing the opportunity of generating hydrological runoff time series. It is one of the most crucial aspects in effectively carrying out the reservoir and hydropower management and providing measures for environmental protection. Various modelling systems can be effectively incorporated based on their capability to accurately predict drought rates [32].

Artificial Neural Networks (ANN), Adaptive Neural-based Fuzzy Inference Systems (ANFIS), Genetic Programming (GP) and Support Vector Machines are some examples which are used now and will be used in the future in sustainability practices. Besides drought management, the effective prediction of floods and rains will also be performed to manage water hazards. The lack of big data in this sector is the only hindrance which has prevented AI from being effectively applicable at the bigger scale. The example of G-Wadi Geoserver has been dealing with this issue in a perfect manner.

G-Wadi Geoserver technology is one classic AI example used for sustainability practices. The application uses ANN technology in order to effectively provide estimation of real-time precipitations on the global scale. It is labeled as Precipitation Estimation using Remote Sensing Information based on the Artificial Neural Networks. The overall system is called Cloud Classification System (G-WADI PERSIANN-CCS6) and has been in use since 2015. The program uses a core algorithm which is supported by NASA and NOAA. It effectively projects and analyzes regional and national cloud conditions and characteristics which are gathered at the international constellation of GEO satellites. The images are taken for providing effective estimation of the rainfall conducted at the 0.04° × 0.04° spatial resolution. This data of LEO satellites will be then further incorporated in adjusting the initial precipitation projection by making use of the ANN algorithm. This tool is a great measure to effectively carry out the sustainability practices while making sure that emergency services and warnings are provided to the areas before any hazardous events occur. It minimizes the hydrological risks in the cases of floods, droughts, and extreme weather conditions [33, 34].

AI technology will be offering many opportunities in the future which could be used in many countries for predicting and tracking storms. This has happened in the case of the Haiyan Super Typhoon which was tracked by Geoserver, where it was established that the storm had the highest precipitation intensity of roughly 361 mm per day. It was recorded on 7 November 2013 [35]. The storm was tracked back to the location of the Philippines. The current technology makes use of the iRain mobile application which involves the general public in gathering regional data for global precipitation estimation. It further permits users to envision real-time global satellite precipitation interpretations and follow extreme precipitation cases on the global scale while reporting the regional rainfall data by incorporating a crowd-sourcing operation to aid the data. It also gives a chance to advance distantly sensed approximations of precipitation. Furthermore, the usage of a crowdsourcing operation aids the app to collect data and encourage more citizens to be involved in scientific research. It has also opened doors for companies to base their practices around the estimation provided by meteorological departments. This application is one of the most critical benefits which AI offered for sustainable development at a global scale [36].

1.6.2   AI and Smart Cities

Sustainable processes in construction are one of the major opportunities to be explored by AI-based services. Not only will they bring in more revenue for companies investing in them, but they will be making sure that cities are well established, not overpopulated, and are capable of handling any natural disasters in a perfect manner.

Many studies have been carried out in order to effectively define the terms of smart cities and what they offer and their dimensions [37]. However, this has not led to a clear, simple definition yet. The classic and broader version is the fact that smart cities can be effectively termed as an "accommodating and appealing urban sustained environment effectively built in a smart and agile administration". Smart cities have their own dimensions which must be respected by AI and all sustainable activities linked to it [38].

The six dimensions which have been offering sustained opportunities for AI-based activities in a smart city are: the economy, agility, atmosphere, individuals, dwelling, and governance. Information technology (IT) aspects have become an integral and significant part of the systems and their usage in building important infrastructure. It is easy to witness the fact that all aspects such as governance efficacy, business innovativeness and cultural growth, and sustainability go hand in hand.

Aspects such as the big data being produced on the Internet of Things (IoT) has a functional role to play in the case of the market cities. They are loaded with big data which can be easily analyzed by the application running on AI to aid the authority, culture, and uptake of a smart city. Smart cities are the opportunity which AI can take hands on with the help of technologies like machine learning. The machine learning tools could be applied for the analysis of the big data which is gathered by the IoT devices and cognitive AI (CV and NLP). This will be a great opportunity for AI-based devices to develop smart cites which are built in order to sustain modern life while complying with all safety standards [38].

When it comes to the economy of smart cities, the AI technologies have a bigger role to play. The economic domain of smart cities will rely heavily on technological innovativeness, business yield, productivity, and smart management. The major work and the yield which one can derive by implementing AI-based services in smart cities are:

- Increasing outcomes and innovation by programming data management and analysis prospects
- Enhancing the efficacy and yield of the current properties, and dropping supplementary charges through pattern acknowledgement
- Maintaining decision-making by investigating bigger bulk of data which includes big data analytics from various causes
- Deriving hypotheses to accelerate well-versed conclusions based on logic, reasoning, and perception using deep machine learning techniques [39]

In relation to the society aspect of smart cities, AI will be mainly focusing on the aspects of public health, welfare, and education. This applies well to the COVID-19 pandemic which has impacted societies and economies all around the world. Major contributions of AI in this sector are:

- Enhancing the health monitoring and analyses using smart sensors and analytical technologies implanted in homes and offices of patients
- Augmenting the public health decisions by using medical imaging analytics in cases of radiology and healthcare actions and services
- Offering self-directed tutoring programs covering subjects such as algebra, grammar, and others
- Effectively organizing customized education options to aid in student growth and widen the curriculum during tough times [40]

When it comes to the aspects related to the environment and surroundings of smart cities, AI will be majorly focusing on the means of transport, energy, land usage, and climate actions. The major contributions which AI-based service can offer are:

- Functioning and channeling smart urban transport arrangements using the Mobility-As-A Service (MaaS) technique, which will be followed by the incorporation of many transport services in this unit on-demand mobility provision
- Enhancing energy production and utilization using local technologies applied in homes and based on tools focusing on environmental matters, energy saving, and lifestyle enhancement actions
- Inspecting variations in natural and manufactured environments using effectively created remote sensing systems using through independent and modern drones. They can be used for carrying out detection services for many objects and tracking all airborne videos.
- Projecting risks linked to climate changes using machine learning algorithms while in combination with climate tools and technologies to predict key upcoming drastic events in precise geographical regions and make sure actions are taken in advance to deal with the events in an effective manner
- AI can be used for more than a solution to the urban environmental concerns. It is a tool for tackling of global planetary environmental struggles and concerns [41].

1.6.3   AI and Climate Change

The use of AI-based tools in tackling climate change issues is one of the most discussed research topics. The area has been one of the leading issues with growing concern due to the fact that it is based on the projection made on the issues arising from the changes in the climate which have wide-scale applications and will impact a lot of people [42].

In comparison to this, AI-based tools which have found their application in environmental sustainability will be offering a lot more services when it comes to aspects like resource preservation and effective pollution management. Machine learning has further found an application in this case as well. With the increase in the global per capita income, the increased dependency on fossil fuels for energy usage and transportation has raised more concerns about global warming and climate alterations.

The AI-based solutions will be offering services which will solve the issues linked to the ecological crises while allowing the enterprises to deal with these issues in an integrated and more engaging manner while carrying out activities which tackle environmental stress in a sustainable manner [43]. The increase in inflation rates and rates of unemployment coupled with decreasing consumer trust will lead to increased interest in businesses focusing on climate issues as well as social and economic issues and suggesting effective solutions.

It has been highlighted that the issues and instabilities in the macro-economic surrounding will be impacting the economy as well as the non-economic part of nature and this has aroused the concern of scientists.

Dealing with draining natural resources and climate change will involve dealing with the issues of increasing populations and ensuring effective sustainable growth practices in all other activities. High fossil fuel interdependency and unlimited clean-energy sources must be developed to deal with the issues of energy resources being wiped out on a regular basis. Since the world has been taking over 25% of its energy from renewable energy resources, AI-based services will have to make sure that the issues of lack of biodiversity and anthropogenic climate change are also controlled in a perfect manner, while ensuring natural disaster management is also covered effectively [44].

Although there are so many encouraging and constructive technological developments and discoveries, technology has also led to a lot of disruption in human society in the cases where people are unable to understand that they must adapt effectively to new technologies. As an example, there are over four billion smartphone users globally, but not all users have access to the internet and mobile services at the exact same speed. Alongside that, the urban perception has to be taken into consideration to highlight the costly tools and technologies that are ineffectively and erratically disseminated in cities at multiple allocations. This might lead to catastrophic effects in urban societies and the formation of high-tech ecological territories which are only available to rich people who can protect themselves from the harm of climate change and environmental degradation. Most of time the role of AI is limited to rich communities; however, we must avoid this and make sure everyone is benefitting from technological advancements, and smart cities are the perfect way to do that [45].

The major contributions which will be made by AI in the case of climate change are:

- AI found its purpose in the sectors of the climate risk mitigation which includes research and development, urban planning, regional development, land usage, construction, suppleness, and energy production and depletion.
- AI tools for ocean health sector are integral parts of the climate change control including functions of the production and preservation of sustainable fishery practices. It also includes pollution censoring and effective diminution and anticipation actions. This is coupled with the services of the habitat and species fortification, and ocean acidification minimization actions to bring in more sustainability.
- AI applications for producing pollution-free and clean air is based on the services of pollutants sifting, filtering, straining, pollution decontaminating, and cleansing.
- Filtering and prevention measures, prompt pollution and threat caution, clean energy, and modern and effective urban management [46].
- AI has popular application in the sector of biodiversity and conservation which is based on the activities surrounding actions like habitat guarding and reinstatement, sustainable trading, pollution filtering, disease control actions for the species while carrying out effective natural capital augmentation.
- AI will be further used for the process of effective supply of clean water and its security which will include actions like effective water supply, analyzing its quality, efficacy management, water catchment control, sanitization, and drought control measures.

- AI will be finding a lot more opportunities in the case of weather and disaster management as well, where it will be effectively carrying out the projection and forecasting as well as the warning for weather and other hazards situations [47].
- AI for smart cities governance is focusing on national and community security, urban authority, and decision-making. It will employ measures like the effective deployment of smart poles which will act as digitalized sensors and as assistive tools for effective decision-making. This is a great way to deal with management and planning for disasters and pandemics. The use of AI tools, such as predictive analytics, will make sure the future is safer for all communities around the globe [48].

1.6.4   AI and Environmental Sustainability

AI has so many important applications in environmental sustainability businesses and practices. Environmental sustainability can be viewed as the actions and resources required to sustain a healthy ecosystem. This includes all activities leading to lower-impact transportation and balanced agricultural resources. It also includes preservation of environmental resources and materials such as effective and safe biodiversity, management of water resources, effective energy usage, and renewable energy sources. Additionally, it entails careful consumption of raw materials including food, minerals, land, and effective management and treatment of waste. Integration of AI-based tools will further enhance the credibility of dealing with pollution and making sure that environmentally suitable materials are used effectively at all times.

As an example, rule-based tools like ARIES1 are effective for modeling ecosystem actions. The software is designed to use various ML models for carrying out data analysis to aid experts in understanding the intricate, nonlinear links among various system variables. The more famous ML tools for biodiversity which are commonly used to achieve environmental sustainability are the ANN and BN which work effectively for ecosystems and their related actions. This tool is a great option to effectively carry out the sustainability practices while making sure that emergency services and warnings are provided to the areas before any hazard occurs [33].

More and more ML models are known to enhance the prediction abilities and the optimization of water resource conservation for future generations as well as the current areas where there is water scarcity. It observed that ANN, more exclusively the ANFIS which is a category of ANN-based on FL, as well as the SVM have major application in ML models for sustainability applications. There are a number of experts who are utilizing decision trees such as the random forest as well as tools like multiple regression and spline regression in order to predict environmental sustainability. One other example to consider here is the GA, which is the most significant EC optimization method.

These algorithms will also find an effective integration in the FL systems for suitable decision support linked to the projecting or optimization services. The usage of the Ensemble paradigms or hybrid paradigms coalesce numerous models to generate more perfect outcomes. Widespread permutations incorporate ANN alongside various models which are more beneficial in the statistical or time series. They have been further augmenting a number of models alongside the NC algorithms. Many other trends and averages have also resurfaced. Fundamentally, the AI-based services and the intuition, cognition and robotics are mostly overseen parts of AI. Many other pattern recognition and classification methodologies relied on the ML tools including the ANN and clustering. There has been a lot of renewable energy research which has been highlighted in the energy conservation sector. Alongside that, many studies have focused on renewable energy sources as well as hybrid energy sources. The usage of solar energy is the most prevalently considered renewable energy source. The increase of the energy production and financial probability of market disposition.

1.6.5   Impacts of AI in Transportation

The opportunities which the transport sector will have are numerous. Transport, with AI-based-autonomous vehicles, will be offering a lot more benefits in terms of energy efficacy and the effective and smooth navigation systems followed by ecofriendly driving. The AI-based electric vehicles will further increase the rebound impacts of enhanced vehicle miles. The GHG emissions will be reduced by -1.7% in the case of the transport sector which will have positive impacts on the environment [13].

AI-based interventions will be targeting the transport sector with making sure that the aspects like cargos and public are allowed to effectively mobilize more securely, effectively, and sustainably in an enhanced global world. The AI technologies allow effective and better traffic prediction, instantaneous journey preparation, and autonomous vehicles. The expected GPD gain from the sector has been projected from $3.6 – $5.2 trillion USD. The fossil fuel exhaustive divisions of transport will allow the AI tools to make use of the renewables since they are more economical and encourage the trend from fossil fuels to bio-energy resources [49].

The major AI environmental impacts in the transport sector are autonomous vehicles and semi-autonomous transportation, as well as more vehicle sharing. This coupled with autonomous deliveries, trucking and autonomous delivery robots is a great prospective as well. The more effective traffic optimization will reduce the jams, queuing, and smart toll pricing. This is a very beneficial prospect since effective prediction and logistics planning as well as the maintenance for vehicles will bring in more vehicles, while the AI and IoT technologies will find more ground at the global scale. This will revolutionize the future [50].

1.6.6   Opportunities in Disaster Forecasting and Deforestation Forecasting

The deterrence of illegal deforestation and forest crisis has caused over 80,000 to 150,000 square kilometers of the global forests to shrink. The significant increase in the tropical deforestation because of the illegal actions also top the list. Technology companies and NGOs have been incorporating AI tools to address the issue by continuously monitoring and supervising the forest crisis. AI has the capability to detect and evaluate satellite data using ground sensors for effective supervision of forest conditions. Early warning systems will minimize the deforestation and will further allow the saving of 32 million hectares of forest in the next 10 years and the reduction of 29 Gt CO_2 emissions [51]. Figure 1.7 illustrates the AI prediction models that could be used for disaster forecasting.

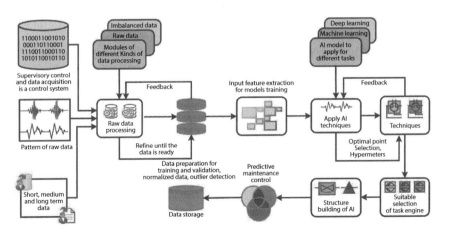

Figure 1.7 Prediction models for AI [7].

1.6.7   Opportunities in the Energy Sector

The energy sector has so many opportunities for AI-based activities in order to bring in more suitability at the most suitable acceptance rate. The classic example is the case of NextEra Energy, which is an American *Fortune* 200 energy company. It has been successfully implementing machine learning for the optimization of operations standards in the wind turbine fleet. The main goals of the company are to carry out successful maximization of the output and implement effective predictive maintenance. The other example is the French oil and gas company, Total, which collaborated with Google Cloud to collectively work on the development of AI tools to provide more effective and accurate subsurface data analysis for oil and gas evaluation and production [52].

Opportunities are increasing for AI-based tools. The American startup AppOrchid, for example, has been using deep learning and natural language processing in its applications. The main aim is to analyze the grid behavior while considering multiple wind scenarios. The Canadian company Utilities Kingston is a multi-utility contributor. It has been steering AI and geospatial analysis for optimization of leak assessment actions. The aim is to decease the time and money in this process by over 50%. The case of the Pacific Gas & Electric company is also encouraging for considering the opportunities which AI has in the energy sector. The employment of machine learning for enhancing effectiveness in the load reduction projections is an innovative approach. The EDF Energy Company from the UK has been providing its services to over 5 million consumers and has been utilizing Amazon's Alexa in carrying out the account balance data and the meter readings for consumers. These Energy transition trends are encouraging for a brighter future for AI applications in the energy sector to achieve sustainability [53].

1.7   Conclusion and Future Direction

This chapter has explored all the aspects and limitations of developing and deploying AI technologies to make present and future cities more sustainable. The analysis has shown that, while AI technology is evolving and becoming an integral part of urban services, spaces, and operations, we still need to find ways to integrate AI in our cities in a sustainable manner, and also to minimize the negative social, environmental, economic, and political externalities that the increasingly global adoption of AI is triggering. In essence, the city of AI is not a sustainable city. Both the development of AI and the development of cities need to be improved and better aligned towards sustainability as the overarching goal.

AI Applications for sustainability practices are extremely effective today and also for the future. AI can provide provisions for culturally motivated administrations as well as corporate practices in reducing the consumption and disruption of the natural resource. The significance of AI tools is not only seen in how they will enable the society to reduce its consumption of energy, water, and land; AI will further focus on facilitating and fostering environmental governance. There will be challenges as well as opportunities for businesses and societies in incorporating AI in their sustainability practices. Careless human actions are impacting Earth in a bad way and have resulted in harming all natural resources. There is an urgent need to resolve these issues immediately and work towards a more sustainable future. AI technology applications will be looking at tons of opportunities in the future in which it could be used in other countries for predicting and tracking the storms. The introduction of AI-based practices in smart cities will handle overpopulated areas effectively. The sustainable processes in construction are a major opportunity to be explored by the AI-based services; not only will they bring in more revenue for the companies investing in them, they will be making sure that the cities are well established, not overpopulated and adept at handling natural disasters in a perfect manner. The AI-based solutions will be offering services which will solve the issues linked to the ecological crises while allowing the enterprises to deal with these issues in an integrated and more engaging manner while carrying out activities which tackle environmental stress in a sustainable manner. AI will be revealing more opportunities for weather and disaster management, projection and forecasting, as well as weather warnings and other hazards situations. Energy transition trends are another encouraging domain for AI in the energy sector as it will help increase sustainability.

It can be concluded that AI-based sustainability interventions will be facing a number of challenges and opportunities. The climate, the society and the public need the sustainable practices to overcome all environmental challenges of the future. AI technologies will be of great help, since they have proved effective in predicting global climate change using machine learning and other analysis tools. All of these applications will be of great help to the entire global economy in the upcoming years.

References

1. K. Toniolo, E. Masiero, M. Massaro and C. Bagnoli, "Sustainable Business Models and Artificial Intelligence: Opportunities and Challenges," in *Knowledge, People, and Digital Transformation*, 2020, pp. 103-117.

2. R. Nishant, M. Kennedy and J. Corbett, "Artificial intelligence for sustainability: Challenges, opportunities, and a research agenda," *International Journal of Information Management,* vol. 54, 2020.

3. E. Brynjolfsson and A. Mcafee, "The business of artificial intelligence: how AI fits into your data science team," *Harv. Bus. Rev.,* pp. 1-20, 2017.

4. J. R. Doppa, J. Rosca and P. Bogdan, "Autonomous Design Space Exploration of Computing Systems for Sustainability; Opportunities and Challenges," *IEEE Design & Test, vol. 36, issue 5,* pp. 35-43, 2019.

5. R. R. Davenport TH, "Artificial intelligence for the real world: don't start with moon shots," *Harv. Bus. Rev.,* vol. 96, no. 1, p. 108–116, 2018.

6. R. Abduljabbar, H. Dia, S. Liyanage and S. & Bagloee, "Applications of artificial intelligence in transport: An overview," *Sustainability,* vol. 11, no. 1, p. 189, 2019.

7. T. Ahmad, D. Zhang, C. Huang, H. Zhang, N. Dai, Y. Song and H. Chen, "Artificial intelligence in sustainable energy industry: Status Quo, challenges and opportunities," *Journal of Cleaner Production,* vol. 289, pp. 1-27, 2021.

8. M. Saqib and A. Saleem, "Power-quality issues and the need for reactive power compensation in the grid integration of wind power," *Renewable and Sustainable Energy Rev.,* vol. 43, pp. 51-56, 2019.

9. M. Raza and A. Khosravi, "A review on artificial intelligence based load demand forecasting techniques for smart grid and buildings," *Renewable and Sustainable Energy Rev.,* vol. 50, pp. 1352-1372, 2015.

10. A. Mellit and S. Kalogirou, "Artificial intelligence techniques for photovoltaic applications: a review. Prog.," *Prog. Energy Combust. Sci.,* vol. 34, pp. 574-632, 2008.

11. P. Engels, M. Kunkis and S. Altstaedt, "A new energy world in the making imaginary business futures in a dramatically changing world of decarbonized energy production," *Energy Res. Soc. Sci.,* vol. 60, 2020.

12. Y. Duan, J. Edwards and Y. Dwivedi, "Artificial intelligence for decision making in the era of Big Data—evolution, challenges and research agenda," *Int. J. Inf. Manage.,* vol. 48, p. 63–71, 2019.

13. P. Vié, A. Bollack, D. A. Bujak, J. Buvat and N. Manchanda, "Intelligent Automation in Energy and Utilities: The next digital wave," *Capgemini,* 2019.

14. E. Commission, "The 2030 Agenda for sustainable development and SDGs," 2017.

15. W. R. H. H. S. L. Fleming A, "The sustainable development goals: a case study," *Mar Policy,* vol. 86, p. 94–103, 2017.

16. M. Huang and R. Rust, "Artificial intelligence in service," *J. Serv. Res.,* vol. 21, no. 2, p. 155–172, 2018.

17. J. Gillham, "How AI can enable a Sustainable Future," *PricewaterhouseCoopers,* p. 8, 2020.

18. C. Herweijer, B. Combes and J. Gillham, "How AI can enable a Sustainable Future," *PWC,* 2020.

19. A. Buis, "Study confirms climate models are getting future warming projections right," 2020.
20. A. Z˙elazna, M. Bojar and E. Bojar, "Corporate Social Responsibility towards the Environment in Lublin Region, Poland: A Comparative Study of 2009 and 2019," *Sustainability*, vol. 13, p. 4463, 2020.
21. N. R. Sanders, T. Boone, R. Ganeshan and J. D. Wood, "Sustainable Supply Chains in the Age of AI and Digitization: Research Challenges and Opportunities," *Journal of Business Logistics*, vol. 40, no. 3, pp. 229-240, 2019.
22. S. E. Windolph, "Assessing Corporate Sustainability Through Ratings: Challenges and Their Causes," *Journal of Environmental Sustainability*, vol. 1, no. 1, 2011.
23. C. Muntaner, "Digital platforms, gig economy, precarious employment and the invisible hand of social class," *International Journal of Health Services*, vol. 48, no. 4, pp. 597-600, 2018.
24. E. T. Albert, "AI in talent acquisition: a review of AI-applications used in recruitment and selection," *Strategic HR Review*, vol. 18, no. 5, pp. 215-221, 2019.
25. W. Wilkinson, I. Podhorska and A. Siekelova, "Does the Growth of Artificial Intelligence and Automation Shape Talent Attraction and Retention?," *Psychosociological Issues in Human Resource Management*, vol. 1, no. 1, pp. 30-35, 2016.
26. V. Masson-Delmotte, P. Zhai, H. O. Pörtner, D. Roberts, J. Skea, P. R. Shukla and S. Connors, "IPCC 2018: Summary for policymakers," *Global Warming*, 2018.
27. S. B. Kotsiantis, I. Zaharakis and P. Pintelas, "Supervised machine learning: A review of classification techniques," *Emerging artificial intelligence applications in computer engineering, 160, 3–24.,* vol. 160, pp. 3-24, 2007.
28. F. Alrukaibi, R. Alsaleh and T. & Sayed, "Applying machine learning and statistical approaches for travel time estimation in partial network coverage," *Sustainability*, vol. 11, no. 4, 2019.
29. G. Torbert, "Statistician raises red flag about reliability of machine learning techniques," *Digital Trends*, 2019.
30. M. Belkin, D. Hsu, S. Ma and S. Mandal, "Reconciling modern machine-learning practice and the classical bias–variance trade-off," *Proceedings of the National Academy of Sciences of the United States of America*, vol. 116, no. 32, p. 15849–15854, 2019.
31. D. Kolokotsa, K. Gobakis, S. Papantoniou, C. Georgatou and N. Kampelis, "Development of a web based energy management system for University Campuses: The CAMP-IT platform," *Energy and Buildings*, vol. 123, pp. 119–135, 2016.
32. I. M. Cockburn, Henderson, R. and S. S., "The Impact of Artificial Intelligence on Innovation," 2017.
33. M. K. E. B. Horowitz, G. C. Allen and P. Scharre, "Strategic Competition in an Era of Artificial Intelligence," *World Robotics 2017*, 2018.

34. UNESCO, "The use of AI for environmental management and disaster risk reduction," *Artificial intelligence for sustainable development: challenges and opportunities for UNESCO's science and engineering programmes,* pp. 18-20, 2018.

35. S. Rasp, M. S. Pritchard and P. Gentine, "Deep learning to represent sub-grid processes in climate models," *Proceedings of the National Academy of Sciences,* 2018.

36. P. Biggs, J. Garrity, C. LaSalle and A. Polomska, "Harnessing the Internet of Things for Global Development," *A contribution to the ITU/UNESCO Broadband Commission for Sustainable Development,* 2015.

37. V. Albino, U. Berardi and R. M. Dangelico, "Smart cities–definitions, dimensions, and performance," *Proceedings IFKAD,* p. 1723–1738, 2013.

38. J. Corbett and S. Mellouli, "Winning the SDG battle in cities: How an integrated information ecosystem can contribute to the achievement of the 2030 sustainable development goals," *Information Systems Journal,* vol. 27, no. 4, p. 427–461, 2017.

39. Z. Allam and Z. A. Dhunny, "On big data, artificial intelligence and smart cities," *Cities,* vol. 89, pp. 80-91, 2019.

40. R. Giffinger, C. Fertner, H. Kramar and E. Meijers, "City-ranking of European medium-sized cities," 2007.

41. R. G. Hollands, "Will the real smart city please stand up? Intelligent, progressive or ntrepreneurial?," *City,* vol. 12, no. 3, p. 303–320, 2008.

42. M. Ghallab, D. Nau and P. Traverso, *Automated planning and acting,* Cambridge University Press, 2016.

43. D. J. Jeon, S. J. Ki, Y. Cha, Y. Park and J. H. Kim, "New methodology of evaluation of best management practices performances for an agricultural watershed according to the climate change scenarios: A hybrid use of deterministic and decision support models," *Ecological Engineering,* vol. 119, pp. 73-89, 2018.

44. W. J. Raseman, J. R. Kasprzyk, F. L. Rosario-Ortiz, J. R. Stewart and B. Livneh, "Emerging investigators series: A critical review of decision support systems for water treatment: Making the case for incorporating climate change and climate extremes.," *Environmental Science Water Research & Technology,* vol. 3, no. 1, p. 18–36, 2017.

45. A. Ullah, N. Salehnia, S. Kolsoumi, A. Ahmad and T. Khaliq, "Prediction of effective climate change indicators using statistical downscaling approach and impact assessment on pearl millet (Pennisetum glaucum L.) yield through Genetic Algorithm in Punjab, Pakistan," *Ecological Indicators,* vol. 90, p. 569–576, 2018.

46. P. Chamoso, J. F. De Paz, S. Rodríguez and J. Bajo, "Smart cities simulation environment for intelligent algorithms evaluation," *International Symposium on Ambient Intelligence.,* vol. Springer, p. 177–187, 2016.

47. F. Aymen and C. Mahmoudi, "A novel energy optimization approach for electrical vehicles in a smart city," *Energies,* vol. 12, no. 5, p. 929, 2019.

48. J. F. De Paz, J. Bajo, S. Rodríguez, G. Villarrubia and J. M. Corchado, "Intelligent system for lighting control in smart cities," *Information Sciences,* vol. 372, p. 241–255, 2016.
49. D. Elliott, W. Keen and L. Miao, "Recent advances in connected and auto-mated vehicles," *Journal of Traffic and Transportation Engineering (English Edition),* vol. 6, no. 2, pp. 109-131, 2019.
50. Q. Demlehner, D. Schoemer and S. Laumer, "How can artificial intelligence enhance car manufacturing? A Delphi study-based identification and assess-ment of general use cases," *International Journal of Information Management,* vol. 58, 2021.
51. Y. Duan, J. S. Edwards and Y. K. Dwivedi, "Artificial intelligence for decision making in the era of Big Data – evolution, challenges and research agenda," *International Journal of Information Management,* vol. 48, pp. 63-71, 2019.
52. Y. K. Dwivedi, L. Hughes, E. Ismagilova, G. Aarts, C. Coombs, T. Crick, Y. Duan, R. Dwivedi, J. Edwards and A. Eirugi, "Artificial Intelligence (AI): Multidisciplinary perspectives on emerging challenges, opportunities, and agenda for research, practice and policy," *International Journal of Information Management,* vol. 57, 2021.
53. G. D. Sharma, A. Yadav and R. Chopra, "Artificial intelligence and effective governance: A review, critique and research agenda," *Sustainable Futures,* vol. 2, 2020.

2

Recent Applications of Machine Learning in Solar Energy Prediction

N. Kapilan[1]*, R.P. Reddy[2] and Vidhya P.[3]

[1]Department of Mechanical Engineering, Nitte Meenakshi Institute of Technology, Bangalore, India
[2]Department of Mechanical Engineering, Global Academy of Technology, Bangalore, India
[3]Department of Computer Science, SRSMN Government First Grade College, Barkur, India

Abstract

Renewable energy sources are getting attention in recent years due to an increase in global warming and greenhouse gas emission caused by the burning of fossil fuels for electrical power production. Among the renewable energy sources, solar energy is preferred as its potential is high. However, there are a few challenges in solar energy conversion due to variability and uncertainty with solar radiation which results in lower energy conversion, intermittent power supply, etc. The solar photovoltaic systems and solar thermal systems are most widely used to tap the solar energy. The challenges faced with these devices can be overcome with the help of machine learning, which is used to predict the solar radiation, solar power and faculty solar modules and to optimize and control the solar photovoltaic systems. This chapter discusses basic concepts of solar energy, solar energy conversion methods, different types of machine learning techniques used in solar photovoltaic systems, machine learning algorithms, challenges, and opportunities in solar energy production. This chapter will be useful to faculty members, research scholars, working professionals, government officials and non-government organizations.

Keywords: Renewable energy source, solar energy, PV system, ML, challenges, review

Corresponding author: kapil_krecmech@yahoo.com

Pandian Vasant, Gerhard-Wilhelm Weber, Joshua Thomas, José Antonio Marmolejo-Saucedo and Roman Rodriguez-Aguilar (eds.) Artificial Intelligence for Renewable Energy and Climate Change, (33–52) © 2022 Scrivener Publishing LLC

2.1   Introduction

The rate of consumption of fossil fuels is high in recent years due to industrialization and population growth. Energy is generated by the burning of fossil fuels which results in increases greenhouse gases; however, there is an increase in energy demand [1]. Hence research work is being carried out in various countries to find alternative energy sources which are renewable fuels and carbon dioxide neutral. The growth of economic and social developments of any country depends upon the availability of energy sources. Fossil fuels are depleting and hence research work is focused to find renewable energy sources which are sustainable [2]. It is necessary to identify suitable alternative energy sources to meet the energy demand of the world and safeguard the environment. These energy sources should be sustainable, reliable, and affordable. Also, it is necessary to reduce CO_2 emission from conventional energy sources and to minimize greenhouse gas emissions and mitigate climate change [3]. It is reported that the renewable energy sources such as wind energy, solar energy, etc., can supply two-thirds of world energy demand, and significantly reduce greenhouse gas emissions and limit global surface temperature within the limit. Hence most countries have formulated renewable energy policies which promote the usage of renewable energy sources, and it is estimated that the demand of renewable energy sources will grow sixfold in the near future. Among renewable energy sources, the highest growth is estimated in solar photovoltaic (PV) power plant due to solar energy potential and easily availability. It is reported that the hybrid renewable energy sources can significantly reduce emissions, and it is estimated that the energy supplied by renewable energy sources may increase from 14.00% in 2015 to 63.00% in 2050. It is estimated that USD 120 trillion will be invested in the renewable energy sector by 2050 [4].

2.2   Solar Energy

The sun is a large sphere of very hot gases, and the heat is produced by various nuclear fusion reactions, which convert hydrogen atoms to helium atoms. The sun radiates the solar energy as electromagnetic waves, of which 99% have wavelengths and varies from 0.2 to 4 μm. The sun radiates about 3.8 X 1026 W of energy into space. Out of this about 1.7 X 1017 W power is intercepted by the Earth. In Earth's atmosphere, the average solar radiation is around 1.35 kW/m². On a bright sunny day, the solar radiation is about

1 kW/m^2. On entering the Earth's atmosphere, part of the solar energy is absorbed in the atmosphere and gets converted into heat. Some of the solar energy is scattered through the atmosphere, which gives a bluish colour to the sky. The rest of the energy reaches the Earth directly. On reaching the Earth, part of the energy is reflected. The solar radiation on a particular location on Earth is affected by latitude, time of the day and year, seasonal variation, and atmospheric clarity. The solar radiation which is received by the Earth can be classified into direct, diffuse, and reflected radiation and is shown in Figure 2.1. Direct radiation is the radiation received from the sun and reaches Earth's surface without scattering. The component of solar energy which is scattered in the atmosphere is called diffuse radiation. The energy content of diffuse radiation is lower than the direct radiation. The total radiation which is reflected by the Earth's surface is called reflected radiation [5–7].

The energy supplied by the sun is inexhaustible, non-toxic, and environmentally friendly. Solar energy can meet the energy demand of humankind. Electrical energy can be produced from solar energy using solar PV technology and heat energy using a solar thermal system such as a solar water heating system. The solar-based heating system is used in various industrial and domestic applications [8]. Hence, solar energy is widely used in many countries [9, 10].

In recent years, solar PV systems have been widely used and different techniques have increased the efficiency a of solar PV panel [11]. A solar water heating system is an example of a solar-based heating system, and several modifications has been carried out to improve the efficiency of this type of system using machine learning (ML) technique [12]. The amount of solar energy produced by the solar energy conversion devices depends

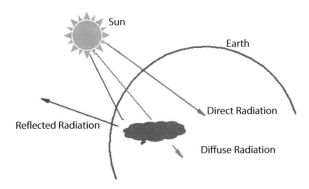

Figure 2.1 Different types of solar radiation.

upon various factors such as, air temperature, azimuth angle, wind speed, etc. The solar azimuth angle is important as it affects solar energy production. The air temperature affects the solar PV energy and the higher temperature reduces the power produced by the solar PV system [13]. Similarly, a solar PV panel exposed to low temperature reduces the amount of electrical power produced [14]. Wind speed is associated with air temperature, and it affects the energy conversion efficiency [15].

The drawbacks of the solar PV system are intermittent power production, low energy conversion efficiency, higher cost, etc. Hence various techniques were used to optimize the power production and reduce the cost of energy produced. The efficiency of the solar PV panel is affected by the ambient air, relative humidity, wind speed and insolation [16]. There are a few challenges in integrating renewable energy sources with an actual power system due to the quality of energy, networking, protection, and management of power system, etc. The main problem with a renewable energy system is continuous variation in energy produced [17].

It is necessary to predict the short- and long-term production of energy from a solar PV system to study the feasibility of installation of a solar PV energy system and to calculate return on investment. A significant amount of research work has been carried out in this aspect [18, 19]. A few studies were carried out to study the effect input variables such as solar irradiance on the power produced [20]. The solar PV power production is affected by weather conditions and the time of the day, which affect stability of the grid. Hence it is necessary to forecast the energy produced so that it will be easy to balance the grid performance at lower cost [21]. This helps to overcome the power shortage issues, uncertainty, and reduce the energy cost [22].

2.3   AI, ML and DL

Artificial intelligence (AI) techniques are becoming popular in various areas of engineering and technology to solve practical problems. In a renewable energy system, AI techniques can be used to design a model of a problem, which can be analyzed to predict the performance and control it effectively. An AI system can be an alternative to understand and solve a complex and difficult problem. AI systems are designed to handle data which are incomplete and problems which are nonlinear. They can learn from examples and fault tolerant. Once trained, AI can predict and generalize it quickly. Due to these characteristics, AI systems are used in various applications in signal processing, forecasting, control, optimization, robotics, pattern recognition, power systems, manufacturing, etc. The ML use statistical methods to improve the performance of a system and learn by using experience. The ML algorithms are classified into reinforcement, unsupervised and supervised learnings. The ML technique selection can vary, based on the data sets and type of applications. The reinforcement learning method is utilized to bring high dimensional into lower dimensional data for visualization. The deep learning (DL) is the subset of ML and is used to provide knowledge using data, observations (using multilayer neural network) to computers and using [23–25]. Figure 2.2 relates AL, ML and DL.

The AI and data analytics can be used to predict the power generated by the renewable energy sources and to operate the renewable energy conversion devices effectively [26]. Several ML models were developed to predict the power generated by the solar PV system considering several important weather factors. In this model, historic hourly data was used without and with data manipulation. The manipulation work was performed with the help of recursive feature elimination [27]. The wind speed prediction is gaining popularity as it helps in predicting the power generated by the windmill and due to increase in wind energy demand. The ANN technique was used to predict the performance of the wind turbine based on data obtained from the metrological department [28]. The multiple nonparametric tree-based ML method was effective in predicting performance of the wind turbine using weather data variables [29]. The fuzzy logic controller was developed for wind turbine [30]. There is a need for preprocessing data, and optimization process parameters are very important in increasing the performance of wind speed forecasting and stability. The data pretreatment technique is necessary to identify the influence of wind speed series, and to minimize noise interference [31].

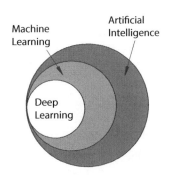

Figure 2.2 Relation between DL, ML and AI.

2.4   Data Preprocessing Techniques

The important steps involved in energy forecasting are preprocessing of data, selection of model, training model, testing of trained model, and forecasting of required parameter. The removal of data with missing values and data exceptions due to lack of data are done in the preprocessing step. In energy predictions using ML, various data preprocessing techniques are used [32, 33].

2.5   Solar Radiation Estimation

The abundant renewable energy available on Earth's surface is called solar radiation. Its energy content is higher than other renewable energy sources such as wind energy, biomass energy, etc. Hence solar radiation has the potential to meet the energy demand using solar PV panels. However, there are various factors which result in uncertainty in power production [34].

The solar radiation reaches the Earth in the form of electromagnetic radiation produced by the sun's nuclear fusion reaction. The solar radiation is converted into electrical energy using a solar PV system. The controlling and scheduling of solar PV power plants can be improved with solar radiation forecasting [35]. The energy produced by the solar PV system can be predicted using weather data. The meteorological data like solar radiation intensity, solar sunshine duration, speed of the wind, air humidity, air temperature, etc., are given as inputs to predict the energy generated by the PV system using different models. The sizing of the PV system depends on the solar radiation data, and solar energy production is predicted using AI models [36].

The solar radiation measurement is essential to increase solar energy conversion. Solar radiation is measured using a device called pyranometer [37]. Figure 2.3 shows the pyranometer with data logger used to measure solar radiation; it consists of thermopile sensor with black coating. The solar radiation is absorbed by the black coating and heat energy is converted into electrical energy in micro volts, and finally solar radiation is displayed in W/m^2 as shown in the figure.

The sunshine recorder is used to measure the sunshine duration. It measures hours of sunshine and not hours of daylight. Figure 2.4 shows the sunshine recorder and in this device, solar radiation is focused on the card by using the glass sphere. The burning of the card depends on the radiation intensity. The gaps recorded in the cards show the time at which the sun is covered by clouds.

Figure 2.3 Pyranometer with data logger.

Figure 2.4 Sunshine recorder.

Figures 2.5 and 2.6 show the solar radiation recorded by the pyranometer and sunshine recorder burnt strip, respectively. These data can be used as inputs to predict the solar energy produced by the solar PV power plant.

The solar radiation prediction using hourly data is complex and difficult as compared to daily or monthly data. Hence, the estimation models related to hourly data are much fewer [38]. The ANN is a computing technique based on a collection of connected nodes, inspired by the biological neural networks that constitute animal brains.

The hourly solar radiation can be predicted with ANN models like generalized regression neural network (NN), Elman back propagation NN,

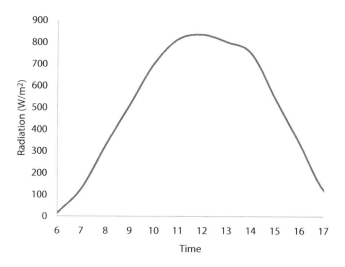

Figure 2.5 Solar radiation at different day times.

Figure 2.6 Sunshine recorder burnt strip.

feed-forward back propagation NN, and cascade-forward back propagation NN. The solar radiation is predicted based on parameters like temperature, sunshine, latitude, longitude, humidity, hour, day, and month in these models. It is reported that the generalized regression neural network provides better prediction as compared to other techniques [39]. Figure 2.7 depicts ANN architecture which uses different layers for the prediction of solar radiation.

The predictive variables such as insolation clearness index, specific humidity and radiative flux and response variable such as solar insolation can be obtained from NASA database [40]. The ANN model which uses sunshine duration, latitude, altitude, and longitude as inputs results in mean error value between 6.50 to 19.10% [41]. Another ANN model was used to estimate diffuse radiation using mean air temperature, relative humidity, maximum air temperature, and day [42]. The hourly global solar radiation was forecasted using wind speed, humidity, air temperature and soil temperature [43]. The global and diffuse radiation was measured

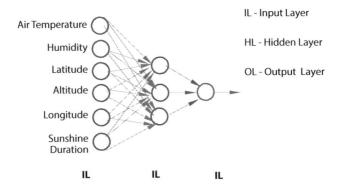

Figure 2.7 Architecture of ANN.

using four input parameters such as latitude, longitude sunshine and day [44]. It is suggested that ANN, random forest, regression tree, support-vector regression and gradient boosting have significant potential in the solar radiation prediction. The accuracy of forecasting can be enhanced with ensemble forecast or hybrid approaches [45]. It is reported that the ANN gives better results for both short-term and real-time predictions [46]. The ML gives 27 to 30% higher accuracy in forecasting renewable energy availability with reference to conventional method [47]. Figure 2.8 shows the ML steps involved in solar radiation prediction.

The ML algorithms such as support vector regression, m5, linear and non-linear regression, random forests were most widely used to estimate solar radiation at various geographic areas of the world [48]. These models were used to estimate solar radiation at various geographical locations [39]. It is reported that the random forest algorithm gives accurate prediction and hence it has great potential in forecasting renewable energy as this model considers accuracy factors such as hour angle, elevation angle, declination angle, zenith, and azimuth angles as the inputs [47]. Some data-driven ML models use meteorological sensor station data as the pyranometer is expensive and needs regular maintenance [37].

It is reported that the daily average data is required to develop comprehensive design, and monthly average data can be used for draft design. However, hourly average data gives precise results and is used for result-oriented designs [49]. In the conventional method, human experience can be used for prediction; however, the inaccuracy may be high. The ML based on supervised learning can be used to predict the solar irradiation using unstructured data with better accuracy [34]. The prediction of the performance of renewable energy system by a single ML model cannot be

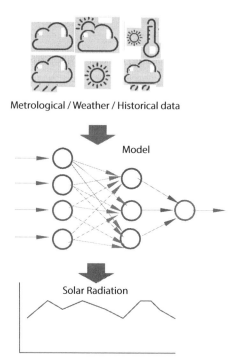

Figure 2.8 ML steps involved in solar radiation prediction.

improved due to diversified datasets, performance indicators, time steps, settings, etc. The hybrid ML model overcomes these limitations with deep learning technique and support-vector regression [50].

The ML algorithms depend on data; however, scaling, cleaning, scaling, normalization, and reduction affects energy prediction accuracy [51]. For example, bird droppings, dirt and dust on the solar PV panel minimizes solar radiation received by the panels and power production [52]. Similarly, faculty solar PV module and overheating may reduce power produced [53]. Figure 2.9 shows the dusts and other impurities deposited on the solar PV panel.

The hybrid deep learning method uses deep time-series clustering to identify irregular patterns and provides good clustering performance. This feature dynamically utilizes the weighted features for forecasting. The simulation results based on this method reveal that this method gives accurate results as compared to other models and this method minimizes the root mean square error [35]. The sky type (sunny or cloudy) can be predicted using meteorological data like sunshine hour, cloud cover, diffuse fraction and clearness index [54]. The hourly average solar radiation was predicted

Figure 2.9 Solar PV panel deposited with dust and other impurities.

using ML algorithms such as multilayer feed forward NN, M5 rules algorithms, support vector machines and nearest neighbors with selected data groups for each target location. It is reported that this feature selection method is successful for target locations [50].

2.6   Solar Power Prediction

Solar power is produced by converting the sun radiation into electrical energy using solar PV or solar thermal systems. The solar PV system produces electrical energy from the solar energy while in the solar thermal system, heat energy is used to produce steam using solar energy. The energy possessed by the steam is converted into electrical energy using steam turbine and generator. Figure 2.10 shows the schematic of the solar PV power plant.

The smart grids can be operated at optimized condition by forecasting of renewable energy as energy demand and energy consumption may vary frequently [46]. Various techniques are used to predict the solar power using solar radiation datasets which are based on hourly, daily, weekly, monthly data due to change in climate condition in different countries.

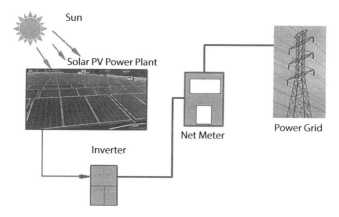

Figure 2.10 Schematic of Solar PV power plant.

The feedforward ANN is used by many researchers in the prediction of solar PV electrical energy production [55]. Different types of models were developed to predict the solar energy production and it is necessary to understand the impact of various factors which affect solar energy generation [56].

The ANN was developed to forecast energy output from a solar PV system using solar irradiance which was recorded using a weather station. The ML technique can be used to predict solar PV system under various weather conditions. Also, this technique can be used to optimize integration of solar PV plant with various power systems [57]. There are a few limitations in the algorithms used in the precise determination of solar energy production and it is suggested that the hybrid algorithm minimizes resources of manual parameter adjustment. Also, this hybrid algorithm is superior to other methods [58]. The AI algorithms are efficient in forecasting solar power as compared to other models [59].

The power output of hybrid solar PV and wind systems can be predicted using the ML method using seven weather data which affect the hybrid system significantly. The recursive feature elimination using cross-validation was used with historic hourly data as input. The input data was used with and without data manipulation. It is reported that the feature selection technique using linear regression model results in better performance as compared to other models and is effective in improving the efficiency of smart grids by accurately predicting the power produced by hybrid system [27]. Figure 2.11 depicts the solar power plant installed on the building roof.

Figure 2.11 Rooftop solar PV power plant.

The deep learning approach is most effectively used in forecasting power produced by the solar and wind turbines. The deep learning prediction models use historical data to estimate the energy produced by smart grids [60]. The estimation of solar power production can be influenced by various factors, which can be obtained from satellites. Using this data, deep learning prediction models can predict the energy produced considering solar factors, electrical factors, and atmospheric and geological factors [61]. To reduce data errors related to numerical weather predictions (NWP), it is suggested to use NWP data from several reliable sources available [62].

2.7   Challenges and Opportunities

The life span of solar PV panel is 25 to 30 years and the power produced by the panels gradually decreases due to various types of failures and aging of the solar PV panels. Hence, the ML system should have features to detect the few undetectable faults which directly and indirectly affect the solar PV plants. Also, it is necessary to develop a low-cost Internet of Things (IOT) system for remote monitoring of solar PV power plant. If an IOT system is used, then there are challenges in data security and privacy, and these aspects should be addressed [63].

The accuracy of an ML model is good for sunny days; however, accuracy is low for cloudy days [25]. The ML system should have a feature which considers load management, classification of customer and analysis. There are a few challenges in integrating the AI with an energy management system [64]. An AI system which is inspired by biological things should be developed for energy production, distribution of energy and effective energy management [65].

The power produced by the solar PV panel is intermittent and hence energy storage systems such as battery storage systems, fuel cells, etc., are used [66]. A robust ML system must be developed for estimating the performance of the energy storage systems. Also, it is necessary to develop advanced control strategies for a solar PV power plant [67]. New techniques must be developed for fast charging of batteries without affecting the battery performance and minimizing battery degradation [68].

2.8   Future Research Directions

The power produced by the solar PV panel decreases with aging and hence it is necessary to develop a suitable ML system for power production with respect to aging. The aging also depends upon environmental conditions and maintenance and hence these aspects also should be considered in developing an ML system.

The energy produced by the solar PV system is affected by dust, bird droppings, etc. Hence, a suitable IOT system can be integrated with an ML system to carry out regular cleaning work. This enhances the life of the solar PV system and increases power production.

The performance of the hybrid renewable energy systems can be improved with the ML system which also improves the grid performance and ensures continuous power supply. Hence further research work can be carried out in these areas using a suitable ML system.

In recent years, most countries are interested in utilizing solar PV systems for power generation. Hence, there are a lot of opportunities for local entrepreneurs to start their own enterprises to meet the local demand in developing an ML system according to local climate conditions. Also, the integration of a solar PV system with the IOT will also generate local employment and research opportunities.

2.9   Conclusion

Conventional fuels are burnt to produce electrical energy; however, energy production from conventional fuel sources causes global warming directly and indirectly. Hence, there is a need to minimize greenhouse gas emissions and to mitigate climate change. Most countries are considering solar energy as the renewable replacement to the fossil fuel. The challenges faced in solar energy conversion devices can be overcome using computer technologies like big data, ML and IOT. The utilization of sensors, IOT systems and smart grids with an ML system helps to enhance the performance of a solar PV system and balance energy production and energy demand. The ML technique is popular in predicting solar radiation, solar energy production, load demand, peak load, power quality estimation, power demand, potentials risks, energy storage, optimization of energy storage system, battery charging and discharging prediction, production cost, energy pricing, etc. However, there are a few challenges which can be overcome with the help of the development of a hybrid system and a low-cost IOT system.

Acknowledgement

The authors thank Mr. Nagaraja T, Managing Director, M/s Bluevolt Services, Bangalore, India, for his valuable suggestions.

References

1. Johannes Schmidt, Katharina Gruber, Michael Klingler, Claude Klöckl, Luis Ramirez Camargo, Peter Regner, Olga Turkovska, Sebastian Wehrle and Elisabeth Wetterlund, A new perspective on global renewable energy systems: why trade in energy carriers matters, *Energy Environment Science*, 12, 2022-2029, 2019.
2. K.A. Abed, A.K. El Morsi, M.M. Sayed, A.A. ElShaib, M.S. Gad, Effect of waste cooking-oil biodiesel on performance and exhaust emissions of a diesel engine, *Egyptian Journal of Petroleum*, 27(4), 985-989, 2018.
3. Oliver Inderwildi, Chuan Zhang, Xiaonan Wang and Markus Kraft, The impact of intelligent cyber-physical systems on the decarbonization of energy, *Energy & Environmental Science*, 2020, DOI: 10.1039/c9ee01919g
4. Dolf Gielen, Francisco Boshell, Deger Saygin, Morgan D. Bazilian, Nicholas Wagner, RicardoGorini, The role of renewable energy in the global energy transformation, *Energy Strategy Reviews*, 24, 38-50, 2019.
5. Daryl R. Myers, Solar Radiation, Practical Modeling for Renewable Energy Applications, CRC Press, 2017.
6. Soteris A. Kalogirou, *Solar Energy Engineering*, Academic Press, 2013.
7. C. Julian Chen, *Physics of Solar Energy*, Wiley, 2002.

8. King, P.; Sansom, C.; Comley, P., Photogrammetry for Concentrating Solar Collector Form Measurement, Validated Using a Coordinate Measuring Machine. *Sustainability*, 12, 196, 2019.

9. Shafeek, H, Maintenance Practices in Cement Industry. *Asian Trans. Eng.* 1, 10–20, 2012.

10. Kiesecker, J.; Baruch-Mordo, S.; Heiner, M.; Negandhi, D.; Oakleaf, J.R.; Kennedy, C.M.; Chauhan, P., Renewable Energy and Land Use in India: A Vision to Facilitate Sustainable Development. *Sustainability*, 12, 281, 2019.

11. Muhammad Badar Hayat, Danish Ali, Keitumetse Cathrine Monyake, Lana Alagha, Niaz Ahmed, Solar energy—A look into power generation, challenges, and a solar-powered future, *International Journal Energy Research*, 43(3), 1049-1067, 2019.

12. Hao Li, Zhijian Liu, Kejun Liu, Zhien Zhang, "Predictive Power of Machine Learning for Optimizing Solar Water Heater Performance: The Potential Application of High-Throughput Screening", *International Journal of Photoenergy*, 2017, Article ID 4194251, 1-10, 2017.

13. Ibrahim, S.; Daut, I.; Irwan, Y.; Irwanto, M.; Gomesh, N.; Farhana, Z. Linear Regression Model in Estimating Solar Radiation in Perlis. *Energy Procedia*, 18, 1402–1412, 2012.

14. Dupré, O.; Vaillon, R.; Green, M.A. Thermal Behavior of Photovoltaic Devices; Springer Science and Business Media: Berlin/Heidelberg, Germany, 2017.

15. Jacques, S.; Caldeira, A.; Ren, Z.; Schellmanns, A.; Batut, N. Impact of the cell temperature on the energy efficiency of a single glass PV module: Thermal modeling in steady-state and validation by experimental data. *Renew. Energy Power Qual. J.* 1, 291–294, 2013.

16. Adeh, E.H., Good, S.P., Calaf, M. *et al.* Solar PV Power Potential is Greatest Over Croplands. *Sci Rep* 9, 11442, 2019.

17. R. Hudson, G. Heilscher, PV grid integration–system management issues and utility concerns. *Energy Procedia*. 25, 82-92, 2012.

18. Abujubbeh, M., Marazanye, V.T., Qadir, Z., Fahrioglu, M., Batunlu, C., 2019. Techno-economic feasibility analysis of grid-tied PV-wind hybrid system to meet a typical household demand: Case study - amman, Jordan. In: *2019 1st Global Power, Energy and Communication Conference. GPECOM, Nevsehir, Turkey*, pp. 418–423.

19. Zhang, Hongyi, *et al.*, Beyond empirical risk minimization. arXiv preprint arXiv:1710.09412, 2017.

20. Das, Utpal Kumar, *et al.* Forecasting of photovoltaic power generation and model optimization: A review. *Renew. Sustain. Energy Rev.* 81, 912–928, 2018.

21. Al-Turjman, F., Qadir, Z., Abujubbeh, M., Batunlu, C., Feasibility analysis of solar photovoltaic-wind hybrid energy system for household applications. *Comput. Electr. Eng.* 86, 106743, 2020.

22. Antonanzas, Javier, *et al.*, Review of photovoltaic power forecasting. *Sol. Energy* 136, 78–111, 2016.
23. Wolfgang Ertel, *Introduction to Artificial Intelligence,* Springer, 2017.
24. Sudharsan Ravichandiran, Hands-On Deep Learning Algorithms with Python: Master deep learning algorithms with extensive math by implementing them using TensorFlow, McGraw Hill, 2019.
25. Adel Mellit, Alessandro Massi Pavan, Emanuele Ogliari, Sonia Leva and Vanni Lughi, Advanced Methods for Photovoltaic Output Power Forecasting: A Review, *Appl. Sci.* 10, 487, 1-22, 2020.
26. Mekyung Lee, Gang He, An empirical analysis of applications of artificial intelligence algorithms in wind power technology innovation during 1980–2017, *Journal of Cleaner Production*, 297, 126536, 2021.
27. Z. Qadir, S.I. Khan, E. Khalaji *et al.*, Predicting the energy output of hybrid PV–wind renewable energy system using feature selection technique for smart grids. *Energy Reports* 2021, https://doi.org/10.1016/j.egyr.2021.01.018.
28. P.J.Zucatelli, E.G.S.Nascimento, G.Y.R.Aylas, N.B.P.Souza, Y.K.L.Kitagawa, A.A.B.Santos, A.M.G.Arce, D.M.Moreira, Short-term wind speed forecasting in Uruguay using computational intelligence, *Heliyon*, 5(5), e01664, 2019.
29. Bhuiyan Md Abul Ehsan, Fatema Begum, Sheikh Jawad Ilham, Raihan Sayeed Khan, Advanced wind speed prediction using convective weather variables through machine learning application, *Applied Computing and Geosciences*, 1, 100002, 2019.
30. Vasant, Pandian, Zelinka, Ivan, Weber, Gerhard-Wilhelm, Intelligent Computing and Optimization, *Proceedings of the 2nd International Conference on Intelligent Computing and Optimization 2019* (ICO 2019), Springer, 2019.
31. Zhenkun Liu, Ping Jiang, Lifang Zhang, Xinsong Niu, A combined forecasting model for time series: Application to short-term wind speed forecasting, *Applied Energy*, 259, 114137, 2020.
32. Jung-Pin Lai, Yu-Ming Chang, Chieh-Huang Chen and Ping-Feng Pai, A Survey of Machine Learning Models in Renewable Energy Predictions, *Appl. Sci.* 10, 5975, 2020.
33. Wang, G.; Jia, G.; Liu, J.; Zhang, H. A hybrid wind power forecasting approach based on Bayesian model averaging and ensemble learning. Renew. *Energy*, 145, 2426–2434, 2020.
34. J. E. T. Akinsola, Supervised Machine Learning Algorithms: Classification and Comparisons, *International Journal of Computer Trends and Technology*, 48(3), 128-138, 2017.
35. Chun Sing Lai, Cankun Zhong, Keda Pan, Wing W.Y.Ng, Loi Lei Lai, A deep learning based hybrid method for hourly solar radiation forecasting, *Expert Systems with Applications*, 177, 114941, 2021.
36. A. Mellit, Artificial intelligence techniques for modelling and forecasting of solar radiation data: a review, *International journal of Artificial Intelligence and Soft Computing*, 1, 52–76, 2008.

37. Ivana Nizetic Kosovic, ToniMastelic, DamirIvankovic, Using Artificial Intelligence on environmental data from Internet of Things for estimating solar radiation: Comprehensive analysis, *Journal of Cleaner Production*, 266, 121489, 2020.

38. J. Zhang, L. Zhao, S. Deng, W. Xu, and Y. Zhang, A critical review of the models used to estimate solar radiation, *Renewable and Sustainable Energy Reviews.*, 70, 314–329, 2017.

39. T. Khatib, A. Mohamed, K. Sopian and M. Mahmoud, Assessment of Artificial Neural Networks for Hourly Solar Radiation Prediction, *International Journal of Photoenergy*, 1-7, 2012.

40. NASA, https://power.larc.nasa.gov/, 2021.

41. M. Mohandes, S. Rehman and T. Halawani, Estimation of Global Solar Radiation Using Artificial NeuralNetworks, *Renewable Energy*, 14, 179–84, 1998.

42. S. Rehman and M. Mohandes, Estimation of diffuse fraction of global solar radiation using artificial neural networks, *Energy Sources*, 31, 974–84, 2009.

43. J. Lazzús, A. Ponce and J. Marín, Estimation of global solar radiation over the City of La Serena using a neural network, *Applied Solar Energy*, 47(1), 66–73, 2011.

44. Voyant, C.; Notton, G.; Kalogirou, S.; Nivet, M.-L.; Paoli, C.; Motte, F.; Fouilloy, A. Machine learning methods for solar radiation forecasting: A review. *Renew. Energy*, 105, 569–582.

45. Imane Jebli, Fatima-Zahra Belouadha, Mohammed Issam Kabbaj, AmineTilioua, Prediction of solar energy guided by pearson correlation using machine learning, *Energy*, 224, 120109, 2021.

46. Kusum Tharani, Neeraj Kumar, Vishal Srivastava, Sakshi Mishra & M. Pratyush Jayachandran, Machine learning models for renewable energy forecasting, *Journal of Statistics and Management Systems*, 23:1, 171-180, 2020.

47. C. Voyant, G. Notton, S. Kalogirou *et al.*, Machine learning methods for solar radiation forecasting: a review, *Renewable Energy*, 105, 569–582, 2017.

48. T. Khatib, A. Mohamed, and K. Sopian, A review of solar energy modeling techniques, *Renewable and Sustainable Energy Reviews*, 16(5), 2864–2869, 2012.

49. G. Notton, C. Paoli, S. Vasileva, M. L. Nivet, J.-L. Canaletti, and C. Cristofari, Estimation of hourly global solar irradiation on tilted planes from horizontal one using artificial neural networks, *Energy*, 39(1), 166–179, 2012.

50. Tasdemir, Sakir, Yaniktepe, Bulent, Effective Estimation of Hourly Global Solar Radiation Using Machine Learning Algorithms, *International Journal of Photoenergy*, Article ID 8843620, 2020.

51. C. V. G. Zelaya, Towards explaining the effects of data preprocessing on machine learning," in *2019 IEEE 35th International Conference on Data Engineering*, 2086–2090, Macao, 2019.

52. Giovanni Cipriani, Antonino D'Amico, Stefania Guarino, Donatella Manno, Marzia Traverso and Vincenzo Di Dio, Convolutional Neural Network for

Dust and Hotspot Classification in PV Modules, *Energies*, 13, 6357, 1-17, 2020.

53. Barun Basnet, Hyunjun Chun, and Junho Bang, An Intelligent Fault Detection Model for Fault Detection in Photovoltaic Systems, *Journal of Sensors*, Article ID 6960328, 2020.

54. Jamel Chakchak, Numan Sabit Cetin, Investigating the impact of weather parameters selection on the prediction of solar radiation under different genera of cloud cover: A case-study in a subtropical location, *Measurement*, 176, 109159, 2021.

55. Adrian Gligora, Cristian-Dragos Dumitrua,, Horatiu-Stefan Grif, Artificial intelligence solution for managing a photovoltaic energy production unit, *Procedia Manufacturing* 22, 626–633, 2018.

56. Jose Manuel Barrera, Alejandro Reina, Alejandro Maté, and Juan Carlos Trujillo, Solar Energy Prediction Model Based on Artificial Neural Networks and Open Data, *Sustainability*, 12, 6915, 2020.

57. Mohammad H. Alomari, Jehad Adeeb, and Ola Younis, Solar Photovoltaic Power Forecasting in Jordan using Artificial Neural Networks, *International Journal of Electrical and Computer Engineering*, 8(1), 497–504, 2018.

58. Na Dong Jian-Fang, ChangAi-Guo Wu Zhong-Ke Gao, A novel convolutional neural network framework based solar irradiance prediction method, *International Journal of Electrical Power & Energy Systems*, 114, 105411, 2020.

59. Huaizhi Wang, Yangyang Liu, Bin Zhou, Canbing Li, Guangzhong Cao, Nikolai Voropai, Evgeny Barakhtenko, Taxonomy research of artificial intelligence for deterministic solar power forecasting, *Energy Conversion and Management*, 214, 112909, 2020.

60. Sheraz Aslam, Herodotos Herodotou, Syed Muhammad Mohsin, Nadeem Javaid, Nouman Ashraf, Shahzad Aslam, A survey on deep learning methods for power load and renewable energy forecasting in smart microgrids, *Renewable and Sustainable Energy Reviews*, 144, 110992, 2021.

61. Jose Manuel Barrera, Alejandro Reina, Alejandro Maté, and Juan Carlos Trujillo, Solar Energy Prediction Model Based on Artificial Neural Networks and Open Data, *Sustainability*, 12, 6915, 2020.

62. Ganesh V. Karbhari, Dr. Pragya Nema, IoT & Machine Learning Paradigm for Next Generation Solar Power Plant Monitoring System, *International Journal of Advanced Science and Technology*, 29(03), 6894-6902, 2020.

63. Adel Mellit, Soteris Kalogirou, Artificial intelligence and internet of things to improve efficacy of diagnosis and remote sensing of solar photovoltaic systems: Challenges, recommendations and future directions, *Renewable and Sustainable Energy Reviews*, 143, 110889, 2021.

64. Aparna Kumari, Rajesh Gupta, Sudeep Tanwar, Neeraj Kumar, Blockchain and AI amalgamation for energy cloud management: Challenges, solutions, and future directions, *Journal of Parallel and Distributed Computing*, 143, 148-166, 2020.

65. Sunil Kr.Jha, Jasmin Bilalovic, Anju Jha, Nilesh Patel, Han Zhang, Renewable energy: Present research and future scope of Artificial Intelligence, *Renewable and Sustainable Energy Reviews,* 77, 297-317, 2017.

66. Amy J.C. Trappey, Paul P.J. Chen, Charles V. Trappey and Lin Ma, A Machine Learning Approach for Solar Power Technology Review and Patent Evolution Analysis, *Applied. Science.* 9, 1478, 1-25, 2019.

67. TianhanGao, WeiLu, Machine learning toward advanced energy storage devices and systems, *Science*, 24(1), 101936, 2021.

68. University of Cambridge, www.sciencedaily.com/releases/2020/04/2004060 92833.htm 2020.

Mathematical Analysis on Power Generation – Part I

G. Udhaya Sankar[1]*, C. Ganesa Moorthy[2] and C.T. Ramasamy[3]

[1]Department of Physics, Alagappa University, Karaikudi, India
[2]Department of Mathematics, Alagappa University, Karaikudi, India
[3]Department of Mathematics, Alagappa Government Arts College, Karaikudi, India

Abstract

Computing processes using electronic processors also become parts of artificial intelligence. Instrumentation for temperature measurement is based on mathematical analysis and algorithms for implementation of mathematical analysis. Thermocouples are used to generate current from heat and used to produce heat from current. Temperature is measured when a thermocouple generates current from heat; classical method s measure voltages, then temperatures are computed by using a formula that considers temperature as a tenth degree polynomial of voltage in which the coefficients of the polynomial depend on the thermocouple used and they should be evaluated first so that the thermocouple can be used. This chapter provides a mathematical analysis and computing methods to understand that first two coefficients are the most significant ones. These ideas propose another format in the form that temperature is a scalar multiple of a scalar power of voltage, which also involves two parameters. Methods are discussed to find two parameters in both methods, they are evaluated for known data, and they are found to be good ones for computing temperature in terms of voltage measured in a thermocouple. This approach simplifies algorithms without compromising accuracy in measurement of temperature, but with a less computation time. These two coefficient methods are suggested for implementation in measurement of temperature using thermocouples.

Keywords: Planck's distribution, polynomials, voltmeter, ammeter, thermocouple

*Corresponding author: udhaya.sankar.20@gmail.com

Pandian Vasant, Gerhard-Wilhelm Weber, Joshua Thomas, José Antonio Marmolejo-Saucedo and Roman Rodriguez-Aguilar (eds.) *Artificial Intelligence for Renewable Energy and Climate Change*, (53–86) © 2022 Scrivener Publishing LLC

3.1 Introduction

The Seebeck effect and the Peltier effect are used to generate current and heat in a thermocouple, respectively; current from heat and heat from current. They are the basics for the theory of thermoelectric effects [2, 4, 15]. On the other hand, it is possible to produce light from electricity and electricity from light. They are the basics of photovoltaic theory. Both theories are related because heat produces light and light produces heat. This connection is always justified by a Quantum theory of black body radiation. This connection is to be used in this chapter to derive a formula which provides a linear relationship between product of current with voltage and heat in a thermocouple. The fundamentals for this connection are Planck's distribution law for black body radiation and the photovoltaic equation of Einstein. Both of them are to be used; Planck's distribution is to be used in terms of its consequence, namely, Wien's displacement law.

Existing calculation methods [11] for conversion of voltage to temperature uses a theoretical relation assuming that temperature is a polynomial of voltage in a thermocouple; they find the unknown coefficients by using data to fix polynomial, and then they use the polynomial as a formula for conversion of voltage to temperature. There is always nonlinearity in the relation connecting voltage and temperature in a thermocouple. But, when temperature to be measured is locally fixed, there is linearity. This linear relation is derived in this chapter which is not theoretical linearization. Theory of vector spaces may refer to this type of linear relation $T = a + bV$ as affine relation, but it is mentioned here only as a linear relation to avoid a term "affine mapping", which is not commonly used in theoretical physics. Multiplicative analysis is also used to derive relations of the type $T = aV^b$ and of the type $T = ab^V$. It is observed that the relation of the type $T = aV^b$ is more appropriate for temperature measurement than the other two types of relations.

Major thermoelectric applications of thermocouples are construction of small electricity generators, small refrigerators, and temperature sensors for industries [12, 14, 17, 19, 21–25]. Temperature sensors for a wide range of temperature are made by using two major principles. One is done by using heat-voltage relation in a thermocouple. The second one is done by using heat-resistance relation. The first is used in thermocouple-temperature sensors. The second is used in resistance-temperature detectors which have many variations. This chapter focuses on measurement through thermocouples. Applications of photovoltaic theory are generation of electricity and producing light using electricity. It is also possible to use this theory for temperature measurement by using thermocouples. Photovoltaic theory has already been used for temperature measurement without using thermocouples [8] in terms of Planck's distribution law for black body radiation.

A theoretical formula for conversion of voltage to temperature for a thermocouple-temperature sensor is derived in this chapter. This formula is temperature dependent so that it is a localized conversion. At this cost, the theoretical formula provides a linear relationship between voltage and temperature in a thermocouple. The derivation is based on Einstein's photovoltaic equation, Wien's displacement formula, and basic theory for thermoelectric effects. This particular linear relationship between temperature and voltage is derived from a relation between temperature and product of voltage with current. The main aspect is the observation of the importance of current along with voltage in conversion to temperature for measurement by using a thermocouple. Two more types of formulae related with the linear formula are discussed, and it is concluded that the formula of the type "temperature = a constant times of voltage with a constant power" is the most advantageous for measurement of temperature in a classical thermocouple.

3.2   Methodology for Derivations

As a consequence of theory in [1], it can be stated that if a real valued function f which is differentiable on an open interval (a, b) is strictly monotonically increasing when $f'(c) > 0$, for every c in (a, b), and it is strictly decreasing when $f'(c) < 0$, for every c in (a, b). Let us first apply this fact to understand the relationship between maximum efficiency of a thermoelectric generator and figure of merit. The maximum efficiency η of a electricity generator is given in [5] by

$$\eta = \frac{(T_c - T_h)\left((1 + ZT)^{\frac{1}{2}}\right) - 1}{T_c + (1 + ZT)^{\frac{1}{2}} T_h}$$

where ZT is the figure of merit, T_c and T_h are temperatures at cold end and hot end, respectively. Let us give a notation K for ZT at present so that

$$\eta = \frac{(T_c - T_h)\left((1+K)^{\frac{1}{2}}\right) - 1}{T_c + (1+K)^{\frac{1}{2}} T_h}.$$

To explore whether $\dfrac{d\eta}{dK} > 0$ or $\dfrac{d\eta}{dK} < 0$, it is sufficient to check whether

$$\left[T_c + (1+K)^{\frac{1}{2}} T_h \right](T_c - T_h)\left(\frac{1}{2}(1+K)^{-\frac{1}{2}} \right)$$

$$-\left[(T_c - T_h)\left((1+K)^{\frac{1}{2}}\right) - 1 \right]\frac{1}{2}(1+K)^{-\frac{1}{2}} T_h,$$

is positive or negative, or whether

$$\left[T_c + (1+K)^{\frac{1}{2}} T_h \right](T_c - T_h) - \left[(T_c - T_h)\left((1+K)^{\frac{1}{2}}\right) - 1 \right] T_h$$

is positive or negative, or whether $T_c (T_c - T_h) + (T_c - T_h) T_h$ is positive or negative, and hence whether $-(T_h + T_c)$ is positive or negative, because $(T_c - T_h) < 0$. So, maximum efficiency η of electricity generation strictly decreases when ZT strictly increases, and when T_c and T_h are fixed. The maximum value of coefficient of performance for refrigeration is given in [5] by

$$\phi = \frac{(1+ZT)^{\frac{1}{2}} T_c - T_h}{(T_c - T_h)\left(1 + (1+ZT)^{\frac{1}{2}}\right)}$$

and, with $K = ZT$, this becomes

$$\phi = \frac{(1+K)^{\frac{1}{2}} T_c - T_h}{(T_c - T_h)\left(1 + (1+K)^{\frac{1}{2}}\right)}.$$

To explore whether $\dfrac{d\phi}{dK} > 0$ or $\dfrac{d\phi}{dK} < 0$, it is sufficient to check whether

$$(T_c - T_h)\left(1 + (1+K)^{\frac{1}{2}}\right)\frac{1}{2}(1+K)^{-\frac{1}{2}}T_c$$

$$-\left[(1+K)^{\frac{1}{2}}T_c - T_h\right](T_c - T_h)\frac{1}{2}(1+K)^{-\frac{1}{2}},$$

is positive or negative, or whether

$$\left[(1+K)^{\frac{1}{2}}T_c - T_h\right] - \left(1 + (1+K)^{\frac{1}{2}}\right)T_c$$

is positive or negative, or whether $-(T_h + T_c)$ is positive or negative. So, maximum value of coefficient of performance ϕ strictly decreases when ZT strictly increases, and when T_c and T_h are fixed. With these unknown illustrations for applications for positivity and negativity of first order derivatives, let us consider a known illustration for zero first order derivatives. A particular case of theory in [1] is the following. If f is a real valued function which is twice differentiable on (a, b) for which its second order derivative is continuous on (a, b), and if $f'(c) = 0$ and $f''(c) < 0$ for some c in (a, b), then f has a local maximum at c. Let us recall how to apply this result to derive Wien's displacement law from Planck's distribution law for black body radiation. When $u(\lambda)$ denotes the intensity of radiation-rays with wavelength λ, the Planck's distribution is given by

$$u(\lambda) = \frac{8\pi hc}{\lambda^5} \frac{1}{\exp\left(\dfrac{hc}{\lambda kT}\right) - 1}, \tag{3.1}$$

where h is the Planck's constant, k is the Boltzmann's constant, c is the velocity of light in vacuum, and the temperature of the black body T is measured in Kelvin. It is possible to find a value λ_{max} such that $u'(\lambda_{max}) = 0$, by solving the equation $u'(\lambda) = 0$ for $\lambda = \lambda_{max}$, and it can be verified that $u''(\lambda_{max}) < 0$. This derivation provides a relation

$$\lambda_{max} = \frac{b}{T}, \tag{3.2}$$

where b is the Wien's constant. This is called Wien's displacement law.

The function $u(\lambda)$ given in (3.1) is actually a function of λ and T, when T is also considered as a variable. So, T may be considered implicitly as a function of $u(\lambda)$ and λ. However, if rays emitted from a source have a single wavelength, then there is a possibility to consider in this special case, T as a function of λ alone as:

$$T = \frac{b}{\lambda}, \tag{3.3}$$

and let us write the same in the form:

$$T = av, \tag{3.4}$$

where $a = \dfrac{b}{c}$ is a constant. Left side of (3.4) represents temperature of the source which emits rays with only one frequency v, and this may also be considered as the temperature that can be produced by a light ray with frequency v which hits a matter. This provides a way to use the formula (3.4) along with Einstein's photovoltaic equation [7].

Let us recall Einstein's photovoltaic equation:

$$hv = \phi + KE_{max}, \tag{3.5}$$

where $KE_{max} = \dfrac{1}{2}mv^2$ is the maximum kinetic energy of an electron which produces a voltage in a photovoltaic effect, m is the mass of an electron, v is the maximum velocity reached by the electron which moves due to a light ray with frequency v, and ϕ is a work function. From (3.4), the equation (3.5) becomes

$$\frac{h}{a}T = \phi + KE_{max}. \tag{3.6}$$

If this equation is divided by time to get energy divided by time or to get power, then KE_{max} can be replaced by an expression in the form IV, where I represents current and V represents voltage. Thus, the equation (3.6) can be simplified to the following form:

$$T = \psi + c_2 IV, \tag{3.7}$$

where c_2 is a constant, and ψ is a function associated with ϕ. The reason stated for usage of (3.4) for temperature of matters is applicable even for the formula (3.7). Some more details are needed. The derivation reveals that c_2 depends only on the thermocouple-devise used and the scale used for temperature. Let us observe that (3.7) is applicable only for temperature measured in Kelvin. The relation (3.7) is applicable also for other units like Centigrade because of linear transformation relations between Kelvin and other units. For thermocouple-temperature sensor application purpose, I and V depend on T, and hence I should also be a function of T so that I and V should be interrelated so that IV may also be replaced by a function of V alone. For localized values of T or V in some neighborhoods, (3.7) may be written as:

$$T = c_1 + c_2 IV,$$
(3.8)

where c_1 is a localized constant. It may be localized further in the form:

$$T = c_3 + c_4 V,$$
(3.9)

where c_3 and c_4 are localized constants, because I is a function of V. In multiplicative analysis [9], a formal rule for conversion from additive analysis to multiplicative analysis suggests that addition should be replaced by multiplication, and multiplication should be replaced by exponentiation. If this formal rule is applied, then (3.9) may be converted to the form:

$$T = \alpha V^\beta,$$
(3.10)

where α and β are localized constants, or (3.9) may be converted to the form:

$$T = \alpha \beta^V,$$
(3.11)

where again α and β are localized constants.

3.3   Energy Discussions

The format (3.8) is an expected one although it was not derived by others; because the capacity of a thermoelectric generator is measured by its power in the form IV. There is nothing wrong in using (3.9) because I is a function of V corresponding to T. A continuous real valued function with a real variable can be approximated by means of a polynomial. This is an approximation result in mathematics. So, companies [10, 20] manufacturing thermocouple-temperature sensors report use of polynomial approximation procedure to convert voltage to temperature. That is, let us begin with an assumption that

$$T = a_0 + a_1 V + a_2 V_2 + \cdots + a_{10} V_{10}, \qquad (3.12)$$

where a_0, a_1, a_2, $\cdots$ a_{10} are (globalized) constants to be determined for a thermocouple-temperature sensor. These constants may be found by many mathematical methods based on measurement of different observed values of V in the thermocouple-temperature sensor and the corresponding actual temperature measurement done by some other reliable instrument. Once this is done, (3.12) provides a formula for the thermocouple-temperature sensor, which can be used for measurement of T. A major observation that should be noted is that there is an ultimate ready-made table for conversion [10, 18] on forgetting existence of all theories used for computation purposes. When the formula (3.9) is applied; the reliable temperature range should be divided and found as $T_1 < T_2 < \cdots < T_n$ or equivalently the reliable voltage range should be divided and found as $V_1 < V_2 < \cdots < V_n$ such that c_3 and c_4 are fixed in each divided range: V_i to V_{i+1}. This will help us to create the ready-made table for conversion for any new type of thermocouple. For example, let us consider Table 4 given in [13], and let us consider the following pairs of observed values provided in the table:

(419.5°C, 3443.6μV), (630.5°C, 5546.2μV), (650°C, 5747.6μV), (700°C, 6269.8μV), (1000°C, 9581.1μV), and (1050°C, 10162.6μV) for readings of a specific thermocouple in which reference temperature is 0°C. If the first two pairs of values are substituted in (3.9), and two equations are solved for c_3 and c_4, then the following equation is obtained

$$T = 73.97804147246267 + 0.1003519452106915 \ V; \qquad (3.13)$$

this relation can be used for measuring temperature in the voltage range: 3443.6μV to 5546.2μV. If the second two pairs of values are substituted in (3.9), and two equations are solved for c_3 and c_4, then the following equation is obtained

$$T = 99.67445423209498 + 0.0957487552661815 \ V; \qquad (3.14)$$

this relation can be used for measuring temperature in the voltage range: 5747.6μV to 6269.8μV. If the third two pairs of values are substituted in (3.9), and two equations are solved for c_3 and c_4, then the following equation is obtained:

$$T = 146.829919857524 + 0.08904719501336 \ V; \qquad (3.15)$$

this relation can be used for measuring temperature in the voltage range: $9581.1\mu V$ to $10162.6\mu V$. If this is done for all pairs of values given in that table, it can be found that the values of c_3 are increasing with the increasing values of the ranges of voltage. This increasing relation was checked for many tables, which could be due to increase in resistance for an increase in temperature. When (3.9) is used, c_4 also varies. But, if it is possible to use (3.8), then c_2 is fixed for all values of voltages, and only c_1 should be found and tabulated. For this purpose, the design of a thermocouple should include a voltmeter as well as an ammeter. But present thermocouples include only voltmeter, and temperatures are found only by using voltages. A technical problem in including an ammeter should be discussed. Let us consider the Figure 3.1, which provides a simplified form of a thermocouple which includes only a voltmeter.

Let us recall the following law of the third metal mentioned in the book [8] for thermocouples: "Introduction of a third metal C into a circuit comprising of two dissimilar metals A and B does not affect the resulting emf in the circuit when both ends of the third metal are kept at the same temperature". This is followed in Figure 3.1. For a better measurement of temperature by using (3.8), there is a need to connect a voltmeter as well as an ammeter with a thermocouple. If they are connected in serial then it would affect voltmeter readings, and if they are connected in parallel, then it would affect ammeter readings. To avoid this problem, only one measurement of voltage and current should be observed at a time. For example, a Single Pole Double Throw switch as given in Figure 3.2 or a Double Pole Double Throw switch as given in Figure 3.3 may be used to reach this aim. So, there is a possibility to use more advantageous (3.8) instead of (3.9).

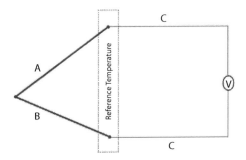

Figure 3.1 Classical thermocouple with a voltmeter.

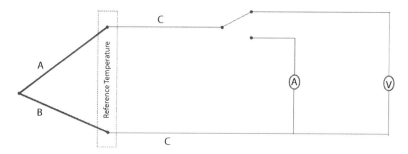

Figure 3.2 Thermocouple with a voltmeter, an ammeter, and an SPDT switch.

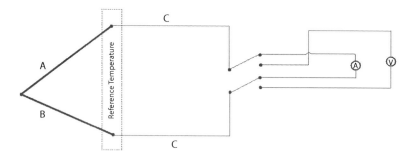

Figure 3.3 Thermocouple with a voltmeter, an ammeter, and a DPDT switch.

Let us discuss the possibility of using (3.10) and (3.11) instead of (3.9). Let us consider again first two pairs, second two pairs, and third two pairs from: (419.5°C, 3443.6μV), (630.5°C, 5546.2μV), (650°C, 5747.6μV), (700°C, 6269.8μV), (1000°C, 9581.1μV), and (1050°C, 10162.6μV), which were used above, but for finding the constants α and β in the equations (3.10) and (3.11), and to find the following equations in order for the corresponding ranges of voltages mentioned above.

$$T = (0.39708171201196)V^{0.85491694169749} \tag{3.16}$$

$$T = (0.40656221710069)V^{0.8521872095634} \tag{3.17}$$

$$T = (0.5048904666312)V^{0.82804794795444} \tag{3.18}$$

$$T = (215.239194172032)(1.00019380248768)^V \qquad (3.19)$$

$$T = (287.522799144298)(1.00014192499218)^V \qquad (3.20)$$

$$T = (447.583386770912)(1.00008390749969)^V \qquad (3.21)$$

The coefficients of equations derived for (3.9), (3.10) and (3.11) for localized three ranges of voltages reveal that the format (3.10) is a most suitable representation for localized measurement of temperature through a thermocouple of the type given in Figure 3.1. This conclusion is arrived in view of the almost closed coefficients for equations corresponding to (3.10). The closeness of coefficients for (3.1) was confirmed through some more data. A separate analysis is to be done to confirm more suitability of (10) by analyzing the six formulae (3.16)-(3.21) just now derived from (3.10) and (3.11), and three similar formulae (3.13)-(3.15) which were already derived from (3.9).

3.4   Data Analysis

Formulae (3.13), (3.16) and (3.19) were used to derive values for temperatures T1, T2, and T3, respectively, corresponding to the (discrete) voltages in the Range 1: $3443.6\mu V$ to $5546.2\mu V$. They are given as graphs in the Figures 3.4(a), 3.4(b), and 3.4(c), respectively, based on supplementary data. They are compared by graphs in the Figure 3.4(d). Notations T1, T2, T3 are used for same T obtained through different formulae.

Formulae (3.14), (3.17) and (3.20) were used to derive values for temperatures T1, T2, and T3, respectively, corresponding to the voltages in the Range 2: $5747.6\mu V$ to $6269.8\mu V$. They are given as graphs in the Figures 3.5(a), 3.5(b), and 3.5(c), respectively, based on supplementary data. They are compared by graphs in the Figure 3.5(d).

Formulae (3.15), (3.18) and (3.21) were used to derive values for temperatures T1, T2, and T3, respectively, corresponding to the voltages in the Range 3: $9581.1\mu V$ to $1016.2\mu V$. They are given as graphs in the Figures 3.6(a), 3.6(b), and 3.6(c), respectively, based on supplementary data. They are compared by graphs in the Figure 3.6(d).

The comparisons made in Figures 3.4(d), 3.5(d), and 3.6(d) ensure that almost all equations (3.9), (3.10) and (3.11) provide almost same data.

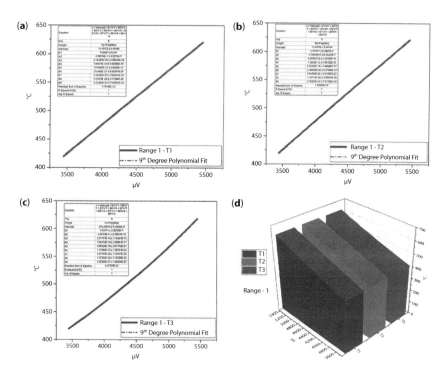

Figure 3.4 Voltage – Temperature relations. (a): for (3.13), (b): for (3.16), (c): for (3.19), (d): overall comparisons for Range – 1 (T1, T2, T3).

This was also verified directly from data obtained from the nine formulae. In solving coefficients for equations (3.9), (3.10) and (3.11) for Range 1, an importance was given to the relation for c_3 and c_4 obtained from the pair $(419.5°C, 3443.6\mu V)$, to find c_3 after finding c_4. This given importance had a reflection in the data corresponding to end values, along with truncation errors. The differences in coefficients of nine formulae found reveal that the equations (3.9), (3.10) and (3.11) provide only localized relations. The coefficient values of c_4 decrease in (3.13), (3.14) and (3.15). This means that the slopes of the straight lines corresponding to (3.9), (3.14) and (3.15) decrease. This means that the derivatives of the unknown actual curve which provide an unknown actual formula to find temperature from voltage decrease as voltages increase. To provide an interpretation for this meaning, let us recall few known things from mathematical analysis [16]. A real valued function $f:(a, b) \to \mathbb{R}$ on an interval is said to be convex, if $f(\theta x + (1 - \theta)y) \le \theta f(x) + (1 - \theta) f(y)$ for every x, y in (a, b), and for all θ satisfying $0 \le \theta \le 1$. A real valued function $f:(a, b) \to \mathbb{R}$ on an interval is

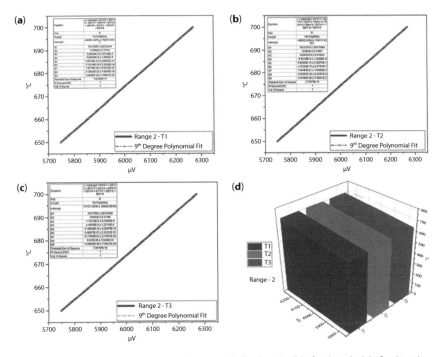

Figure 3.5 Voltage – Temperature relations. (a): for (3.14), (b): for (3.17), (c): for (3.18), (d): overall comparisons for Range – 2 (T1, T2, T3).

said to be concave, if $f(\theta x + (1 - \theta) y) \geq \theta f(x) + (1 - \theta) f(y)$ for every x, y in (a, b), and for all θ satisfying $0 \leq \theta \leq 1$. When the function f is also differentiable, then f is convex (or, concave) if and only if the derivative of f is increasing (decreasing, respectively). Thus, the unknown actual formula to find temperature from voltage should be a concave function. From the definition of derivatives, it is known that the second order derivative is negative (non-positive) when the first order derivative decreases. To use this fact, after fixing graphs for data obtained from formulae, another graph was fixed by using ninth degree polynomial fit for each fixed graph. They also suggest (3.10) as a better candidate for finding localized formulae. Moreover, the second order derivatives obtained directly from (3.16), (3.17) and (3.18) are also found as negative, without referring to data/graph obtained from these formulae. This second order derivative method also gives a fruitful information about β in (3.10): $0 < \beta < 1$. The second order derivatives obtained directly from (3.19), (3.20) and (3.21) are found to be positive; the same information is also obtained from the graphs for them. So, (3.11) is not a better candidate for formula derivation, even though

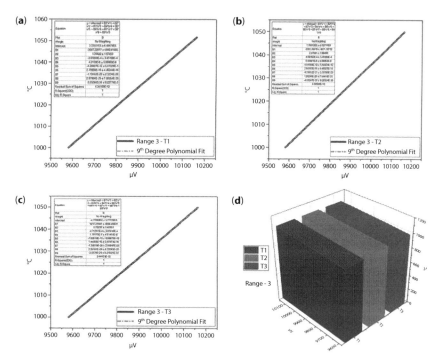

Figure 3.6 Voltage – Temperature relations. (a): for (3.15), (b): for (3.18), (c): for (3.21), (d) overall comparisons for Range – 3 (T1, T2, T3).

data provide obtained from (3.19), (3.20) and (3.21) are good approximations. Geometry for convex functions [16], concave functions and graphs obtained also lead to the same conclusions.

Thermocouple is always being a thrust research area [3, 6]. It is concluded that an ammeter should also be used in addition to a voltmeter in a thermocouple to measure temperature by using the formula (3.8), in which an analysis about the constant c_1 is required. However, the formulae (3.9), (3.10) and (3.11) may also be used because current in a thermocouple-temperature sensor depends on voltage. It is concluded that the type (3.10) localized formula is better than the other two formulae. All theory and suggestions are provided in view of industrial applications of thermocouple for measurement of temperature. Let us continue to search for actual formula based on a concave function for conversion of voltage to temperature in a thermocouple.

Acknowledgement

The authors thank RUSA Theme based project fellowship (Ref: Alu/RUSA/ Project Fellow –Science/2019) for financial support. The chapter has been written with the financial support of RUSA – phase 2.0 grant sanctioned vide Letter No. F. 24-51/2014-U, Policy (TNMulti-Gen), Dept. of Edn, Govt. of India.

References

1. Apostal TM. *Mathematical Analysis*. Narosa Pub. House, New Delhi, India. 1994.
2. Gajdarus, Tomás. Thermocouple Arrangement and Method for Measuring Temperatures. U.S. Patent Application 16/614,096, filed June 4, 2020.
3. Gather, Florian. Design and test of an apparatus for measuring the thermoelectric figure of merit ZT of solids. PhD diss., Universitätsbibliothek, 2015.
4. Goldsmid, H. Julian. The thermoelectric and related effects. *Introduction to Thermoelectricity*, Springer, Berlin, Heidelberg, 2010.
5. Gonçalves, A. P., and C. Godart. Alternative strategies for thermoelectric materials development. In *New Materials for Thermoelectric Applications: Theory and Experiment*, pp. 1-24. Springer, Dordrecht, 2013.
6. Kee, Yoong Yen, Yutaka Asako, Tan Lit Ken, and Nor Azwadi Che Sidik. Uncertainty of Temperature measured by Thermocouple. *Journal of Advanced Research in Fluid Mechanics and Thermal Sciences* 68, 1, 2020.
7. Lamb Jr, Willis E., and Marlan O. Scully. *The photoelectric effect without photons*. Miami Univ. Coral Gables FL Center for Theoretical Studies, 1968.
8. Sostmann, Henry E. Temperature Measurement. *Kirk-Othmer Encyclopedia of Chemical Technology*, John Wiley & Sons, England, 2000.
9. Moorthy, C. Ganesa, and G. Udhaya Sankar. Planck's Constant and Equation for Magnetic Field Waves. *Natural and Engineering Sciences* 4, 2, 2019.
10. Potter, David. Measuring temperature with thermocouples–a tutorial. *National Instruments Corporation*, 1996.
11. Powell, Robert L. *Thermocouple reference tables based on the IPTS-68*. Vol. 125. US National Bureau of Standards, 1974.
12. Radajewski, M., S. Decker, and L. Krüger. Direct temperature measurement via thermocouples within an SPS/FAST graphite tool. *Measurement* 147, 2019.

13. Roeser, William Frederick, and S. T. Lonberger. *Methods of Testing Thermocouples and Thermocouple Materials.* Vol. 590. US Department of Commerce, National Bureau of Standards, 1958.
14. Root, Waleri, Thomas Bechtold, and Tung Pham. Textile-integrated thermocouples for temperature measurement. *Materials* 13, 3, 2020.
15. Rowe, David Michael, ed. *Thermoelectrics Handbook: Macro to Nano.* CRC Press, United States, 2018.
16. Rudin, Walter. Real and complex analysis. *Bull. Amer. Math. Soc* 74, 1968.
17. Santos, M. C., J. S. Araujo Filho, M. A. S. Barrozo, M. J. Jackson, and A. R. Machado. Development and application of a temperature measurement device using the tool-workpiece thermocouple method in turning at high cutting speeds. *International Journal of Advanced Manufacturing Technology* 89, 8, 2017.
18. Shenker, Henry. *Reference tables for thermocouples.* No. 561. US Department of Commerce, National Bureau of Standards, 1955.
19. Souza, T. J., J. A. C. C. Medeiros, and A. C. Gonçalves. Identification model of an accidental drop of a control rod in PWR reactors using thermocouple readings and radial basis function neural networks. *Annals of Nuclear Energy* 103, 2017.
20. Wu, Joseph. A basic guide to thermocouple measurements. *Texas Instrum.*, 2018.
21. Xu, Zuwei, Xin Tian, and Haibo Zhao. Tailor-making thermocouple junction for flame temperature measurement via dynamic transient method. *Proceedings of the Combustion Institute* 36, 3, 2017.
22. Özmen, Ayşe, Gerhard Wilhelm Weber, İnci Batmaz, and Erik Kropat. RCMARS: Robustification of CMARS with different scenarios under polyhedral uncertainty set. *Communications in Nonlinear Science and Numerical Simulation* 16, 12, 2011.
23. Pandian Vasant, Ivan Zelinka, and Gerhard-Wilhelm Weber (Eds.). *Intelligent Computing & Optimization.* Springer, 2018.
24. Pandian Vasant, Ivan Zelinka, Gerhard-Wilhelm Weber (Eds.). Intelligent Computing and Optimization, *Proceedings of the 2nd International Conference on Intelligent Computing and Optimization* (ICO 2019), Springer, 2019.
25. Pandian Vasant, Ivan Zelinka, Gerhard-Wilhelm Weber (Eds.). Intelligent Computing and Optimization, *Proceedings of the 3rd International Conference on Intelligent Computing and Optimization* (ICO 2020), Springer, 2020.

Supplementary

Range- 1- T1

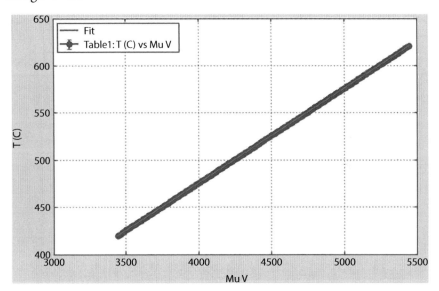

Residual Plot:

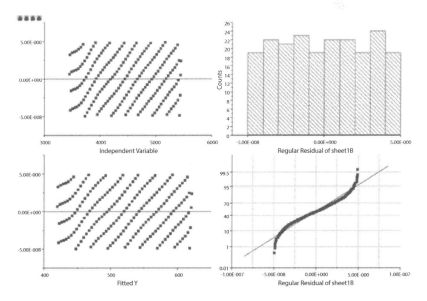

Polynomial Fit:

		Value	Standard Error	t-Value	Prob>|t|
B	Intercept	74.19123	0.48496	152.98428	0
B	B1	0.09991	0.001	99.4186	0
B	B2	4.05676E-7	9.2279E-7	0.43962	0.66069
B	B3	-2.16483E-10	4.92825E-10	-0.43927	0.66094
B	B4	7.40074E-14	1.68699E-13	0.4387	0.66136
B	B5	-1.68091E-17	3.8385E-17	-0.43791	0.66192
B	B6	2.53662E-21	5.80561E-21	0.43692	0.66264
B	B7	-2.45262E-25	5.62842E-25	-0.43576	0.66348
B	B8	1.37879E-29	3.17386E-29	0.43442	0.66445
B	B9	-3.43384E-34	7.93167E-34	-0.43293	0.66553
B					

Number of Points	210
Degrees of Freedom	200
Residual Sum of Squares	1.73189E-13
R-Square(COD)	1
Adj. R-Square	1

		DF	Sum of Squares	Mean Square	F Value	Prob>F
B	Model	9	716167.11609	79574.12401	9.18926E19	0
B	Error	200	1.73189E-13	8.65947E-16		
B	Total	209	716167.11609			

Range- 1- T2

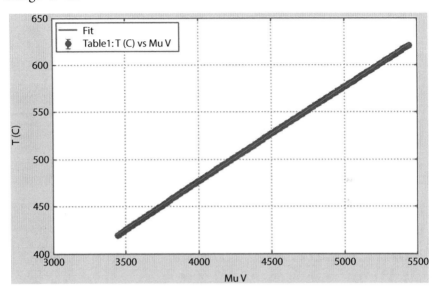

Residual Plot:

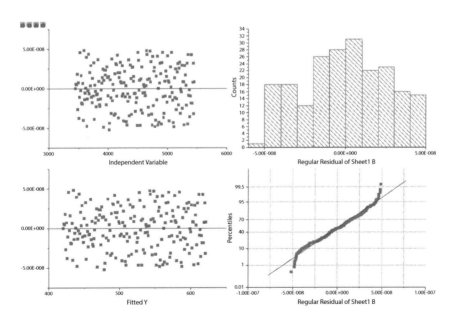

Polynomial Fit:

		Value	Standard Error	t-Value	Prob>|t|
B	Intercept	11.64516	0.44104	26.4037	0
B	B1	0.14797	9.13937E-4	161.90534	0
B	B2	-1.79016E-5	8.39224E-7	-21.33113	0
B	B3	5.30301E-9	4.48195E-10	11.83192	0
B	B4	-1.2855E-12	1.53422E-13	-8.37886	9.32587E-15
B	B5	2.30252E-16	3.49089E-17	6.59581	3.69619E-10
B	B6	-2.90858E-20	5.27986E-21	-5.50882	1.103E-7
B	B7	2.44568E-24	5.11872E-25	4.77792	3.42299E-6
B	B8	-1.22774E-28	2.88644E-29	-4.25348	3.23055E-5
B	B9	2.78391E-33	7.21338E-34	3.85937	1.53356E-4
B					

Number of Points	210
Degrees of Freedom	200
Residual Sum of Squares	1.43242E-13
R-Square(COD)	1
Adj. R-Square	1

		DF	Sum of Squares	Mean Square	F Value	Prob>F
B	Model	9	717488.31456	79720.92384	1.11309E20	0
B	Error	200	1.43242E-13	7.1621E-16		
B	Total	209	717488.31456			

Range- 1- T3

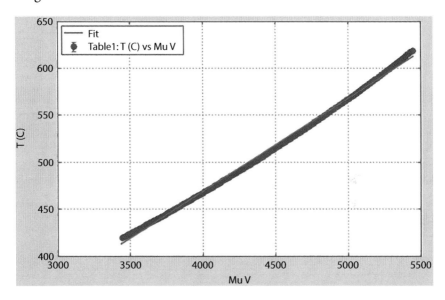

Residual Plot:

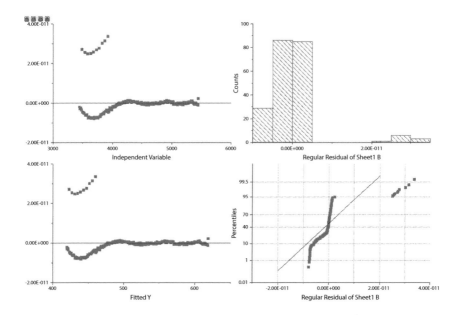

Polynomial Fit:

		Value	Standard Error	t-Value	Prob>|t|
B	Intercept	215.23914	1.13422E-4	1.89769E6	0
B	B1	0.04171	2.35035E-7	177462.70478	0
B	B2	4.04123E-6	2.15821E-10	18724.87917	0
B	B3	2.61117E-10	1.15261E-13	2265.43525	0
B	B4	1.26212E-14	3.94551E-17	319.88728	0
B	B5	4.96634E-19	8.97744E-21	55.3202	0
B	B6	1.47086E-23	1.35781E-24	10.83258	0
B	B7	5.67916E-28	1.31637E-28	4.31426	2.51532E-5
B	B8	1.17932E-33	7.42299E-33	0.15887	0.87393
B	B9	6.00385E-37	1.85505E-37	3.23649	0.00142
B					

Number of Points	210
Degrees of Freedom	200
Residual Sum of Squares	9.47335E-21
R-Square(COD)	1
Adj. R-Square	1

		DF	Sum of Squares	Mean Square	F Value	Prob>F
B	Model	9	700356.37873	77817.37541	1.64287E27	0
B	Error	200	9.47335E-21	4.73668E-23		
B	Total	209	700356.37873			

Range- 2- T1

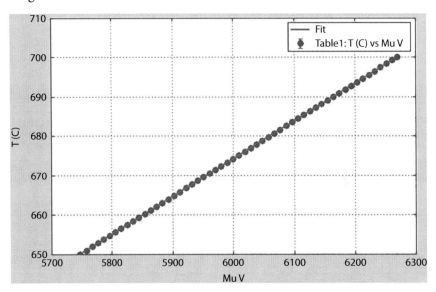

Residual Plot:

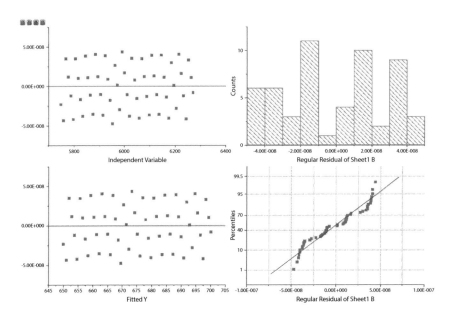

Polynomial Fit:

		Value	Standard Error	t-Value	Prob>|t|
B	Intercept	-84068.14374	172372.74747	-0.48771	0.62812
B	B1	129.42055	262.22594	0.49355	0.62403
B	B2	-0.08823	0.17749	-0.49712	0.62153
B	B3	3.50836E-5	7.01438E-5	0.50017	0.6194
B	B4	-8.96024E-9	1.78353E-8	-0.50239	0.61785
B	B5	1.52435E-12	3.02542E-12	0.50385	0.61683
B	B6	-1.72749E-16	3.42336E-16	-0.50462	0.61629
B	B7	1.25756E-20	2.49138E-20	0.50476	0.61619
B	B8	-5.33625E-25	1.05805E-24	-0.50435	0.61648
B	B9	1.00566E-29	1.99761E-29	0.50343	0.61712
B					

Number of Points	55
Degrees of Freedom	55
Residual Sum of Squares	4.22483E-14
R-Square(COD)	1
Adj. R-Square	1

		DF	Sum of Squares	Mean Square	F Value	Prob>F
B	Model	9	11947.98361	1327.55373	1.41402E18	0
B	Error	45	4.22483E-14	9.3885E-16		
B	Total	54	11947.98361			

Range- 2- T2

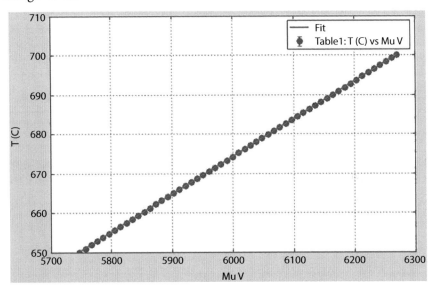

Residual Plot:

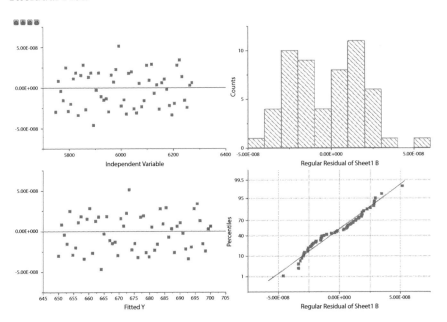

Polynomial Fit:

		Value	Standard Error	t-Value	Prob>|t|
B	Intercept	-68562.23904	134617.45051	-0.50931	0.61302
B	B1	100.21312	204.78984	0.48935	0.62697
B	B2	-0.06483	0.13861	-0.46768	0.64227
B	B3	2.44541E-5	5.478E-5	0.44641	0.65744
B	B4	-5.92145E-9	1.39288E-8	-0.42512	0.67277
B	B5	9.54353E-13	2.36276E-12	0.40391	0.68819
B	B6	-1.02362E-16	2.67354E-16	-0.38287	0.70362
B	B7	7.04481E-21	1.94569E-20	0.36207	0.71899
B	B8	-2.82251E-25	8.26303E-25	-0.34158	0.73425
B	B9	5.01495E-30	1.56007E-29	0.32146	0.74935
B					

Number of Points   55

Degrees of Freedom   45

Residual Sum of Squares   2.57676E-14

R-Square(COD)   1

Adj. R-Square   1

		DF	Sum of Squares	Mean Square	F Value	Prob>F
B	Model	9	11947.13364	1327.45929	2.31825E18	0
B	Error	45	2.57676E-14	5.72614E-16		
B	Total	54	11947.13364			

Range- 2- T3

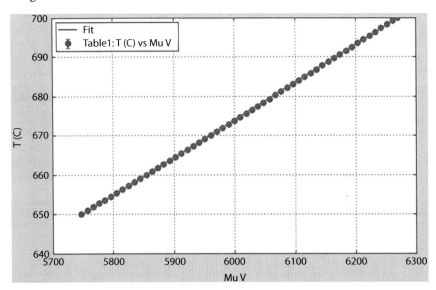

Residual Plot:

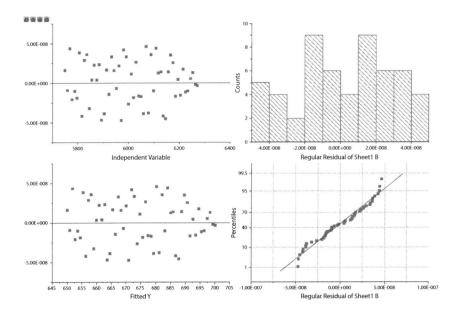

Polynomial Fit:

		Value	Standard Error	t-Value	Prob>|t|
B	Intercept	41731.12335	166923.85436	0.25	0.80372
B	B1	-63.57982	253.93668	-0.25038	0.80344
B	B2	0.04338	0.17188	0.25238	0.8019
B	B3	-1.72378E-5	6.79265E-5	-0.25377	0.80083
B	B4	4.40099E-9	1.72715E-8	0.25481	0.80003
B	B5	-7.48565E-13	2.92979E-12	-0.2555	0.7995
B	B6	8.48271E-17	3.31515E-16	0.25588	0.79921
B	B7	-6.17558E-21	2.41263E-20	-0.25597	0.79914
B	B8	2.621E-25	1.0246E-24	0.25581	0.79927
B	B9	-4.94096E-30	1.93447E-29	-0.25542	0.79956
B					

Number of Points   55

Degrees of Freedom   45

Residual Sum of Squares   3.96195E-14

R-Square(COD)   1

Adj. R-Square   1

		DF	Sum of Squares	Mean Square	F Value	Prob>F
B	Model	9	11949.40631	1327.71181	1.50802E18	0
B	Error	45	3.96195E-14	8.80432E-16		
B	Total	54	11949.40631			

Range- 3- T1

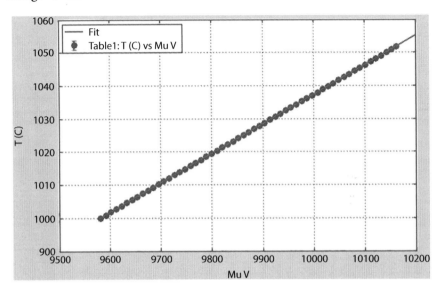

Residual Plot:

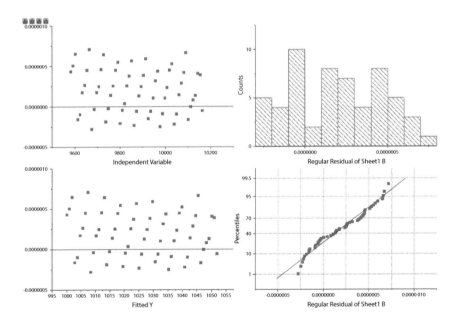

Polynomial Fit:

		Value	Standard Error	t-Value	Prob>|t|
B	Intercept	3.33551E6	6.48674E6	0.5142	0.60952
B	B1	-3007.22917	4940.41466	-0.6087	0.54565
B	B2	1.20422	1.67453	0.71914	0.47561
B	B3	-2.81069E-4	3.45138E-4	-0.81437	0.41954
B	B4	4.2139E-8	5.06805E-8	0.83146	0.40992
B	B5	-4.20827E-12	5.61328E-12	-0.7497	0.45717
B	B6	2.79936E-16	4.46244E-16	0.62731	0.53349
B	B7	-1.19602E-20	2.3234E-20	-0.51477	0.60913
B	B8	2.97804E-25	7.00054E-25	0.4254	0.67249
B	B9	-3.29244E-30	9.22774E-30	-0.3568	0.72284
	B				

Number of Points	57	
Degrees of Freedom	47	
Residual Sum of Squares		3.96195E-14
R-Square(COD)	1	
Adj. R-Square	1	

		DF	Sum of Squares	Mean Square	F Value	Prob>F
B	Model	9	13227.58513	1469.73168	1.59103E16	0
B	Error	47	4.34169E-12	9.23764E-14		
B	Total	56	13227.58513			

Range- 3- T2

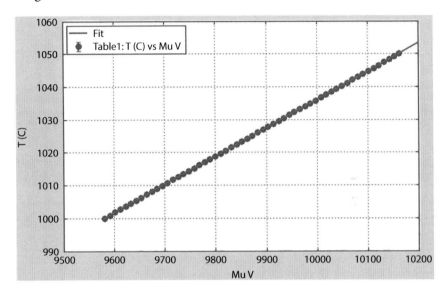

Residual Plot:

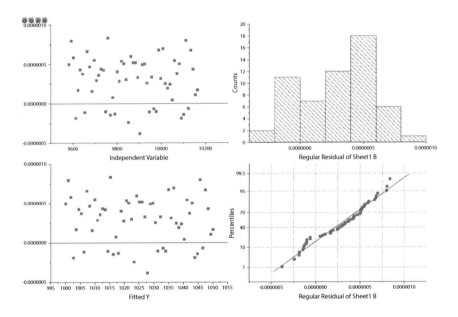

Polynomial Fit:

		Value	Standard Error	t-Value	Prob>|t|
B	Intercept	7.78012E6	6.52716E6	1.19196	0.23926
B	B1	-6361.30419	4971.19732	-1.27963	0.20696
B	B2	2.27981	1.68496	1.35303	0.18252
B	B3	-4.68162E-4	3.47288E-4	-1.34805	0.1841
B	B4	6.03481E-8	5.09963E-8	1.18338	0.24261
B	B5	-5.01598E-12	5.64826E-12	-0.88806	0.37903
B	B6	2.64365E-16	4.49025E-16	0.58875	0.55885
B	B7	-8.23652E-21	2.33788E-20	-0.35231	0.72618
B	B8	1.26246E-25	7.04416E-25	0.17922	0.85853
B	B9	-4.91247E-31	9.28524E-30	-0.05291	0.95803
B					

Number of Points	57	
Degrees of Freedom	47	
Residual Sum of Squares		4.39596E-12
R-Square(COD)	1	
Adj. R-Square	1	

		DF	Sum of Squares	Mean Square	F Value	Prob>F
B	Model	9	12332.92158	1370.32462	1.4651E16	0
B	Error	47	4.39596E-12	9.35311E-14		
B	Total	56	12332.92158			

Range- 3- T3

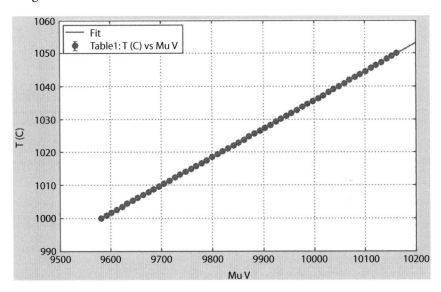

Residual Plot:

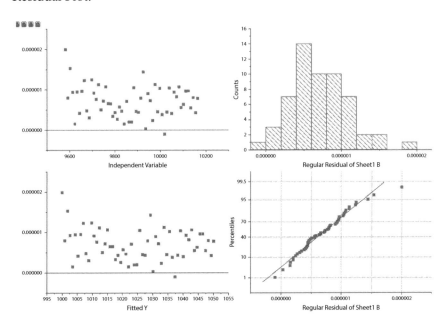

Polynomial Fit:

		Value	Standard Error	t-Value	Prob>|t|
B	Intercept	-4.71692E6	5.77778E6	-0.81639	0.4184
B	B1	1217.27601	4400.45931	0.27662	0.78328
B	B2	0.75297	1.49151	0.50483	0.61603
B	B3	-4.71707E-4	3.07416E-4	-1.53442	0.13163
B	B4	1.16175E-7	4.51415E-8	2.57357	0.01328
B	B5	-1.62619E-11	4.99979E-12	-3.25252	0.00212
B	B6	1.40066E-15	3.97473E-16	3.5239	9.59181E-4
B	B7	-7.38919E-20	2.06947E-20	-3.57057	8.34344E-4
B	B8	2.20141E-24	6.23543E-25	3.53049	9.40534E-4
B	B9	-2.8479E-29	8.21921E-30	-3.46493	0.00114
	B				

Number of Points   57

Degrees of Freedom   47

Residual Sum of Squares   3.44451E-12

R-Square(COD)   1

Adj. R-Square   1

		DF	Sum of Squares	Mean Square	F Value	Prob>F
B	Model	9	12333.72847	1370.41427	1.86991E16	0
B	Error	47	3.44451E-12	7.32875E-14		
B	Total	56	12333.72847			

4

Mathematical Analysis on Power Generation – Part II

G. Udhaya Sankar[1]*, C. Ganesa Moorthy[2] and C.T. Ramasamy[3]

[1]Department of Physics, Alagappa University, Karaikudi, India
[2]Department of Mathematics, Alagappa University, Karaikudi, India
[3]Department of Mathematics, Alagappa Government Arts College,
Karaikudi, India

Abstract

This is second part for finding suitable methods to evaluate temperature from observations of a thermocouple. Evaluation for measurement is a part of artificial intelligence. A voltmeter is attached with a thermocouple to measure voltage, and the previous part of this chapter observed that two parameter formulas are suitable to evaluate temperature from voltage measured in a thermocouple. This part finds that a particular type of one parameter formulas are the best ones, but the reduction in number of parameters costs in a different way. Theoretical de Broglie law is considered for mathematical analysis, and it is theoretically derived that temperature is a constant multiple of the square root of power generated in a thermocouple. That is, temperature is a constant multiple of the square root of the product of voltage and current. The cost for effective use of this formula is that one ammeter should also be attached with a thermocouple in addition to attachment of a voltmeter. However, this one parameter formula is the best one in terms of exactness. This theoretical exact formula is also an exact formula for practical purpose. The practical exactness is verified through observed data available in a few articles. Because of this exactness of the formula, it is suggested for implementation in measuring temperature by using a thermocouple.

Keywords: Thermocouple, ammeter, voltmeter, de Broglie law, power for electricity

---

*Corresponding author: udhaya.sankar.20@gmail.com

Pandian Vasant, Gerhard-Wilhelm Weber, Joshua Thomas, José Antonio Marmolejo-Saucedo and Roman Rodriguez-Aguilar (eds.) *Artificial Intelligence for Renewable Energy and Climate Change*, (87–116) © 2022 Scrivener Publishing LLC

4.1   Energy Analysis

Thermocouples are generally used for three purposes: temperature measurement [7, 9, 14, 15], electricity generation [3, 5, 12, 17] and refrigeration [1, 4, 16, 18]. Theory for thermocouples begins in general with the Seebeck effect, Peltier effect, Seebeck coefficient, Peltier coefficient, Figure of merit, etc. In thermocouple – temperature sensors, heat is converted to voltage, voltage is measured, and then voltage is converted into temperature. There is no exact analytic formula which is applicable for conversion of voltage to temperature for these sensors, even though there are theories and equations for thermocouples [33, 34]. However, it is possible to get approximate localized formulae as well as approximate globalized polynomial formulae. For approximate polynomial formulae the existence of polynomial approximations in the form

$$T = a_0 + a_1 V + a_2 V^2 + \cdots + a_n V^n, \tag{4.1}$$

are assumed and coefficients are found by using observed voltages V for known temperatures T. It can be observed that the equations of the form

$$T = \alpha V^{\beta}, \tag{4.2}$$

are more suitable in deriving localized formulae for conversion of voltages to temperatures, where the constants α and β are need to be determined locally. For practical purposes, it is normally one used to consider the other counter – relation

$$V = b_0 + b_1 T + b_2 T^2 + \cdots + b_m T^m, \tag{4.3}$$

to obtain relations to obtain voltages from temperatures. Although these relations are derived for thermocouples, the relations may be considered as measurement of voltages for thermoelectric generators using thermocouples. The purpose of this chapter is to analyze a counter – relation for (4.2) in the form

$$V = \alpha T^{\beta}, \tag{4.4}$$

so that it is applicable for localized measurement of voltages from temperatures for a thermocouple – electric generator. It is possible to derive (4.4) directly from (4.2). That is, if (4.2) is assumed then (4.2) implies that

$$\alpha^{-\left(\frac{1}{\beta}\right)}T^{\left(\frac{1}{\beta}\right)} = V,\qquad(4.5)$$

which may be considered in the form of (4.4). So, let us justify again that (4.4) is a suitable form of localized formula for conversion of temperature to voltage, but in a different approach by using the de Broglie law along with theory for thermoelectric effects. It can also be observed that the actual unknown globalized formula as well as (4.2) for conversion of voltages to temperatures are given by means of concave functions. In this chapter, it will be observed that the actual unknown globalized formula as well as (4.4) for conversion of temperatures to voltages are given by means of convex functions. Temperature is directly proportional to square root of power generated in a thermoelectric generator. Equivalently, temperature is directly proportional to square root of power consumed in a thermocouple. These proportionalities are converted as analytic formulae. These equivalent formulae are derived by using the de Broglie law. Concavity of a function of voltage giving temperature is observed. "Voltage = a constant times of temperature with a power" is considered as a good localized formulae for conversions of temperature to voltage in a thermoelectric generator.

4.2   Power Efficiency Method

Let us recall the de Broglie law in the form

$$\lambda = \frac{h}{p},\qquad(4.6)$$

where λ is the wavelength of an electron, h is the Planck's constant, and p is the linear momentum of the electron. Let us recall the Wien's displacement law in the form

$$T = \frac{b}{\lambda},\qquad(4.7)$$

where b is the Wien's constant, λ is the wavelength of the light ray radiated with maximum intensity from a black body with temperature T. In view of the possibility of conversion of light energy into heat energy and heat energy into light energy, it is possible to assume that when a beam of light rays with single wavelength λ hits a solid portion of a thermocouple, then there is a temperature $T = \dfrac{b}{\lambda}$, which makes a movement of electrons with linear momentum p given in (4.6). So, (4.7) and (4.6) imply the relation $\dfrac{h}{p} \propto \dfrac{b}{T}$. On considering this relation for unit time, on considering $p = \sqrt{2mE}$ with m as the mass of an electron and E as the kinetic energy of moving electron, and on replacing E per unit time by power, there is a relation in the form $T = \alpha\sqrt{IV}$, where I is the current and V is the voltage in the thermocouple, where α is a positive constant. So, based on the de Broglie law, there is a new formula

$$T = \alpha\sqrt{IV}, \tag{4.8}$$

for thermocouples, where α is a constant which depends only on the thermocouple chosen. This becomes $V = \dfrac{1}{\alpha^2 I}T^2$, which again justifies (4.4). The relation (4.8) can be used for temperature measurements, when an arrangement is made to measure current as well as voltage separately in a thermocouple.

It can be verified that $\alpha > 0$ and $0 < \beta < 1$ in (4.2) for a thermocouple. So, (4.5) implies that $\alpha > 0$ and $\beta < 1$ in (4.4) for a thermocouple. To interpret these facts and to justify again that (4.4) is a suitable form for conversion, some mathematical parts are required.

Let us first recall some parts from [11]. A real valued function $f: (a, b) \to \mathbb{R}$ is said to be convex, if $f(\theta x + (1 - \theta)y) \leq \theta f(x) + (1 - \theta) f(y)$, for every x and y in the interval (a, b). A real valued function $f: (a, b) \to \mathbb{R}$ is said to be concave, if $f(\theta x + (1 - \theta) y) \geq \theta f(x) + (1 - \theta) f(y)$, for every x and y in the interval (a, b). If a function $f: (a, b) \to \mathbb{R}$ is differentiable, then it is f is convex (concave, respectively) if and only if its derivative is an increasing function (a decreasing function, respectively). Proposition 1 in [6] states that if $f: (a, b) \to (c, d) \subseteq \mathbb{R}$ has an inverse function $f^{-1}: (c, d) \to (a, b) \subseteq \mathbb{R}$, the function f is twice differentiable, $f'(x) \neq 0$ for every x, and if f and f^{-1} are increasing functions, then convexity of one of them implies the convexity of the other in these functions f and f^{-1}. In general, if temperature T increases then voltage V increases, and vice versa, in a thermocouple. It can further be observed that the function in the unknown exact formula for conversion of voltage to temperature is a concave function, and that the right-hand side functions in localized formulae in the form of (4.2) are also concave functions. So, the function in the unknown exact formula for conversion of temperature to voltage should be a convex function in view of Proposition 1 in [6]. It can be observed that $\alpha > 0$ and $\beta > 1$ in (4.4) for a thermocouple. So, the first order derivative is positive and it is not equal to zero at all points. The left-hand side function of (4.5) has derivative which is an decreasing function so that this function is concave. Hence, again by Proposition 1 in [6], this function for (4.4) is also convex, because the inverse function is concave, which can be obtained by interchanging the roles of V and T in (4.5). Thus the right-hand side function of (4.4) is convex, which agrees with the convexity of the function in the unknown exact formula. This fact also justifies the form of (4.4) for conversion of temperature to voltage.

4.3   Data Analysis

Let us consider the following observed values of a thermocouple with respect to 0°C re ference temperature given in Table 4 of [10]:

(650°C, 5747.6μV), (700°C,6269.8μV), (750°C,6800.5μV),
(800°C, 7339.7μV), (850°C,7887.3μV), (900°C, 8443.4μV),
(950°C, 9008.0μV), (1000°C, 9581.1μV), (1050°C, 10162.6μV),

Let us substitute the first and second pairs in (4.5), the second and third pairs in (4.4), the third and fourth pairs in (4.4),…, and the eighth and ninth pairs in (4.4), separately to solve for the unknown constants α and β, and to obtain the following equations.

$$V = (2.875214942) \ T^{1.173451081}, \tag{4.9}$$

$$V = (2.79661142) \ T^{1.177682285}, \tag{4.10}$$

$$V = (2.712987744) \ T^{1.182268029}, \tag{4.11}$$

$$V = (2.630116732) \ T^{1.18690888}, \tag{4.12}$$

$$V = (2.545624039) \ T^{1.19174969}, \tag{4.13}$$

$$V = (2.453397624) \ T^{1.197176404}, \tag{4.14}$$

$$V = (2.365729519) \ T^{1.202483428}, \tag{4.15}$$

$$V = (2.282636807)\ T^{1.207659519}, \qquad (4.16)$$

Formula (4.9) is applicable in the Range 1: 650°C to 700°C. Formula (4.10) is applicable in the Range 2: 700°C to 750°C. Formula (4.11) is applicable in the Range 3: 750°C to 800°C. Formula (4.12) is applicable in the Range 4: 800°C to 850°C. Formula (4.13) is applicable in the Range 5: 850°C to 900°C. Formula (4.14) is applicable in the Range 6: 900°C to 950°C. Formula (4.15) is applicable in the Range 7: 950°C to 1000°C. Formula (4.16) is applicable in the Range 8: 1000°C to 1050°C. This means that these localized formulae can be used to find voltage values V, corresponding to given temperature values T which are given only in the respective ranges. Tables for the pair of values (T, V) were found by using these values and curves were drawn for these eight ranges. The decreasing values of α of (4.4) in (4.9)-(4.16) justify that the unknown function involved in the unknown actual formula for conversion of temperature to voltage should be concave [31, 32]. However, the increasing values of β of (4.4) in (4.9)-(4.16) compensate the increasing values of α so that these equations represent almost straight lines. This is justified by the Figures 4.1–4.8, which also provide ninth degree polynomial fits to check again the concavity of the curves. The values of β of (4.4) in (4.9)-(4.16) are greater than 1. So, the curves in the Figures 4.1–4.8 should be concave.

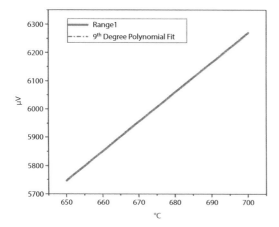

Equation	$y = \text{Intercept} + B1*x^1 + B2*x^2 + B3*x^3 + B4*x^4 + B5*x^5 + B6*x^6 + B7*x^7 + B8*x^8 + B9*x^9$
Plot	B
Weight	No Weighting
Intercept	-643908.52877 ± 4.1162
B1	6734.98143 ± 53017.555
B2	-28.8783 ± 303.84159
B3	0.0619 ± 1.01735
B4	-5.33811E-5 ± 0.00219
B5	-4.545E-8 ± 3.16346E-6
B6	1.67699E-10 ± 3.05005E-
B7	-1.84305E-13 ± 1.8975E-
B8	9.70301E-17 ± 6.91538E-
B9	-2.06975E-20 ± 1.1254E-
Residual Sum of Square	4.43531E-12
R-Square(COD)	1
Adj. R-Square	1

Figure 4.1 Temperature-Voltage graph for Range 1: 650°C to 700°C

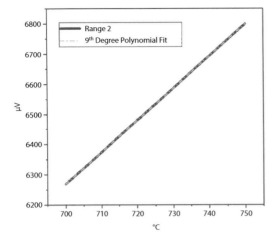

Figure 4.2 Temperature-Voltage graph for Range 2: 700°C to 750°C.

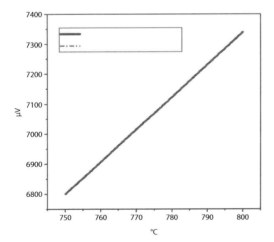

Figure 4.3 Temperature-Voltage graph for Range 3: 750°C to 800°C.

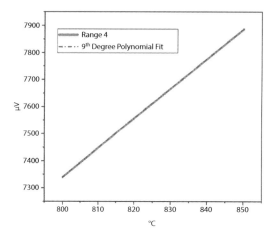

Equation	y = Intercept + B1*x^1 + B2*x^2 + B3*x^3 + B4*x^4 + B5*x^5 + B6*x^6 + B7*x^7 + B8*x^8 + B9*x^9
Plot	B
Weight	No Weighting
Intercept	1.19422E6 ± 7.80322E6
B1	-7107.2701 ± 69374.455
B2	5.81474 ± 260.61276
B3	0.06468 ± 0.52673
B4	-2.65032E-4 ± 5.95709E
B5	4.99853E-7 ± 3.99391E-
B6	-5.48129E-10 ± 4.12646
B7	3.59579E-13 ± 3.8098E-
B8	-1.31612E-16 ± 1.72855
B9	2.07714E-20 ± 3.12498
Residual Sum of Square	3.36438E-12
R-Square(COD)	1
Adj. R-Square	1

Figure 4.4 Temperature-Voltage graph for Range 4: 800°C to 850°C.

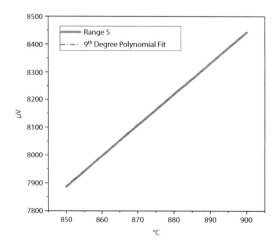

Equation	y = Intercept + B1*x^1 + B2*x^2 + B3*x^3 + B4*x^4 + B5*x^5 + B6*x^6 + B7*x^7 + B8*x^8 + B9*x^9
Plot	B
Weight	No Weighting
Intercept	-1.72152E6 ± 8.27856E
B1	15329.44123 ± 66452.5
B2	-59.10561 ± 218.90333
B3	0.12835 ± 0.36191
B4	-1.6967E-4 ± 2.80545E-
B5	1.36135E-7 ± 3.27678E-
B6	-5.95434E-11 ± 5.47028
B7	7.44772E-15 ± 4.29709
B8	4.09867E-18 ± 1.69835
B9	-1.31389E-21 ± 2.7574E
Residual Sum of Square	2.93809E-12
R-Square(COD)	1
Adj. R-Square	1

Figure 4.5 Temperature-Voltage graph for Range 5: 850°C to 900°C.

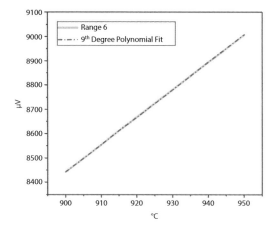

Figure 4.6 Temperature-Voltage graph for Range 6: 900°C to 950°C.

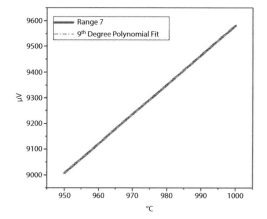

Figure 4.7 Temperature-Voltage graph for Range 7: 950°C to 1000°C.

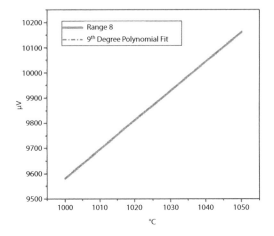

Equation	y = Intercept + B1*x^1+ B2*x^2 + B3*x^3 + B4*x^4 + B5*x^5 + B6*x^6 + B7*x^7 + B8*x^8 + B9*x^9
Plot	B
Weight	No Weighting
Intercept	-6.13535E7 ± 5.59597E7
B1	389094.17262 ± 353515 28185
B2	-927.12063 ± 844.99655
B3	0.74792 ± 0.78102
B4	9.23695E-4 ± 0.00117
B5	-2.89355E-6 ± 2.79052E-
B6	3.19294E-9 ± 2.96637E-
B7	-1.88942E-12 ± 1.72895
B8	5.97564E-16 ± 5.41805E
B9	-7.97608E-20 ± 7.18261
Residual Sum of Square	9.40372E-11
R-Square(COD)	1
Adj. R-Square	1

Figure 4.8 Temperature-Voltage graph for Range 8: 100°C to 1050°C.

Let us consider (4.8) again in which α is a constant which depends on a particular thermocouple for which observations are made. Thus, $=\dfrac{T}{\sqrt{IV}}=\dfrac{T}{\sqrt{Power}}$, and it should remain unchanged for all observations of a particular thermocouple or equivalently for all observations of a particular thermoelectric generator. This was checked for all observations made in the chapters [2, 8, 13, 19-30]. In view of these positive conclusions, it is declared that (4.8) is the first applicable analytic formula for conversions in thermocouples and thermoelectric generators. So, this chapter provides a partial verification of the famous de Broglie's law.

The form (4.8) provides a general analytic formula for conversions of power or current and voltage to temperature. If only a voltmeter is used for simplification purpose, then the general formula for temperature to voltage conversions contains a concave function of temperature. The equation (4.4) provides a good form of localized formulae for conversions of temperature to voltage.

Acknowledgement

The authors thank RUSA Theme based project fellowship (Ref: Alu/RUSA/ Project Fellow –Science/2019) for financial support. The chapter has been written with the financial support of RUSA – phase 2.0 grant sanctioned vide Letter No. F. 24-51/2014-U, Policy (TNMulti-Gen), Dept. of Edn., Govt. of India.

References

1. Diaz-Londono, Cesar, Diana Enescu, Fredy Ruiz, and Andrea Mazza. Experimental modeling and aggregation strategy for thermoelectric refrigeration units as flexible loads. *Applied Energy,* 272, 2020.
2. Ferreira-Teixeira, S., and A. M. Pereira. Geometrical optimization of a thermoelectric device: Numerical simulations. *Energy Conversion and Management,* 169, 2018.
3. Karalis, George, Lazaros Tzounis, Eleftherios Lambrou, Leonidas N. Gergidis, and Alkiviadis S. Paipetis. A carbon fiber thermoelectric generator integrated as a lamina within an 8-ply laminate epoxy composite: Efficient thermal energy harvesting by advanced structural materials. *Applied Energy,* 253, 2019.
4. Kizilkan, Onder, Shoaib Khanmohammadi, and Morteza Saadat-Targhi. Solar based CO2 power cycle employing thermoelectric generator and absorption refrigeration: Thermodynamic assessment and multi-objective optimization. *Energy Conversion and Management,* 200, 2019.
5. Lund, Anja, Yuan Tian, Sozan Darabi, and Christian Müller. A polymer-based textile thermoelectric generator for wearable energy harvesting. *Journal of Power Sources,* 480, 2020.
6. Mršević, Mila. Convexity of the inverse function. *Teaching of Mathematics,* 20, 2008.
7. Nishihara, Yu, Shunta Doi, Sho Kakizawa, Yuji Higo, and Yoshinori Tange. Effect of pressure on temperature measurements using WRe thermocouple and its geophysical impact. *Physics of the Earth and Planetary Interiors,* 298, 2020.
8. O'Halloran, Steven, and Matthew Rodrigues. AC 2012-3976: Power and Efficiency Measurement in a Thermoelectric Generator. In *American Society for Engineering Education.* 2012.
9. Radajewski, M., S. Decker, and L. Krüger. Direct temperature measurement via thermocouples within an SPS/FAST graphite tool. *Measurement,* 147, 2019.
10. Roeser, Wm F., and S. T. Lonberger. Methods of testing thermocouples and thermocouple materials. *National Bureau of Standards Handbook,* 2, 1961.
11. Rudin, Walter. Real and complex analysis. *Bull. Amer. Math. Soc.,* 74, 1968.
12. Shen, Yongting, Trevor Hocksun Kwan, and Qinghe Yao. Performance numerical analysis of thermoelectric generator sizing for integration into

a high temperature proton exchange membrane fuel cell. *Applied Thermal Engineering*, 178, 2020.

13. Shittu, Samson, Guiqiang Li, Xudong Zhao, Xiaoli Ma, Yousef Golizadeh Akhlaghi, and Emmanuel Ayodele. High performance and thermal stress analysis of a segmented annular thermoelectric generator. *Energy Conversion and Management*, 184, 2019.

14. Tang, Yu-Qing, Wen-Zhen Fang, Hong Lin, and Wen-Quan Tao. Thin film thermocouple fabrication and its application for real-time temperature measurement inside PEMFC. *International Journal of Heat and Mass Transfer*, 141, 2019.

15. Tian, Bian, Yan Liu, Zhongkai Zhang, Libo Zhao, Zhaojun Liu, Peng Shi, Qijing Lin, Qi Mao, Dejiang Lu, and Zhuangde Jiang. WRe26–In2O3 probe-type thin film thermocouples applied to high temperature measurement. *Review of Scientific Instruments*, 91, 7, 2020.

16. Wantha, Channarong. Experimental investigation of the influence of thermoelectric subcooler on the performance of R134a refrigeration systems. *Applied Thermal Engineering*, 180, 2020.

17. Yang, S. M., J. Y. Wang, and M. D. Chen. On the improved performance of thermoelectric generators with low dimensional polysilicon-germanium thermocouples by BiCMOS process. *Sensors and Actuators A: Physical*, 306, 2020.

18. Zhang, Feng, Xiayu Xu, Lei Cheng, Lu Wang, Zhongbing Liu, and Ling Zhang. Global moment-independent sensitivity analysis of single-stage thermoelectric refrigeration system. *International Journal of Energy Research*, 43, 15, 2019.

19. Zhu, Qing, and Zhifeng Ren. A double four-point probe method for reliable measurement of energy conversion efficiency of thermoelectric materials. *Energy*, 191, 2020.

20. RajKumar, G., G. Udhaya Sankar, G. Ravi, C. Ganesa Moorthy, and S. Sekar. Portable Network Graphics Approach to the Authentication of Halftone Images with Henon Map Encryption. *Smart Science*, 8, 2, 2020.

21. Udhaya Sankar, G., C. Ganesa Moorthy, and G. RajKumar. Smart storage systems for electric vehicles–a review. *Smart Science*, 7, 1, 2019.

22. Udhaya Sankar, G., C. Ganesa Moorthy, and G. RajKumar. Synthesizing graphene from waste mosquito repellent graphite rod by using electrochemical exfoliation for battery/supercapacitor applications. *Energy Sources, Part A: Recovery, Utilization, and Environmental Effects*, 40, 10, 2018.

23. Moorthy, C. Ganesa, G. Udhaya Sankar, and G. Rajkumar. Two Expressions for Electrostatic Forces and for Magnetic Forces to Classify Electromagnetic Waves. *Imperial Journal of Interdisciplinary Research*, 3, 10, 2017.
24. Moorthy, C. Ganesa, G. Udhaya Sankar, and G. RajKumar. A Design for Charging Section of Electrostatic Precipitators by Applying a Law for Electric Field Waves. *Imperial Journal of Interdisciplinary Research*, 3, 6, 2017.
25. Moorthy, C. Ganesa, G. Udhaya Sankar, and G. RajKumar. Temperature of Black Holes and Minimum Wavelength of Radio Waves. *International Journal of Scientific Research in Science, Engineering and Technology*, 4, 4, 2018.
26. Moorthy, C. Ganesa, and G. Udhaya Sankar. Planck's Constant and Equation for Magnetic Field Waves. *Natural and Engineering Sciences*, 4, 2, 2019.
27. Sankar, G. Udhaya, and C. Ganesa Moorthy. Network Modelling on Tropical Diseases vs. Climate Change. In *Climate Change and Anthropogenic Impacts on Health in Tropical and Subtropical Regions*, pp. 64-92. IGI Global, 2020.
28. Moorthy, C. Ganesa, G. Udhaya Sankar, and G. Rajkumar. Rotating Bodies Do Have Magnetic Field. *International Journal of Scientific Research in Science, Engineering and Technology*, 2, 6, 2016.
29. UdhayaSankar, G., C. GanesaMoorthy, and G. RajKumar. Global Magnetic Field Strengths of Planets from a Formula. *International Journal of Scientific Research in Science, Engineering and Technology*, 2, 6, 2016.
30. Moorthy, C. Ganesa, G. Udhaya Sankar, and Graj Kumar. What Is the Polarity of an Electromagnetic Wave? *Indian J. Sci. Res,* 13, 1, 2017.
31. Pandian Vasant, Ivan Zelinka, and Gerhard-Wilhelm Weber (Eds.). *Intelligent Computing & Optimization,* Springer, 2018.
32. Pandian Vasant, Ivan Zelinka, Gerhard-Wilhelm Weber (Eds.). Intelligent Computing and Optimization, *Proceedings of the 2nd International Conference on Intelligent Computing and Optimization* (ICO 2019), Springer, 2019.
33. Pandian Vasant, Ivan Zelinka, Gerhard-Wilhelm Weber (Eds.). Intelligent Computing and Optimization, *Proceedings of the 3rd International Conference on Intelligent Computing and Optimization* (ICO 2020), Springer, 2020.
34. Kara, Güray, Ayşe Özmen, and Gerhard-Wilhelm Weber. Stability advances in robust portfolio optimization under parallelepiped uncertainty. *Central European Journal of Operations Research*, 27, 1, 2019.

Supplementary - II

Range 1:

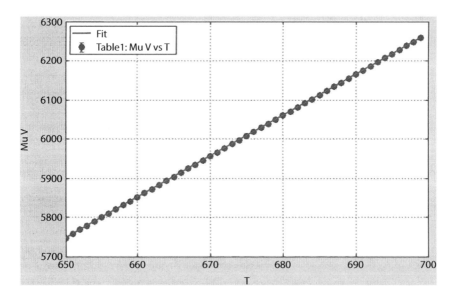

9th degree Polynomial fit:

		Value	Standard Error	t-Value	Prob>|t|
B	Intercept	-643908.52877	4.1162E6	-0.15643	0.87646
B	B1	58620.37546	46351.85345	1.26468	0.21313
B	B2	-28.8783	303.84159	-0.09504	0.92474
B	B3	0.0619	1.01735	0.06085	0.95178
B	B4	-5.33811E-5	0.00219	-0.02433	0.98071
B	B5	-4.5457E-8	3.16346E-6	-0.01437	0.9886
B	B6	1.67699E-10	3.05005E-9	0.05498	0.95642
B	B7	-1.84305E-13	1.8975E-12	-0.09713	0.9231
B	B8	9.70301E-17	6.91538E-16	0.14031	0.8891
B	B9	-2.06975E-20	1.1254E-19	-0.18391	0.85499

B

Number of Points   51

Degrees of Freedom   41

Residual Sum of Squares   4.43531E-12

R-Square(COD)   1

Adj. R-Square   1

		DF	Sum of Squares	Mean Square	F Value	Prob>F
B	Model	9	1.20534E6	133926.17262	1.23801E18	0
B	Error	41	4.43531E-12	1.08178E-13		
B	Total	50	1.20534E6			

Residual Plot:

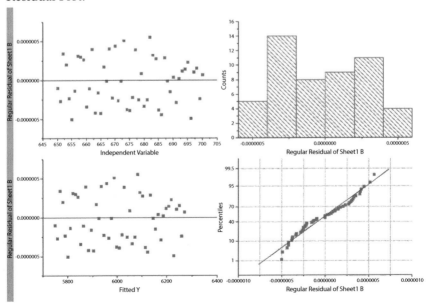

Range 2:

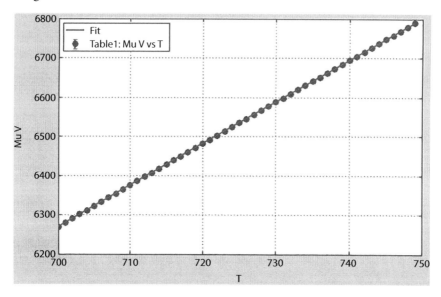

9th degree Polynomial fit:

		Value	Standard Error	t-Value	Prob>|t|
B	Intercept	-4.81373E6	3.9781E6	-1.21006	0.23319
B	B1	58620.37546	46351.85345	1.26468	0.21313
B	B2	-317.01349	241.48606	-1.31276	0.19656
B	B3	0.99958	0.74086	1.34923	0.18467
B	B4	-0.00202	0.00148	-1.36774	0.17884
B	B5	2.73261E-6	2.00469E-6	1.36311	0.18029
B	B6	-2.45678E-9	1.84315E-9	-1.33292	0.18992
B	B7	1.41889E-12	1.10956E-12	1.27878	0.20816
B	B8	-4.77649E-16	3.96098E-16	-1.20589	0.23477
B	B9	7.14057E-20	6.36835E-20	1.12126	0.2687

B

Number of Points   51

Degrees of Freedom   41

Residual Sum of Squares   4.21267E-12

R-Square(COD)   1

Adj. R-Square   1

		DF	Sum of Squares	Mean Square	F Value	Prob>F
B	Model	9	1.20534E6	133926.17262	1.23801E18	0
B	Error	41	4.43531E-12	1.08178E-13		
B	Total	50	1.20534E6			

Residual Plot:

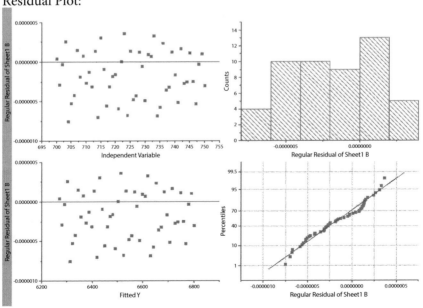

Range 3:

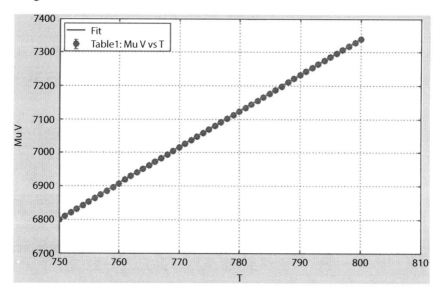

9th degree Polynomial fit:

		Value	Standard Error	t-Value	Prob>|t|
B	Intercept	-3.07242E6	3.2689E6	-0.93989	0.35278
B	B1	19492.78542	29472.13556	0.6614	0.51206
B	B2	-17.22798	113.51887	-0.15176	0.88012
B	B3	-0.19828	0.26317	-0.75342	0.4555
B	B4	8.66384E-4	5.01477E-4	1.72767	0.09158
B	B5	-1.73852E-6	8.29926E-7	-2.09478	0.04241
B	B6	2.02741E-9	9.58682E-10	2.11478	0.04057
B	B7	-1.41416E-12	6.8574E-13	-2.06223	0.04556
B	B8	5.50314E-16	2.7434E-16	2.00596	0.05149
B	B9	-9.23364E-20	4.7163E-20	-1.95781	0.05708

B

Number of Points	51
Degrees of Freedom	41
Residual Sum of Squares	4.16879E-12
R-Square(COD)	1
Adj. R-Square	1

		DF	Sum of Squares	Mean Square	F Value	Prob>F
B	Model	9	1.28508E6	142787.11221	1.40431E18	0
B	Error	41	4.16879E-12	1.01678E-13		
B	Total	50	1.28508E6			

Residual Plot:

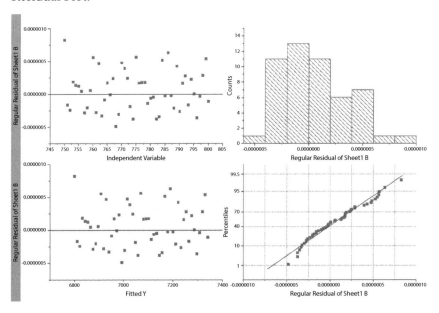

Range 4:

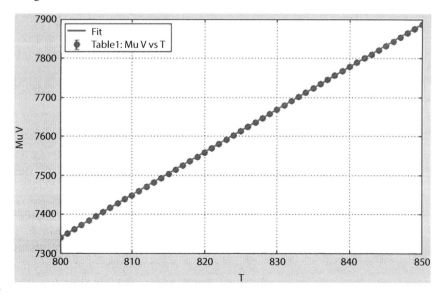

9th degree Polynomial fit:

		Value	Standard Error	t-Value	Prob>|t|
B	Intercept	1.19422E6	7.80322E6	0.15304	0.87912
B	B1	-7107.2701	69374.45595	-0.10245	0.9189
B	B2	5.81474	260.61276	0.02231	0.98231
B	B3	0.06468	0.52673	0.12279	0.90287
B	B4	-2.65032E-4	5.95709E-4	-0.4449	0.65873
B	B5	4.99853E-7	3.99391E-7	1.25154	0.21783
B	B6	-5.48129E-10	4.12646E-10	-1.32833	0.19142
B	B7	3.59579E-13	3.8098E-13	0.94383	0.35079
B	B8	-1.31612E-16	1.72855E-16	-0.7614	0.45077
B	B9	2.07714E-20	3.12498E-20	0.66469	0.50997

B

Number of Points   51

Degrees of Freedom   41

Residual Sum of Squares   3.36438E-12

R-Square(COD)1

Adj. R-Square   1

		DF	Sum of Squares	Mean Square	F Value	Prob>F
B	Model	9	1.32543E6	147270.31656	1.79471E18	0
B	Error	41	3.36438E-12	8.20579E-14		
B	Total	50	1.32543E6			

Residual Plot:

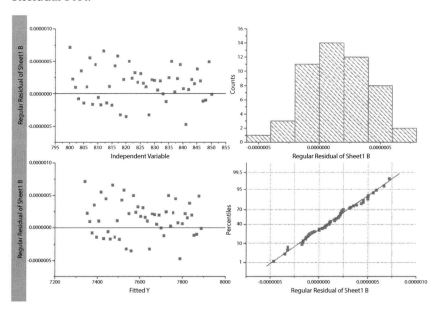

Range 5:

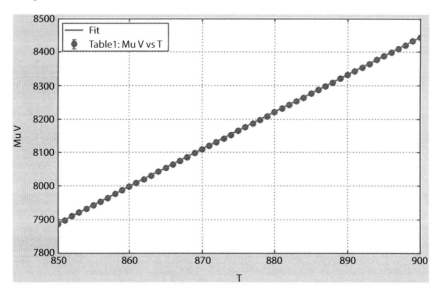

9th degree Polynomial fit:

		Value	Standard Error	t-Value	Prob>|t|
B	Intercept	-1.72152E6	8.27856E6	-0.20795	0.8363
B	B1	15329.44123	66452.52602	0.23068	0.81871
B	B2	-59.10561	218.90333	-0.27001	0.78851
B	B3	0.12835	0.36191	0.35466	0.72467
B	B4	-1.6967E-4	2.80545E-4	-0.60479	0.54865
B	B5	1.36135E-7	3.27678E-7	0.41546	0.67997
B	B6	-5.95434E-11	5.47028E-10	-0.10885	0.91385
B	B7	7.44772E-15	4.29709E-13	0.01733	0.98626
B	B8	4.09867E-18	1.69835E-16	0.02413	0.98086
B	B9	-1.31389E-21	2.7574E-20	-0.04765	0.96223

B

Number of Points 51

Degrees of Freedom 41

Residual Sum of Squares 2.93809E-12

R-Square(COD) 1

Adj. R-Square 1

		DF	Sum of Squares	Mean Square	F Value	Prob>F
B	Model	9	1.36637E6	151819.00245	2.11858E18	0
B	Error	41	2.93809E-12	7.16608E-14		
B	Total	50	1.36637E6			

Residual Plot:

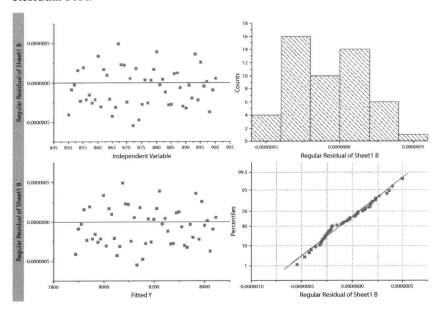

Range 6:

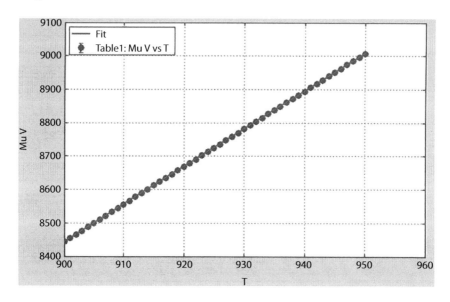

9th degree Polynomial fit:

		Value	Standard Error	t-Value	Prob>|t|
B	Intercept	-3.9432E6	9.06149E6	-0.43516	0.66573
B	B1	28691.09943	67571.68689	0.4246	0.67335
B	B2	-82.67476	203.93234	-0.4054	0.68729
B	B3	0.10552	0.29878	0.35317	0.72577
B	B4	-6.17999E-6	2.14461E-4	-0.02882	0.97715
B	B5	-1.69255E-7	3.90146E-7	-0.43382	0.66669
B	B6	2.47039E-10	5.4427E-10	0.45389	0.6523
B	B7	-1.71571E-13	3.81957E-13	-0.44919	0.65566
B	B8	6.15788E-17	1.38841E-16	0.44352	0.65972
B	B9	-9.19576E-21	2.09802E-20	-0.43831	0.66346

B

Number of Points	51
Degrees of Freedom	41
Residual Sum of Squares	3.55766E-12
R-Square(COD)	1
Adj. R-Square	1

		DF	Sum of Squares	Mean Square	F Value	Prob>F
B	Model	9	1.409E6	156555.62638	1.80422E18	0
B	Error	41	3.55766E-12	8.67721E-14		
B	Total	50	1.409E6			

Residual Plot:

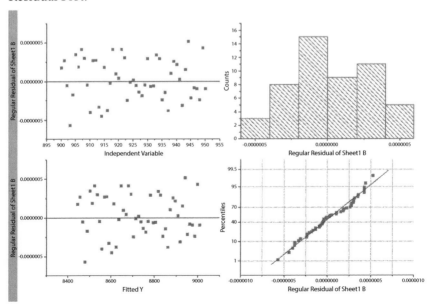

Range 7:

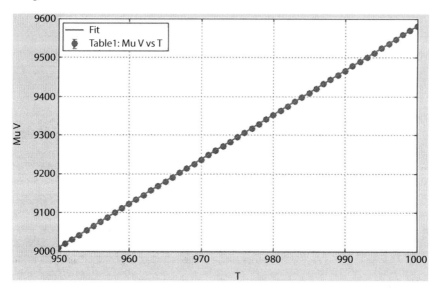

9th degree Polynomial fit:

		Value	Standard Error	t-Value	Prob>|t|
B	Intercept	-1.22973E6	1.26906E7	-0.0969	0.92328
B	B1	10544.91734	87644.5877	0.12031	0.90482
B	B2	-40.43115	239.71635	-0.16866	0.86689
B	B3	0.09133	0.29533	0.30925	0.7587
B	B4	-1.3405E-4	1.76862E-4	-0.75793	0.45283
B	B5	1.32783E-7	5.12413E-7	0.25913	0.79683
B	B6	-8.88676E-11	6.49353E-10	-0.13686	0.89181
B	B7	3.8775E-14	4.1932E-13	0.09247	0.92677
B	B8	-1.00092E-17	1.41928E-16	-0.07052	0.94412
B	B9	1.16399E-21	2.00902E-20	0.05794	0.95408

B

Number of Points	51
Degrees of Freedom	41
Residual Sum of Squares	3.33599E-12
R-Square(COD)	1
Adj. R-Square	1

		DF	Sum of Squares	Mean Square	F Value	Prob>F
B	Model	9	1.45174E6	161304.7557	1.98247E18	0
B	Error	41	3.33599E-12	8.13656E-14		
B	Total	50	1.45174E6			

Residual Plot:

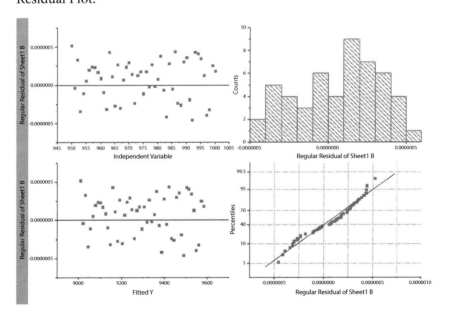

Range 8:

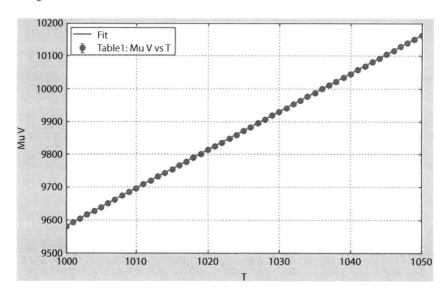

9th degree Polynomial fit:

		Value	Standard Error	t-Value	Prob>|t|
B	Intercept	-6.13535E7	5.59597E7	-1.09639	0.27931
B	B1	389094.17262	353515.28185	1.10064	0.27747
B	B2	-927.12063	844.99655	-1.09719	0.27896
B	B3	0.74792	0.78102	0.95762	0.34387
B	B4	9.23695E-4	0.00117	0.79157	0.43317
B	B5	-2.89355E-6	2.79052E-6	-1.03692	0.30585
B	B6	3.19294E-9	2.96637E-9	1.07638	0.28805
B	B7	-1.88942E-12	1.72895E-12	-1.09281	0.28086
B	B8	5.97564E-16	5.41805E-16	1.10291	0.2765
B	B9	-7.97608E-20	7.18261E-20	-1.11047	0.27327

B

Number of Points	51
Degrees of Freedom	41
Residual Sum of Squares	9.40372E-11
R-Square(COD)	1
Adj. R-Square	1

		DF	Sum of Squares	Mean Square	F Value	Prob>F
B	Model	9	1.49461E6	166067.74668	7.24052E16	0
B	Error	41	9.40372E-11	2.29359E-12		
B	Total	50	1.49461E6			

Residual Plot:

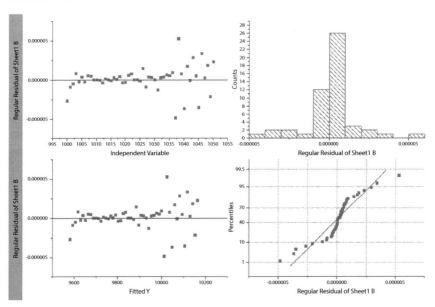

5

Sustainable Energy Materials

G. Udhaya Sankar

Department of Physics, Alagappa University, Karaikudi, India

Abstract

The Co-precipitation, Microwave-assisted solvothermal and Sol-Gel methods are chosen for investigation of the Zn-CuO nanoparticles for energy harvesting applications. The synthesized nanoparticles are examined by different characterization techniques like X-ray diffraction, FTIR, Raman, UV, SEM, EDAX and application studies. The structural nature is confirmed by XRD as monoclinic crystalline nature on C2/c space group. All vibrational and rotational phenomena of Zn-CuO nanoparticles are investigated by FTIR and Raman. Through UV analysis, the band gap values of the materials via different methods are calculated as 2.64eV, 2.67eV and 2.69eV. The performance of the Zn-CuO nanomaterials depending on the variations in the morphological shapes is analyzed by SEM. The energy harvesting applications depend on thermal conductivity, electrical conductivity, Seebeck coefficient, power factor and figure of merit. The maximum Seebeck coefficient for Zn-CuO is obtained in the Co-precipitation method, and the power factor range also increases to 1.287×10^{-4} $\mu Wcm^{-1}K^{-2}$, which is higher than other known methods.

Keywords: Energy materials, nanoparticles, seebeck coefficient, raman spectrum

5.1 Introduction

Nanotechnology has pulled in numerous specialists from different fields like biotechnology, physical sciences, material sciences, and designing [1–3, 33–35]. The oxides of transition metals are an extensive elegance of semiconductors, which have applications in attractive stockpiling media,

Email: udhaya.sankar.20@gmail.com

Pandian Vasant, Gerhard-Wilhelm Weber, Joshua Thomas, José Antonio Marmolejo-Saucedo and Roman Rodriguez-Aguilar (eds.) *Artificial Intelligence for Renewable Energy and Climate Change*, (117–136) © 2022 Scrivener Publishing LLC

thermal-based vitality change, and hardware. Among all metal oxide nanoparticles, Copper oxide is one of the p-type semiconductors; researchers' attention in copper oxide materials happens due to its low cost, excellent reactivity, high stability, industrial and commercial applications. In nanotechnology, analysing morphology of micrometer to nanometer size materials has been an uncommon challenge for analysts for a long time [24]. The Copper oxide nanoparticles have many key applications in various fields, such as thermal resistors, gas sensors, seductive storage media, near-infrared filters, photoconductive, photothermal and thermoelectric applications [9–11, 25]. There are many materials doped with CuO nanoparticles that are done by a lot of researchers in our world. Among the metals like Fe, Mn, Ni doped materials show magnetic and capacitive properties [21–23]. However, Zn doped CuO gives us a predominant nature for transportation properties [2, 11]; which has been more useful to thermoelectric applications by finding carrier concentration coefficient of the Seebeck effect and power factor. Research work for Zn doped at 1%, 2% up to 10% were reported in literature [2–4, 7, 8]. Based on literature reports, Zn doped at 8% with CuO is more effective for many applications [9–14].

S. G. Rejith and C. Krishnan [26] reported that Zn doped CuO was synthesized by Microwave-assisted solvothermal method and obtained band gap value as 2.65 eV for 2%. Here, microwave irradiation was applied for 20 minutes to enhance the spherical shaped morphology. The Zn^{2+} doping in CuO gives good band properties with different morphology. Variation of the electrical properties with respect to doped Zn (%) in CuO was reported by R.O. Yathisha et al. [2]; they discussed about crystalline size of the particles at different percentage of dopant and also reported good conductivity nature at 8% of Zn doping for spongy morphology. J. Jayaprakash et al. [27] synthesized the Zn-CuO nanoparticles via the Sol-Gel method. They obtained p-type semiconductor having maximum band gap value as 2.17 eV at 6-10 % Zn – doped. The Clustered morphology was obtained for FESEM and stretched vibrational properties of monoclinic phase of CuO was reported at 524 cm^{-1} through FTIR studies. Natpast Chaithanathan et al. [28] reported the Zn-CuO nanoparticles prepared by the Co-precipitation method. They reported that 8% of Zn gave 21nm to 30nm size crystalline particles for temperature above 500 and obtained quasi sphere morphology through SEM. L. Muthaiyan et al. [29] reported enhanced electronic transport properties at 8% of Zn doped CuO from DFT studies.

The present work gives a detailed account of comparative studies of three different methods (Sol-Gel method, Microwave-assisted solvothermal method and Co-precipitation method are shown in Figure 5.1 below) at

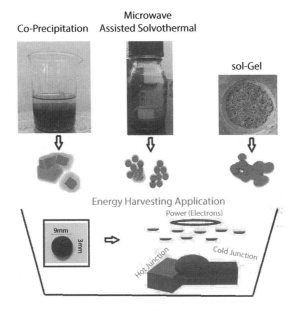

Figure 5.1 Comparative work of three methods.

8% of Zn doped CuO. The results and discussion part will be discussed by analyzing its structural, functional, optical and morphological properties by using X-ray diffraction (XRD) spectroscopy, Fourier transform infrared (FTIR) spectroscopy, ultraviolet (UV) spectroscopy, and scanning electron microscopy (SEM). The different methods provide good results on thermal conductivity, electrical conductivity, Seebeck coefficient, power factor and figure of merit at 8% of Zn doped CuO nanostructures for energy harvesting application (Thermoelectric Application).

5.2   Different Methods

The used chemicals are laboratory grade materials that are purchased from Merck, Alfa.

List of Materials: $CuCl_2 . 2H_2O$, $(CH_3COO)_2Cu . H_2O$, NaOH, Urea, $(CH_3COO)_2Zn . 2H_2O$, HCL, Methoxyethanol, Citric acid.

5.2.1   Co-Precipitation Method

The copper chloride dihydrate and zinc chloride were taken in the ratio 1: 2/3. The compounds were stirred well with 200ml distilled water for 10 minutes. Then 0.4M of NaOH was added as reducing agent. While stirring the solution, the temperature was maintained at 60 and also the pH was maintained between 11 to 13 for 2 hours. After completing the process the solution was sonicated for 15 minutes and then stirred again for 1 hour to get fine nanoparticle. A brown black precipitation was formed during the temperature and pH maintenance. The precipitated materials were washed well to get maximum purity of Zn-CuO. Then, the collected samples were dried at 110 for 18 hours. Afterwards the sample was annealed at 380 for 5 hours.

5.2.2 Microwave-Assisted Solvothermal Method

The copper acetate and zinc acetate were taken in the ratio of 1: 2/3 and 200ml of ethylene glycol was used as a solvent. Those mixtures were stirred well for 20 minutes, then Urea was added to reduce acetates in both precursors. The solution was maintained between 70-85 while stirring the mixtures. The solution was kept in 300W microwave for fifteen minutes. During this period, the greenish blue solution turned into brownish black solution. Here, the microwave played a major role in preparations of Zn-CuO for decomposing the hydroxyl compounds. Now the nanoparticles were filtered and washed well for few times. Then, the sample was dried at 110 for 18 hours. Afterwards the sample was annealed at 380 for 5 hours.

5.2.3 Sol-Gel Method

10g of copper acetate monohydrate was taken and it was dissolved in 60ml of 2 methoxyethanol and it was maintained under constant stirring at 70 for dissolving the copper ion completely. Now 0.08M of Zinc acetate was added to the solution and stirred well for 4 hrs; a greenish dark yellow gel was obtained at the beginning. Afterwards, 0.43M of citric acid was added along with 4.5ml of concentrated HCL as stabilizer. The gel became yellowish brown in colour while the stabilizer stabled the gel formation. The gel was kept at room temperature for a few days and then the gel was dried at 150 to get pure Zn-CuO gel.

5.3 X-Ray Diffraction Analysis

The diffraction peaks (2 theta) were recorded from 10^0 to 80^0 and Figure 5.2 shows the typical powder XRD pattern of Zn doped CuO nanoparticles synthesis by different methods. The Zn-CuO nanoparticles come under monoclinic crystal system and C2/c space group for Microwave-assisted solvothermal method, Sol-Gel method and co-precipitation method [1–4]; this was confirmed with the help of JCPDS card no. 05-0661, 45-0937 and 80-0076. The Zn doped in CuO varies the 2θ value in minor peaks of CuO phase. The two

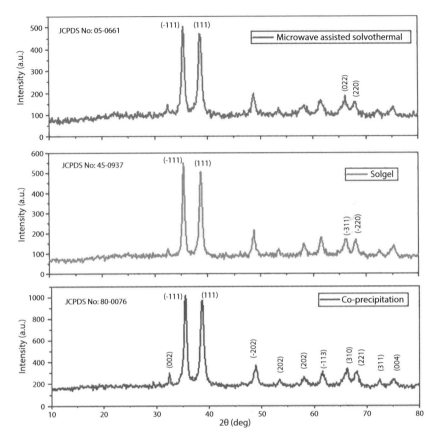

Figure 5.2 XRD analysis for Zn-CuO nanoparticles for different methods.

major peaks of CuO was confirmed with 2θ and hkl values of (-111) and (111) which is shown in Figure 5.2. The other CuO minor peaks show the slight variation on 2θ as 35.50⁰, 38.77⁰, 48.44⁰, 53.45⁰, 58.42⁰, 61.48⁰, 72.47⁰ and 75.16⁰ for Co-precipitation method, 35.47⁰, 38.77⁰, 48.45⁰, 53.52⁰, 58.27⁰, 61.47⁰, 72.42⁰ and 75.21⁰ for Microwave-assisted solvothermal method, 35.49⁰, 38.74⁰, 48.75⁰, 53.47⁰, 58.34⁰, 61.54⁰, 72.42⁰ and 75.04⁰ for Sol-Gel method, which is due to Zn doped. In Co-precipitation method, the 2θ value varied at 32.51⁰, 65.97⁰ and 68.27⁰ for Zn-CuO nanoparticles. In Microwave-assisted solvothermal method, the 2θ value varied at 65.93⁰ and 68.25⁰ which are due to Zn doped in lattice, and the corresponding hkl values are (310) and (211). In Sol-Gel method, the 2θ value varied at 66.19⁰ [hkl-(-311)] and 67.96⁰ [hkl-(-220)]. By using the Debye - Scherer's formula (5.1) and the Bragg's law equation (5.2), the average crystalline size (D) and the inter-planar spacing (d) of the sample is calculated and is shown in Table 5.1 below.

Table 5.1 Crystalline size of Zn-CuO.

Experimental method	Crystal system	Space group	Cell parameters ($a \neq b \neq c$)			d-spacing value (d) ($*10^{-10}$)	Crystalline size (D) (nm)
			a	b	c		
Co-precipitation Method	Monoclinic	C2/c	4.69	3.45	5.17	1.786	22.65
Microwave-Assisted Solvothermal Method	Monoclinic	C2/c	4.68	3.43	5.13	1.688	23.18
Sol-Gel Method	Monoclinic	C2/c	4.68	3.42	5.13	1.498	22.70

The Debye - Scherer's formula

$$\text{Crystalline size} (D) = \frac{k\lambda}{\beta cos\theta} \tag{5.1}$$

where,

D is the particle size perpendicular to the reflecating phase
β is the full diameter at half maximum of the peak
θ is the glancing angle
λ is the wavelength of radiation
k is the Scherer's constant.

Bragg's law equation $(n\lambda = 2dsin\theta)$

$$d = \frac{n\lambda}{2sin\theta} \tag{5.2}$$

where, d is inter-planar spacing.

5.4   FTIR Analysis

The FTIR analysis of Zn- CuO nanoparticles were examined in the range of 4000 cm^{-1} to 400 cm^{-1} which is shown in Figure 5.3. The FTIR spectra were employed for the detection of functional groups/chemical species

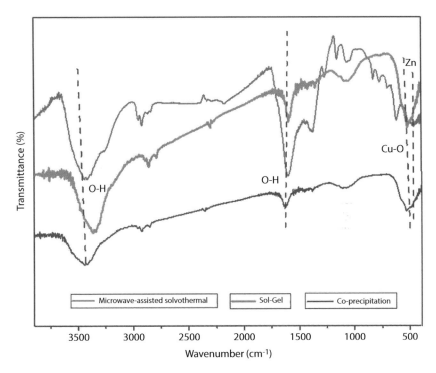

Figure 5.3 FTIR Analysis of Zn-CuO nanoparticles.

which were present in the synthesized samples. It is also interpreted that the changes in vibrational, absorption band, intermolecular and intramolecular interaction owing to effect of Zn doped into CuO lattice [2, 3]. The sharp and strong peaks also show that samples were highly crystalline in nature. The backgrounds of KBr and air spectra were eliminated while taking FTIR spectra. For different methods all the samples exhibited a strong absorption peak at around 400 to 550 cm^{-1}, which is described as the presence of CuO and Zn nanoparticles vibration (Table 5.2). Peak positioned at 580 cm^{-1} corresponds to Cu-O vibration of monoclinic crystal structure [6]. The presence of two broad peaks at 1670 cm^{-1} and 3470 cm^{-1} corresponds to the bending and stretching modes of hydroxyl groups present in the -OH molecules. The peak appeared at 2258 cm^{-1} is due to C=O species absorbed from the atmosphere. Further, peak obtained at 1300 to 1400 cm^{-1} represents C-H asymmetric stretching vibration.

Table 5.2 Mode of vibration for different methods.

Wavelength (cm⁻¹)	Assignment
3500 - 3750 cm^{-1}	O-H stretching mode
1600 - 1700 cm^{-1}	O-H stretching, bending mode
2258 cm^{-1}	C=Ostretching
1392 cm^{-1}	C-Hasymmetric stretching
525 cm^{-1}	Cu-O stretching
473 cm^{-1}	Zn stretching with CuO

5.5 Raman Analysis

Raman spectroscopy is a technique used to determine the vibrational modes of molecules. Figure 5.4 shows the Raman spectra for Zn-CuO nanoparticles. Here, the CuO Raman shift at Y+Z, Z+Y polarization

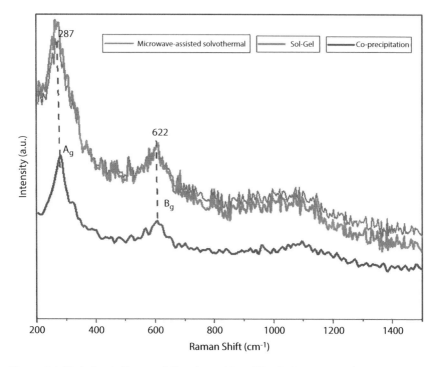

Figure 5.4 Variation in Raman shift at Ag and Bg of Zn-CuO nanoparticles.

spectra are from Wilsons F-G method [6]. The transverse mode of vibration shows acoustic nature from the data set and it involves Cu-O, Cu-Cu, O-O stretches. The Zn-CuO Raman shift was taken place at two places and it can be represented as A_g band and B_g band from group theory [5]. In the Microwave-assisted solvothermal, Sol-Gel and Co-precipitation methods, the A_g band shifted between 287 cm^{-1} and 292 cm^{-1} as well as the B_g band of Zn-CuO shifted between 622 cm^{-1} and 625 cm^{-1}. The Zn slows down the vibrational properties at B_{g1} (330-340 cm^{-1}) in CuO nanoparticles. But, the secondary B_g band is due to electronic density variation in the Zn-CuO phase because of electron-phonon interaction. Hence, it stretches Zn-Cu-O in $(x^2 - y^2)$ (ref: [5]).

5.6 UV Analysis

UV-Visible spectrophotometer is normally used to determine the optical absorption spectra. In order to investigate the different method effects on the optical properties of Zn-CuO nanoparticles, the absorption spectra in the range of 300nm to 500nm is shown in Figure 5.5. In different methods, the absorbance peaks between 391 nm and 393 nm exhibit the red shit due to Zn doping in CuO nanostructures [7]. The Zn effectively enhances

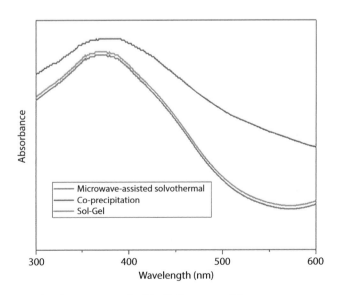

Figure 5.5 UV Absorbance spectra for Zn-CuO nanoparticles.

the optical nature and also enhances the band gap of CuO nanoparticles which is shown in Figure 5.6 for different methods.

The band gap has been calculated using Tauc relation

$$\alpha = A\left(h\nu - E_g\right)^n$$

where,

$h\nu$ = photon energy, α = Absorption Coefficient, A = Constant E_g = Energy Band Gap.

The amount of n in this equation depends on the transition characteristics. The amount of n for electronic transition is $\frac{1}{2}$ and 2 for direct and indirect transition [7, 8]. The value of band gap interprets the α. The band gap values for Co-precipitation, Microwave-assisted solvothermal

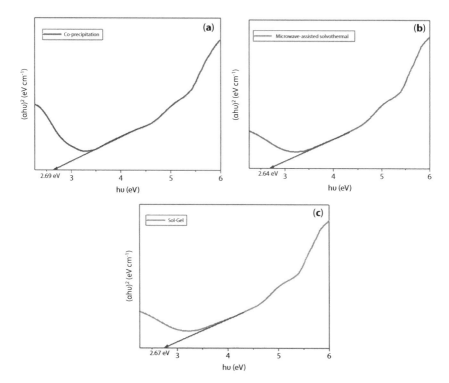

Figure 5.6 Band gap of Zn-CuO, (a) Co-precipitation method, (b) Microwave-assisted solvothermal method, (c) Sol-Gel method.

and Sol-Gel method of Zn-CuO are 2.69 eV, 2.64 eV and 2.67 eV, respectively. The band gap value is increased in Co-precipitation method than Microwave-assisted solvothermal method. It also reveals a more strong absorption and long wavelength, while the sample has a colour change from yellowish to light red. And it may enhance the transportation properties for thermoelectric application.

5.7   SEM Analysis

The Co-precipitation method, Microwave-assisted solvothermal method and Sol-Gel method form a significant framework for morphology and quality of resultant nanomaterial (Zn-CuO) that is shown in Figure 5.7(a-f) with the range of 1m-5m along with 15kV magnification. The prepared nanomaterials through Microwave-assisted solvothermal method have a circular sphere like structure with prosperity size distribution which is shown in Figure 5.7(c, d). Similarly for the sample obtained in the Sol-Gel method, the Figure 5.7(e, f) shows the morphology having an elliptical nature combined with circular spheres [30–32]. The circular sphere like nanostructured morphology can arrange effective interfacial sites and mitigate the CuO agglomeration with Zn, resulting in slightly incremented band properties in Sol-Gel rather than in Microwave-assisted solvothermal method. Figure 5.7(a, b) exhibits a great difference in changing shapes to Semi-hexa square like nanostructure, which seems to be high crystalline natured morphology. The anisotropic growth nature in the precipitation method was suggested by Hongyu Zhu [11], and it was enhanced by the doped of Zn in the CuO phase for semi-hexa shape [8–10]. These investigations suggest that multiple nuclei are formed quickly under Co-precipitation pH conditions once the critical spontaneous nucleation concentration was reached; and the semi-hexa square like structure is formed due to anisotropic growth of Zn with monoclinic CuO that are arranged in a specific direction [2, 8, 9, 11].

5.8   Energy Dispersive X-Ray Analysis

To determine the elemental composition of Zn doped CuO nanostructures; EDAX was performed with spectra. The Figure 5.8(a-c) show the EDAX spectra of Co-precipitation, Microwave-assisted solvothemal and Sol-Gel methods, respectively. In the EDAX spectra, the peaks are corresponding to zinc, copper, and oxygen in Zn-CuO nanoparticles. The prepared nanoparticles have no other impurity peaks. The compositional analysis

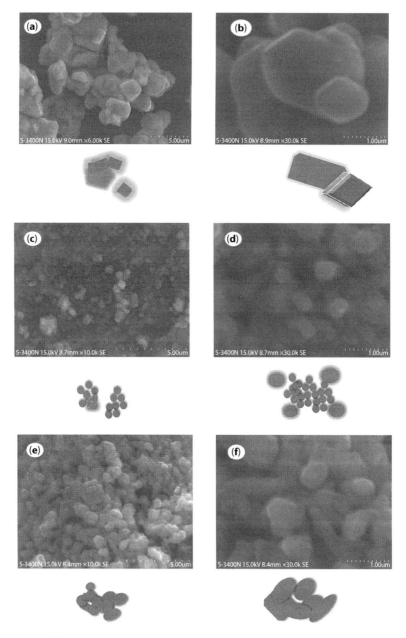

Figure 5.7 The Zn-CuO Morphology of 5μm, 1m (a, b) Co-precipitation method, (b, c) Microwave-assisted Solvothermal method, (d, e) Sol-Gel method.

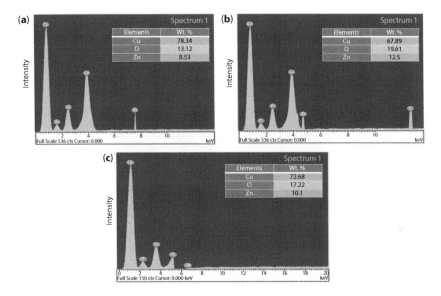

Figure 5.8 EDAX spectra of Zn-CuO (a) Co-precipitation method, (b) Microwave-assisted solvothermal method, (c) Sol-Gel method.

of Zn : Cu : O nanoparticles with atomic ratio 1:3:2 for Co-precipitation and Sol-Gel Methods, 1:3:1 for Microwave-assisted solvothermal method is presented [2, 4, 8]. It is interpreted that 0.0933 - 0.1428 at. % of Zn has entered into the CuO host system. In spectra, the Zn is almost identical to their usual stoichiometry within the experimental error. Therefore, the wt. % of Cu, O and Zn are 78.34%, 13.12%, 8.53% for Co-precipitation method, 67.89%, 19.61%, 12.5% for Microwave-assisted solvothermal method and 72.68%, 17.22%, 10.1% for Sol-Gel method.

5.9   Thermoelectric Application

5.9.1   Thermal Conductivity

The thermal conductivity for materials is due to phonon confinement or phonon scattering mechanisms [12]. The heat flux through the pellet is balanced on the epilayer surface by joule heating with inward electric current.

Therefore, thermal conductivity (k) of the Zn doped CuO is determined by Wiedmannfranz law [13, 14]. The Zn vacancies in CuO would also contribute to the phonon scattering and k. The Zn estimates the hole-carrier concentration in CuO for three methods which is shown on Figure 5.9a. The Microwave-assisted solvothermal, Sol-Gel and Co-precipitation methods deal Zn doped CuO as p-type semiconducting materials; hence, the thermal conduction is generally on the lattice temperature. In Co-precipitation method, the low thermal conductivity state is achieved between 440K and 445K with values from 65.3 kμWm^{-1} K^{-1} to 64.8 kμWm^{-1} K^{-1}. Similarly, Sol-Gel and Microwave-assisted solvothermal methods attain low thermal conductivity between 440K and 445K with values from 101.1 kμWm^{-1} K^{-1} to 99.5 kμWm^{-1} K^{-1}, 81.1 kμWm^{-1} K^{-1} to 79.5 kμWm^{-1} K^{-1}, respectively. According to the Wiedemann-Franz law, for the prepared material, thermal conductivity k is proportional to the temperature with constant Lorentz number (2.4 10^{-8} WΩK^{-2}). From this, the electronic thermal conductivity for the low thermal conductivity temperature 440K is calculated as 36.5 Wm^{-1}K^{-1} for Co-precipitation method of the Zn-CuO. Similarly, it is calculated as 38.61 Wm^{-1}K^{-1} and 37.50 Wm^{-1}K^{-1} at 440K for Sol-Gel and Microwave-assisted solvothermal methods, respectively.

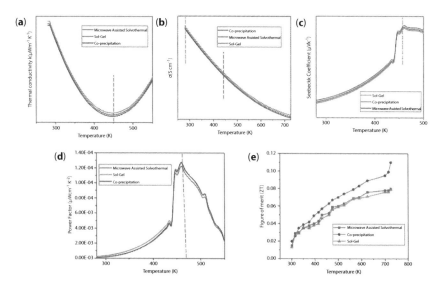

Figure 5.9 Zn-CuO (a) Thermal conductivity, (b) Electric conductivity, (c) Seebeck coefficient, (d) power factor, (e) Figure of merit (ZT).

The theoretical prediction of Lorentz number from the Wiedemann-Franz law is calculated as

$$L = \frac{k}{\sigma T}$$

$$= \frac{\pi^2 k^2}{3e^2}$$

$$= 2.4 \times 10^{-8} \ W\Omega K^{-2}$$

5.9.2   Electrical Conductivity

The electrical conductivity of Zn-CuO indicates the transport behaviour of semiconductor nature with respect to the Band energy [15]. In Co-precipitation, Microwave-assisted solvothermal and Sol-Gel methods, the electric conductivity increases the carrier concentration as $0.276505851\mu n$, $0.193028322\mu n$ and $0.092395285\mu n$; then the carrier mobility is said to be holes. Thus, in all methods the Seebeck increases with respect to decreased conductivity of Zn-CuO. The Figure 5.9b shows the electrical conductivity of Zn-CuO of three methods; the increases in conductivity with respect to decreasing temperature is due to band energy with carrier concentration and it represents the p-type semiconducting material [10, 15]. Hence, the maximum electric conductivity is achieved at low temperature range (300K to 400K) for these methods. In Co-precipitation method, the maximum conductivity is 7.04×10^3 S.cm^{-1} and minimum at higher temperature. This effect deals maximum Seebeck coefficient between the temperature range of 440K to 470K which is shown in Figure 5.9c. Similarly, the Microwave-assisted solvothemal and Sol-Gel methods give maximum conductivity at 7.12×10^3 S.cm^{-1}, 7.25×10^3 S.cm^{-1}. The minimum average conductivity between 440K and 470K is 2.89×10^3 S.cm^{-1} for Co-precipitation method, 3.28×10^3 S.cm^{-1} for Microwave-assisted solvothermal method and 3.40×10^3 S.cm^{-1} for Sol-Gel method.

5.9.3   Seebeck Coefficient

The thermal conductivity of the samples prepared by three methods shows the decreases with increasing temperature and then increases by reaching its max-minimum level. This trend has a good agreement with maximum Seebeck coefficient at nearby temperature of thermal conductivity. This is due to maximum electronic mid-temperature region [16, 17]. The positive sign of the Seebeck coefficient over the measured temperature value confirms the holes [10]. The Seebeck coefficient decreases with increasing temperature below 540K for Co-precipitation method, 545K for Microwave-assisted solvothermal and Sol-Gel methods, which is shown in the Figure 5.9c. The Seebeck coefficient increases above 455K from 188.50 μV.K^{-1} for Co-precipitation method; above 445K from 181.56 μV.K^{-1} for Microwave-assisted solvothermal method; above 460K from 195.88 μV.K^{-1} for Sol-Gel method. It indicates that carriers are uniformly increased between the 440K and 470K, and there is an average maximum 177.63 μV.K^{-1} in the range 440K to 470K for Co-precipitation method. Similarly, there are average maxima 175.78 μV.K^{-1}, 184.63 μV.K^{-1}for sol-gel and Microwave assisted solvothermal methods, respectively. Likewise, Seebeck coefficient has minimum 11.06 μV.K^{-1} for the temperature 280K, which shows the maximum electric conductivity at 7.04 × 10^3 S.cm^{-1} for Co-precipitation method. In the Microwave-assisted solvothermal method, it also shows the maximum electric conductivity at 280K temperature with minimum Seebeck value as 18.05 μV.K^{-1}.

5.9.4   Power Factor

Simple definition for power factor is S^2 σ, the S representation is Seebeck coefficient and the row representation is conductivity [15, 18]. According to the defined equation, the power factor is calculated from measured Seebeck coefficient and electric conductivity of the prepared material (Zn-CuO). Figure 5.9d shows power factor with increased temperature (K). The high value of power factor is calculated as 1.287 × 10^{-4} μ Wcm^{-1}K^{-2} for Co-precipitation method. Similarly, high values of power factor of sol-gel and Microwave-assisted solvothermal methods are calculated as 1.272 10^{-4} μWcm^{-1}K^{-2} and 1.224 × 10^{-4} μWcm^{-1}K^{-2}. The 450K-500K temperature dependent power factor with maximum efficiency of Zn doped Cu$_2$O is 0.46 × 10^{-4}μWm^{-1}K^{-2} -0.60 × 10^{-4}μWm^{-1}K^{-2} for film by F. Ye [19]. In our case, the temperature range 440K - 480K has power factor with maximum efficiency range 1.20 × 10^{-4} μWcm^{-1}K^{-2} – 1.287 × 10^{-4} μWcm^{-1}K^{-2} for Co-precipitation method, 1.092 μWcm^{-1}K^{-2} – 1.112 μWcm^{-1}K^{-2} for Sol-Gel method and 1.00 × 10^{-4}μWcm^{-1}K^{-2} –1.224 × 10^{-4}μWcm^{-1}K^{-2} for Microwave-assisted solvothermal method.

5.9.5   Figure of Merit

The figure of Merit (FOM) is calculated with the formula

$$ZT = \frac{\sigma S^2 T}{k}$$

where, σ is electrical conductivity, S is Seebeck Coefficient, k is Thermal Conductivity, and T is Temperature. Values without dimension are obtained for figure of merit of the material. FOM values for the three methods are calculated by using the ZT formula and the values are between the range 0.02 and 0.11 for Co-precipitation method, 0.015 and 0.08 for Microwave-assisted solvothermal method and 0.013 and 0.079 for Sol-Gel method. The different values obtained for different methods depend on the morphology of material [20]. Figure 5.9e shows FOM values for Zn-CuO FOM from 280K to 700K for three methods. The increase of dimensionless values of FOM with increase of temperature is due to increased power factor and decreased thermal conductivities.

5.10   Limitations and Future Direction

This research work was not limited in nanotechnology. Most of the materials were examined by many researchers in the world. Here, the copper-based material is directed for sustainable energy harvesting application. The renewability of the energy from the heat sink or climatic change condition leads this application to future progress. The future scope is energy source from the temperature difference.

5.11   Conclusion

The Zn-CuO nanoparticles were synthesized by Co-precipitation, Sol-Gel and Microwave-assisted solvothermal methods. In three methods, the prepared Zn-CuO nanoparticles were investigated by XRD, and it is confirmed as C2/c space group and they have monoclinic crystal nature of CuO with crystalline size range between 22.65nm and 23.18nm. The dense crystalline grains were observed by SEM between the scale range of 1 μm up to 500nm in the Co-precipitation method; circular and elliptical grains were observed in the sol-gel method and the smooth surfaced grains were observed in the Microwave-assisted solvothermal method. The EDS spectra confirm the presence of zinc doped copper oxide. The doped of Zn influences the reduction in lattice thermal conductivity to get higher values for ZT. Furthermore, the Semi-Hexa morphology gives dense feature of Zn-CuO nanoparticle grains and thus it reduces the thermal conductivity as 64.8 kμWm^{-1} K^{-1}. Similarly, the thermal conductivity is reduced also in other methods in view of Zn-CuO morphology. The reduced thermal conductivity increases the Seebeck and power factor of the Zn-CuO. Hence, the dimensionless highest FOM values of the prepared materials are 0.11 for Co-precipitation method, 0.079 for Sol-Gel method and 0.08 for Microwave-assisted solvothermal method.

Acknowledgement

The author acknowledges financial support from RUSA TBRP (Ref: Alu/RUSA/Project Fellow –Science/2019, dated at 11.04.2019).

References

1. Lipson, H. Elements of X-ray diffraction. *Contemporary Physics* 20, 1, 1979.
2. Yathisha, R. O., and Y. Arthoba Nayaka. Structural, optical and electrical properties of zinc incorporated copper oxide nanoparticles: doping effect of Zn. *Journal of Materials Science* 53, 1, 2018.
3. Udhaya Sankar, G., C. Ganesa Moorthy, and G. RajKumar. Synthesizing graphene from waste mosquito repellent graphite rod by using electrochemical exfoliation for battery/supercapacitor applications. *Energy Sources, Part A: Recovery, Utilization, and Environmental Effects* 40,10, 2018.
4. Mishra, Abhaya Kumar, Arpan Kumar Nayak, Ashok Kumar Das, and Debabrata Pradhan. Microwave-assisted solvothermal synthesis of cupric oxide nanostructures for high-performance supercapacitor. *Journal of Physical Chemistry C* 122, 21, 2018.
5. Deng, Yilin, Albertus D. Handoko, Yonghua Du, Shibo Xi, and Boon Siang Yeo. In situ Raman spectroscopy of copper and copper oxide surfaces during electrochemical oxygen evolution reaction: identification of CuIII oxides as catalytically active species. *Acs Catalysis* 6, 4, 2016.
6. Guha, Soumyendu, Dale Peebles, and J. Terence Wieting. Raman and infrared studies of cupric oxide. *Bulletin of Materials Science* 14, 3, 1991.
7. Wattoo, Abdul Ghafar, Zhenlun Song, M. Zubair Iqbal, Muhammad Rizwan, Ahmad Saeed, Sajjad Ahmad, Akbar Ali, and Nazir A. Naz. Effect

of zinc concentration on physical properties of copper oxide (Cu 1– x Zn x O). *Journal of Materials Science: Materials in Electronics* 26, 12 2015.

8. Yathisha, R. O., Y. Arthoba Nayaka, P. Manjunatha, H. T. Purushothama, M. M. Vinay, and K. V. Basavarajappa. Study on the effect of Zn2+ doping on optical and electrical properties of CuO nanoparticles. *Physica E: Low-dimensional Systems and Nanostructures* 108, 2019.

9. Walia, Sumeet, Sivacarendran Balendhran, Hussein Nili, Serge Zhuiykov, Gary Rosengarten, Qing Hua Wang, Madhu Bhaskaran, Sharath Sriram, Michael S. Strano, and Kourosh Kalantar-zadeh. Transition metal oxides–Thermoelectric properties. *Progress in Materials Science* 58, 8, 2013.

10. Pei, Yanzhong, Heng Wang, and G. Jeffrey Snyder. Band engineering of thermoelectric materials. *Advanced Materials* 24, 46, 2012.

11. Zhu, Hongyu, Taichao Su, Hongtao Li, Qiang Hu, Shangsheng Li, and Meihua Hu. Thermoelectric properties of BiCuSO doped with Pb. *Solid State Communications* 278, 2018.

12. Beyer, H., *et al.* High thermoelectric figure of merit ZT in PbTe and Bi2Te3-based superlattices by a reduction of the thermal conductivity. *Physica E: Low-dimensional Systems and Nanostructures* 13, 2002.

13. Chandrasekaran, P., *et al.* The impact of sintering temperature on structural, morphological and thermoelectric properties of zinc titanatenanocrystals. *Materials Research Express* 4, 2017.

14. Lan, Chun-Yen, *et al.* Grain growth behavior and enhanced thermoelectric properties of PbTe consolidated by high-density pulse current. *Journal of Alloys and Compounds* 8, 2020.

15. Feng, Yining, *et al.* Metal oxides for thermoelectric power generation and beyond. *Advanced Composites and Hybrid Materials* 1, 2018.

16. Salah, Numan, *et al.* Nanocomposites of CuO/SWCNT: Promising thermoelectric materials for mid-temperature thermoelectric generators. *Journal of the European Ceramic Society* 39, 2019.

17. Fauziah, Khotimatul, *et al.* Effect of Phonon-Drag Contributed Seebeck Coefficient on Si-Wire Thermopile Voltage Output. *IEICE Transactions on Electronics* 102, 2019.

18. Tato, Masahiko, *et al.* Reactive templated grain growth and thermoelectric power factor enhancement of textured CuFeO2 ceramics. *ACS Applied Energy Materials* 3, 2020.

19. Ye, F., *et al.* The electrical and thermoelectric properties of Zn-doped cuprous oxide. *Thin Solid Films* 603, 2016.

20. Liu, Wei-Di, *et al.* Promising and Eco-Friendly Cu_2X-Based Thermoelectric Materials: Progress and Applications. *Advanced Materials* 32, 2020.

21. Sinan, Neriman, and Ece Unur. Fe3O4/carbon nanocomposite: investigation of capacitive & magnetic properties for supercapacitor applications. *Materials Chemistry and Physics* 183, 2016.

22. Feng, Xuansheng, *et al.* Hierarchical CoFe 2 O 4/NiFe 2 O 4 nanocomposites with enhanced electrochemical capacitive properties. *Journal of Materials Science* 53, 2018.

23. Gholizadeh, Ahmad, and Elahe Jafari. Effects of sintering atmosphere and temperature on structural and magnetic properties of Ni-Cu-Zn ferrite nanoparticles: Magnetic enhancement by a reducing atmosphere. *Journal of Magnetism and Magnetic Materials* 422, 2017.

24. Maynard, Andrew D., *et al.* Safe handling of nanotechnology. *Nature* 444, 2006.

25. Hessel, Colin M., *et al.* Copper selenide nanocrystals for photothermal therapy. *Nano Letters* 11, 2011.

26. Rejith, S. G., and C. Krishnan. Optical, thermal and magnetic studies on zinc-doped copper oxide nanoparticles. *Materials Letters* 106, 2013.

27. Jayaprakash, J., *et al.* Synthesis and characterization of cluster of grapes like pure and Zinc-doped CuO nanoparticles by sol–gel method. *Spectrochimica Acta Part A: Molecular and Biomolecular Spectroscopy* 136, 2015.

28. Chaithanatkun, Natpasit, Korakot Onlaor, and Benchapol Tunhoo. Comparative study of post-sintering temperature on properties of copper doped zinc oxide nanoparticles prepared by co-precipitation process. *Materials Today: Proceedings* 4, 2017.

29. Muthaiyan, L., S. Sriram, and D. Balamurugana. The Electronic Transport Properties of CuO and Zn Doped CuO Nanotubes. *International Journal of Nanoelectronics & Materials* 11, 2018.

30. Khalil, André, *et al.* Chromosome territories have a highly nonspherical morphology and nonrandom positioning. *Chromosome Research* 15, 2007.

31. Li, Jian, *et al.* Ordered honeycomb-structured gold nanoparticle films with changeable pore morphology: From circle to ellipse. *Langmuir* 21, 2005.

32. Wang, Tieqiang, *et al.* Morphology-controlled two-dimensional elliptical hemisphere arrays fabricated by a colloidal crystal based micromolding method. *Journal of Materials Chemistry* 20, 2010.

33. Udhaya Sankar, G., C. Ganesa Moorthy, and G. RajKumar. Smart storage systems for electric vehicles–a review. *Smart Science* 7, 1, 2019.

34. Udhaya Sankar, G., R. Yuvakkumar, G. Ravi, G. RajKumar and C. Ganesa Moorthy. Preparation of CuO -Mn (x= 0.03, 0.05, 0.07) and MATLAB modelling for sustainable energy harvesting applications. *Journal of Physics: Conference Series*, 1850, no. 1, p.012025. IOP Publishing, 2021.

35. Udhaya Sankar, G., C. Ganesa Moorthy, C. T. Ramasamy and G. RajKumar.A review on recent opportunities in MATLAB software based modelling for thermoelectric applications. *International Journal of Energy Applications and Technologies.* 8, 2, 2021.

6

Soft Computing Techniques for Maximum Power Point Tracking in Wind Energy Harvesting System: A Survey

TigiluMitikuDinku[1,2], Mukhdeep Singh Manshahia[2*]
and Karanvir Singh Chahal[3]

[1]Department of Mathematics, Bule Hora University, Bule Hora, Ethiopia
[2]Department of Mathematics, Punjabi University Patiala, Punjab, India
[3]Harold M. Brathwaite S. School, Brampton, Ontario, Canada

Abstract

The research based on soft computing is concerned with the integration of knowledge, techniques and methodologies from many complementary AI tools such as ANN, FL, EA and many others in a complementary hybrid framework for solving complex problems. SC can be applied in a wide area of applications such as in forecasting, optimization and control, robotics, natural language processing and many others. This chapter presents brief descriptions of different MPPT techniques with the main focus on FL, ANN and Neuro fuzzy methods in detail.

Keywords: Maximum power point tracking, wind energy harvesting system, artificial neural networks, fuzzy logic

6.1 Introduction

The operation of a Wind Energy Harvesting System (WEHS) mostly depends on weather conditions which cause the variation of electric generation [1]. Therefore, an appropriate controller should be adopted to improve the effectiveness and reliable performance of a WEHS. MPPT controllers are an algorithm used for generating maximum available power from wind turbines under variable wind speed. The point at which a wind turbine can produce maximum power is called "maximum power point".

---

*Corresponding author: mukhdeep@gmail.com

Pandian Vasant, Gerhard-Wilhelm Weber, Joshua Thomas, José Antonio Marmolejo-Saucedo
and Roman Rodriguez-Aguilar (eds.) *Artificial Intelligence for Renewable Energy and Climate Change*,
(137–170) © 2022 Scrivener Publishing LLC

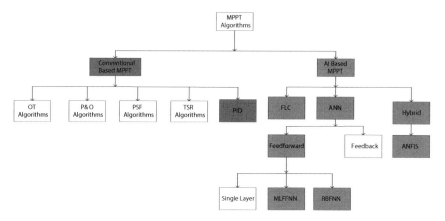

Figure 6.1 Maximum power point algorithms.

In [2] MPPT methods were classified into those that use sensors and those that do not use sensors to track the maximum power. [3] classified MPPT methods into two categories, i.e., classic methods which contain OTC, P&O, TSR, PID, etc., and intelligent methods (adaptive methods) such as FL, ANN, EA and the hybrid of these methods such as Neuro-Fuzzy and many others. Ref. [4] categorized MPPT techniques into IPC, DPC and soft computing methods. Some researchers categorized both IPC and DPC as classical (conventional) methods. The main drawbacks associated with classic methods are large convergence time, fluctuations in the steady state and possible failure to track MPP in rapidly changing wind conditions and load demand. Moreover, the tracking performance is slow and it may give rise to continuous oscillation around operating point [2]. Maximum power point algorithms are shown in Figure 6.1.

6.1.1   Conventional MPPT Control Techniques

Mostly conventional methods depend on the knowledge of the wind turbine characteristics C_{P_opt}, λ_{opt} and information about wind speed, generator torque and power signal feedback values to find the optimum speed [4].

i) Tip Speed Ratio Technique
The TSR control method maintains the TSR value at a fixed optimum value so that maximum power can be obtained from the system. The method needs prior knowledge of the optimal value of TSR λ_{opt} either through experiment from the turbine power and speed characteristics or theoretically and stores it as a reference [5]. Figure 6.2 shows the block diagram representation of the TSR.

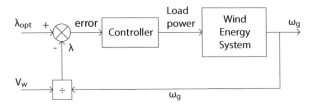

Figure 6.2 The block diagram of the TSR control.

This method is simple to implement but its main drawback is it requires the knowledge of measured (estimated) value of wind speed and the generator speed information prior to fixing the reference value of TSR [6, 7]. Some research has made interest on estimation of wind speed using soft computing techniques like ANN, FL and ANFIs, etc., to improve the reliability [8].

The other version of the TSR method is the control of the rotational speed of the generator to maintain the value of the TSR at the optimum value so that the extracted power will be at maximum level. The optimal rotational speed is obtained as

$$\omega_{m\_opt} = \frac{\lambda_{opt} V_w}{R} \tag{6.1}$$

The controller forces the mechanical power of the generator to track maximum mechanical p as shown in Figure 6.3 [9].

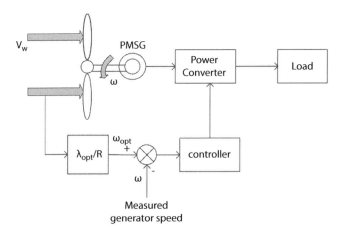

Figure 6.3 Block diagram of the TSR control.

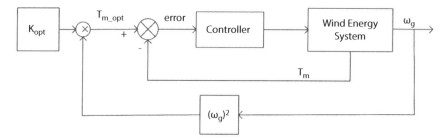

Figure 6.4 The block diagram of optimal torque control MPPT method.

ii) Optimal Torque Control

The block diagram of WEHS with OTC is shown in Figure 6.4. The mechanical torque of the turbine can be determined as a function of λ and ω_m. If the rotor is running at $\lambda = \lambda_{opt}$, it will also run at $C_p = C_{P\_opt}$. From the tip speed formula, we have

$$V_w = \frac{\omega_m R}{\lambda_{opt}}$$ (6.2)

The optimum mechanical torque can be given as [5]

$$T_{m\_opt} = \frac{P_{m\_max}}{\omega_m} = K_{opt}\omega^2{}_m$$ (6.3)

where $K_{opt} = \frac{1}{2}\rho\pi R^5 \frac{C_{P\_opt}}{\lambda_{opt}^3}$ is a constant.

iii) Power Signal Feedback

The PSF control algorithm requires the knowledge of wind turbine's maximum power curve as function of the rotor speed, and tracks this curve through its control mechanisms as shown in Figure 6.5. Then, the obtained recorded data for maximum output power and the corresponding rotor speed must be implemented in a lookup table. This data provides the necessary information about wind turbine maximum power curve for efficient tracking.

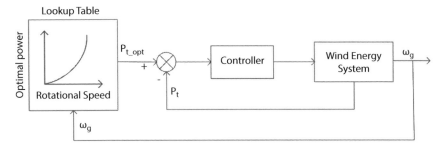

Figure 6.5 The block diagram of a wind energy system with the power signal feedback control technique.

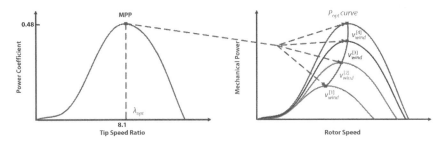

Figure 6.6 Characteristics of turbine mechanical power as a function of the rotor speed for a series of wind speeds [5, 10].

The optimum power (reference power), P_{m_opt}, is generated either using a recorded power–speed curve as shown in Figure 6..6, or using the expression of mechanical power equation of the wind turbine,

$$P_{m\_opt} = \frac{1}{2}\rho\pi R^2 C_{P\_opt} V^3{}_w \qquad (6.4)$$

iv) Perturbation and Observation/Hill-Climb Control

The P&O method is a control algorithm continuously which tracks the optimum power point of the wind power-speed characteristics. The block diagram of P&O algorithm is shown in Figure 6.7.

If the power increases due to perturbation, then the controller continued to move in that direction otherwise the direction will be reversed. After the peak power is obtained the power at the next instant decreases and hence

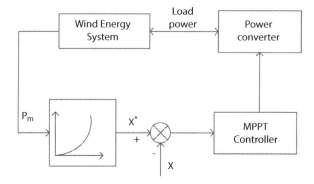

Figure 6.7 Hill climb search MPPT control strategy.

direction of the perturbation reverses. When the steady state is reached, the method oscillates around the optimal point. To keep the power variation small, the perturb size needs to be kept small [5, 8]. This method is simple, flexible and preferred over PSF and OTC methods.

6.2 Other MPPT Control Methods

Many of the problems associated with the above-mentioned methods have been solved by means of AI control and hybrid methods. An adaptive based MPPT algorithm which plays a vital role for maximum power extraction is categorized under this category. In addition to conventional algorithms, PID controllers, AI methods like ANN, FLC and neuro fuzzy methods have also been attempted in literature to achieve MPPT in WEHS applications.

6.2.1 Proportional Integral Derivative Controllers

PID controllers are the most commonly used controllers in industrial control processes as they have a simple structure and robust performance in a wide range of operating conditions [11]. Conventionally, PI controllers are most commonly used to control the generator converters. However, PI controllers offer less robustness, and their tuning requires an accurate knowledge over the dynamic model parameters. The basic form of the conventional PID controller is shown in Figure 6.8 [11].

The main function of the proportional compensator is to introduce a gain that is proportional to the error reading which is produced by

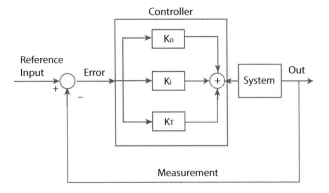

Figure 6.8 Block diagram of PID controller [11].

comparing the system's output and input. The conventional PID control process is written in the time domain and S-domain as [11]:

In time domain

$$u(t) = K_p \left[e(t) + \frac{1}{T_i} \int_0^t e(t)dt + T_d \frac{de(t)}{dt} \right] \qquad (6.7)$$

In S-domain it is given by

$$G_{controller} = \frac{U(s)}{R(s)} = K_P + \frac{K_I}{s} + K_D s \qquad (6.8)$$

where K_p is the proportional action coefficient, K_I is the integral action coefficient and K_D is the differential action coefficient. Larger values of K_p typically mean faster response since the larger the error, the larger the proportional term compensation. An excessively large proportional gain will lead to process instability and oscillation. However, if K_p is increased beyond the normal range, process variable starts oscillating at a higher rate and it will cause instability of the system [4].

To design and tune the PID controller parameters (K_p, K_i and K_d), the Ziegler-Nichols tuning method is the most commonly used method. In this method, the ultimate gain of a proportional controller and the ultimate period of oscillation are used to represent the dynamic characteristic of the process. The following procedure is used to determine the ultimate gain and period [12]. The steps for tuning a PID controller are as follows:

Table 6.1 Ziegler Nichols method.

PID Type	K_p	T_i	T_d
P	$0.5K_{cr}$	∞	0
PI	$0.45\ K_{cr}$	$\dfrac{P_{Cr}}{1.2}$	0
PID	$0.6\ K_{cr}$	$\dfrac{P_{Cr}}{1.2}$	$\dfrac{P_{Cr}}{8}$

i)   First set the integrator and differentiator gains to 0.
ii) Increase K_p from 0 to some critical value (ultimate gain) $K_{cr} = K_p$ at which sustained oscillations occur.
iii) Record the value K_{cr} and the corresponding period of sustained oscillation, P_{cr}
iv) The controller gains are now specified as in Table 6.1.

6.2.2   Fuzzy Logic Controller

A classical (crisp) set is a collection of separate objects. In classical set theory the membership of element x of a crisp sub set A in the universal set U is defined by

$$\mu_A(x) = \begin{cases} 0, & if \ \ x \notin A \\ 1, & jf \ \ x \in A \end{cases} \tag{6.9}$$

Here the element either belongs to the set or not. The universal set U is a crisp set. Such types of set are also called Boolean set (crisp set). Therefore, the boundary of set A is sharp and well defined.

The concept of fuzzy set theory was first introduced by Lotif A. Zadeh, a professor at the University of California at Berkeley [13], as a means of representing and manipulating data that was not precise, but rather fuzzy. It was designed to mathematically represent uncertainty and vagueness and to provide formalized tools for dealing with the imprecision intrinsic to many real-life problems.

Fuzzy set is characterized by assigning continuous grades of MF to an element in a set. Unlike classical set theory, the elements of fuzzy set can belong to the set with a partial degree of membership and such a set does not have crisp (clearly defined) boundaries. FL deals with finding an approximate rather than exact and precise solution to problems. A fuzzy set A of a universe of discourse U is represented as

$$\mu_A : U \to [0, 1] \tag{6.10}$$

where $\mu_A(x)$ is a degree (grade) of membership of element x in set A. A MFs are curves that defines how each point in the universe of discourse is mapped to a membership value (or degree of membership) between 0 and 1. Since $\{0, 1\} \in [0, 1]$, crisp sets are special case of fuzzy sets. Fuzzy set A is often represented as a set of ordered pairs as

$$A = \{(x, \mu_A(x)) \,|\, x \in U\} \tag{6.11}$$

where the first part x represents the element and the second part determines the grade of membership. The most commonly used MFs in control theory are triangular, trapezoidal, Gaussian, generalized bell and sigmoidal Z- and S-functions.

i) Triangular Membership Function
Three parameters $\{a, b, c\}$ with, $a < b < c$, describes a triangular membership function by

$$\mu_{Tri}(x) = \begin{cases} 0, & x \leq a \\ \dfrac{x-a}{b-a}, & a \leq x \leq b \\ \dfrac{c-x}{c-b}, & b \leq x \leq c \\ 0, & c \leq x \end{cases} \tag{6.12}$$

or alternatively it can also be represented as

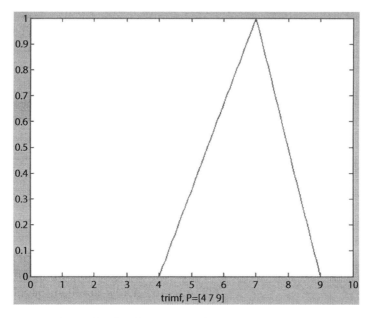

Figure 6.9 Triangle membership function (a=4, b=7, c=9).

$$\mu_{Tri}(x) = max\left(min\left(\frac{x-a}{b-a}, \frac{c-a}{c-b} \right), 0 \right) \qquad (6.13)$$

Triangle membership function is shown in Figure 6.9.

ii) Trapezoidal Membership Function

Three parameters {a, b, c, d}, a< b < c <d, describes a trapezoidal member-ship function as

$$\mu_{Trap}(x) = \begin{cases} 0, & x \le a \\ \dfrac{x-a}{b-a}, & a \le x \le b \\ 1, & b \le x \le c \\ \dfrac{d-x}{d-c}, & c \le x \le d \\ 0, & d \le x \end{cases} \qquad (6.14)$$

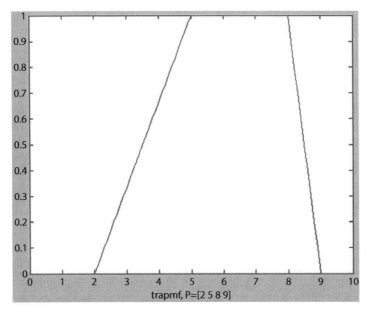

Figure 6.10 Trapezoidal Membership Function (a=2, b=5, c=8, d=9).

or by an alternative formula to Equation (6.14)

$$\mu_{Trap}(x) = max\left(min\left(\frac{x-a}{b-a}, 1, \frac{d-x}{d-c} \right), 0 \right) \quad (6.15)$$

Trapezoidal membership function is shown in Figure 6.10.

iii) Gaussian Membership Function

A Gaussian MF has two parameters, i.e., c and σ which are responsible for its center and width respectively and given by

$$\mu_{Gauss}(x) = exp\left[-\left(\frac{x-c}{2\sigma} \right)^2 \right] \quad (6.16)$$

Gaussian membership function is shown in Figure 6.11.

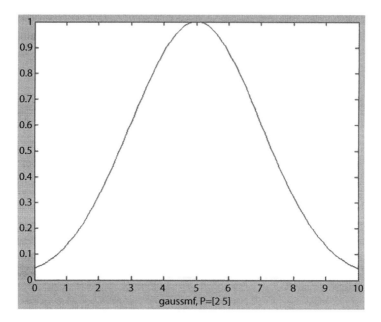

Figure 6.11 Gaussian membership function (σ=2, c=5).

iv) Generalized Bell-Shaped Membership Function

A generalized bell-shaped membership function has three parameters, i.e., a, b and c are responsible for its width, its slopes and its center, respectively, and expressed as

$$\mu_{Bell}(x) = \frac{1}{1 + \left|\dfrac{x-c}{a}\right|^{2b}} \tag{6.17}$$

Generalized bell membership function is shown in Figure 6.12.

v) Sigmoidal Membership Function

A sigmoidal membership function has two parameters, i.e., a-responsible for its slope at the crossover point $x = c$;

$$\mu_{Sigm}(x) = \frac{1}{1 + exp\left[-a(x-c)\right]} \tag{6.18}$$

Sigmoidal membership function is shown in Figure 6.13.

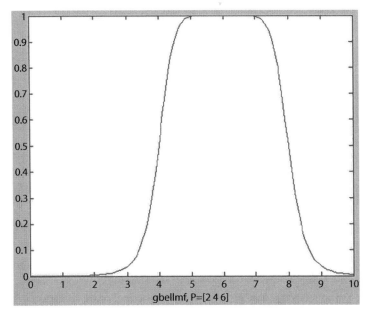

Figure 6.12 Generalized bell membership function (a=2, b=4, c=6).

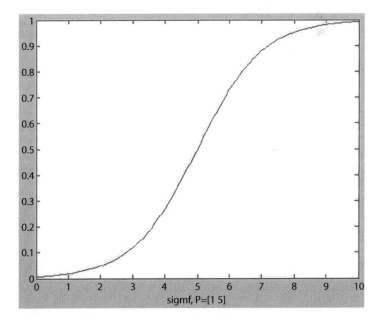

Figure 6.13 Sigmoidal Membership Function (a=1, c=5).

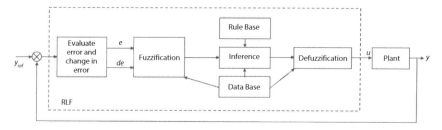

Figure 6.14 Basic structure of fuzzy control system.

6.2.2.1   Fuzzy Inference System

The main goal of fuzzy logic is to implement such types of human knowledge in the form of a computer program to make a decision about the system or process. Therefore, fuzzy reasoning mechanism is linked to human reasoning through linguistic variables [14].

FLC is an advanced control method that comes about through the application of fuzzy set theory [15]. FLC appears very useful for nonlinear control of a process/plant which varies in time. Moreover, it is an appropriate tool when determination of mathematical model of the system is difficult to develop due to lack of quantitative data regarding the input-output relations or when human understanding of the process is very different from its model. It uses human knowledge and expertise to deal with uncertainties in the process of control. Today almost everywhere we can find fuzzy logic application. There are three different types of FIS [16].

A)   Mamdani Fuzzy Inference System

Mamdani FIS were originally designed to imitate the performance of human operators in charge of controlling certain industrial processes [17, 18]. The aim was to convert (represent) the human operator's experience into a set of linguistic IF-THEN rules that could be used by a machine to automatically control the process. To implement Mamdani fuzzy model one must go through the following six steps as shown in Figure 6.14.

B)   Takagi-Sugeno fuzzy model

TSK fuzzy models or Sugeno models were first proposed as a systematic approach capable of generating fuzzy rules from a given input-output data set [19, 20]. The input membership functions of this model can be linguistic variables, but the output must be linear or constant. Considering a system having two input and a single output, a typical fuzzy rule in a Takagi-Sugeno fuzzy model has the following form

$$\text{If } x \text{ is } A \text{ and } y \text{ is } B \text{ then } z = f(x, y),$$

where A and B are the fuzzy set in the premise (antecedent) functions and $z = f(x, y)$ is the function in the conclusion (consequent). This function is usually polynomial expression of x and y, but it can be any linear or nonlinear function. The order of the polynomial defines the order of the model. When this function is a first-order polynomial, i.e., $z = px + qy + r$, the resulting FIS is first-order Sugeno fuzzy model. If $f(x, y)$ is a constant, the fuzzy model is called zero-order Sugeno fuzzy model which is a special case of Mamdani FIS described above.

C) Tsukamoto Model fuzzy model

Tsukamoto fuzzy model was proposed by Tsukamoto [21], where the consequent of each fuzzy IF-THEN rule is represented by a fuzzy set with a monotonic membership function. Since it is not transparent as either the Mamdani or Sugeno fuzzy model, Tsukamoto fuzzy model is not often used.

The flowchart of implementing FLC is given in Figure 6.15 below.

6.2.2.2   Advantages and Disadvantages of Fuzzy Logic Controller

Fuzzy logic does not require knowledge of the underlying physical process as a precondition for its application and reduces possible difficulties in the modelling and analysis of complex data. A higher degree of tolerance is one of the advantages of a fuzzy logic system in control application [23]. It can also be understood and implemented by a non-specialist in control theory. For a complex system, it required a long time to find the correct membership function and rules that give a reliable solution.

6.2.3   Artificial Neural Network

Computers can outperform humans in mental functions in limited areas such as in the speed of mathematical calculations [40]. Understanding the working principles of biological neurons is essential to understand the

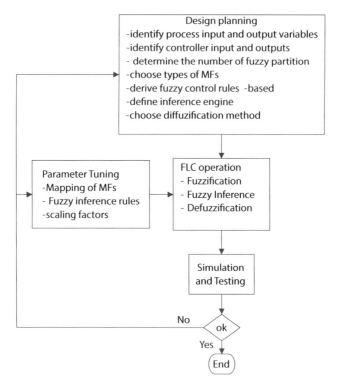

Figure 6.15 Flow chart of FLC design [22].

operation of artificial neurons and the analogy between ANNs and biological networks [24].

6.2.3.1 Biological Neural Networks

The human nervous system consists of billions of neurons of various types and lengths relevant to their location in the body. Our brain contains around 100 billion interconnected neurons which process information in the form of electric signals. It is estimated that each neuron may receive stimuli from as many as 10,000 other neurons. Groups of neurons are organized into subsystems and the integration of these subsystems forms the brain [40]. The neurons contain three major functional units called dendrites, cell body and axon as shown in Figure 6.16. Information/stimuli from the external body is received with the help of dendrites. The junction point of an axon with a dendrite of another neuron is called a

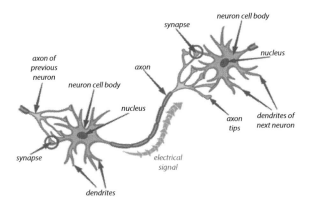

Step 1: External signal received by dendrites	**Step 2**: External signal processed in the neuron cell body	**Step 3**: Processed signal converted to an output signal and transmitted through the Axon	**Step 4**: Output signal received by the dendrites of the next neuron through the synapse

Figure 6.16 Neuron of nerve cell [25].

synapse. A synapse works like a valve controlling the rate of flow of information and is necessary to parameterize all these synapses to achieve a goal. The neuron receives information at the synapses from a large number of other neurons by means of electrochemical transmitters called neurotransmitters, which are released by arriving nerve impulses [25].

The history of ANN began many years ago with scientific attempts to study the working principles of the human brain. ANNs are a new trend inspired by the functionality of a biological neural network that allow a computer to emulate the structure and operation of the biological nervous system to recognize difficult, confusing patterns. An ANN is a complex network composed of massively interconnected elementary processing units called artificial neurons (nodes) that are grouped in layers, and assigned weights to these interconnections to perform a specific task [26]. The design of ANN resembles the human brain system in the construction of architectural structures, learning and operating techniques [25].

The first model of the neurons was produced by neurophysiologist Warren McCulloch and mathematician Walter Pitts in 1943 and is still used today in ANN [27] as shown in Figure 6.17. When the sum of inputs

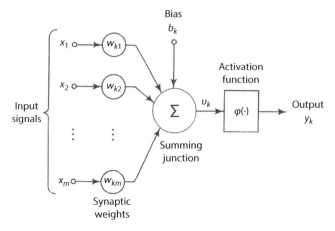

Figure 6.17 McCulloch-Pitts model of an artificial neuron.

reaches a threshold value, a neuron fires and the signal travels down the axon to the other neurons. The amount of signal transmitted depends upon the synaptic weights (strength) of the connections.

As we observe from Figure 6.17 the model of any neuron has three basic elements [28], i.e., connection links or the synaptic weights, the adder for summing the input signals and activation function for limiting the amplitude of the output of a neuron. The information relevant to the input–output mapping of the network is stored in the weights. A signal x_j at the input of synapse j connected to neuron k is multiplied by the synaptic weight w_{kj} from unit input k to unit j. The subscript (k) refers to the neuron in question and j refers to the input end of the synapse to which the weight refers.

A neural k may be described mathematically by equations (6.19) and (6.20)

$$v_k = \sum_{j=1}^{m} w_{kj} x_j \qquad\qquad (6.19)$$

$$y_k = \varphi(v_k + b_k) \qquad\qquad (6.20)$$

where $x_1, x_2, \dots, x_m$ are the input signals, $w_{k1}, w_{k2}, \dots, w_{km}$ are the synaptic weights of neuron k, v_k is the linear combiner output due to the input signals, $\varphi(.)$ is the activation function (transfer function) and y_k is the output signal of the neuron. The neuronal model also includes an externally applied bias, b_k which provides the effect of increasing or lowering the net input of the activation function, depending on whether it is positive or negative, respectively.

6.2.3.2   Architectures of Artificial Neural Networks

The connections between neurons with other neurons will form a layered pattern, so-called network architecture, which consists of three different layers, i.e., input layers, hidden layers and output layers. The input neurons receive the data (information), signals, features, or measurement either from input files or directly from electronic sensors in real-time applications [29]. These inputs are usually normalized within the limit values produced by activation functions. This normalization results in better numerical precision for the mathematical operations performed by the network. After a neuron performs its function, it passes its output to all of the neurons in the layer after it. Too many hidden layer neurons can result in 'over-training' (or lack of generalization) and lead to large 'verification' errors, whereas too few neurons can result in large training and verification errors [41]. The obtained result of this layer is sent to the output layer which plays a role in determining the validity of data that are analyzed based on the existing limits in the activation function. The output layer neurons send information directly to the outside world, or to a secondary computer process, or to other devices such as mechanical control system.

The graphical illustration and mathematical form of MATLAB built-in functions are shown in Table 6.2 [26].

Considering the arrangement of neurons as well as how they are interconnected and how its layers are composed, the architectures of ANNs can be divided into two (Figure 6.18), i.e., feed-forward and feedback (recurrent) networks [24].

i) Feed-forward Network

FFNN architecture has one or more hidden layers, whose computation nodes are called hidden neurons or hidden units. MLP and RBF are the most common types of feed-forward network architecture having one or more hidden layers as shown in Figure 6.18. The information always flows in a single direction from the input layer to the output layer; no loops are formed by the network connections (thus, unidirectional) [3].

Table 6.2 MATLAB built-in transfer functions.

Function name	Graphicl illustration	Mathematical form
Linear	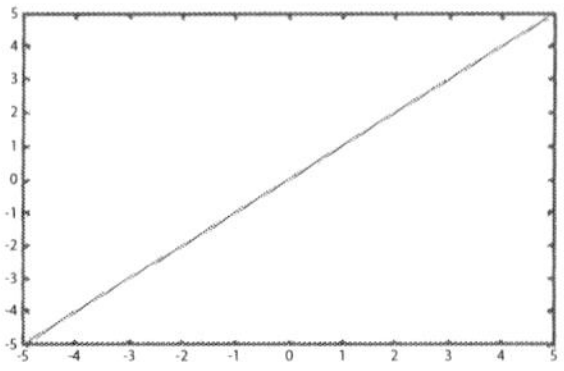	$f(x)=x$
Hyperbolic Tangent Sigmoid	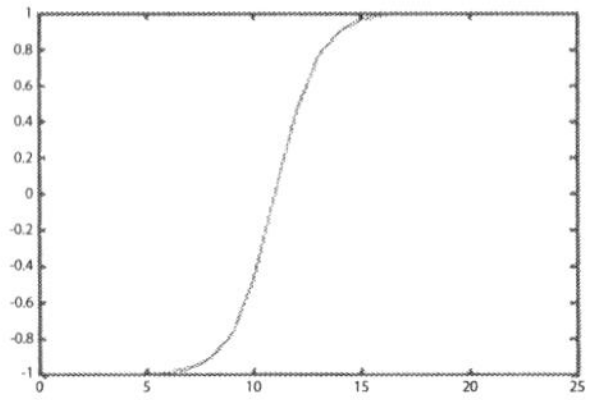	$f(x) = \dfrac{e^x - e^{-x}}{e^x + e^{-x}}$
Logistic Sigmoid	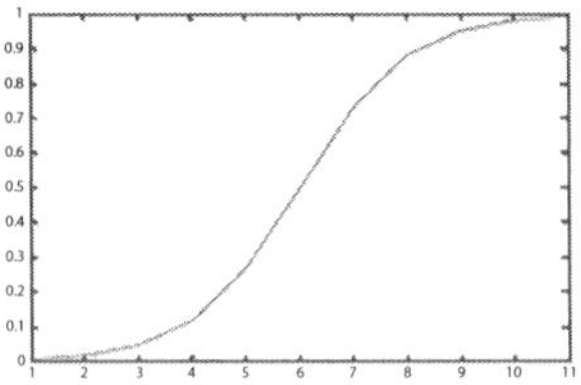	$f(x) = \dfrac{1}{1 + e^{-x}}$
Gausian RBF	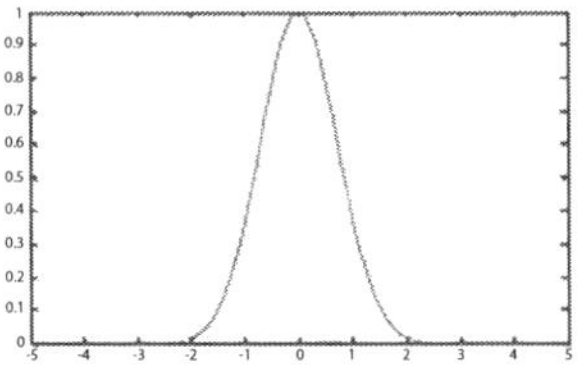	$\varphi_j(x) = \exp\left(-\dfrac{1}{2\sigma_j^2}\left\|x - x_j\right\|^2\right)$

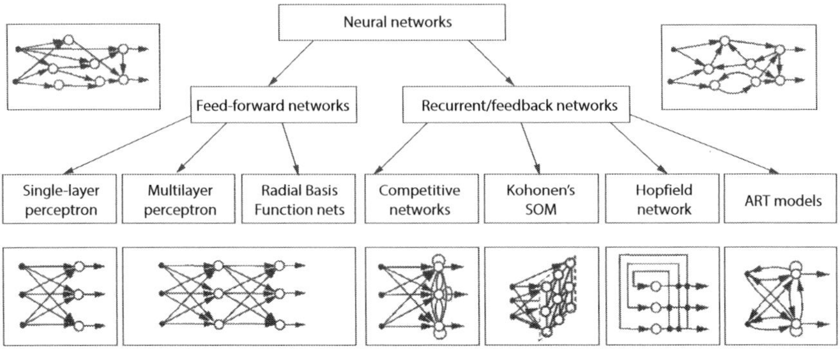

Figure 6.18 A taxonomy of feed-forward and recurrent/feedback network architectures [30].

ii) Recurrent Network

RNN is an FFNN having one or more hidden layers with at least one feedback loop as shown in Figure 6.18. The presence of feedback loops has a profound impact on the learning capability of the network and on its performance.

The advantages of ANN with respect to other models are its speed, simplicity, and ability of modeling a multivariable problem to solve complex relationships between the variables; and it can extract the nonlinear relationships among these variables by means of training data [1]. These systems are able to adapt to learn how to deal with situations that they have not previously encountered and, in extreme cases, are able to learn to survive when the environment in which they operate changes [5].

6.2.3.3 *Training of Artificial Neural Networks*

ANNs are not programmed to perform specific tasks on computers. Rather they are trained with respect to data sets until they learn the patterns presented to them. After they are trained, they are ready for prediction or classification of a new pattern presented to them [24]. Once a network has been structured for a particular application, it is ready to be trained. To start this process, the initial weights are chosen randomly and then the training or learning begins. During the training process of ANNs, each complete presentation of all the samples belonging to the training set, in order to adjust the synaptic weights and thresholds, will be called training epoch. Learning methods of ANN are categorized into supervised learning and unsupervised learning.

i) Supervised Learning

In supervised learning the network is provided with a training data set of both input and correct output or target. When the inputs are supplied to the network, it compares the output with the targets. This training is considered complete when the neural network reaches a user-defined performance level [31]. When no further training is necessary, the weights are frozen for the underlying application. During the training of a network, the same set of data is processed many times, as the connection weights are ever refined. Then the learning rule helps the network to adjust the weights and biases of the network to move the network outputs closer to the targets.

ii)   Unsupervised Learning

In the case of the unsupervised learning (Adaptive training) method, the weights and biases are modified in response to the network inputs only without target outputs available. The networks use no external influences to adjust their weights. Instead, they internally monitor their performance [24, 32].

6.2.3.4   Radial Basis Function

Architecture of RBF networks is similar to MLP networks but it uses RBFs as an activation function. Due to their good approximation capabilities, faster learning algorithms and simpler network structures, RBF networks are used in function approximation, time series prediction, control and others [33, 34]. RBF structure is shown in Figure 6.19.

Modified BP-based RBF network training flowchart is shown in Figure 6.20.

The comparison of FL and ANN is given in Table 6.3 below.

6.2.4   Neuro-Fuzzy Inference Approach

Hybrid neuro-fuzzy systems are systems for which more than one technology is employed to solve the problem. A neuro-fuzzy system is a neural network that is functionally equivalent to a fuzzy inference model trained by neural network learning algorithm. In a neuro-fuzzy system, neural networks extract fuzzy rules automatically from numerical data, and the membership functions are adjusted adaptively through the learning process. Training helps the system to develop fuzzy IF-THEN rules and determine parameters of membership functions for input and output variables of the system. There are several different types of hybrid neuro-fuzzy systems developed in literature. Among the hybrid neural networks types ANFIS is the most efficient network so most researchers

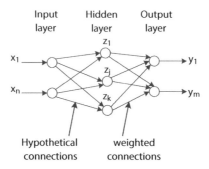

Figure 6.19 RBF structure.

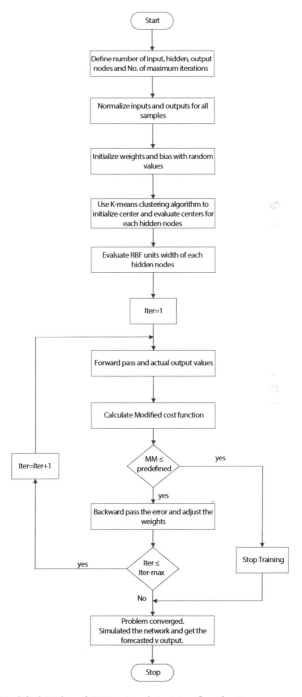

Figure 6.20 Modified BP-based RBF network training flowchart.

Table 6.3 Comparing neural networks and fuzzy systems.

Fuzzy system	Neural network
Merits	
✓ Does not require mathematical model of the system ✓ Requires prior knowledge ✓ Simple to implement and interpret	✓ Does not require mathematical model of the system ✓ Does not requires rule-based knowledge ✓ Different learning algorithms available
Demerit	
✓ Rules must be available ✓ Cannot learn ✓ No means for tuning ✓ Sematic problems in interpreting tuned system ✓ Adaptation to modified environment can be difficult	✓ Black box ✓ Rules cannot be extracted ✓ Determine heuristic parameters ✓ Adaptation to modified environment can be difficult and relearning may be necessary ✓ No need of prior knowledge usage ✓ No guarantee that learning converges

give more attention to using it to model different real-life systems [42]. A two–input first-order Sugeno fuzzy model with two rules is shown in Figure 6.21.

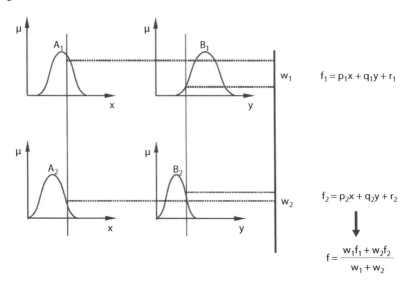

Figure 6.21 A two–input first-order Sugeno fuzzy model with two rules.

6.2.4.1 Adaptive Neuro-Fuzzy Approach

The ANFIS is trained mostly by the combination of least-square method and the back-propagation algorithm. The ANFIS architecture is shown in Figure 6.22. This model is called a first-order Takagi-Sugeno fuzzy model [35].

6.2.4.2 Hybrid Training Algorithm

The ANFIS training algorithm is used to change all the adjustable parameters to compare ANFIS output with trained data. Each training period of the network is divided into two phases [37]. The two passes in the hybrid learning algorithm are mentioned in Table 6.4.

i)   Forward pass to determine the antecedent membership function parameters
ii) Backward pass to determine the consequent parameters $[p, q, r]$

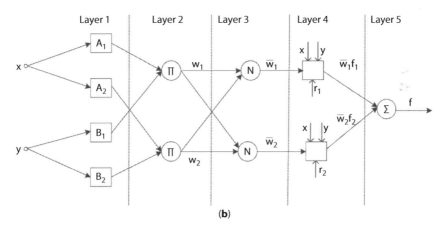

(b)

Figure 6.22 Equivalent ANFIS architecture [36].

Table 6.4 The two passes in the hybrid learning algorithm.

	Forward pass	**Backward pass**
Premise Parameters	Fixed	Gradient Descent
Consequent parameters	Least-squares estimator	Fixed
Signals	Node outputs	Error signals

Table 6.5 Advantages and disadvantages of MPPT techniques.

Methodology	Description	Advantage	Limitations
PID proposed in 1911 by Elmer Sperry	✓ It is a kind of device used to control different process variables in industrial applications. ✓ It acts on the error between the desired signal and the controlled signal. ✓ It has three parameters to be tuned, i.e., proportional, integral and derivative gains need to be tuned to give better performance.	✓ Easy to implement in hardware as well as though microcontrollers, PLC, etc. ✓ No fancy codes to design… can be written by a middle-level programmer. ✓ Can be improved by combining with other methods such as FLC, ANN, GA and others.	✓ Low capability to handle the difficulties of a multi-modal search landscape. ✓ It may not assure the desired performance for a changing environment/operating points. ✓ Less effective with large number of variables and relatively less convergence rate. ✓ *influenced by the controller tuning parameters and the controller error.* ✓ Not suited for advance applications of nonlinear plants such as defense, robotics, financial models, etc.

(Continued)

Table 6.5 Advantages and disadvantages of MPPT techniques. (*Continued*)

Methodology	Description	Advantage	Limitations
FLC Developed by Lotif Zadeh in 1965	✓ It combines the expert experience of a human operator with the design of the controller that does not need any mathematical model of the system to be controlled. ✓ The design process for an FLC consists of four blocks, i.e., fuzzification, rule base, inference mechanism and defuzzification	✓ Few control parameters ✓ Simple to design ✓ Fast convergence rate as compared to PI. ✓ easy to be understood because it uses linguistic terms and the structure of IF-THEN rules. ✓ use of linguistic variables instead of numerical variables, which provide imprecise and qualitative communication ✓ flexible operation, user-friendly, interface, and simplicity of implementation	✓ High ignorance of the abundant source ✓ fuzzy logic by itself cannot learn. ✓ In contrast to FLC it difficult to understand. ✓ Constriction of the control rules depend on the expert knowledge on the area. ✓ tuning of the fuzzy rule parameters and the high cost of implementation

(*Continued*)

Table 6.5 Advantages and disadvantages of MPPT techniques. (*Continued*)

Methodology	Description	Advantage	Limitations
MLFFNN Proposed by Rumelhart, Hinton, and Williams in 1986	✓ It is a family of intelligent algorithms inspired by the performance of biological neural network. ✓ It is feed-forward network having large number of processing elements called neurons. ✓ The neurons are arranged into layers called input layers, one or more hidden layers and output layers which uses gradient descent-based delta learning rule. ✓ The neurons work together to solve problems.	✓ Has great ability to solve nonlinear optimization problems. ✓ Stable convergence characteristics as compared to FLC and ANN. ✓ Memory less algorithm ✓ Neural networks have been applied successfully to speech recognition, image analysis and adaptive control, in order to construct software agents or autonomous robots & in the control of machines. ✓ can be used for time series prediction, classification, and control and identification purposes.	✓ Slow searching speed in the last iteration. ✓ It has relatively complex operator. ✓ Determining the no. of hidden layer and number of neurons in each layer is difficult ✓ Several tests to determine the optimal network architecture have been carried. ✓ it is usually difficult to develop an insight about the meaning associated with each neuron and each weight.

(*Continued*)

Table 6.5 Advantages and disadvantages of MPPT techniques. (*Continued*)

Methodology	Description	Advantage	Limitations
RBFNN First developed Broomhead and Lowe in 1988	✓ It is a type of FFNN which uses radial basis function as an activation function. ✓ It consists of three layers: an input layer, a hidden layer with nonlinear RBF activation function and a linear output layer. ✓ It is determined by the distance between the input and the prototype vector. ✓ Two types of training carried out. In forward pass unsupervised training and in backward pass supervised types of training process are carried out supervised to update the weights.	✓ Easy to implement for the problem at hand. ✓ Time of computation is relatively less. ✓ It has good capability in maintain the diversity of the population. ✓ Neural networks can learn from data.	✓ It is easy to fall into local optimum in high-dimensional space. ✓ It has a low convergence rate in the iterative process. ✓ Can converge prematurely and can be trapped in to local minima especially with complex problems.
ANFIS First proposed by J.S. Roger in 1993	✓ Describing and cognitive behaviour of human mind ✓ ANFIS structure is tuned automatically by least-square estimation & the back propagation algorithm.	✓ It incorporates both qualitative and quantitative knowledge in one framework. ✓ It is simple to design	✓ The determination of the convenient parameters

To track the MPPT with ANFIS requires input and output data sets. These input and output data sets are taken from the system operating constraints. There are two possible ways to collect training data. One is collecting data from the real-time system; another one is from simulation by developing an accurate dynamic model for WEHS using conventional methods like P&O, PI, IcnCon methods, FLC and so on. Collecting data from the real-time system was very difficult due to the irregular nature of weather and the inability to control the weather conditions [38]. Therefore, the training data were collected in this work from simulation of the system

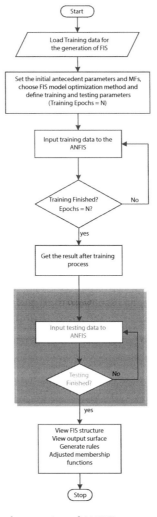

Figure 6.23 Flowchart of implementation of ANFIS.

in Matlab/Simulink using FLC technique [39]. Advantage and disadvantage of MPPT techniques are mentioned in Table 6.5.

The flowchart of ANFIS implementation is shown in Figure 6.23.

6.3 Conclusion

This chapter provides a brief descriptions of different MPPT techniques with the main focus on soft computing techniques. Because of the absence of systematic tools to deal with ill-defined and uncertain systems, not all complex real-world problems can be modelled using conventional modelling approaches. For such reasons, intelligent systems or soft computing techniques emerged to deal with such problems as a better alternative to a conventional model-based control approach. Advantages and disadvantages of each MPPT technique are also provided in this study.

References

1. D. Biswas, S. S. Sahoo, P. M. Tripathi and K. Chatterjee, "Maximum Power Point Tracking for Wind Energy System by Adaptive Neural-Network Based Fuzzy Inference System," in *4th Int'l Conf. on Recent Advances in Information Technology*, 2018.
2. S. Marmouh, M. Boutoubat and L. Mokrani, "MPPT fuzzy logic controller of a wind energy conversion system based on a PMSG," in *8th International Conference on Modelling, Identification and Control (ICMIC)*, Algeria, 2016.
3. J. Aymen, Z. ONS and M. M. Nejib, "Performance assessment of a Wind Turbine with variable speed wind using Artificial Neural Network and Neuro-Fuzzy Controllers," *International Journal of Systems Application, Engineering & Development,* vol. 1, pp. 167-172, 2017.
4. J. P. Ram, N. Rajasekar and M. Miyatake, "Design and overview of maximum power point tracking techniques in wind and solar photovoltaic systems: A review," *Renewable and Sustainable Energy Reviews,* vol. 73, pp. 1138-1159, 2017.
5. M. A. Abdullah, A. H. M. Yatim, C. W. Tan and R. Saidur, "A review of maximum power point tracking algorithms for wind energy systems," *Renewable and Sustainable Energy Reviews,* vol. 16, no. 5, pp. 3220-3227, 2012.
6. J. Pavalam, R. R. Kumar and K. Umadevi, "Design and development of MPPT for wind electrical power system under variable speed generation using fuzzy logic," in *International Conference on Engineering Technology and Science*, 2014.

7. D. Kumar and K. Chatterjee, "A review of conventional and advanced MPPT algorithms for wind energy systems," *Renewable and Sustainable Energy Reviews,* vol. 55, pp. 957-970, 2016.

8. K. Belmokhtar, H. Ibrahim and M. L. Doumbia, "A Maximum Power Point Tracking Control Algorithms for a PMSG-based WECS for Isolated Applications: Critical Review," *Wind Turbines: Design, Control and Applications,* p. 199, 2016.

9. M. B. H. Kumar, B. Saravanan, P. Sanjeevikumar and F. Blaabjerg, "Review on control techniques and methodologies for maximum power extraction from wind energy systems," *IET Renewable Power Generation,* vol. 12, no. 14, pp. 1609-1622, 2018.

10. H. H. Mousa, A. R. Youssef and E. E. Mohamed, "Variable step size P&O MPPT algorithm for optimal power extraction of multi-phase PMSG based wind generation system," *International Journal of Electrical Power & Energy Systems, 108,* pp. 218-231, 2019.

11. O. O. Mengi and I. H. Altas, "Fuzzy logic control for a wind/battery renewable energy production system," *Turk. J. Elec. Eng. & Comp. Sci.,* vol. 20, no. 2, pp. 187-206, 2012.

12. R. A. Kadhim, "Design and Simulation of Closed Loop Proportional Integral (PI) Controlled Boost Converter and 3-phase Inverter for Photovoltaic (PV) Applications," *Al-Khwarizmi Engineering Journal,* vol. 15, no. 1, pp. 10-22, 2019.

13. L. Zadeh, "Fuzzy sets," *Information and Control,* vol. 8, no. 3, pp. 338-353, 1965.

14. N. Chakraborty and M. D. Barma, "Modelling of Stand –Alone Wind Energy Conversion System using Fuzzy Logic Controller," *International Journal of Innovative Research In Electrical, Electronics, Instrumentation and Control Engineering,* vol. 2, no. 1, pp. 861-868, 2014.

15. E. C. Perez, I. Algredo-Badillo and V. H. G. Rodriguez, "Performance analysis of ANFIS in short term wind speed prediction," *arXiv preprint,* pp. 1212-2671, 2012.

16. J. F. Chen, Q. H. Do, T. V. A. Nguyen and T. T. H. Doan, "Forecasting Monthly Electricity Demands by Wavelet Neuro-Fuzzy System Optimized by Heuristic Algorithms," *Information,* vol. 9, no. 3, p. 51, 2018.

17. E. H. Mamdani, "Application of fuzzy logic to approximate reasoning using linguistic synthesis," *In Proceedings of the sixth international symposium on Multiple-valued logic. IEEE Computer Society Press,* pp. 196-202, 1976.

18. E. H. Mamdani and S. Assilian, "An experiment in linguistic synthesis with a fuzzy logic controller," *International Journal of Human-Computer Studies,* vol. 51, no. 2, pp. 135-147, 1999.

19. T. Takagi and M. Sugeno, "Fuzzy identification of systems and its applications to modeling and control," *IEEE Transactions on Systems, Man, and Cybernetics,* vol. 15, no. 1, pp. 116 - 132, 1985.

20. M. Sugeno and G. Kang, "Structure identification of fuzzy model," *Fuzzy Sets and Systems,* vol. 28, no. 1, pp. 15-33, 1988.

21. Y. Tsukamoto, "An approach to fuzzy reasoning method," *Advances in Fuzzy Set Theory and Applications,* pp. 137-149, 1979.

22. P. Jindal and E. G. Singh, "Design Fuzzy Logic Controller For Doubly-Fed Induction Generator Based Wind Power Generation System: A Comparison," *International Journal of Science Technology & Engineering,* vol. 2, no. 01, pp. 148-156, 2015.

23. A. D. Jadhav and S. Nair, "Battery Management using Fuzzy Logic Controller," in *In Journal of Physics: Conference Series (Vol. 1172, No. 1, p. 012093).* IOP Publishing, 2019.

24. I. Basheera and M. Hajmeerb, "Artificial neural networks: fundamentals, computing, design, and application," *Journal of Microbiological Methods,* vol. 43, pp. 3-31, 2000.

25. K. Karabacak and N. Cetin, "Artificial neural networks for controlling wind–PV power systems: A review," *Renewable and Sustainable Energy Reviews,* vol. 29, p. 804–827, 2014.

26. M. H. Al Shamisi, A. H. Assi and H. A. Hejase, "Using MATLAB to Develop Artificial Neural Network Models for Predicting Global Solar Radiation in Al Ain City-UAE," *Rijeka: INTECH Open Access Publisher,* 2011.

27. W. S. McCulloch and W. Pitts, "A logical calculus of the ideas immanent in nervous activity," *Bulletin of Mathematical Biophysics,* vol. 5, no. 4, pp. 115-133, 1943.

28. P. Fuangkhon, "An incremental learning preprocessor for feed-forward neural network," *Artificial Intelligence Review,* vol. 41, no. 2, pp. 183-210, 2014.

29. H. H. El-Tamaly and A. Y. Nassef, "Tip speed ratio and Pitch angle control based on ANN for putting variable speed WTG on MPP," in *Eighteenth International Middle East Power Systems Conference (MEPCON),* 2016.

30. K. Raza, "Analysis of microarray data using artificial intelligence based techniques," In *Handbook of Research on Computational Intelligence Applications in Bioinformatics, IGI Global,* pp. 216-239, 2016.

31. E. Cam and O. Yildiz, "Prediction of wind speed and power in the central Anatolian region of Turkey by adaptive neuro-fuzzy inference systems (ANFIS)," *Turkish Journal of Engineering and Environmental Sciences,* vol. 30, no. 1, pp. 35-41, 2006.

32. A. P. Marugán, F. P. G. Marquez, J. M. P. Perez and D. Ruiz-Hernández, "A survey of artificial neural network in wind energy systems," *Applied Energy,* vol. 228, pp. 1822-1836, 2018.

33. K. Kumar, N. R. Babu and K. R. Prabhu, "Design and analysis of RBFN-based single MPPT controller for hybrid solar and wind energy system," *IEEE Access, 5,* pp. 15308-15317, 2017.

34. A. S. Yilmaz and Z. Ozer, "Pitch angle control in wind turbines above the rated wind speed by multi-layer perceptron and radial basis function neural

networks," *Expert Systems with Applications,* vol. 36, no. 6, pp. 9767-9775, 2009.

35. J. S. Jang, "ANFIS: Adaptive network based fuzzy inference system," *IEEE Trans. Syst. Man Cybern,* vol. 23, p. 665–685, 1993.

36. R. Sitharthan and M. Geethanjali, "ANFIS based Wind Speed Sensor-less MPPT Controller for Variable Speed Wind Energy Conversion Systems," *Australian Journal of Basic and Applied Sciences,* vol. 8, no. 18, pp. 14-23, 2014.

37. Y. O. a. I. Guney, "Adaptive neuro-fuzzy inference system to improve the power quality of variable-speed wind power generation system," *Turk J. Elec. Eng. & Comp. Sci.,* vol. 18, no. 4, pp. 625-645, 2010.

38. A. Padmaja and M. Srikanth, "Design of MPPT Controller using ANFIS and HOMER based sensitivity analysis for MXS 60 PV module," *International Journal of Innovative Research in Advanced Engineering (IJIRAE),* vol. 11, no. 2, pp. 40-50, 2014.

39. A. Ali, A. Moussa, K. Abdelatif, M. Eissa, S. Wasfy and O. P. Malik, "ANFIS Based Controller for Rectifier of PMSG Wind Energy Conversion System Energy Conversion System," in *2014 IEEE Electrical Power and Energy Conference IEEE,* 2014.

40. S. A. Kalogirou, "Artificial neural networks in renewable energy systems applications: *A review," Renewable and sustainable energy reviews,* vol. 5, no. 4, pp. 373-401, 2001.

41. S. A. Kalogirou, "Artificial neural networks in energy applications in buildings," *International Journal of Low-Carbon Technologies,1(3),* vol. 1, no. 3, pp. 201-216, 2006.

42. A. B. Asghar and X. Liu, "Online Estimation of Wind Turbine Tip Speed Ratio by Adaptive Neuro-Fuzzy Algorithm," *International Journal of Advanced Computer Science and Applications,* vol. 9, no. 3, pp. 28-33, 2018.

Section II
CLIMATE CHANGE

7

The Contribution of AI-Based Approaches in the Determination of CO_2 Emission Gas Amounts of Vehicles, Determination of CO_2 Emission Rates Yearly of Countries, Air Quality Measurement and Determination of Smart Electric Grids' Stability

Mesut Toğaçar

*Technical Sciences Vocational School, Computer Technologies Department,
Fırat University, Elazig, Turkey*

Abstract

To make the globalized world more livable, many countries have started to take various measures and have made the necessary legal arrangements in this regard. Any initiative that can harm the ecological balance of countries on a global scale harms both living things and the country's economy. Today, technological infrastructure services play a more environmentally friendly role. In a world where people live more intensely, it is now possible to provide automatic control of systems that can harm the environment with AI-based technologies. Four datasets are used in this paper. The first dataset includes vehicle features in the calculation of the CO_2 emission gas amount of vehicles. The second dataset shows the annual CO_2 emission gas measurement amounts of the countries. The third dataset consists of air quality measurement data and the fourth dataset contains data created on the determination of the stability of smart electricity networks. Proposed approaches consist of machine learning methods and AI models designed using open-source codes. The models designed for this study are as follows: long short-term memory

Email: mtogacar@firat.edu.tr: ORCID: 0000-0002-8264-3899

Pandian Vasant, Gerhard-Wilhelm Weber, Joshua Thomas, José Antonio Marmolejo-Saucedo and Roman Rodriguez-Aguilar (eds.) *Artificial Intelligence for Renewable Energy and Climate Change*, (173–216) © 2022 Scrivener Publishing LLC

(LSTM), bidirectional LSTM, convolutional neural network (CNN), CNN-based LSTM model, and recurrent neural network (RNN). It has been observed that proposed approaches contribute to all the experimental analyzes.

Keywords: Air quality measurement, artificial intelligence, carbon dioxide emission, deep learning, machine learning, smart grids, sustainable world

7.1   Introduction

The rapid increase of the world population can disrupt the supply and demand balance in parallel with technological developments [1]. Especially in the face of rapid population growth in developing countries, energy demand increases in direct proportion [2]. It has brought various problems with it. Meeting the global energy demand can cause various environmental problems. Problems such as the deterioration of ecological balance, global warming, climate change, and poor quality of life can be cited as examples [3]. Failure to take adequate preventive measures that may harm nature in energy production, in line with unconscious and excessive energy consumption, causes the increase of gases such as carbon dioxide (CO_2) that cause global warming in the air [4]. On the other hand, besides unconsciously consumed electrical energy, many people cannot use electrical energy today. Nevertheless, a sustainable living standard is only possible by using sustainable energy [5, 6]. For a sustainable energy vision, the technological infrastructure must be constructive. For this, new ideas and new systems may be needed. It is possible to produce systems that can minimize the use of any system that may harm the environment in energy consumption and maintain the sustainability of the ecological balance [7]. Many international organizations carry out various projects by providing financial funds [8]. As the motto of these projects, the Organisation for Economic Co-operation and Development (OECD) has determined a green growth strategy for sustainable development. In line with the aim of this strategy, countries take joint decisions to develop practical tools of policies that can pave the way for sustainable development [9].

Energy is directly related to the global economy. For this reason, many global companies and organizations have to catch and adopt innovations by the green-sustainable strategy. It is important to adopt technological developments to energy production, to keep the CO_2 concentration at the desired level, to ensure ecological balance, and for a sustainable economy. Minimizing emission rates will positively affect global warming and improve air quality [10, 11]. The European Union (EU) is turning towards green technology and taking serious steps in this regard. However, unlike the EU, China and the US were delayed in taking impressive steps [12]. Despite this, innovative approaches are used in the fields of energy production and consumption [13]. There have been several studies in the artificial intelligence-based literature. Some of these studies are examined below.

Samaher Al-Janabi et al. [14] used deep learning approaches to transforming wind energy into renewable electrical energy. In their study, they proposed a hybrid model that uses deep learning architectures together with the cuckoo optimization method. The aim they wanted to realize with the model they suggested was to reduce the energy cost, reduce the need for manpower and reduce foreign dependency. Analyzes were performed using the datasets they created. The iteration number of the model proposed for each analysis and the error margin of energy production were calculated. Their proposed model has achieved better results than traditional approaches. Thanongsak Xayasouk et al. [15] used data on particulate matter emissions that cause air pollution. They measured the particulate matter emission contrast using long short-term memory (LSTM) and deep autoencoder (DAE) approaches. They analyzed the proposed model with hourly data they obtained at 25 stations in Seoul, South Korea. They used the root mean square error (RMSE) for numerical evaluation in the analyzes. They obtained the best results in the measurement of air concentration with the DAE approach. R. Janarthanan et al. [16] used air monitoring data covering 240 cities of India to measure air quality with deep learning models. In their proposed approach, they used a combination of gray-level co-occurrence matrix (GLCM) with support vector regression (SVR) and LSTM methods. The approach they proposed in the process of classifying air quality has yielded successful results. Thus, they planned to implement a system that could raise the awareness of the people of India about air quality. Qingchun Guo et al. [17] proposed an approach to measure air efficiency in Xi'an and Lanzhou, China, using air pollution index data. They determined the linear or nonlinear correlation relation of these data between the meteorological parameters with artificial neural networks (ANN) and wavelet ANN models. The meteorological data they used consisted of 16 parameter features. They found a direct relationship with the average temperature, average water vapor pressure, minimum temperature, and maximum temperature parameters in the analysis performed with the proposed approach. They analyzed that they saw a direct link with parameters. In experimental analysis, they observed that the performance of the wavelet ANN model was more efficient than the ANN model. They achieved correlation success of 88.46% in the city of Xi'an, and correlation success of 89.06% in the city of Lanzhou. Ajit Bhat et al. [18] used machine learning methods to detect air pollutants that cause air pollution. Sulfur oxides, carbon dioxide (CO_2), nitrogen oxides, carbon monoxide (CO), etc. They carried out their analysis on the pollutants. They collected data in two ways; they used open access data on the internet and obtained data using sensors. They used random forest regression (RFR), decision tree regression (DTR), and linear regression (LR) methods in the analysis of the level of CO in the air. They achieved the best performance result with the RFR method. Asiye K. Ozcanlı et al. [19] examined compilation studies to increase efficiency by using artificial intelligence-based techniques in smart electrical networks. They compared the contributions of artificial intelligence approaches and machine learning methods to stabilize and solve complex problems, unstable and nonlinear solutions they encountered in traditional electrical grids. Ali Kashif Bashir et al. [20] aimed to increase electricity efficiency by using machine learning methods in line with the prediction of smart grid stability. They used SVM, decision trees, k-Nearest Neighbor (kNN), Logistic Regression, Naive Bayes and Neural Networks approaches to minimize the energy lost during the power distribution of smart grids. Decision Tree gave the best performance among machine learning methods. Their overall accuracy success was 99.96%.

The goals aimed to be achieved in this paper can be listed as follows:

- The contribution of artificial intelligence approaches to increase air efficiency;
- Analysis and correlations of cause - result relationships of CO_2 emission gas conditions produced by vehicles;
- Successful evaluation of countries' CO_2 emission measurements by years with artificial intelligence techniques;
- Calculating the contribution rates of deep learning models in smart grids to achieve sufficient efficiency in energy production.

The other sections of this study are as follows. Information about datasets is given in the second section. Detailed information about the artificial intelligence approaches used in conducting the experimental analysis is given in the third section. The experiments and analysis results are expressed in the fourth section. Explanations about the Discussion and conclusion are included in the last two sections, respectively.

7.2   Materials

This section consists of detailed information about the datasets used for experiments. Four datasets were used for experimental analyzes. Information about these datasets is as follows, respectively.

7.2.1   Classification of Air Quality Condition in Gas Concentration Measurement

Most people have to perform their daily activities indoors due to their work. Gas concentration rates may change over time in the area of work. This situation can adversely affect the health and work of the people in the environment. In this dataset, the data obtained by monitoring the daily changes in indoor gas concentration were recorded. The dataset consists of values obtained through six sensors. Each sensor (MQ) is low-cost and reacts to different types of gases. In addition, other data type was acquired using the CO_2 gas sensor type (MG-811). The dataset contains information describing the condition of the indoor environment (four categories) [21]. The dataset consists of 1,845 samples in total and the summary information of the four categories is given in Table 7.1.

Explanations of each category are given below:

- Activity areas and activities of individuals in the normal situation category; fresh air, sleeping, reading, rest, etc.
- Preparing meals: People in this category engage in activities such as cooking meat, cooking pasta, and frying vegetables.

Table 7.1 Condition category of the environment according to gas concentration rates in measuring air quality (dataset #1).

Number	Categories	Number of images
#1	Normal situation	595
#2	Preparing meals	515
#3	Presence of smoke	195
#4	Cleaning - activity	540
	Total	1845

There are one or two people in the activity areas and these people use the compulsory air circulation effectively.
- Presence of smoke: Their field of activity is a closed environment and it is to wait by burning paper and wood for a short time in this environment.
- Cleaning - activity: Activity areas are a closed environment. The activities they carry out are cleaning with the use of ammonia or alcohol sprays. Also, it is to perform cleaning using liquid detergent. Compulsory air circulation can be enabled or disabled depending on the environment.

Seven feature values were obtained for each user in the creation of the dataset. The first six values consisted of sensors. The seventh value includes the action index obtained by calculating the first six values [21]. In the experimental analysis of dataset #1, 80% was separated as training data and 20% was separated as test data.

7.2.2 CO_2 Emission of Vehicles

The second dataset (dataset #2) contains information on the amount of CO_2 emission gas generated depending on the various attribute of the vehicles. Data has been generated from government of Canada websites. The dataset includes information that measures the effects on CO_2 emission gas, taking into account the different attributes of vehicles in Canada, and

Table 7.2 Features that make up dataset #2 and obtained from each vehicle.

Number	Features name	Number	Features name
1	Make	7	Fuel Type
2	Model	8	Fuel Consumption City (L/100 km)
3	Vehicle Class	9	Fuel Consumption Hwy (L/100 km)
4	Engine Size (L)	10	Fuel Consumption Comb (L/100 km)
5	Cylinders	11	Fuel Consumption Comb (mpg)
6	Transmission	12	CO_2 Emissions(g/km)

Table 7.3 Sample representation of string format features in dataset #2.

Make	Model	Vehicle class	Transmission	Fuel type
ACURA	ILX	COMPACT	AS5	Z
ACURA	ILX	COMPACT	M6	Z
ACURA	ILX HYBRID	COMPACT	AV7	Z
ACURA	MDX 4WD	SUV - SMALL	AS6	Z
ACURA	RDX AWD	SUV - SMALL	AS6	Z

it was collected over 7 years and made available. The information of 7,385 vehicles in total is included and there are 12 features for each vehicle [22]. These features are given in Table 7.2.

Five of the features consist of string contents and the others consist of numerical values. An example representation of the string structured features is given in Table 7.3. An example representation of the numerical structured features is given in Table 7.4. The fuel type feature category of the dataset consists of five class types. These types are; "X = Normal gasoline, Z = High quality gasoline, D = Diesel, E = Ethanol (E85), N = Natural gas" [22]. Graphic representation of these Fuel Types is shown in Figure 7.1.

7.2.3   Countries' CO_2 Emission Amount

This dataset (dataset #3) consists of data containing values of CO_2 emission rates of countries yearly. The data includes emission amounts between 1960 and 2014. The data includes the CO_2 emission rates of 264 countries in total [23]. The first five sample data of countries on a yearly and country basis are given in Table 7.5.

In this study, the change of CO_2 amounts of countries was measured by artificial intelligence techniques.

7.2.4   Stability Level in Electric Grids

This dataset (dataset #4) contains data from local stability analyzes of the four-node star system that implements the concept of decentralized smart grid control. The dataset is multivariate and consists of ten thousand grid analyzes. There are fourteen features for each grid in the dataset. All values

Table 7.4 Sample representation of numerical value features in dataset #2.

Engine size	Cylinders	Fuel consumption city	Fuel consumption hwy	Fuel consumption comb (L/100 km)	Fuel consumption comb (mpg)	CO_2 emissions
2.0	4	9.9	6.7	8.5	33	196
2.4	4	11.2	7.7	9.6	29	221
1.5	4	6.0	5.8	5.9	48	136
3.5	6	12.7	9.1	11.1	25	255
3.5	6	12.1	8.7	10.6	27	244

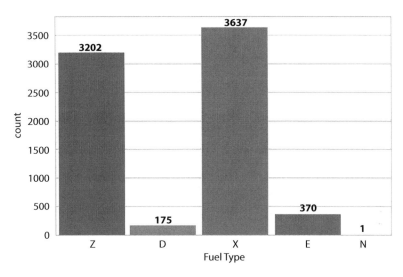

Figure 7.1 Graphical representation of fuel types in dataset #2.

Table 7.5 Change of countries' CO_2 emission amounts by years.

Country name	Country code	1960	1961	2012	2013	2014
Aruba	ABW	NaN	NaN	13.155542	8.351294	8.408363
Afghanistan	AFG	0.046060	0.053604	0.350371	0.315602	0.299445
Angola	AGO	0.097472	0.079038	1.330843	1.330843	1.291328
Albania	ALB	1.258195	1.374186	1.692908	1.692908	1.978763
Andorra	AND	NaN	NaN	5.916597	5.900753	5.832170

of these features are actual data values [24, 25]. The fourteen features that make up the dataset are given in Table 7.6.

Numerical information about the types in the Stabf feature of the dataset is shown in Figure 7.2. 6380 electrical grid is unstable and 3620 electrical grid is stable [25]. In the analyzes performed 80% of the dataset was used as training data and 20% of the dataset was used as test data.

7.3   Artificial Intelligence Approaches

In this section, detailed information about machine learning methods and deep learning models used for experimental analysis is given. It also includes

Table 7.6 Features that make up the electrical grid dataset.

Number	Features name	Explanation	Number	Features name	Explanation
1	Tau #1	Tau: Participant's reaction time	9	G_1	G: Coefficient proportional to price elasticity
2	Tau #2		10	G_2	
3	Tau #3		11	G_3	
4	Tau #4		12	G_4	
5	P_1	P: Nominal power consumed/ produced	13	Stab	Stab: The maximal real part of the characteristic equation root
6	P_2				
7	P_3		14	Stabf	Stabf: the stability label of the system
8	P_4				

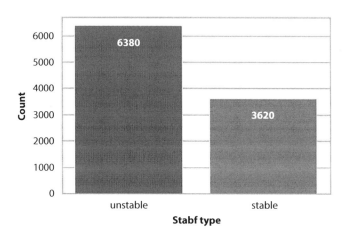

Figure 7.2 Features that make up the electrical grid dataset.

information about the architectural structures of the approaches used for analysis, and information about preferred parameters and parameter values.

7.3.1   Machine Learning Methods

Machine learning is an approach that enables learning based on types of data with various software-based algorithms and deals with the design and development processes. Machine learning is a sub-branch of artificial intelligence. In general, machine learning methods are classified in four ways according to learning approaches:

1. Supervised learning with all the input samples that make up the first dataset and the labels showing the accuracy of each input.
2. Unsupervised learning, where each input learns on its own, without the truth labels, with all the input samples that make up the dataset.
3. Semi-supervised learning where the training of the dataset with missing data takes place and the methods are learned with missing data.
4. Reinforcement learning complements the learning with reward-punishment feedback from the environment [26].

7.3.1.1 Support Vector Machine

SVM method is a popular machine learning approach preferred for regression and classification processes. This method processes the input samples, places them on the coordinate plane, and performs classification between types using hyper lines. The maximum margin area (w) is determined by optimizing [27]. The explanation showing the binary and multiple classification processes of the SVM method is given in Figure 7.3. The most

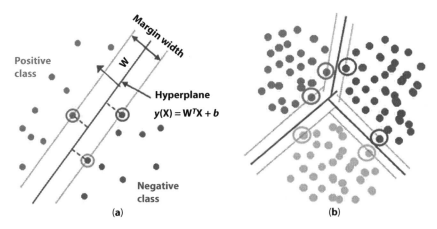

Figure 7.3 SVM classification process; (a) binary classification process and (b) multiple classification process [29].

important criterion in SVM methods is setting the decision limit. The following equations are used for this critical step. Thanks to the mathematical formula in Eq. (7.1), problems that may occur during the classification process are minimized. The bias variable is represented by b. The X and Y variables in Eq. (7.2) represent the feature values, and the labeling process is performed with this equation [27, 28].

$$u = \vec{w} \cdot \vec{x} - b \tag{7.1}$$

$$y_i(\vec{w} \cdot \vec{x}_i - b) \geq 1, \forall i \tag{7.2}$$

One of the cases where the SVM method is successful is the multiple classification process. It uses the probability-based maximum voting process in the multi-classification process. The input sample is labeled with the class with the highest number of votes. In this process, the input type is represented by the variable K and the number of matches is calculated using the formula $K(K-1)/2$. For example, considering the representation in Figure 7.3(b), K = 3 in a dataset with three classes. Therefore, the number of matches is three (red-blue, red-yellow, blue-yellow). In the next step, probability values (0-1) are given as much as the number of matches for each input sample. In the last step, each input data is labeled to the class with the higher probability value (high score) [28].

SVM method was used in the Sklearn library, with default values preferred in the analysis of this study. The preferred method of SVM is linear. Other preferred parameter values are as follows: the maximum number of iterations was selected as 1,000, the cut scaling value was selected one, and the tolerance parameter value 10^{-4} was selected.

7.3.1.2   eXtreme Gradient Boosting (XG Boost)

Extreme gradient boosting (XG Boost) is an open-source approach that enables efficient and effective implementation of the gradient boost algorithm. This approach enabled the applied machine learning community to move towards gradient boosting more generally. The XG Boost method is among the methods used in winning solutions for classification and regression problems in machine learning competitions. In this method, the gain parameter is used and it contributes to the process performance with this parameter. The gain parameter is calculated according to Eq. (7.3). It facilitates the partitioning process with an approach similar to the tree-root relationship in the classification process. XG Boost scales beyond billions of instances using far fewer resources than existing systems [30]. The process of estimating the output value of the tree structure created in this method is calculated according to Eq. (7.4).

$$Gain = left\ similarity + right\ similarity - root\ similarity \qquad (7.3)$$

$$Newguess = initial\ predicted\ value + learning\ rate\ x\ output\ value$$

$$(7.4)$$

XG Boost method was used in the Sklearn library, with default values preferred in the analysis of this study. Other preferred parameter values are as follows; the maximum depth size of 100 was chosen, and the number of samples (estimation value) that the algorithm could work on was 1,000, and the learning rate 10^{-1} was chosen.

7.3.1.3   Gradient Boost

Gradient Boost, typically capable of generating a prediction model in the form of a collection of weak prediction models such as decision trees; is the machine learning method preferred for the solution of classification and regression problems. This method is based on combining the best possible model approach with the previous model approaches and performing the process steps, thus minimizing the overall prediction error. The change in the outcome estimate for each sample input in the data set depends on how much it affects the overall estimation error. The steps to be followed in my classification process in the gradient boost method are as follows:

- Placing a simple linear regression or decision tree on the data,
- Calculating error residues according to Eq. (7.5),
- Placing a new model on error residues as target variable with the same input variables,
- Adding the predicted residues to previous estimates,
- Placing another model in the remaining residues [31].

$$Error = actual\ target\ value - estimated\ target\ value \qquad (7.5)$$

Gradient Boost method was used in the Sklearn library, with default values preferred in the analysis of this study. Other preferred parameter values are as follows; the maximum depth size of 100 was chosen, and the number of samples (estimation value) that the algorithm could work on was 1,000, and the learning rate 10^{-1} was chosen.

7.3.1.4   Decision Tree

Decision tree (DT) is the popular machine learning method preferred for the solution of classification and prediction problems. DT is a flowchart-like tree structure where each internal node expresses a test on an attribute, each branch represents a result of the test, and each leaf node holds a class label. The general design of DT is shown in Figure 7.4. Decision trees can handle both continuous and categorical variables. This method provides a clear indication of which areas are most important for estimation or classification. As with all analytical methods, the DT method has limitations that users should be aware of. Its main disadvantage is that it may not be successful, especially when using a small dataset. This problem may limit the generalizability and robustness of the resulting models [32].

DT method is a machine learning approach that is preferred in classification operations consisting of a root, inner node, and leaf nodes. In the classification process, nodes are divided into sub-nodes using recursive methods, and this situation continues until it does not affect the classification process. In the classification process, the "Entropy" method called information gain measurement is used to separate the data features. The uncertainties of the data are measured by the entropy method and the data properties are classified with the obtained probability values [33]. The formula used for measuring entropy (E) is given in Eq. (7.6). While N variable expresses the data number in Eq. (7.6); P is i refers to the probability value of the data.

$$E = -\sum_{i=1}^{N} P_i \log_2 P_i \qquad (7.6)$$

Other important parameters preferred for the DT method in the experimental analysis are as follows: the criterion value "Gini" was selected, and the maximum depth value 100 was selected. Other parameter values are default values accepted in the Sklearn library.

7.3.1.5   Random Forest

Random Forest (RF) is a machine learning method that includes more than one decision tree in its algorithm structure. The general design of the RF

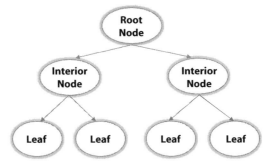

Figure 7.4 Decision tree method's root-leaf link.

method is shown in Figure 7.5. To classify a new object from an input vector, insert the input vector into each of the trees in the forest. Each tree in the RF approach performs classification and the result is calculated by voting. In the RF method, each input data chooses the classification with the highest number of votes. This method generally works more efficiently with large data sets. The margin of error is important in the calculation of efficiency, and the formula for the mean square error (MSE) given in Eq. (7.7) is used in the RF method [34]. In this equation; variable N represents the number of data points, variable f_i represents the value returned by the method. The actual value for each i at the data point represents the variable y_i. In addition, it makes predictions about which variables are important in the classification and the created forests are recorded to be used in other data inputs.

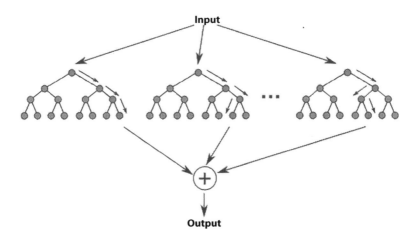

Figure 7.5 Working principle of the RF method [35].

$$MSE = \frac{1}{N}\Sigma_{i=1}^{N}\left(f_i - y_i\right)^2 \qquad (7.7)$$

The RF method creates multiple sets of decision trees and then combines these clusters to make the classification process more accurate. It aims to bring together as many different decision trees as possible, thus creating a low-correlation forest community. In the classification process, random nodes are selected and the best node is chosen among randomly selected variables. The Gini parameter is used to measure the homogeneity of classes. If the Gini measurement value of the lower node is lower than the Gini measurement value of the parent node, the branch with the nodes is considered successful. The Gini measurement is calculated according to Eq. (7.8). All data are represented by variable G_i and selected data are represented by lm. Also, p_i variable represents the square of the selected data divided by the number of elements smaller and larger than itself [36].

$$Gini(Gi) = 1 - \sum_{i=1}^{lm} p_i^2 \qquad (7.8)$$

Other important parameters preferred for the RF method in the experimental analysis are as follows: the criterion value "Gini" was selected, and the maximum depth value 100 was selected. Also, the minimum sample split value was chosen as 4, and the number of trees was set as 1,000. Other parameter values are default values accepted in the Sklearn library.

7.3.2   Deep Learning Methods

Artificial intelligence technologies have made their name permanent in many fields of engineering and applied science over time. Today, artificial intelligence and its sub-branches; machine learning, deep learning, and statistical methods have started to attract attention [37]. Deep learning models include hidden layers in their architectural structure, and they can realize the learning situation without true labels. Deep learning models have learning weights and these weights are updated with each iteration or epoch [38]. Thanks to the weight updates, the learning success of the model increases. In deep learning models, feed-forward and feedback approaches have been developed for updating weight and other parameter values. In some models, operations are carried out by keeping the histories of the information thanks to the memory (for example; LSTM) [39].

7.3.2.1   Convolutional Neural Networks

CNN models train input data, classifying, segmentation, natural language processing, speech, etc. It is designed to perform transactions [40]. These are networks with an artificial intelligence-based architecture that can automatically extract the necessary features from datasets and perform image analysis operations. Recently, CNN models have achieved groundbreaking achievements in many areas, from image recognition where pattern recognition processes occur, to signal to process [41]. CNN models played a major role in solving complex problems that artificial neural network (ANN) models could not perform and achieved successful results [42]. The general structure of CNN models consists of three layers. These layers are the input layer, the hidden layers and the output layer [43]. This situation is shown in Figure 7.6.

CNN models are multilayer meshes that process input data from convolutional, pooling, normalization, dropout, and fully connected layers to the output layer. The purpose of these models is to process the features extracted from the input data by layers and transfer the best features to the activation function in the last layer [44]. If the functions of these layers are explained;

The convolution layer enables activation maps to be created by circulating filters ($2{\times}2$, $3{\times}3$, $5{\times}5$, $7{\times}7$, etc.) over the input data. The filter resolution is smaller than the size and volume of the input data. Each filter is shifted across the width and height of the input data. The values of the activation map are created by calculating the output values during each step between the input data and the filter. The output volume of the convolution layer is formed by stacking the activation maps of the filters along the depth dimension. The activation functions decide whether to activate the features derived from the input data. Thus, by filtering the transfer of each feature to the next layer, it ensures that the features it deems efficient are transferred [45]. The pooling layer allows the input data to be processed regionally

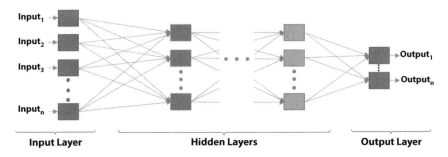

Figure 7.6 The general layer structure of CNN models.

within the frame of the preferred filter size and to be transferred to the next layer by drawing the maximum value or average value from the relevant region. The pooling layer lowers the cost of the model by reducing the number of input features. Using an incorrect pooling layer can lead to the loss of important information in the CNN models [45, 46]. Normalization converts these values to a specific standard range using statistical methods if there are large differences between input values from the previous layer. In this way, deep learning models provide faster training and prevent models from overfitting. The dropout layer is intended to dilute neurons below a certain threshold value. Thus, it is aimed to increase the success

Table 7.7 The architectural structure of the CNN model was designed for this study.

Layer		Filter/value	Output shape	Activation
Number	Process step			
1	Convolution	(2, 2)	(None, 1, 1024)	ReLU
2	Batch Normalization	-	(None, 1, 1024)	-
3	Convolution	(2, 2)	(None, 1, 512)	ReLU
4	Batch Normalization	-	(None, 1, 512)	-
5	Convolution	(2, 2)	(None, 1, 256)	ReLU
6	Batch Normalization	-	(None, 1, 256)	-
7	Pooling	Maximum	(None, 256)	ReLU
8	Dense	-	(None, 128)	ReLU
9	Dropout	0.25	(None, 128)	-
10	Dense	-	(None, 64)	ReLU
11	Dropout	0.2	(None, 64)	-
12	Dense	-	(None, 16)	ReLU
13	Dropout	0.1	(None, 16)	-
Output	Dense	(Number of classes)	(None, Number of classes)	Softmax

of the model by deactivating the neurons with less efficiency in the model [47]. In the fully connected layer, it is the layer where the neurons obtained as output from all previous layers are fully connected and the flattening process takes place. In other words, it tries to collect all the features from the previous layer in a single dimension or vector array. In the dense/fully connected layer, each input value is generated as output after processing by activation functions. It also contributes to the classification process with the dense/fully connected layer [48].

Finally, the CNN model used in this study is designed in Python software. The general design, layer information, and preferred parameter information of the CNN model used in the experimental analysis of this study are given in Table 7.7. In the compilation of the CNN model, ADAM was chosen as the optimization method and the loss activation function "categorical cross-entropy" was preferred.

7.3.2.2   Long Short-Term Memory

Unlike the recurrent neural network (RNN) model, the LSTM model works with linear interaction using private and multilayer neural networks instead of using a single neural network. Input data can be easily switched between layers along the linear chain. LSTM model realizes information transitions between layers with special gates. If this model is to be used in an information network structure, the transfer of information is provided by "input gates". If the information is unnecessary or if sufficient space is to be created in the memory, the "forgetting gate" is used. If "forgetting and input" gates are to be merged by LSTM, then "update gates" are used. After all, the LSTM model takes the data as input and processes it. It performs prediction and classification steps by transferring the processed data to "output gates". The operation steps of the LSTM model are shown in Figure 7.7.

The LSTM model is designed in Python language, and detailed information about the designed model is given in Table 7.8. In the compilation of

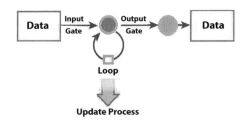

Figure 7.7 The process steps and design of the LSTM model.

Table 7.8 The architectural structure of the LSTM model was designed for this study.

Number	Layer	Value/output shape	Activation
#1	LSTM	(None, 1, 400)	ReLU
	Dropout	0.3	-
#2	LSTM	(None, 200)	ReLU
	Dropout	0.2	-
#3	LSTM	(None, 100)	ReLU
	Dropout	0.2	-
#4	LSTM	(None, 50)	ReLU
	Dropout	0.2	-
#5	Dense	(None, Number of classes)	Softmax

the LSTM model, ADAM was chosen as the optimization method and the loss activation function "categorical cross-entropy" was preferred.

7.3.2.3 Bi-Directional LSTM and CNN

The most important feature that distinguishes the Bi-LSTM model from the LSTM model is its ability to provide bidirectional transmission of information by using a gateway between the previous layer and the next layer. Hence, the Bi-LSTM model is similar to bidirectional recurrent neural networks (Bi-RNN). However, the most important feature that distinguishes the Bi-LSTM model from the Bi-RNN model is the gates used in its architecture as a memory unit. The Bi-LSTM model, just like the architectural structure of the LSTM model, obtains results by processing the input data from the input gates, update gates, and output gates [49]. In Bi-LSTM models, the number of hidden units and their functioning are calculated according to Eq. (7.9) and Eq. (7.10). In these equations, L and H inputs are used for the number of hidden units. Here; t represents the time value x^t, is the sequence input, θ_h the activation function of the hidden unit, the weight values of the hidden unit, and the variable represents the activation function of the h unit at time t [50, 51].

$$a_h^t = \sum_{l=1}^{L} x_l^t w_{lh} + \sum_{h'=1,t>0}^{H} b_{h'}^{t-1} w_{h'h} \tag{7.9}$$

Table 7.9 The architectural structure of the LSTM & CNN model was designed for this study.

Number	Layer	Value/output shape
#1	Convolutional	(None, 1, 1024)
	Batch Normalization & ReLU	(None, 1, 1024)
#2	Convolutional	(None, 1, 512)
	Batch Normalization & ReLU	(None, 1, 512)
#3	Convolutional	(None, 1, 256)
	Batch Normalization & ReLU	(None, 1, 256)
#4	Bidirectional LSTM	(None, 1, 512)
#5	Bidirectional LSTM	(None, 1, 512)
#6	Maximum Pooling	(None, 512)
#7	Dense (Activation: Softmax)	(None, Number of classes)

$$b_h^t = \theta_h \left(a_h^t \right) \tag{7.10}$$

In the proposed approach, a hybrid model is created by using the layers of the Bi-LSTM model and CNN model together. The LSTM & CNN model used for this study is designed in Python language and model information is given in Table 7.9. In the compilation of the LSTM & CNN model, the ADAM optimization method was chosen and the lost function MSE was preferred.

7.3.2.4   Recurrent Neural Network

Since there is no memory status in CNN models, the output of the previous layer is forgotten. RNN models keep the past process steps in memory with their forward and backward feeder structure, unlike CNN models. Therefore, RNN models are used more frequently in time series (e.g., change of financial values, weather) with this feature. On the other hand, RNN models are preferred for sequential data such as text, sound, and stock prices. In RNNs, as in the LSTM model, the input data is rotated through a loop and the update process is performed according to historical data values. Gated repetitive units (GRU) are used to avoid problems in

Table 7.10 The architectural structure of the RNN model was designed for this study.

Number	Layer	Value/output shape	Activation/parameter
#1	LSTM	(None, 1, 128)	ReLU / return sequences (true)
	Dropout	0.25	-
#2	LSTM	(None, 1, 256)	ReLU / return sequences (true)
	Dropout	0.2	-
#3	LSTM	(None, 1, 256)	ReLU / return sequences (true)
	Dropout	0.2	-
#4	LSTM	(None, 1, 512)	ReLU / return sequences (true)
#5	Flatten	(None, 512)	-
#6	Dense	(None, 512)	ReLU / -
	Dropout	0.3	-
#7	Dense	(None, 256)	ReLU / -
	Dropout	0.25	-
#8	Dense	(None, 128)	ReLU / -
#9	Dense	(None, Number of classes)	Softmax / ADAM optimizer

propagating the first error that occurs in RNN models back to the network. There are two gates in the structure of GRUs. These gates are the update gate and the reset gate, respectively [52].

The RNN model designed for this study was designed in Python programming language, and the recommended design is given in Table 7.10. The loss function preferred in the compilation phase of the experimental analysis: "categorical cross-entropy" and optimization method is ADAM.

7.3.3   Activation Functions

The activation function directly affects the network performance of AI-based models and contributes to these networks with nonlinear features. The main purpose of activation functions is to enable a neuron in neural networks to switch from passive to the active state until it reaches a certain threshold value. With active-passive status, unnecessary data is not included in the training process of the model, and both performance success is increased and time savings are achieved. If the activation function is not used in model training, it means that the model is linearized [53].

7.3.3.1   Rectified Linear Unit

The ReLU function is an activation function that is commonly used in neural networks and converts nonlinear input values into a linear structure. The ReLU function has a functional structure that resets by deriving negative input values. This helps to dilute the input values by the ReLU function. Thus, model training can be performed more easily by not processing the inactive input values by neural networks [54].

It has been observed that the ReLU function generally accelerates the convergence of gradient descent values in deep learning models compared to sigmoid and *tanh* activation functions. It saw that unnecessary observed negative values were reset by the ReLU function. When using the ReLU function in deep learning models, it is directly related to the learning speed of the model, and the model training is negatively affected by excessively increasing or decreasing the learning speed ratio. Sometimes ReLU functions can have a fragile structure because they process negative input values and convert them to zero values. That is, when negative input values are reset, they can now be disabled by the model. As a result, the propagation of the deep learning model cannot be realized and learning becomes difficult. To prevent this situation, the learning speed of the deep learning model should be adjusted correctly. The mathematical formula that produces the output value corresponding to the input value of the ReLU function is specified in Eq. (7.11). In this equation, represents the input value while $f(z)$ represents the output function value [55].

$$f(z) = \max(0, z) \qquad (7.11)$$

7.3.3.2   Softmax Function

Softmax is the activation function that usually functions in the last layer of CNN models. It is preferred by deep learning models in the process of classifying binary or multi-class data sets. It is used to enable features extracted from fully connected layers of models. Thus, at the end of a nonlinear regression process, the normalization process of the properties obtained from the previous layer is realized. Then, it produces probability values between [0,1] by processing the properties that are passed through the normalization process. For classification, probability values of input data are compared and labeled with the class with the highest probability value. Therefore, the sum of probability values obtained for each input data is equal to one. The mathematical formula of the Softmax function is given in Eq. (7.12). In this equation, variable represents the input values while $f(z)$ represents the output function value [56].

$$f(z)_i = \frac{e^{z_i}}{\sum_j e^{z_j}} \tag{7.12}$$

7.4   Experimental Analysis

Jupyter Notebook interface was used in the experimental analysis of the proposed approaches, and the Google Colab server was used as the hardware. A confusion matrix was used for experimental analysis and evaluation of results. The metrics used in the calculation of the confusion matrix are as follows; sensitivity (Se), specificity (Sp), precision (Pre), f-score (F-scr), and Accuracy (Acc). Metrics are calculated with the formulas between Eq. (7.13) and Eq. (7.17). The parameters used in these equations; true positive (TP), true negative (TN), false positive (FP), false negative (FN) [57].

$$Se = \frac{TP}{TP + TN} \tag{7.13}$$

$$Sp = \frac{TN}{TN + TP} \tag{7.14}$$

$$Pre = \frac{TP}{TP + FP} \qquad (7.15)$$

$$F\text{-scr} = \frac{2xTP}{2xTP + FP + FN} \qquad (7.16)$$

$$Acc = \frac{TP + TN}{TP + TN + FP + FN} \qquad (7.17)$$

Four datasets were used in experimental analyzes. The dataset of each analysis was enumerated (please see the Materials section, dataset #1, ..., dataset #4). In the experimental analyzes, 80% of the dataset was separated as training data in the analyzes performed by deep learning models and machine learning methods, and 20% was separated as test data. Therefore, four experimental analyzes were performed for four datasets.

In the first experimental analysis, analyzes were performed using data from dataset #1. In this experiment, the measurement of air quality was examined with artificial intelligence-based approaches. In the experimental analysis carried out, a classification process was carried out about the situation in the room by monitoring the change in indoor gas concentration. A total of 1,845 samples were used for four target conditions (a normal situation, preparing meals, presence of smoke, cleaning), and ambient gas concentration ratios were calculated using data sensors for each. The aim of this study is that artificial intelligence-based approaches can successfully measure the value of air efficiency in the environment. Since 6 sensors were used in the analysis of dataset #1, each sensor gave a feature. Dataset #1 containing 6 features was analyzed with machine learning methods in the first step. In the first step SVM, XG Boost, Gradient Boost, Decision Tree, and RF methods were used. The XG Boost method gave the best performance, and the overall accuracy success achieved was 97.02%. In this step, the confusion matrices obtained from machine learning methods and used in calculating the measurement values are shown in Figure 7.8. The number equivalents of the class types expressed from the confusion matrices in Figure 7.8 are as follows: "1: Normal situation, 2: Preparing meals, 3: Presence of smoke, 4: Cleaning - activity". Overall accuracy achievements obtained from other machine learning methods are as follows: 88.07% success was achieved with the SVM method, 94.85% success was achieved with the Gradient Boost method, 94.85% success was achieved with the Decision Tree method and 96.20% success was achieved

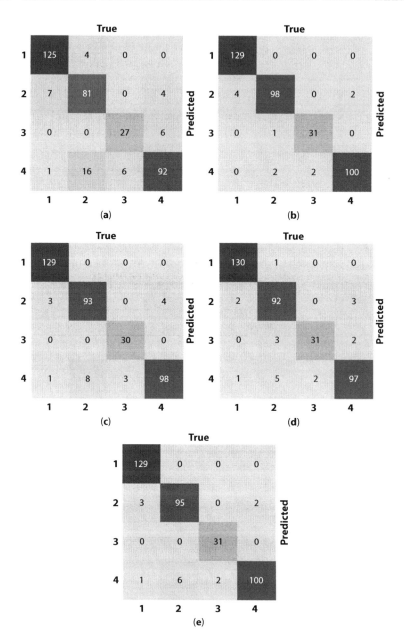

Figure 7.8 Confusion matrices obtained by machine learning methods of dataset #1; (a) SVM, (b) XG boost, (c) gradient boost, (d) decision tree, (e) RF.

Table 7.11 Analysis results of dataset #1 with machine learning methods (%).

Machine learning	Class	Se	Sp	Pre	F-scr	Acc	Overall acc
SVM	Normal	96.89	96.15	93.98	95.41	96.43	88.07
	Preparing meals	88.04	92.42	80.19	83.93	91.29	
	Presence of smoke	81.81	98.02	81.81	81.81	96.43	
	Cleaning	80	95.88	90.19	84.79	90.78	
XG Boost	Normal	100	98.28	96.99	98.47	98.89	97.02
	Preparing meals	94.23	98.85	97.02	95.60	97.54	
	Presence of smoke	96.87	99.39	93.93	95.38	99.16	
	Cleaning	96.15	99.23	98.03	97.08	98.35	
Gradient Boost	Normal	100	98.22	96.99	98.47	98.87	94.85
	Preparing meals	93	96.98	92.07	92.53	95.89	
	Presence of smoke	100	99.07	90.90	95.23	99.15	
	Cleaning	89.09	98.43	96.07	92.45	95.62	
Decision Tree	Normal	99.23	98.65	97.74	98.48	98.87	94.85
	Preparing meals	94.84	96.62	91.08	92.92	96.15	
	Presence of smoke	86.11	99.37	93.93	89.85	98.03	
	Cleaning	92.38	98.06	95.09	93.71	96.41	
RF	Normal	100	98.26	96.99	98.47	98.88	96.20
	Preparing meals	95	97.74	94.05	94.52	96.99	
	Presence of smoke	100	99.38	93.93	96.87	99.43	
	Cleaning	91.74	99.22	98.03	94.78	96.99	

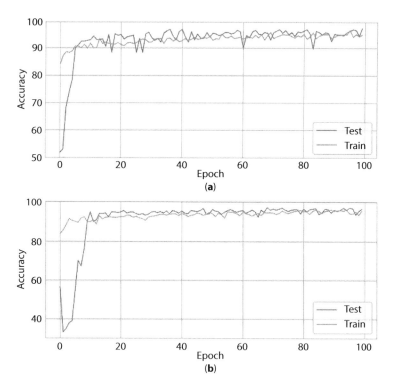

Figure 7.9 Training-test success graphs obtained for dataset #1 of CNN and LSTM & CNN models; (a) CNN, (b) LSTM & CNN.

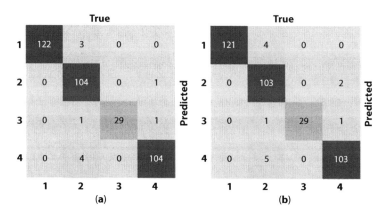

Figure 7.10 Confusion matrices obtained for dataset #1 of CNN and LSTM & CNN models; (a) CNN, (b) LSTM & CNN.

with the RF method. Detailed analysis results are given in Table 7.11. In the second step of the first experiment, dataset #1 was analyzed by CNN and (LSTM & CNN) models. The training of the models was carried out with an epoch value of 100. In the second step of the first experiment, the best success was achieved with the designed CNN model. The training-test success graphs obtained in the second step are shown in Figure 7.9 and the confusion matrices are shown in Figure 7.10. An overall accuracy success rate of 97.29% was achieved with the CNN model. An overall accuracy success rate of 96.47% was achieved by the LSTM & CNN hybrid model. The overall accuracy success achieved with the CNN model gave more successful results than other methods used for the first experiment. The successes of the CNN model based on class is as follows: 99.17% accuracy success was achieved for normal class, 97.55% accuracy success was achieved for preparing meals class, 99.44% accuracy success was achieved for the presence of the smoke class, and 98.35% accuracy success was obtained for cleaning class. Detailed analysis results are given in Table 7.12.

In the second experiment, correlational measurements of CO_2 emission amounts in vehicles depending on various attribute conditions were analyzed. The second experiment consists of two steps. In the first step, all features (12 features) of dataset #2 were examined and the relational

Table 7.12 Analysis results of dataset #1 with deep learning models (%).

Deep learning	Class	Se	Sp	Pre	F-scr	Acc	Overall acc
CNN	Normal	97.60	100	100	98.78	99.17	97.29
	Preparing meals	99.04	96.95	92.85	95.85	97.55	
	Presence of smoke	93.54	100	100	96.66	99.44	
	Cleaning	96.29	99.22	98.11	97.19	98.35	
LSTM & CNN	Normal	96.80	100	100	98.37	98.88	96.47
	Preparing meals	98.09	96.19	91.15	94.49	96.73	
	Presence of smoke	93.54	100	100	96.66	99.44	
	Cleaning	95.37	98.82	97.16	96.26	97.80	

dimensions of some features were investigated using artificial intelligence techniques. Analyzes were performed using the libraries of the python software language "Pandas, Seaborn, Numpy, Sklearn" in correlation measurement. In the first step of the second experiment, the connection between the attributes of the vehicles and their fuel consumption and CO_2 emission amounts were analyzed. Dozens of vehicle data were used in the analysis. The graphical results show the top three types of attributes that have the highest consumption and the highest emission rates. "Lamborghini, Rolls Royce, and Bentley" took the first three places in the CO_2 emission rates in Canada based on vehicle brands, respectively. The ranking of vehicle classes according to fuel consumption is as follows: "van-passenger,

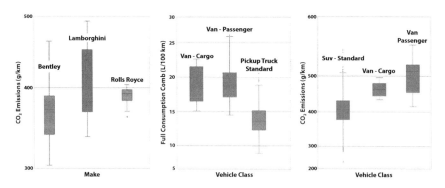

Figure 7.11 The relationship graphs with the attribute of the vehicles and the amount of CO_2 emission gas and fuel consumption.

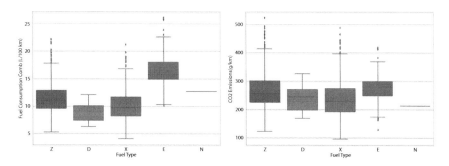

Figure 7.12 Comparison of fuel types according to fuel consumption and CO_2 emission amounts.

van-cargo, pickup truck-standard". Likewise, vehicle classes in the top three according to CO_2 emission amounts are as follows: "van-passenger, van-cargo, SUV-standard". Also, the analysis of CO_2 emission amounts and fuel consumption rates of fuel types were performed. "E-Ethanol (E85)" took first place in the relationship between fuel type - fuel consumption. "Z = High-quality gasoline, E = Ethanol (E85)" took place in the first two places in the relationship between fuel type and CO_2 emission amounts. In addition, since there is one data for "N = Natural gas" fuel type, it was not included in the analysis. The relationships between the characteristics, emission amounts, fuel consumption, and types of the vehicles are shown in Figure 7.11 and Figure 7.12.

In the second step of the second experiment, fuel types were analyzed based on vehicle attributes. In this step, the classification of fuel types was carried out using machine learning methods and deep learning models. The XG Boost method gave the best performance with 94.65% in the

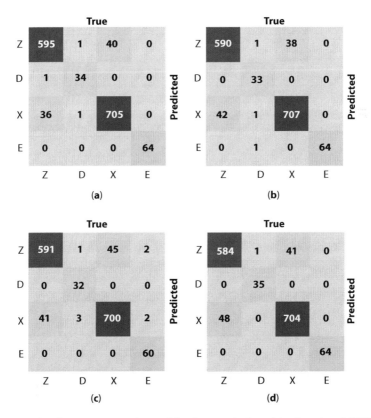

Figure 7.13 Confusion matrices obtained for dataset #2 of machine learning; (a) XG boost, (b) gradient boost, (c) decision tree, (d) RF.

Table 7.13 Analysis results of dataset #2 with machine learning methods (%).

Machine learning	Fuel type	Se	Sp	Pre	F-scr	Acc	Overall acc
XG Boost	Z	93.55	95.59	94.14	93.84	94.71	94.65
	D	97.14	99.85	94.44	95.77	99.78	
	X	95.01	94.54	94.63	94.82	94.77	
	E	100	100	100	100	100	
Gradient Boost	Z	93.79	95.03	93.35	93.57	94.50	94.38
	D	100	99.78	91.66	95.65	99.78	
	X	94.26	94.75	94.89	94.58	94.50	
	E	98.46	100	100	99.22	99.92	
Decision Tree	Z	92.48	95.07	93.51	92.99	93.95	93.63
	D	100	99.70	88.88	94.11	99.71	
	X	93.83	93.81	93.95	93.89	93.82	
	E	100	99.69	93.75	96.77	99.71	
RF	Z	93.29	94.35	92.40	92.84	93.90	93.90
	D	100	99.92	97.22	98.59	99.92	
	X	93.61	94.33	94.49	94.05	93.97	
	E	100	100	100	100	100	

analysis of fuel types based on machine learning methods. The general accuracy success of other machine learning methods is as follows: 94.38% success was achieved with gradient boost, 93.63% success was achieved with a decision tree, 93.90% success was achieved with RF. Accuracy achievements obtained by the XG Boost method based on fuel types are as follows: accuracy success achieved in Z fuel type was 94.71%, accuracy success achieved in D fuel type was 99.78%, accuracy success achieved in X fuel type was 94.77% and accuracy success achieved in E fuel type was 100%. The confusion matrices obtained in the process of classifying the fuel types of dataset #2 with machine learning methods are shown in Figure 7.13, and the detailed analysis results are given in Table 7.13. In the second step of the second experiment, the analyzes performed with

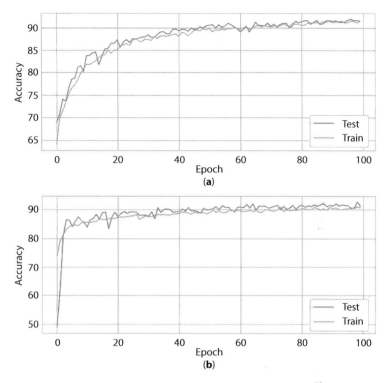

Figure 7.14 Training-test success graphs obtained for dataset #2 of deep learning models; (a) LSTM, (b) LSTM & CNN.

Table 7.14 Analysis results of dataset #2 with deep learning models (%).

Deep learning	Fuel type	Se	Sp	Pre	F-scr	Acc	Overall acc
LSTM	Z	88.58	93.61	91.19	89.87	91.46	91.46
	D	100	100	100	100	100	
	X	92.45	90.53	90.19	91.31	91.46	
	E	100	100	100	100	100	
LSTM & CNN	Z	93.97	89.36	86.82	90.25	91.33	91.33
	D	100	100	100	100	100	
	X	87.43	95.01	94.27	90.72	91.33	
	E	100	100	100	100	100	

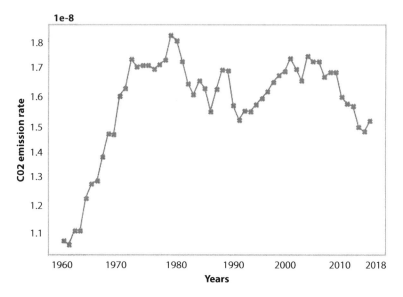

Figure 7.15 Canada's CO_2 emissions rates by years.

machine learning methods were also performed using deep learning models designed in the python language. Analyzes were performed using LSTM and LSTM & CNN models. In these two models, the number of epochs 100 were selected and the resulting training graphics are shown in Figure 7.14. Overall accuracy achievements from the two-deep learning models were over 90%. The overall accuracy success achieved with the LSTM method was 91.46%, and the overall accuracy success achieved with the LSTM & CNN hybrid model was 91.33%. Detailed analysis results obtained with dataset #2 of the two-deep learning models are given in Table 7.14. As a result, in the analyzes performed in dataset #2, successes achieved with machine learning methods were better than those achieved with deep learning models.

In the third experiment, analyzes were carried out by comparing the rates of CO_2 emission amounts of the countries based on statistics. Artificial intelligence-based techniques were used for this. Dataset #3 was used for this experiment. Dataset #3 contains CO_2 data for countries between 1960 and 2018. However, since there was not much information in dataset #3 between 2015 and 2018, the data between 1960 and 2014 were analyzed. In the first analysis, the statistical analysis of the CO_2 emission amount of the Canadian country was carried out over years. The statistical information of Canada's CO_2 emission gas amount by year is shown graphically in Figure 7.15. In the period from 1960 to 1980 in Canada, a remarkable increase

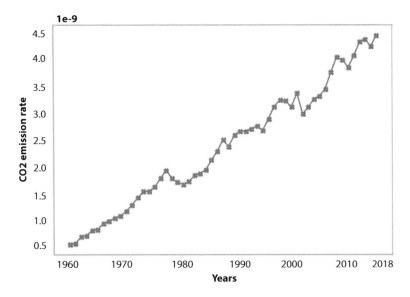

Figure 7.16 Turkey's CO$_2$ emissions rates by years.

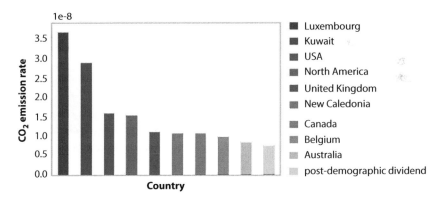

Figure 7.17 The top 10 countries according to the amount of CO$_2$ emission based on 1960.

in the amount of CO$_2$ emission gas was observed. It has been observed that CO$_2$ gas was kept under control between 1980-2018 and the increase observed every year did not increase between these years. This case has been increasing every year since 1960 in Turkey. Turkey's CO$_2$ emissions between the years 1960-2018 are shown in Figure 7.16.

In the analysis of the third experiment, the analyzes were carried out using the CO$_2$ emission amounts of 254 countries in total. Luxembourg was the country with the highest amount of CO$_2$ emissions in 1960. The

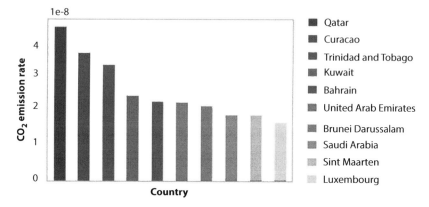

Figure 7.18 The top 10 countries according to the amount of CO_2 emission based on 2014.

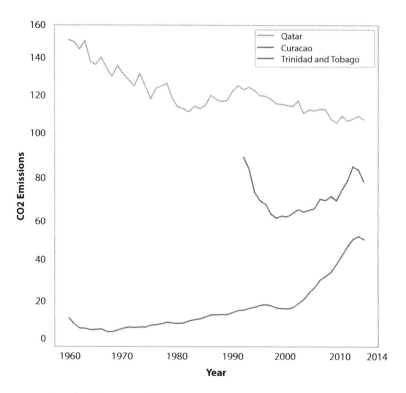

Figure 7.19 Graphical statistics of the three countries with the highest CO_2 emissions between 1960-2014.

top 10 countries with the highest CO_2 emission gas in 1960 are shown in Figure 7.17.

When the 2014 data is analyzed, the top 10 countries with the highest CO_2 emission gas are shown in Figure 7.18. According to the data of 2014, Kuwait was the country with the highest amount of CO_2 emission gas. When Figure 7.18 is examined, it seems that the rate of emission gas is quite high in countries that are generally oil countries. According to the data analysis of 2014, the emission change graph of the top 3 countries with the highest CO_2 emission over years is shown in Figure 7.19.

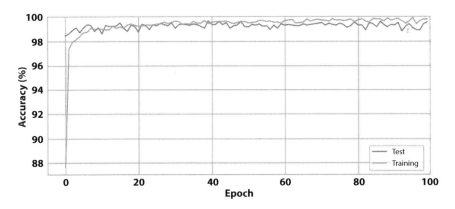

Figure 7.20 Training-test graphics of the RNN model in measuring the stability of electricity grids.

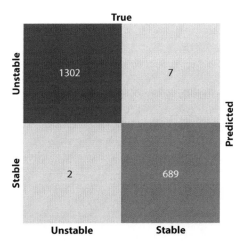

Figure 7.21 Confusion matrix graphic of the RNN model in measuring the stability of electricity grids.

In the last experiment, an artificial intelligence-based approach to measuring energy stability in smart grids was proposed. Dataset #4 is used for the local stability cases of the four-node star system implementing the decentralized intelligent grid control concept. Dataset #4 consists of data consisting of 14 features in total. The last feature contains data that concludes whether the electricity is stable or not. To perform the analysis of the experiment, the stable structure of electrical networks was measured using the RNN model designed in Python language. In total, the RNN model was trained with 13 features and the number of epochs of the RNN model in training was 100 preferred as in other experiments. An overall accuracy success of 99.55% was achieved in the stability measurement criteria obtained with the RNN model. The training-test accuracy graphs of the RNN model are shown in Figure 7.20. The confusion matrix of this success is shown in Figure 7.21. The successes obtained from other confusion matrix parameters were as follows: Sensitivity success was 99.85%, specificity success was 98.99%, precision success was 99.47%, and f-score success was 99.66%.

7.5   Discussion

The study aimed to contribute to sustainable energy, development, and living standards with innovative approaches. Our study consisted of four categories and analyzes were carried out using different artificial intelligence approaches for each category. The results obtained in this study show us that it has been successful in measuring the factors that cause renewable energy and climate change. The first three experiments consisted of studies directly related to climate change. For this, artificial intelligence-based

Table 7.15 Literature studies and analysis results performed using dataset #4.

Study	Year	Models/methods	Acc (%)
Marian Gorzałczany *et al.* [58]	2020	Strength pareto evolutionary algorithm	85.50
Farhad Balali *et al.* [59]	2020	kNN, linear regression, SVM	96.90
Dorin Moldovan *et al.* [60]	2019	Optimization & feature selection methods	93.80
This study	2021	RNN	99.55

analyzes were carried out regarding the measurement of air efficiency and the amount of CO_2 emission gas used. The last experiment consisted of a study directly related to energy efficiency. Also, some studies have been carried out in the literature on the stability of smart energy grids and some studies using dataset #4 have been found. Analyzes of other studies using the same dataset with the RNN model we suggested for dataset #4 are given in Table 7.15. The success we performed in the fourth experiment gave more successful results than other researchers' studies.

Marian Gorzałczany et al. [58] used the strength Pareto evolutionary algorithm (SPEA) for stability measurement in smart grids. The best test accuracy success achieved by their analysis without using artificial intelligence-based approaches was 85.5%. Farhad Balali et al. [59] used machine learning methods (SVM, linear regression, kNN) to measure the stability structures of smart grids. In their study, they carried out their analysis using artificial intelligence-based machine learning methods. However, the fact that they were limited to machine learning methods in their studies limited their success. Perhaps they could have achieved a better result using deep learning approaches. The best success they achieved in their study was with the SVM method; an accuracy success rate of 96.9% was achieved. Dorin Moldovan et al. [60] performed analyzes for stability in electrical grids by using the binary particle swarm optimization method and feature selection algorithm together. Their approach was interesting, but their use of optimization without using deep learning approaches has limited their success. In addition, the number of features of dataset #4 used for power grids is limited, although their use of feature selection algorithms did not increase the success they would achieve. Their overall accuracy success as a result was 93.8%.

7.6   Conclusion

Sustainable development has been included in the plans and program processes of most countries. In a globalized world, the energy requirement increases in direct proportion to the population. In such a case, ways of saving are sought and it is aimed to realize more environmentally friendly energy consumption. Recently, many artificial intelligence-based approaches have attracted attention for sustainable energy and factors affecting climate change. In this study, experimental analyzes that address both issues were carried out. Experimental analyzes have shown that artificial intelligence approaches give promising results in measuring air efficiency, CO_2 emissions, and smart electricity grids. The computer hardware used during the experimental analyzes were not sufficient. However, successful results have been obtained by using the existing hardware facilities. If the approaches used in experimental analyzes are used fully, it is predicted that they will contribute to the country's economy and that individuals can transition to a cleaner and more economical living standard.

In future studies, artificial intelligence-based analyzes will be planned by examining different data sets, including renewable energy and climate change issues. Efficiency in transaction analysis will be achieved by using metaheuristic optimization methods in the approaches to be proposed in the future, and the time of transaction analysis will be saved [61–63].

Funding

There is no funding source for this book section.

Ethical Approval

This book section does not contain any data, or other information from studies or experimentation, with the involvement of human or animal subjects.

Conflicts of Interest

The author declares that there is no conflict of interest related to this paper.

References

1. Fróna D, Szenderák J, Harangi-Rákos M. The Challenge of Feeding the World. *Sustain.* 2019; 11. doi:10.3390/su11205816.
2. Klasen S, Lawson D. *The impact of population growth on economic growth and poverty reduction in Uganda.* Göttingen: Georg-August-Universität Göttingen, Volkswirtschaftliches Seminar, 2007.
3. Omer AM. Energy use and environmental impacts: A general review. *J Renew Sustain Energy.* 2009; 1:53101. doi:10.1063/1.3220701.
4. Manta AG, Florea NM, Bădîrcea RM, Popescu J, Cîrciumaru D, Doran MD. The Nexus between Carbon Emissions, Energy Use, Economic Growth, and Financial Development: Evidence from Central and Eastern European Countries. *Sustain.* 2020;12. doi:10.3390/su12187747.
5. Panwar NL, Kaushik SC, Kothari S. Role of renewable energy sources in environmental protection: A review. *Renew Sustain Energy Rev.* 2011;15:1513–24. doi:10.1016/j.rser.2010.11.037.

6. Krepl V, Shaheen HI, Fandi G, Smutka L, Muller Z, Tlustý J, vd. The Role of Renewable Energies in the Sustainable Development of Post-Crisis Electrical Power Sectors Reconstruction. *Energies*. 2020;13. doi:10.3390/en13236326.

7. Spencer J. The Sustainable Development Goals. Des. Glob. Challenges Goals, Abingdon, Oxon; New York, NY: Routledge, 2021. | *Series: Design for social responsibility: Routledge*; 2021, s. 12–25. doi:10.4324/9781003099680-3.

8. Zhan JX, Santos-Paulino AU. Investing in the Sustainable Development Goals: Mobilization, channeling, and impact. *J Int Bus Policy*. 2021;4:166–83. doi:10.1057/s42214-020-00093-3.

9. Littig B. Good work? Sustainable work and sustainable development: a critical gender perspective from the Global North. *Globalizations*. 2018;15:565–79. doi:10.1080/14747731.2018.1454676.

10. Guo M, Nowakowska-Grunt J, Gorbanyov V, Egorova M. Green Technology and Sustainable Development: Assessment and Green Growth Frameworks. *Sustain*. 2020;12. doi:10.3390/su12166571.

11. Chen S-Y. True sustainable development of green technology: The influencers and risked moderation of sustainable motivational behavior. *Sustain Dev*. 2019;27:69–83. doi:10.1002/sd.1863.

12. Fortuński B. Sustainable Development and Energy Policy: Actual CO2 Emissions in the European Union in the Years 1997–2017, Considering Trade with China and the USA. *Sustain*. 2020;12. doi:10.3390/su12083363.

13. Gielen D, Boshell F, Saygin D, Bazilian MD, Wagner N, Gorini R. The role of renewable energy in the global energy transformation. *Energy Strategy Rev*. 2019;24:38–50. doi:10.1016/j.esr.2019.01.006.

14. Al-Janabi S, Alkaim AF, Adel Z. An Innovative synthesis of deep learning techniques (DCapsNet & DCOM) for generation electrical renewable energy from wind energy. *Soft Comput*. 2020;24:10943–62. doi:10.1007/s00500-020-04905-9.

15. Xayasouk T, Lee H, Lee G. Air Pollution Prediction Using Long Short-Term Memory (LSTM) and Deep Autoencoder (DAE) Models. *Sustain*. 2020;12. doi:10.3390/su12062570.

16. Janarthanan R, Partheeban P, Somasundaram K, Navin Elamparithi P. A deep learning approach for prediction of air quality index in a metropolitan city. *Sustain Cities Soc*. 2021;67:102720. doi:10.1016/j.scs.2021.102720.

17. Guo Q, He Z, Li S, Li X, Meng J, Hou Z, *et al*. Air Pollution Forecasting Using Artificial and Wavelet Neural Networks with Meteorological Conditions. *Aerosol Air Qual Res*. 2020;20:1429–39. doi:10.4209/aaqr.2020.03.0097.

18. Bhat A, Manek AS, Mishra P. Machine Learning based Prediction System for Detecting Air Pollution. *Int J Eng Res Technol*. 2019;8:155–9.

19. Ozcanli AK, Yaprakdal F, Baysal M. Deep learning methods and applications for electrical power systems: A comprehensive review. *Int J Energy Res*. 2020;44:7136–57. doi:10.1002/er.5331.

20. Bashir AK, Khan S, Prabadevi B, Deepa N, Alnumay WS, Gadekallu TR, *et al*. Comparative analysis of machine learning algorithms for

prediction of smart grid stability†. *Int Trans Electr Energy Syst.* 2021;n/a:e12706. doi:10.1002/2050-7038.12706.

21. Gambi E. Air Quality dataset for ADL classification. Mendeley Data 2020. doi:10.17632/kn3x9rz3kd.1.

22. Podder D. CO2 Emission by Vehicles. Kaggle 2020. https://www.kaggle.com/debajyotipodder/co2-emission-by-vehicles?select=CO2+Emissions_Canada.csv (access: 15 April 2021).

23. Murray E. CO2 Emissions per capita dataset. data.world 2019. https://data.world/makeovermonday/2019w22 (access: 15 April 2021).

24. Schäfer B, Grabow C, Auer S, Kurths J, Witthaut D, Timme M. Taming instabilities in power grid networks by decentralized control. *Eur Phys J Spec Top.* 2016;225:569–82. doi:10.1140/epjst/e2015-50136-y.

25. Arzamasov V. Electrical Grid Stability Simulated DataSet. UCI Mach Learn Repos 2018. https://archive.ics.uci.edu/ml/datasets/Electrical+Grid+Stability+Simulated+Data+# (access: 15 April 2021).

26. Webb ME, Fluck A, Magenheim J, Malyn-Smith J, Waters J, Deschênes M, vd. Machine learning for human learners: opportunities, issues, tensions, and threats. *Educ Technol Res Dev.* 2020. doi:10.1007/s11423-020-09858-2.

27. Huang S, Cai N, Pacheco PP, Narrandes S, Wang Y, Xu W. Applications of Support Vector Machine (SVM) Learning in Cancer Genomics. *Cancer Genomics Proteomics.* 2017;15:41–51. doi:10.21873/cgp.20063.

28. Toğaçar M, Ergen B, Sertkaya M. Zatürre Hastalığının Derin Öğrenme Modeli ile Tespiti. *Fırat Üniversitesi Mühendislik Bilimleri Dergisi.* 2019; 31(1): 223-230.

29. Wu H, Wang L, Zhao Z, Shu C, Lu C. Support Vector Machine based Differential Pulse-width Pair Brillouin Optical Time Domain Analyzer. *IEEE Photonics J.* 2018;10:1–11. doi:10.1109/jphot.2018.2858235.

30. Ibrahem Ahmed Osman A, Najah Ahmed A, Chow MF, Feng Huang Y, El-Shafie A. Extreme gradient boosting (Xgboost) model to predict the groundwater levels in Selangor Malaysia. *Ain Shams Eng J.* 2021. doi:10.1016/j.asej.2020.11.011.

31. Natekin A, Knoll A. Gradient boosting machines, a tutorial. *Front Neurorobot.* 2013;7:21. doi:10.3389/fnbot.2013.00021.

32. Ahmed AM, Rizaner A, Ulusoy AH. A novel decision tree classification based on post-pruning with Bayes minimum risk. *PLoS One.* 2018;13:e0194168.

33. Mienye ID, Sun Y, Wang Z. Prediction performance of improved decision tree-based algorithms: a review. *Procedia Manuf.* 2019;35:698–703. doi:10.1016/j.promfg.2019.06.011.

34. Prihandoko P, Bertalya B, Setyowati L. City Health Prediction Model Using Random Forest Classification Method. *2020 Fifth Int. Conf. Informatics Comput.* 2020, s. 1–5. doi:10.1109/icic50835.2020.9288542.

35. Bakshi C. Random Forest Regression. Gitconnected 2021. https://levelup.gitconnected.com/random-forest-regression-209c0f354c84 (access: 16 April 2021).

36. Aldrich C. Process Variable Importance Analysis by Use of Random Forests in a Shapley Regression Framework. *Miner.* 2020;10. doi:10.3390/min10050420.

37. Cioffi R, Travaglioni M, Piscitelli G, Petrillo A, De Felice F. Artificial Intelligence and Machine Learning Applications in Smart Production: Progress, Trends, and Directions. *Sustain.* 2020;12. doi:10.3390/su12020492.

38. Koutsoukas A, Monaghan KJ, Li X, Huan J. Deep-learning: investigating deep neural networks hyper-parameters and comparison of performance to shallow methods for modeling bioactivity data. *J Cheminform.* 2017;9:42. doi:10.1186/s13321-017-0226-y.

39. Van Houdt G, Mosquera C, Nápoles G. A review on the long short-term memory model. *Artif Intell Rev.* 2020;53:5929–55. doi:10.1007/s10462-020-09838-1.

40. Cai L, Gao J, Zhao D. A review of the application of deep learning in medical image classification and segmentation. *Ann Transl Med.* 2020;8:713. doi:10.21037/atm.2020.02.44.

41. Liu YH. Feature Extraction and Image Recognition with Convolutional Neural Networks. *J Phys Conf Ser.* 2018;1087:062032. doi:10.1088/1742-6596/1087/6/062032.

42. Salah Alaloul W, Hannan Qureshi A. Data Processing Using Artificial Neural Networks. Dyn. Data Assim. - Beating Uncertainties, IntechOpen; 2020. doi:10.5772/intechopen.91935.

43. Kim K, Jeong J. Real-Time Monitoring for Hydraulic States Based on Convolutional Bidirectional LSTM with Attention Mechanism. *Sensors (Basel).* 2020;20:7099. doi:10.3390/s20247099.

44. Gong W, Chen H, Zhang Z, Zhang M, Wang R, Guan C, vd. A Novel Deep Learning Method for Intelligent Fault Diagnosis of Rotating Machinery Based on Improved CNN-SVM and Multichannel Data Fusion. *Sensors (Basel).* 2019;19. doi:10.3390/s19071693.

45. Diamant A, Chatterjee A, Vallières M, Shenouda G, Seuntjens J. Deep learning in head & neck cancer outcome prediction. *Sci Rep.* 2019;9:2764. doi:10.1038/s41598-019-39206-1.

46. Arı A, Hanbay D. Deep learning-based brain tumor classification and detection system. *Turk J Elec Eng Comp Sci.* 2018;26:2275–86. doi:10.3906/elk-1801-8.

47. Garbin C, Zhu X, Marques O. Dropout vs. batch normalization: an empirical study of their impact to deep learning. *Multimed Tools Appl.* 2020;79:12777–815. doi:10.1007/s11042-019-08453-9.

48. Yamashita R, Nishio M, Do RKG, Togashi K. Convolutional neural networks: an overview and application in radiology. *Insights Imaging.* 2018;9:611–29. doi:10.1007/s13244-018-0639-9.

49. Elfaik H, Nfaoui EH. Deep Bidirectional LSTM Network Learning-Based Sentiment Analysis for Arabic Text. *J Intell Syst.* 2021;30:395–412. doi:10.1515/jisys-2020-0021.

50. Zhang C, Biś D, Liu X, He Z. Biomedical word sense disambiguation with bidirectional long short-term memory and attention-based neural networks. *BMC Bioinformatics*. 2019;20:502. doi:10.1186/s12859-019-3079-8.

51. Yulita IN, Fanany MI, Arymuthy AM. Bi-directional Long Short-Term Memory using Quantized data of Deep Belief Networks for Sleep Stage Classification. *Procedia Comput. Sci.* 2017;116:530–8. doi:10.1016/j.procs.2017.10.042.

52. Singh U, Kedas S, Prasanth S, Kumar A, Semwal VB, Tikkiwal VA. Design of A Recurrent Neural Network Model for Machine Reading Comprehension. *Procedia Comput Sci*. 2020;167:1791–800. doi:10.1016/j.procs.2020.03.388.

53. Kunc V, Kléma J. On transformative adaptive activation functions in neural networks for gene expression inference. *PLoS One*. 2021;16:e0243915.

54. Banerjee C, Mukherjee T, Pasiliao E. *The Multi-Phase ReLU Activation Function*. Proc. 2020 ACM Southeast Conf., New York, NY, USA: Association for Computing Machinery; 2020, s. 239–242. doi:10.1145/3374135.3385313.

55. Vijayaprabakaran K, Sathiyamurthy K. Towards activation function search for long short-term model network: A differential evolution based approach. *J King Saud Univ - Comput Inf Sci*. 2020. doi:10.1016/j.jksuci.2020.04.015.

56. Hashemi M, Hall M. Criminal tendency detection from facial images and the gender bias effect. *J Big Data*. 2020;7:2. doi:10.1186/s40537-019-0282-4.

57. Demir F. DeepCoroNet: A deep LSTM approach for automated detection of COVID-19 cases from chest X-ray images. *Appl Soft Comput*. 2021;103:107160. doi:10.1016/j.asoc.2021.107160.

58. Gorzałczany MB, Piekoszewski J, Rudziński F. A modern data-mining approach based on genetically optimized fuzzy systems for interpretable and accurate smart-grid stability prediction. *Energies*. 2020;13. doi:10.3390/en13102559.

59. Balali F, Nouri J, Nasiri A, Zhao T. *Data-Intensive Industrial Asset Management*. Cham: Springer International Publishing; 2020. doi:10.1007/978-3-030-35930-0.

60. Moldovan D, Salomie I. Detection of Sources of Instability in Smart Grids Using Machine Learning Techniques. 2019 IEEE 15th Int. Conf. Intell. Comput. Commun. Process., *IEEE*. 2019, s. 175–82. doi:10.1109/iccp48234.2019.8959649.

61. Vasant P, Zelinka I, Weber G.-W. (Eds.). *Intelligent Computing and Optimization, Advances in Intelligent Systems and Computing*. Springer International Publishing, Cham. 2021. https://doi.org/10.1007/978-3-030-68154-8

62. Vasant P, Zelinka I, Weber G.-W. (Eds.). *Intelligent Computing and Optimization, Advances in Intelligent Systems and Computing*. Springer International Publishing, Cham. 2020. https://doi.org/10.1007/978-3-030-33585-4

63. Vasant P, Zelinka I, Weber G.-W. (Eds.). *Intelligent Computing & Optimization, Advances in Intelligent Systems and Computing*. Springer International Publishing, Cham. 2019. https://doi.org/10.1007/978-3-030-00979-3

8

Performance Analysis and Effects of Dust & Temperature on Solar PV Module System by Using Multivariate Linear Regression Model

Sumit Sharma[1]*, J. Joshua Thomas[2] and Pandian Vasant[3]

[1]Arya College of Engineering & IT, Jaipur, India
[2]KDU Penang University College, George Town, Pulau Pinang, Malaysia
[3]University Technology Petronas, Seri Iskandar, Perak, Malaysia

Abstract

Solar energy has enormous potential to serve the present energy demand of the world. Photovoltaic is an elegant process of converting the sun's energy into electricity, and photovoltaic cells become matchless in transforming the sunshine into electrical energy. In this work, an effort had been made to estimate the effects of dust addition and ambient temperature on conversion efficiency of 62 KWp Rooftop SPV module by the use of Capacity Utilization Factor and Performance Ratio parameters.

The operating and electrical performance parameters of SPV array were experimentally collected over an approximately six-month period permitting for usual dust addition. The data were used for the calculation of the CUF, PR, and power conversion efficiency of the SPV systems. A multivariate linear regressions (MLR) model is established to estimate the system's output performance with the consideration of conversion efficiency as the dependent variable and ambient temperature and dust exposure day as the independent variables. Also, the losses due to dust accumulation are estimated. The model can predict conversion efficiency closely, with R^2 values close to 91%. During the days of study, the average efficiency reductions due to dust are 0.872%/day, energy losses are 9.935 kWh/m^2 with an average loss due to dust accumulation of Rs.192.72/day using the MLR model.

Corresponding author: sumitait1111@gmail.com

Pandian Vasant, Gerhard-Wilhelm Weber, Joshua Thomas, José Antonio Marmolejo-Saucedo and Roman Rodriguez-Aguilar (eds.) Artificial Intelligence for Renewable Energy and Climate Change, (217–276) © 2022 Scrivener Publishing LLC

Keywords: SPV, CUF, PR, conversion efficiency

8.1   Introduction

Energy is the leading agent of economic evolution and is vital to the sustenance of the current economy. Solar energy, in spite of having massive potential and growing use, is associated with worry about expenses and questions over acceptability. The research and innovative work have additionally contributed towards better proficiency, moderateness and affordable quality of the products. With the progression of time, a sustainable power source area in India has shown up as a vital player in the photovoltaic power generation capacity. Considering the global challenges of climate change, energy security and sustainable development, a persistent need is felt to accelerate the improvement of superior clean power generation technologies [1]. India is endowed with an immense solar energy potential as it is located in the subtropical region of the globe, thereby receiving ample energy from the sun [2]. Solar energy cannot be availed for a long duration given its intermittent nature. It can be utilized via solar photovoltaic technology which allows direct conversion of sunlight into electricity. Owing to the rising concern and consciousness of natural issues among the scientific group, power generation from solar energy has become significant over the last few years. It can also lead to a decrease in the greenhouse gases (GHGs) that threaten irreversible climate change of the Earth. Nowadays the photovoltaic units are used on a large scale as solar power plants and small units on residential rooftops for purely practical and financial benefits. The environmental influence of electricity generation, considering the greenhouse effect, becomes a key reason to explore functioning of photovoltaic units.

8.1.1   Indian Scenario of Renewable Energy

Globally, India has the fourth-largest electricity generation capacity after the US, China, and Russia. Its Renewable Energy (RE) share improved to 13.15% in 2015 with solar power contribution of 11.62% [3]. The Ministry of Indian Govt. (MNRE) has reported an aspiring solar target of one lac megawatts (MW) installed capacity by 2022, of which 40,000 MW of SPV panel systems are to be installed on rooftops [4]. The India Meteorological Department (IMD) has countrywide stations to measure sunlight-based radiation and the length of daylight every day. In the Indian atmosphere, clear bright sunshine is available from 260 to 300 days in a year. The annual worldwide radiation varies from 1600 to 2200 kWh/sq.m., which is nearly equal to radiation in the subtropical and tropical zones on the globe [5].

The government-upgraded capacity mark of 100 GW set under the National Solar Mission (JNNSM) will primarily include 40 GW through rooftop and 60 GW from large- and medium-scale grid-linked solar power projects.

By 2022 a target of 20,000 MW distribution has been set, to be attained in three phases (I phase up to 2012-13, II phase starts from 2013-17 and the III phase from 2017-22) (Figure 8.1).

Sunlight-based vitality reaching the Earth's surface can be applied specifically by two methods, viz., transforming the sun-powered radiation into the power for valuable purposes by using SPV modules or by warming the medium hotspot for low-temperature heating applications. Solar photovoltaic, which converts the sun radiation directly into electrical energy, is the quickest developing field in the sustainable power source industry. Some of the factors driving the growth of this segment are concerns of the country regarding carbon outflows, energy sustainability and the rising costs of imported fossil fuels.

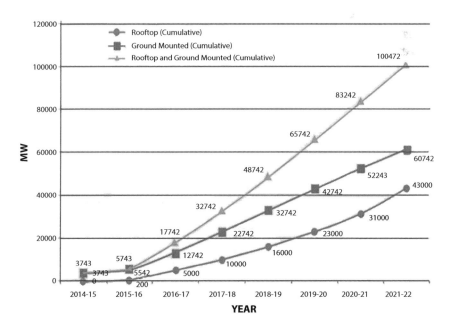

Figure 8.1 Tentative year-wise cumulative targets to be attained by 2022 [6].

8.1.2 Solar Radiation at Earth

The solar constant is an amount of energy that the sun imparts per unit region of Earth that is directly exposed to daylight and perpendicular to it. Its best acceptable value is 1367 W/m². When the sun is close to the zenith, less power reaches the Earth's surface (about 1000 W/m²) even in clear weather, as some amount is reduced by Earth's atmosphere [6].

The sun-powered radiation arriving on the Earth's surface has two constituents: direct or beam radiation, which comes directly from the sun's circle; and diffuse radiation, which comes indirectly (after reflection and refraction). The most shared estimation of sunlight-based radiation is full radiation on a horizontal surface often stated as GHI (global horizontal irradiance) which is the count of the direct and diffuse components. It is measured by pyranometer. Direct solar radiation is generally termed as "sunshine," an amalgamation of bright light and radiant heat.

8.1.3 Solar Photovoltaic Technologies

The Photovoltaic effect is visible when two differently doped or dissimilar semiconducting materials (e.g., germanium, silicon) are in nearby contact with each other, produce an electrical current when visible to daylight. Photovoltaic (PV) cells are semiconductor devices with an internal electric field that separates positive and negative charges generated by absorbed (solar) radiation. As a result of selective transmittance of solar radiation absorbed by the panel absorbers will be emission of the long-wave radiation. And due to the ability of glass to hold long-wave radiation, there is a significant increase in temperature inside the space confined by glass [7]. Semiconductors can exist as doped as well as intrinsic. Doped semiconductors can be P-type (with holes that perform like positively charged particles) or N-type (with electrons as key charge carriers). The quasiparticle is frequently called a "hole" [8, 9]. As a result of the interaction of photons of solar radiation with a semiconductor, electron-hole pairs are formed.

Electric power can be withdrawn by connecting the opposite sides of the PV cell via an external load. PV cells are interrelated to shape PV modules having a power limit of up to several hundred watts. A typical silicon cell produces around 3–4 A current at 0.5 V when fully illuminated, and for commercially accessible silicon PV cells, the conversion efficiencies range from 10 to 18%. The PV voltage output drops with increasing temperature, resulting in a 0.4–0.6%/K decrease in efficiency for silicon PV cells and modules [10].

The planar photovoltaic solar modules with an extended electrical efficiency up to 28% are made with the aid of encapsulation technology with a polysiloxane compound, which increases their service life and advances the performance of the modules [11].

The PV modules generate direct current DC electricity when exposed to sunlight. Then an inverter converts the DC output into AC electricity and feeds into one of the building's AC distribution boards ("ACDB") without influencing the quality of energy supply. Grid-tied frameworks require one or a few inverters to infuse their electrical yield into the mains. The constituents related to this delivery process, such as electrical protection devices, inverters, transformers, monitoring equipment, and wiring are all considered components of the "balance of system" (BOS).

8.1.3.1 Types of SPV Systems

SPV power systems are defined on the basis of their working and purposeful requirements, their possible conformations, and the nature of equipment connection to other power sources and electrical loads. The two primary options are grid-connected and off-grid PV systems.

(a) Grid-connected photovoltaic systems
Grid-connected PV systems are intended to work in parallel with the electric utility grid. In the daytime, the electricity generated by the PV system can either be utilized promptly or be sold to the power supplier. Figure 8.2 shows the configuration of grid-connected SPV system.

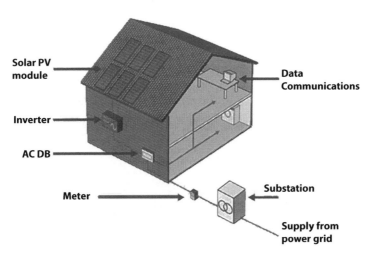

Figure 8.2 Configuration of grid-connected SPV system [10].

When the solar resource is not sufficient or absent, the grid plays the role of the storage system and provides power to meet the energy requirements. Therefore, it is not required to install batteries. For example, a building has two similar (parallel) power supplies, one via the main power grid and the other linked with the solar PV system. The collective power supply feeds all the loads associated to the main AC distribution box. The power grid will provide supply according to the building's claim in the absence of sunlight for generating PV electricity. This system allows more effective consumption of generated energy or power because of the absence of storage losses.

(b) Off-grid photovoltaic systems
For isolated areas or sites which are without power grid station like rural regions or offshore islands, the off-grid SPV systems are used. It requires deep cycle rechargeable batteries such as nickel-cadmium or lithium-ion batteries, lead-acid batteries to store energy for use under situations where there is less or no output from the solar PV system, such as during the night, when it is cloudy, or in the rainy season.

8.1.3.2 *Types of Solar Photovoltaic Cells*

A Photovoltaic system is powered by many crystalline or thin film PV modules. PV cells are prepared by semiconductor materials (light sensitive) that utilize photons to dislocate electrons to flow an electric current and are interconnected to form a PV panel for smooth installation. Figure 8.3 shows different PV module technologies. According to design, cell material and techniques of manufacturing, these are divided into two main groups:

  i)   Single or Mono-crystalline (sc-Si) and
  ii) Multi- or Poly-crystalline (mc-Si).

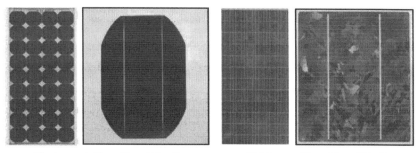

Single-crystalline silicon PV cell   **Multi-crystalline silicon PV cell**

Figure 8.3 Different PV module technologies [10].

The ultra-pure silicon in the form of wafers that are normally 160-200 microns (one fifth of mm) thick, is used as a raw material to prepare the crystalline cells. Thin films are prepared by placing layers of just 0.25 to 2 micrometers thick semiconductor material.

8.1.3.3   Effects of Temperature

The performance of the module is usually evaluated under Standard Test Conditions (STC). All electrical parameters of the solar module depend on temperature. In hot climates, PV cell performance decreases as cell temperature rises. The loss of power is distinct by temperature coefficients. The temperature coefficient signifies the change of power output with changed temperatures. Table 8.1 shows the temperature coefficient and Table 8.2 shows conversion efficiencies of various numerous PV module technologies.

8.1.3.4   Conversion Efficiency

Efficiency of the module shows the ability to obtain electrical energy from solar radiation energy whereas power conversion efficiency indicates maximum accessible electrical power for resistance terms, and it is the ratio of the net AC output energy to the input solar energy. It takes into consideration the energy lost in the cables, inverters, positioning of systems, array mismatch, operating ambient temperature and dust deposition. Standard Test Conditions refer to the following testing conditions: $1000W/m^2$ of sunlight, 25°C cell temperature, spectrum at air mass of 1.5.

Table 8.1 Temperature coefficient of various PV cell technologies [10].

Technology	Temperature coefficient [%/°C]
Crystalline silicon	-0.4 to -0.5
a-Si	-0.21

Table 8.2 Conversion efficiencies of various numerous PV module technologies [10].

Technology	Module efficiency
Mono-crystalline PV module	12.5-15%
Poly-crystalline PV module	11-14%

Figure 8.4 Soiling on top surface of array resulting in mismatch losses [12].

8.1.4   Losses in PV Systems

The difference between the power produced by the modules and power actually received at the grid is sometimes called projected system losses. These losses occurred due to varying insolation levels and ambient temperature, losses in cables, dirt, dust and bird droppings on the modules, losses due to functioning of PV module outside the STC conditions, module degradation, DC losses, mismatch effects, maximum power point tracking losses (MPPT), and inverter losses from conversion of DC to AC, etc. Dust and dirt accumulation are the primary causes of soiling of PV panels. Generally, the dust accumulated on the surface of the panel is washed away with rainfall, still dirt like bird droppings may remain even after rain. Figure 8.4 shows soiling on top surface of array resulting in mismatch losses. The lower edge is the most critical portion of a module. By often repeated water impings in the shallow puddle between glass and frame consecutive evaporation dirt accumulates. Once it causes shielding of the cells, this dirt decreases the generated DC from a particular module. The losses are normally 1%; however, the power is restored by the periodic cleaning of modules [12].

8.1.5   Performance of Solar Power Plants

The Capacity Utilization Factor (CUF) and Performance Ratio (PR) is the most significant factors for assessing the efficiency of a PV plant [13]. The CUF is the ratio of the actual electricity output from the plant, to the highest possible output per year and PR is the ratio of actual energy yield to nominal energy yield or theoretically possible energy outputs [14]. The PR 100% cannot be attained in ideal case as inevitable losses always arise with the operation of PV system. However, the proper functioning of a power plant depends on various constraints including the solar insolation levels, site location, dust accumulation, soiling losses, and technical losses in cabling, environmental factors such as temperature, module mismatch, the inverter losses, MPPT losses and due to module degradation, etc. The projected yield from the solar power plant depends on the design parameters and can be calculated, using standard softwares.

8.2   Literature Review

In the available literature, several studies reported the performance parameters, output of solar PV systems of different capacity installations functions under numerous meteorological conditions. These studies discussed the market potential, technology, overall performance and effective life under the various tropical weather conditions of SPV plants. These terms are helpful in accelerating the diffusion of solar energy, reduced carbon emission, improved energy safety and achieving energy independence.

H. Wang *et al.* [15] shows experimentally that due to the dust deposition on PV modules, the highest power generation efficiency decrease is 5.5% and highest power generation decrease is 35.2% also depending on the local climate condition. N. Manoj *et al.* [16] analyzed the energy loss, and deprivation forecast of roof integrated crystalline solar PV system and estimated to operate with a yearly CF, PR, and energy losses as 16.72%, 77.27%, and −26.5%, respectively. Mouatasim & Darmane [17] proposed different types of regression technique to estimate the power of different types of PV module. The result shows that the association between temperature, solar irradiance and output power is linear and the value of R2 & coefficient of linear correlation are higher in simple and Multiple Linear Regression model. Y. Guan [18] investigated the impact of dust deposition on transmittance of the PV panel and thus disturbing the output power of the PV module. Results shows that with growing dust density, relative power output decreased linearly and relative transmittance reduced logarithmically by 20% within 8 days due to usual dust deposition. A. Allouhi *et al.* [19] investigated the performance and environmental/economical assessment of the two installed technologies (Mono-Si and Poly-Si). The yearly overall efficiency and capacity factor of the system were 12.3% and 20.52%, respectively, for Poly-Si installation and 12.1% and 20.20% for Mono-Si installation, respectively. F. Mejia *et al.* [20] examined the effect of soiling on solar PV panels in USA and observed that the soiling losses are found to be cumulative linearly with time and a reduction in efficiency varies from 7.19% to 5.5% for a period of 108 dry summer days. D. S. Rajput *et al.* [21] determined the influence of accumulated dust particles on the electrical parameters performances of PV panels. It was found that without dust, the maximum and minimum efficiency were 6.38% and 2.29%, respectively, and with dust deposition, the maximum and minimum efficiency were 0.64% and 0.33%, respectively; also, the reduction in power production and efficiency were 92.11% and 89%, respectively, as of dust accumulation. J. Tanesab *et al.* [22] analyzed the influence of dust deposition on the degradation of PV modules positioned in Western Australia. The outcomes indicated that PVs' performance denoted by normalized P_{max} output varied with seasonal weather conditions. Rainfall was the key cause of natural cleaning to wipe off dust particles on PVs' surface. S.A. Sulaiman *et al.* [23] determined the influence of dirt deposition on generation of PV panels. Results reveals that opaque particles, particular in moss, extremely affect the performance of panels, which could decrease the yield and hence the power output by up to 85%. Md. R. Maghami *et al.* [24] studied mitigation of output power loss due to soiling effect on a solar panel. The result predicted that soft shielding (such as air pollution) affects the power produced due to a decrease in current generated by the PV module, but the voltage remains constant. Very often soil patches like bird droppings, leaves and dust patches block some cells of a module, and have a terrible or adverse effect on PV generation. M. S. Vasisht *et al.* [25] conducted experimentation for studying the influence of seasonal climatic differences on 20 kWp solar PV installations. The system daily average yield was almost 80 kWh for the previous two years, which transforms to yearly yield of 28.9 MWh. The CUF of the plant is 16.5%, and average PR of the system is around 85%. PR of the PV plant is correlated with the behaviour of SPV modules in altered seasons, with module temperature (T_{mod}) as the fundamental aspect of comparison. M. Mani *et al.* [26] reviewed the research done on the effect of dust on solar PV performance and made common recommendation for different temperature ranges, environment zones and annual precipitation. They suggested cleaning one time a week or every two weeks depending on the quantity or rate of dust deposition for the Mediterranean climate. A. Ali *et al.* [27] experimentally investigated the consequence of ambient temperature and dust deposition on the efficiency of a PV module (thin film) and found that ambient temperature has a considerable effect on open circuit voltage and a minor influence on short-circuit current. T. A. Hanai *et al.* [28] examined the effect of numerous climatic conditions including solar radiation, dust accumulation, ambient temperature, etc., on the electrical outputs of a thin-film grid-connected PV structure and found that short-circuit current reduces by 0.0413 A/°C and open circuit voltage falls by 2.01 V/°C as the ambient temperature of SPV increases. M. Saidan *et al.* [29] conducted a study on efficiency fall of PV panel due to dust in a restricted experimental arrangement and measured a fall in efficiency of 6.24% for one day, 11.8% for one week and 18.74% for one month of exposures. M. J. Adinoyi *et al.* [30] evaluated the dust effect on the power outputs of PV panels exposed to outdoor environmental conditions for a duration of over six months. The daily evaluated power outputs showed 50% power reduction when systems were left without cleaning for about six months and suggested cleaning at least once every two weeks. A. Bouraiou *et al.* [31] investigated the critical effects of accumulation of sand dust and partial shading for a span of two months on performance of PV panels and observed a 5.1% reduction in power output between clear and dusty days and this was primarily credited to the decrease in short-circuit current. F. Mani *et al.* [32] proposed mathematical modelling based on multiple regression techniques to quantity the effect of unlike particle dimensions on soiling losses in PV systems. Authentication of the regression model shows its adequate accuracy to be used to study the effect of particle sizes on estimated power output. B. S. Kumar *et al.* [33] evaluated the annual performance of 10 MW grid-associated solar PV plant, operating with a seasonal tilt. The annual CUF of 17.68%, yearly performance ratio (PR) of 86.12%, and final yield (YF) of plant ranged from 1.96 to 5.07 h/d with 15798.19 MWh per annum of energy generation. K. Sudhakar *et al.* [34] performed experimentation on energy and exergy analysis of 36 W solar PV module for assessing electrical, thermal and exergy output of solar PV panel. During the day, energy efficiency is found to change from 6% to 9%. The PV exergy efficiency reduces as the ambient temperature increases due to increasing cell temperature and irreversibility whereas the output electricity increases. B. Hammad *et al.* [35] simulate the dust and temperature effects on PV systems, assessing the power losses due to dust deposition and optimizing cleaning regularity are presented by using MLR and ANN models to estimate PV system conversion efficiency; both predict the same nearly with R^2 values 87.7% and 90.0%, the average efficiency declines due to dust are 0.768%/day and 0.607%/day and energy losses are 10.282 kWh/m^2 and 8.140 kWh/m^2, using MLR and ANN models, respectively, for the duration of the study.

8.3   Experimental Setup

In this study the performance analysis and effect of dust deposition and ambient temperature was examined on a 62 KWp grid-connected rooftop solar photovoltaic plant. All the experimental performance parameters like energy yield in kwh/day E_{out}, ambient temperature T_a, (°c) exposure day D_e, Global horizontal irradiance H (kwh/m²/day), were noted on different days for a period of total 176 days, starting from 1st Jan. 2018 and completed on 25th June 2018. During this period the modules were manually cleaned and also by the rainfall. The details of PV modules cleaning are shown in Table 8.3.

Cleaning was not done during the periods between the above six dates of rainfall and manual cleaning; the system was allowed to accumulate dust. The transmittance through PV glass covers reduces and the reflection of incident irradiance on PV modules may increase due to the dust addition. Both effects considerably change PV module current and voltage output. Hence the output electric power, conversion efficiency and energy yield decrease significantly. Moreover, the reduction in the system's output power is affected by other independent and interdependent variables. As the ambient temperature surges, the module temperature also rises, causing the reduction in generated power and vice versa. Therefore, as dust accumulation and/or ambient temperature increase, the output power and conversion efficiency of the PV system decrease. As per the collected data, we calculated the daily system conversion efficiency η (%) and the ambient temperature was averaged over every day for the entire study period.

Table 8.3 Summary of PV modules cleaning.

Cleaning sequence	Day of cleaning	Method of cleaning
1.	1 Jan. 2018	Manually by pressurized water jet
2.	23 Jan. 2018	Due to Rainfall
3.	28 Feb. 2018	Manually by pressurized water jet
4.	5 Apr. 2018	Manually by pressurized water jet
5.	17 May 2018	Manually by pressurized water jet
6.	26 June 2018	Due to Rainfall

8.3.1   Selection of Site and Development of Experimental Facilities

For the present study, the rooftop solar PV modules mounted on Mechanical Engg. Dept. (VISHWAKARMA BLOCK) SKIT, Jaipur (26°55′N latitude, 75°52′ E longitude) has been chosen. The continuous sunshine availability without any interruption and accurate inclination of modules (26°) with correct facing, i.e., south facing are the reasons for choosing this block. The system is grid-connected, consisting of 200 polycrystalline silicon PV modules of nominal power of 310 Wp. These modules are connected in series and form an array to achieve optimal system voltage. Each array consists of 10 module of 310 W so an array having 3100 W and total 20 arrays are mounted on the block with the capacity of 6200 W or 62 KWp. Each module covers an area of 1.94 m² contains 72 cells in it. The module mounting structures are made up of galvanized mild steel. The SPV system is being safeguarded by a lightning arrester, isolator switches and super-earth kits to avoid voltage surges. An array junction box is provided with each module for combining the output of each array. The system is equipped with a data acquisition system which has the remote access facility to collect continuous inputs, outputs and transmit the real-time meteorological data at preset time intervals. The daily global horizontal irradiance, ambient temperature and power output data were collected at an interval of 15 mins. A secondary standard pyranometer was connected with the modules in series, used for measuring solar irradiance.

8.3.2   Methodology

In the present work, a Multivariate Linear Regression (MLR) model is suggested to assess PV system conversion efficiency based on dust deposition and ambient temperature. Regression analysis is broadly used to analyze multifactor data by making a suitable mathematical equation which is obtained using Minitab 17.0 software [36] and relates the dependent variable (i.e., response variable) to a set of independent variables (predictors). Here the ambient temperature (Ta) and the dust effect in terms of exposure days (De) is well-defined as predictors whereas the daily system conversion efficiency is treated as response variable. Thus, the MLR model proposed in present study becomes as follows [36]:

$$\eta_c = \mu_0 + \mu_1 D_e + \mu_2 T_a + \varepsilon_n$$

where η_c is the daily system conversion efficiency of day number n, De is the exposure day n, Ta is the mean daily ambient temperature in day n, μ_0 is the regression model intercept, μ_1 and μ_2 are the regression coefficients and ε_n is the difference between the real and predicted efficiencies of the PV setup of day n. The experimental setup with all measuring instruments is discussed below.

8.3.3   Experimental Instrumentation

The various components and instrumentation of the setup used in this study are as follows:

(a)   Solar PV modules (Cell type: Virtus II Polycrystalline), exported by Renesola India
(b)   PV Grid connected Inverter (Model No. SG50KTL-M) by Sungrow Power Supply Co. Ltd, Bangalore, India
(c)   SR20-D2 secondary standard pyranometer manufactured by Hukseflux
(d)   Lightning Arrestors
(e)   Digital Thermometer used to measure ambient temp. make by Mextech, temperature response $<\pm$ 1°C (-50 to +200°C) (-58~392ºF)
(f)   Data acquisition system (Pinetech).

8.3.3.1   Solar Photovoltaic Modules

These modules are manufactured by ReneSola, a China-based industry and imported by ReneSola India Pvt. Limited, Kolkata. The one PV module (JC310M-24/Ab) of polycrystalline (mc-Si) cell technology having 72 cells (6*12) pcs. in series of dimension 156*156 mm. These cells are covered with low iron, high transmission, tempered glass and placed in anodized aluminum alloy frame. The module has 27 kg Weight, up to 5400 Pa mechanical load capability with overall dimensions of 1956×992×40 mm and the module efficiency, and max. power prescribed by the manufacturer is 16% and 310 W (at STC) respectively. The normal operating cell temperature (NOCT) is 45^0C $\pm$ 2^0C and max. operating temperature ranges -40^0C~ $+85^0$C. Behind the panel there is a provision of junction box with bypass diodes for connectivity purpose. These modules are also ISO9001, ISO14001 Certified [37]. The detailed technical specifications are given in Appendix I. The detailed drawing, PV module are depicted in Figure 8.5.

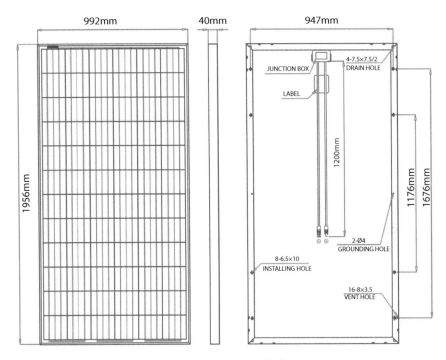

Figure 8.5 Detailed dimensional drawing of module [37].

Figure 8.6 Photographic view of installed PV array.

Figure 8.7 PV grid-connected inverter.

The photographic view of the rooftop plant and installed PV array setup is shown in Figure 8.6. Figure 8.7 shows PV grid-connected inverter.

8.3.3.2 PV Grid-Connected Inverter

The inverter (Model No. SG50KTL-M) is manufactured by Sungrow, a China-based industry and imported by Sungrow Power Supply Co. Ltd, Bangalore. It is a 3-phase string inverter without transformer and an essential unit between the grid and PV strings in the PV system. The detailed specifications of the inverter are specified in Appendix II.

8.3.3.3 Pyranometer

Solar radiation sensor (Model: SR20-D2), manufactured by Hukseflux, is a secondary standard pyranometer having ISO 9060 classification; it allows for rapid data acquisition, easy read-out and error-free apparatus exchange. It measures the solar radiation received by a plane surface from a 180° field of view angle, providing two types of normally used irradiance outputs:

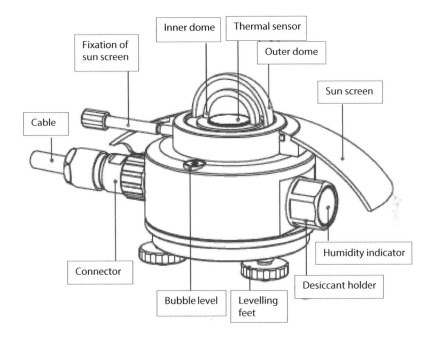

Figure 8.8 Overview of SR20-D2 pyranometer [38].

Figure 8.9 Pyranometer.

Figure 8.8 shows overview of SR20-D2 pyranometer. It is the most precise digital pyranometer available, exclusively verified for temperature and directional response, and temperature response is $<\pm$ 0.4 % (-30 to +50°C) best "zero offset a" and best calibration uncertainty [38]. Detailed specifications of the pyranometer are specified in Appendix III. The view of the mounted pyranometer in series with the modules is shown in Figure 8.9.

8.3.3.4   Digital Thermometer

A Digital thermometer which has temperature ranges from -50°C to 200°C is used to find ambient temperature on the experimental site. It is placed on a wooden surface having some space in between the roof, behind the

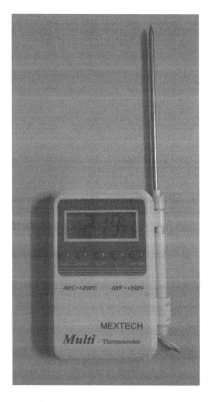

Figure 8.10 Digital thermometer.

module and not in direct contact with sunlight to minimize the heat transfer effects. Figure 8.10 shows the digital thermometer.

8.3.3.5   Lightning Arrester

The solar PV system is safeguarded by super-earth kits, lightning arrester and isolator switches to avoid voltage surges. Figure 8.11 shows the lightning arrester.

Figure 8.11 Lightning arrester.

8.3.3.6   Data Acquisition System

The high-speed data acquisition system was used to accumulate the essential data, and acquired data are shown, analysed, and stored on a computer using appropriate data logger software [39]. The post-processing has been developed in Minitab and arranging and graphical representation of exported data has also done. The system is manufactured and installed with the instruments by Pinetech Solutions pvt. Ltd., Jaipur, and executed by a user ID and password. The technical details of the data acquisition system are shown in Appendix V.

8.3.4   Formula Used and Sample Calculations

Based on the collected data, we calculated the daily system conversion efficiency η (%) for

PV system according to IEC 61724 [40]

(i) The Daily system conversion efficiency [35]:

$$\eta = \frac{E_{out}}{H \times A}$$

Where
E_{out} = Energy yield (daily AC electrical output in kWh/day)
H = Global horizontal irradiance (in kWh/m²/day).
A (Total Area of modules). = 1.94 m² × 200 = 388 m²
T_a = Ambient temperature in °C

(ii) The Capacity Utilization Factor and Performance Ratio is given by [41]:

$$\text{CUF.} = \frac{\textbf{Annual yield (kWh)}}{\textbf{Installed capacity of plant (kW)} \times \textbf{24h} \times \textbf{365 days}} \times \textbf{100}$$

$$\text{PR.} = \frac{\textbf{Annual yield (kWh)}}{\textbf{Nominal energy yield (kWh)}} \times \textbf{100}$$

where Annual yield = Total Energy generation (kWh) in one year (365 days)

And Nominal energy yield = GHI × Rated module efficiency × Total PV area (in m²)

Where GHI is global horizontal irradiance (in kWh/m²)

SAMPLE CALCULATIONS
1 Jan.
The system conversion efficiency:

$$\eta = \frac{E_{out}}{H \times A}$$

$$\eta = \frac{232.38}{4.50 \times 388} = 13.31\%$$

Similarly, the CUF and PR of the plant on 01 Jan. 2018

$$CUF. = \frac{232.38\,(kWh)}{62\,(kW) \times 24\,h \times 01\,day} \times 100$$

$$= 15.61\,\%$$

$$PR. = \frac{232.38\,(kWh)}{5.3 \times 01 \times 0.16 \times 388} \times 100$$

$$= 70.63\,\%$$

Similarly, other calculations are done by the same method as discussed above in the sample calculations.

8.3.5   Assumptions and Limitations

1. The instruments are calibrated for the required measurements by the manufacturer.
2. Modules degrade after a certain period of time due to aging of components and stress due to environmental cycles.
3. The useful life of PV is considered to be a period of 25 years.
4. Fixed module tilt angle of 26° is considered to maximize the irradiation received by the PV module.
5. The spectrum of air mass for the experiment is assumed to be constant and is nearly equal to 1.5 as described in STC.
6. It is suggested that assumption is valid over certain conditions as in this analysis. Here only pressurized water jet cleaning of modules is done but in actual practice so many

process or steps have been taken for performance enhancement, so the effect evaluated in performance improvement shows only the effect of dusting and water cleaning not for the other maintenance actions.

7. The ANOVA tool, used in MLR analysis for validation and significance of the model, is based on some assumptions, such as residuals being normally distributed and having constant variance.

8.4   Results Discussion

8.4.1   Phases of Data Collection

Based on the cleaning dates summarized in Table 8.3, the collected data is divided into three phases:

Phase I: from 1st Jan. to 27th Feb. 2018
Phase II: from 1st Mar. to 5th Apr. 2018
Phase III: from 18th May to 25th June 2018

8.4.2   Variation in Responses Evaluated During Phase I (From 1 Jan. to 27 Feb.) of Study

8.4.2.1   *Effect of Dust and Ambient Temperature on Conversion Efficiency*

Table 8.4 shows the input parameters and responses for phase I during 1 Jan. to 27 Feb. Figure 8.12 shows the variation in ambient temperature and conversion efficiency w.r.t. exposure day. It can be observed that the conversion efficiency gradually decreases with accumulated dust up to on 22 Jan. and after cleaning of modules it increases with certain value and again decrease due to temperature raise and dust deposition up to 27 Feb.

Table 8.4 Calculation for typical set of parameters during phase I.

Date	Exposure day (De)	Today's gen E_{out}	GHI (H)	Conversion efficiency (η_c)	Ambient temp. (Ta)	CUF	PR.
1-Jan-18	1	232.38	4.5	13.31	14.13	15.62	70.63
2-Jan-18	2	221.95	4.37	13.09	15.78	14.92	67.46
4-Jan-18	4	227.85	4.47	13.14	11.27	15.31	69.25
5-Jan-18	5	239.29	4.67	13.21	10.85	16.08	72.73
7-Jan-18	7	244.11	4.86	12.95	11.88	16.41	74.19
8-Jan-18	8	208.38	4.23	12.70	12.25	14.00	63.33
10-Jan-18	10	212.14	4.4	12.43	10.44	14.26	64.48
12-Jan-18	12	223.4	4.48	12.85	11.53	15.01	67.90
14-Jan-18	14	242.12	4.9	12.74	13.66	16.27	73.59
15-Jan-18	15	253.2	5.2	12.55	13.45	17.02	76.96
20-Jan-18	20	224.18	4.47	12.93	12.29	15.07	68.14
22-Jan-18	22	222.5	4.91	11.68	13.42	14.95	67.63

(Continued)

Table 8.4 Calculation for typical set of parameters during phase I. (*Continued*)

Date	Exposure day (De)	Today's gen E_{out}	GHI (H)	Conversion efficiency (η_c)	Ambient temp. (Ta)	CUF	PR.
24-Jan-18	1	262.49	5.25	12.89	10.39	17.64	79.78
25-Jan-18	2	260.05	5.15	13.01	13.55	17.48	79.04
27-Jan-18	4	265.55	5.27	12.99	11.45	17.85	80.71
28-Jan-18	5	260.18	5.2	12.90	12.66	17.49	79.08
29-Jan-18	6	255.59	5.31	12.41	13.77	17.18	77.68
1-Feb-18	9	252.55	5.07	12.84	13.92	16.97	76.76
2-Feb-18	10	250.34	5.23	12.34	14.38	16.82	76.09
4-Feb-18	12	259.28	5.43	12.31	15.62	17.42	78.80
11-Feb-18	19	262.23	5.49	12.31	18.58	17.62	79.70
12-Feb-18	20	255.58	5.53	11.91	19.12	17.18	77.68
14-Feb-18	22	266.81	5.86	11.73	20.35	17.93	81.09
15-Feb-18	23	270.1	5.92	11.76	21.2	18.15	82.09
24-Feb-18	32	239.21	5.29	11.65	22.56	16.08	72.70
25-Feb-18	33	242.57	5.52	11.33	23.18	16.30	73.73
26-Feb-18	34	240.46	5.58	11.11	25.82	16.16	73.08
27-Feb-18	35	238.38	5.63	10.91	26.23	16.02	72.45

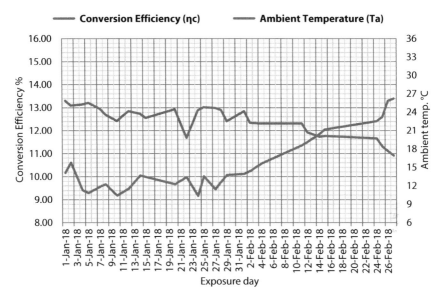

Figure 8.12 Variation in ambient temperature and conversion efficiency w.r.t. exposure day.

8.4.2.2   Capacity Utilization Factor and Performance Ratio

Figure 8.13 shows the variation in CUF and PR due to different energy yields that may be affected by increased ambient temperature and dust accumulation.

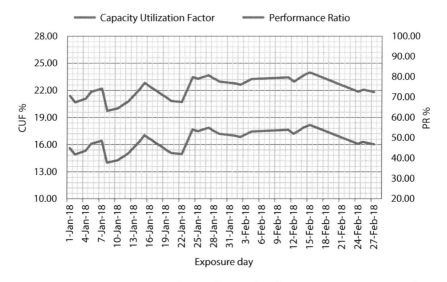

Figure 8.13 Variation in capacity utilization factor and performance ratio w.r.t. exposure day.

8.4.2.3   Evaluation of MLR Model

The complete equation has regression model intercept and associated coefficients with each variable. Regression equation for prediction of daily efficiency:

$$[\eta_c]_n = [13.704 - 0.04020\ D_e - 0.0465\ T_a]_n \qquad (8.1)$$

where η_c is the predicted daily conversion efficiency of nth day.

The least-squares method-based analysis of variance (ANOVA) is used to test the significance of the model [42]. A graphical analysis of the residuals can be used to check the validity of assumptions as shown in Figures 8.14, 8.15 and 8.16. The 4 outliers have been deleted before starting analysis since they have large residual.

Figure 8.14 shows that the analysis exhibits adequate results as the collective normal distribution is nearly a straight line, i.e., the normality hypothesis is contented.

Figure 8.15 shows that the constant variance is satisfied as these residuals are limited within a horizontal band. In other words, this plot shows an arbitrary pattern of residuals on both sides of zero value. This shows that an exact function form is used to model the curvature.

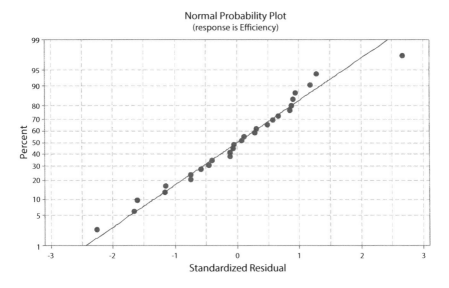

Figure 8.14 Normal probability plot of residuals.

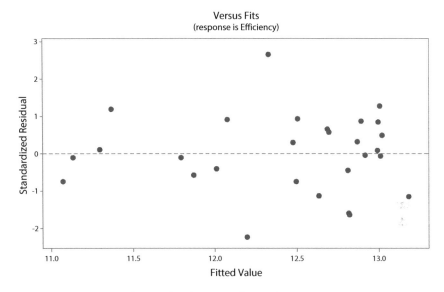

Figure 8.15 Plot for residual v/s fitted values (efficiency).

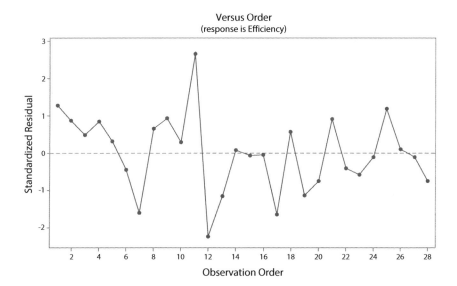

Figure 8.16 Plot for residual v/s order of data.

Figure 8.16 shows clearly that the residuals are arbitrary with order of the data representing independency of variables. Besides, the variables (ambient temperature and dust exposure day) have a smaller p–value showing that they are both significant.

Table 8.5 shows the ANOVA analysis for conversion efficiency.

The model signifies the behavior of data reasonably, because the values of R^2 and adjusted R^2, used to measure goodness-of-fit, are 86.26% and 85.16%, respectively. The VIF value is 3.63 (less than 10) for the two variables, indicating that the multicolinearity does not exist in the model.

The value of large variation inflation factors (VIFs), generally more than 10, shows that the related regression coefficients are poorly assessed due to multicolinearity. The negative signs of model coefficients show the degradation in PV system performance due to accumulation of dust and increasing ambient temperatures.

Figure 8.17 shows a contour curve which shows a two-dimensional carrying every data points that have the same response are linked to generate contour lines of constant responses. A contour curve contains the following essentials:

Table 8.5 ANOVA table: Conversion efficiency v/s exposure day, ambient temperature.

Source	DF	Adj SS	Adj MS	F- value	P- value
Regression	2	10.4921	5.24606	78.47	0.000
Exposure Day	1	1.3506	1.35061	20.20	0.000
Ambient Temp.	1	0.3572	0.35719	5.34	0.029
Error	25	1.6714	0.06686		
Total	27	12.1636			

Term	Coef	SE coef	T-value	P-value	VIF
Constant	13.704	0.222	61.73	0.000	
Exposure Day	-0.04020	0.00894	-4.49	0.000	3.63
Ambient Temp.	-0.0465	0.0201	-2.31	0.029	3.63

S	0.258569
R-sq	86.26%
R-sq (adj)	85.16%
R-sq (pred)	80.69%

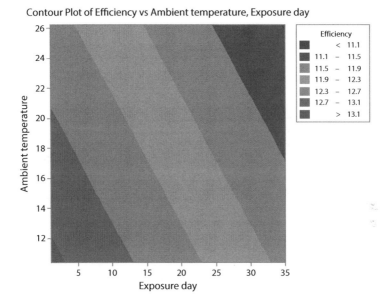

Figure 8.17 Counter plot of conversion efficiency v/s ambient temp. & exposure day.

- Predictors on the x- and y-axes.
- Contour lines that connect points that have the same response value.
- Coloured contour bands that represent ranges of the response values.

Contour plot is used to perceive how a response variable relates to two predictor variables. It is a graphical method for describing a 3-dimensional curve or surface by plotting continuous z slices, called contours, on a 2-dimensional plane. The contour stages are plotted as curves; the area between the lines is colored to show interpolated data. Here the z value (efficiency) is the response that we want to explain or predict and the x and y values are the explanatory variables. Minitab must interpolate and plots response (Z) values at the x-y intersections of the grid, or mesh.

In this graph, darker regions indicate higher z-values. These higher z-values seem to form a fold starting from the top left of the plot to the middle right. Figure 8.17 contour plot of conversion efficiency v/s ambient temp. and exposure day shows the maximum conversion efficiency up to 21°C ambient temperature and 13th day of exposure; after this efficiency may decrease and has its lowest value after 32 days with 26°C ambient temperature, so increasing temperature and dust deposition both have an adverse effect on efficiency.

8.4.3   Variation in Responses Evaluated During Phase II (From 1 March to 5 April)

8.4.3.1   Influence of Dust and Ambient Temperature on Conversion Efficiency

Table 8.6 shows the input parameters and responses for phase II during 1 March to 5 April. Figure 8.18 shows that the conversion efficiency gradually decreases with accumulated dust up to 5 Apr. and after cleaning of modules it increases with certain value and again decreases due to temperature raise and dust deposition. Figure 8.19 shows the variation in CUF and PR due to different energy yields that may affected by increase in ambient temperature and dust accumulation.

8.4.3.2   Capacity Utilization Factor and Performance Ratio

Figure 8.19 shows the variation in CUF and PR due to different energy yields that may be affected by increased ambient temperature and dust accumulation.

8.4.3.3   Evaluation of MLR Model

The complete regression equation of model is:

$$[\eta_c]_n = [13.970 - 0.05480 \, D_e - 0.0424 \, T_a]_n \tag{8.2}$$

where ηc is the predicted daily conversion efficiency of nth day.

Figures 8.20, 8.21 and 8.22 show graphical investigation of the residuals to test the validity of assumptions; also, 5 outliers have high residual so they have been deleted earlier. The collective normal distribution is found to be nearly a straight line as shown in Figure 8.20, so the normality hypothesis is fulfilled.

Figure 8.21 shows that these residuals are contained within a horizontal band, i.e., the constant variance is satisfied. In other words, this plot shows a random pattern of residuals on either side of zero value. This represents that a correct function form is used to form the curvature.

Figure 8.22 shows clearly that the residuals are arbitrary with order of the data representing variable independency. Besides, the variables (ambient temperature and dust exposure day) have a smaller p–value, showing that they are both significant.

Table 8.6 Calculation for typical set of parameters during phase II.

Date	Exposure day (De)	Today's gen E_{out}	GHI (H)	Conversion efficiency (η_c)	Ambient temp. (Ta)	CUF	PR.
1-Mar-18	1	319.54	6.43	12.81	27.6	21.47	97.12
2-Mar-18	2	321.2	6.54	12.66	29.49	21.59	97.62
3-Mar-18	4	287.48	6.05	12.25	30.59	19.32	87.37
8-Mar-18	8	308.18	6.52	12.18	30.94	20.71	93.67
9-Mar-18	9	296.22	6.31	12.10	29.78	19.91	90.03
10-Mar-18	10	288.34	6.18	12.02	31.68	19.38	87.64
11-Mar-18	11	299.39	6.43	12.00	31.95	20.12	90.99
12-Mar-18	13	302.45	6.57	11.86	32.65	20.33	91.92
15-Mar-18	15	304.29	6.61	11.86	30.75	20.45	92.48
16-Mar-18	16	298.87	6.5	11.85	33.74	20.09	90.84
17-Mar-18	17	312.68	6.83	11.80	31.48	21.01	95.03
20-Mar-18	20	281.82	6.23	11.66	30.12	18.94	85.65
21-Mar-18	21	296.15	6.61	11.55	31.57	19.90	90.01

(Continued)

Table 8.6 Calculation for typical set of parameters during phase II. (*Continued*)

Date	Exposure day (De)	Today's gen E_{out}	GHI (H)	Conversion efficiency (η_c)	Ambient temp. (Ta)	CUF	PR.
22-Mar-18	22	310.29	6.98	11.46	29.96	20.85	94.31
24-Mar-18	24	291.6	6.6	11.39	33.62	19.60	88.63
25-Mar-18	25	308.2	7.11	11.17	31.36	20.71	93.67
26-Mar-18	26	306.12	7.09	11.13	34.92	20.57	93.04
29-Mar-18	29	287.2	6.96	10.64	34.79	19.30	87.29
30-Mar-18	30	290.75	6.82	10.99	36.15	19.54	88.37
31-Mar-18	31	281.7	6.67	10.89	34.75	18.93	85.62
1-Apr-18	32	298.7	7.21	10.68	35.58	20.07	90.78
3-Apr-18	34	277.12	6.84	10.44	37.48	18.62	84.23
4-Apr-18	35	265.3	6.62	10.33	36.89	17.83	80.63

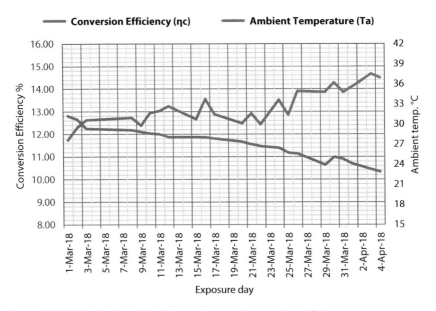

Figure 8.18 Variation in ambient temperature and conversion efficiency w.r.t. exposure day.

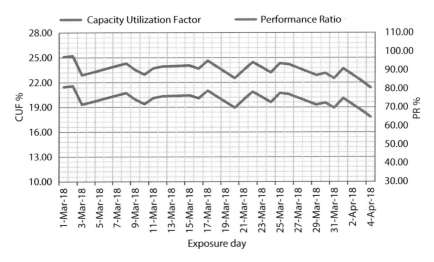

Figure 8.19 Variation in capacity utilization factor and performance ratio w.r.t. exposure day.

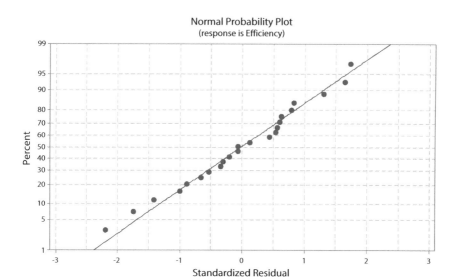

Figure 8.20 Normal probability plot of residuals.

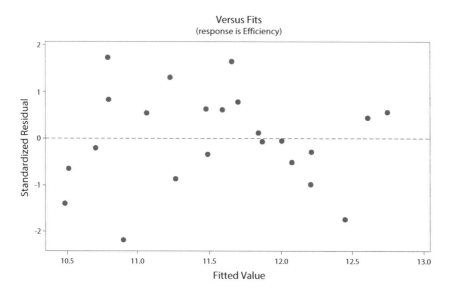

Figure 8.21 Plot for residual v/s fitted values (efficiency).

The model represents the behavior of data reasonably, because the values of R^2 and adjusted R^2, used to measure goodness-of-fit, are 96.93% and 96.62%, respectively.

Table 8.7 shows that the multicollinearity does not exist in the model as the VIF is less than 10 and negative signs of coefficients of the model shows

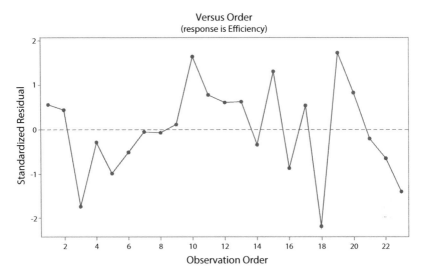

Figure 8.22 Plot for residual v/s order of data.

Table 8.7 ANOVA table: conversion efficiency v/s exposure day, ambient temperature.

Source	DF	Adj SS	Adj MS	F-value	P-value
Regression	2	9.8641	4.93203	315.58	0.000
Exposure Day	1	2.1350	2.13498	136.61	0.000
Ambient Temp.	1	0.0806	0.08062	5.16	0.034
Error	20	0.3126	0.01563		
Total	22	10.1766			

Term	Coef	SE Coef	T-value	P-value	VIF
Constant	13.970	0.536	26.08	0.000	
Exposure Day	-0.05480	0.00469	-11.69	0.000	3.39
Ambient Temp.	-0.0424	0.0187	-2.27	0.034	3.39

S	0.125014
R-sq	96.93 %
R-sq (adj)	96.62 %
R-sq (pred)	95.99 %

Contour Plot of Efficiency vs Ambient temperature, Exposure day

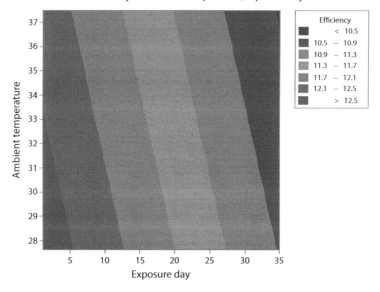

Figure 8.23 Counter plot of conversion efficiency v/s ambient temp. & exposure day.

the degradation in performance due to accumulation of dust and increasing ambient temperatures.

Figure 8.23 contour plot of conversion efficiency v/s ambient temperature and exposure day shows the maximum conversion efficiency up to 32°C ambient temperature and 11th day of exposure; after this, efficiency may significantly decrease and has its lowest value after 35 days with 34°C and greater ambient temperature again increasing temperature and dust deposition; both have an adverse effect on efficiency.

8.4.4 Variation in Responses Evaluated During Phase III (18 May to 25 June)

8.4.4.1 *Effect of Dust and Ambient Temperature on Conversion Efficiency*

Table 8.8 shows the input parameters and responses for phase III during 18 May to 25 June. Figure 8.24 shows that the conversion efficiency gradually decreases with accumulated dust up to 1 June and after cleaning of modules it increases with certain value and again decreases due to temperature raise and dust deposition. Figure 8.25 shows the variation in

Table 8.8 Calculation for typical set of parameters during phase III.

Date	Exposure day (De)	Today's gen E$_{out}$	GHI (H)	Conversion efficiency (η_c)	Ambient temp. (Ta)	CUF	PR.
18-May-18	1	344.68	6.88	12.91	40.28	23.16	104.76
19-May-18	2	329.3	6.82	12.44	40.37	22.13	100.09
21-May-18	4	322.4	6.99	11.89	41.36	21.67	97.99
22-May-18	5	328.39	7.16	11.82	42.79	22.07	99.81
24-May-18	7	329.28	7.27	11.67	42.82	22.13	100.08
25-May-18	8	334.8	7.21	11.97	41.6	22.50	101.76
27-May-18	10	328.16	7.26	11.65	40.07	22.05	99.74
28-May-18	11	342.4	7.51	11.75	41.11	23.01	104.07
29-May-18	12	337.2	7.38	11.78	41.24	22.66	102.49
31-May-18	14	329.2	7.39	11.48	41.31	22.12	100.05
1-Jun-18	15	312.5	7.31	11.02	42.46	21.00	94.98

(Continued)

Table 8.8 Calculation for typical set of parameters during phase III. (*Continued*)

Date	Exposure day (De)	Today's gen E_{out}	GHI (H)	Conversion efficiency (η_c)	Ambient temp. (Ta)	CUF	PR.
2-Jun-18	16	325.12	7.28	11.51	40.79	21.85	98.81
4-Jun-18	18	295.24	6.98	10.90	41.87	19.84	89.73
5-Jun-18	19	304.6	7.48	10.50	42.07	20.47	92.58
7-Jun-18	21	287.2	7.18	10.31	42.34	19.30	87.29
8-Jun-18	22	286.8	7.03	10.51	42.97	19.27	87.17
15-Jun-18	29	289.7	6.79	11.00	40.35	19.47	88.05
20-Jun-18	34	270.2	6.89	10.11	40.81	18.16	82.12
21-Jun-18	35	258.3	6.56	10.15	40.34	17.36	78.51
22-Jun-18	36	261.7	6.32	10.67	39.12	17.59	79.54
25-Jun-18	39	250.5	6.39	10.10	39.44	16.83	76.14

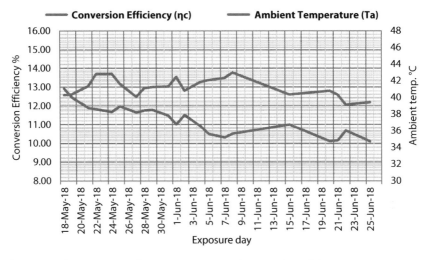

Figure 8.24 Variation in ambient temperature and conversion efficiency w.r.t. exposure day.

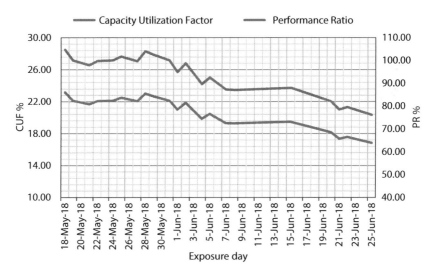

Figure 8.25 Variation in capacity utilization factor and performance ratio w.r.t. exposure day.

CUF and PR due to different energy yields that may be affected by increase in ambient temperature and dust accumulation.

8.4.4.2   *Capacity Utilization Factor and Performance Ratio*

8.4.4.3   Evaluation of MLR Model

The complete regression equation of model is:

$$[\eta_c]_n = [24.52 - 0.07172 \, D_e - 0.2925 \, T_a]_n \qquad (8.3)$$

where η_c is the predicted daily conversion efficiency of nth day.

The collective normal distribution is found to be nearly a straight line as shown in Figure 8.26, so the normality hypothesis is fulfilled. Figure 8.27 shows that these residuals are enclosed within a horizontal band, i.e., the constant variance is contented and shows that a correct function form is used to model the curvature.

Figure 8.28 shows that the residuals are arbitrary with order of the data showing independency of variables. The variables have a smaller p–value, showing that they are both significant.

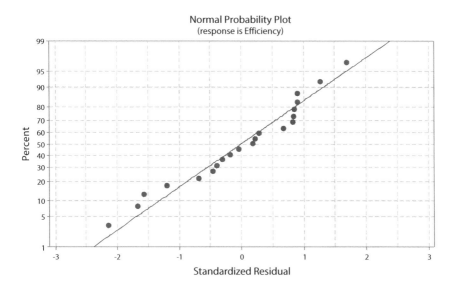

Figure 8.26 Normal probability plot of residuals.

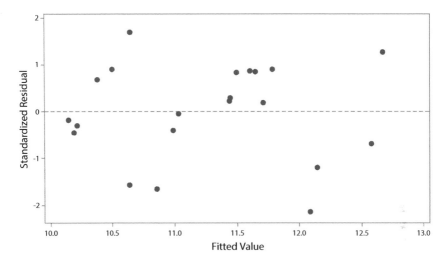

Figure 8.27 Plot for residual v/s fitted values (efficiency).

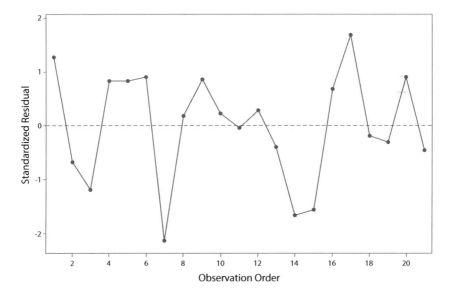

Figure 8.28 Plot for residual v/s order of data.

Table 8.9 shows that the multicollinearity does not exist in the model (VIF is lower than 10). The degradation in PV system performance due to accumulation of dust and increasing ambient temperatures shows by the negative signs of coefficients of the model. The model characterizes

Table 8.9 ANOVA table: conversion efficiency v/s exposure day, ambient temperature.

Source	DF	Adj SS	Adj MS	F-value	P-value
Regression	2	11.9234	5.9617	120.19	0.000
Exposure Day	1	11.9222	11.9222	240.35	0.000
Ambient Temp.	1	1.7762	1.7762	35.81	0.000
Error	18	0.8929	0.0496		
Total	20	12.8162			

Term	Coef	SE coef	T-value	P-value	VIF
Constant	24.52	2.05	11.98	0.000	
Exposure Day	-0.07172	0.00463	-15.50	0.000	1.19
Ambient Temp.	-0.2925	0.0489	-5.98	0.000	1.19

S	0.222718
R-sq	93.03 %
R-sq (adj)	92.26 %
R-sq (pred)	90.42 %

the behavior of data practically, as the values of R^2 and adjusted R^2, used to measure goodness-of-fit, are 93.03% and 92.26%, respectively.

Figure 8.29 contour plot of conversion efficiency v/s ambient temperature and exposure day shows the maximum conversion efficiency up to 40°C ambient temperature and 10th day of exposure. After this, efficiency may significantly decrease and has its lowest value after 39 days with 42°C and greater ambient temperature.

8.4.5 Regression Analysis for the Whole Period

From the obtained results of different phases, we can conclude that the suggested model represents collected data accurately and does not violate the main assumptions.

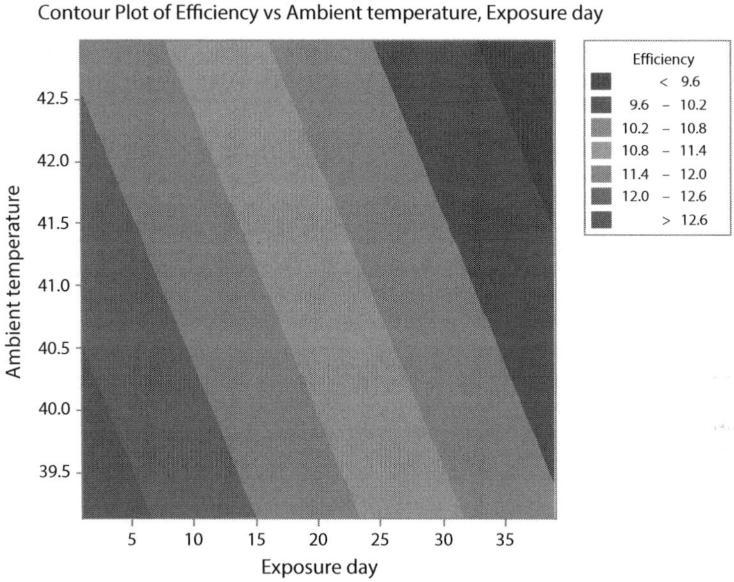

Contour Plot of Efficiency vs Ambient temperature, Exposure day

Figure 8.29 Counter plot of conversion efficiency v/s ambient temp. & exposure day.

The final equation of the model becomes

$$\text{Conversion Efficiency } [\eta_c]_n = [13.7580 - 0.05303\, D_e - 0.03818\, T_a]_n \quad (8.4)$$

where ηc is the predicted daily conversion efficiency of nth day.

Figures 8.30, 8.31 and 8.32 show graphical analysis of the residuals to check the validity of assumptions. The collective normal distribution is found to be almost a straight line as shown in Figure 8.30, so the normality hypothesis is fulfilled.

Figure 8.31 shows that these residuals are confined within a horizontal band, i.e., the constant variance is contented. In other words, a correct function form is used to form the curvature as the plot shows an arbitrary pattern of residuals on both either of zero value. Figure 8.32 shows obviously that the residuals are arbitrary with order of the data representing independency of variables. Besides, the variables (ambient temperature and dust exposure day) have a smaller p–value showing that they are both significant. Figure 8.33 shows the counter plot of conversion efficiency v/s ambient temp. and exposure day. Table 8.10 shows the input parameters and responses for full phase during 1 Jan to 25 June.

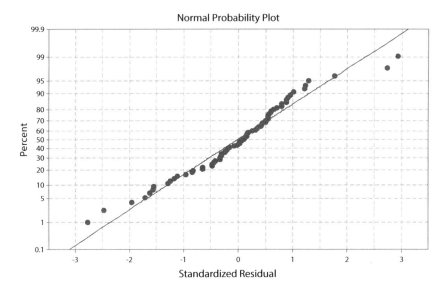

Figure 8.30 Normal probability curve of residuals.

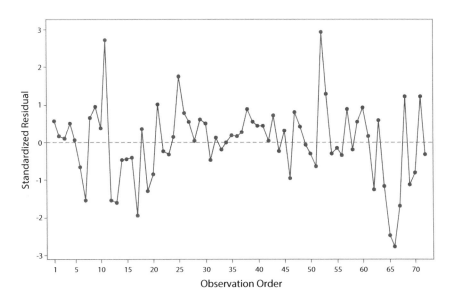

Figure 8.31 Plot for residual v/s order of data.

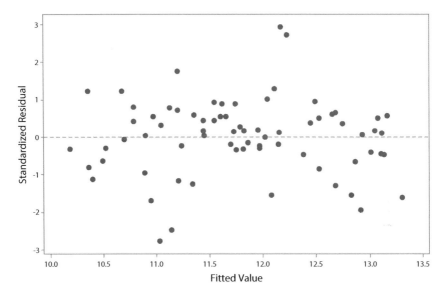

Figure 8.32 Plot for residual v/s fitted values (efficiency).

Contour Plot of Efficiency vs Ambient temperature, Exposure day

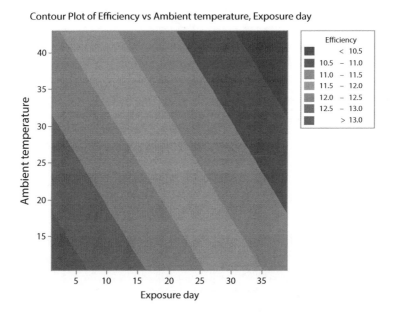

Figure 8.33 Counter plot of conversion efficiency v/s ambient temp. & exposure day.

Table 8.10 Input parameters and responses for full phase during 1 Jan to 25 June.

Date	Exposure day (De)	Today's gen E_{out}	GHI (H)	Conversion efficiency (η_c)	Ambient temp. (Ta)	CUF	PR.
1-Jan-18	1	232.38	4.5	13.31	14.13	15.62	70.63
2-Jan-18	2	221.95	4.37	13.09	15.78	14.92	67.46
4-Jan-18	4	227.85	4.47	13.14	11.27	15.31	69.25
5-Jan-18	5	239.29	4.67	13.21	10.85	16.08	72.73
7-Jan-18	7	244.11	4.86	12.95	11.88	16.41	74.19
8-Jan-18	8	208.38	4.23	12.70	12.25	14.00	63.33
10-Jan-18	10	212.14	4.4	12.43	10.44	14.26	64.48
12-Jan-18	12	223.4	4.48	12.85	11.53	15.01	67.90
14-Jan-18	14	242.12	4.9	12.74	13.66	16.27	73.59
15-Jan-18	15	253.2	5.2	12.55	13.45	17.02	76.96
20-Jan-18	20	224.18	4.47	12.93	12.29	15.07	68.14
22-Jan-18	22	222.5	4.91	11.68	13.42	14.95	67.63
24-Jan-18	1	262.49	5.25	12.89	10.39	17.64	79.78
25-Jan-18	2	260.05	5.15	13.01	13.55	17.48	79.04
27-Jan-18	4	265.55	5.27	12.99	11.45	17.85	80.71

(Continued)

Table 8.10 Input parameters and responses for full phase during 1 Jan to 25 June. (*Continued*)

Date	Exposure day (De)	Today's gen E_{out}	GHI (H)	Conversion efficiency (η_c)	Ambient temp. (Ta)	CUF	PR.
28-Jan-18	5	260.18	5.2	12.90	12.66	17.49	79.08
29-Jan-18	6	255.59	5.31	12.41	13.77	17.18	77.68
1-Feb-18	9	252.55	5.07	12.84	13.92	16.97	76.76
2-Feb-18	10	250.34	5.23	12.34	14.38	16.82	76.09
4-Feb-18	12	259.28	5.43	12.31	15.62	17.42	78.80
11-Feb-18	19	262.23	5.49	12.31	18.58	17.62	79.70
12-Feb-18	20	255.58	5.53	11.91	19.12	17.18	77.68
14-Feb-18	22	266.81	5.86	11.73	20.35	17.93	81.09
15-Feb-18	23	270.1	5.92	11.76	21.2	18.15	82.09
24-Feb-18	32	239.21	5.29	11.65	22.56	16.08	72.70
25-Feb-18	33	242.57	5.52	11.33	23.18	16.30	73.73
26-Feb-18	34	240.46	5.58	11.11	25.82	16.16	73.08
27-Feb-18	35	238.38	5.63	10.91	26.23	16.02	72.45
1-Mar-18	1	319.54	6.43	12.81	27.6	21.47	97.12
2-Mar-18	2	321.2	6.54	12.66	29.49	21.59	97.62

(*Continued*)

Table 8.10 Input parameters and responses for full phase during 1 Jan to 25 June. (*Continued*)

Date	Exposure day (De)	Today's gen E$_{out}$	GHI (H)	Conversion efficiency (η_c)	Ambient temp. (Ta)	CUF	PR.
3-Mar-18	4	287.48	6.05	12.25	30.59	19.32	87.37
8-Mar-18	8	308.18	6.52	12.18	30.94	20.71	93.67
9-Mar-18	9	296.22	6.31	12.10	29.78	19.91	90.03
10-Mar-18	10	288.34	6.18	12.02	31.68	19.38	87.64
11-Mar-18	11	299.39	6.43	12.00	31.95	20.12	90.99
12-Mar-18	13	302.45	6.57	11.86	32.65	20.33	91.92
15-Mar-18	15	304.29	6.61	11.86	30.75	20.45	92.48
16-Mar-18	16	298.87	6.5	11.85	33.74	20.09	90.84
17-Mar-18	17	312.68	6.83	11.80	31.48	21.01	95.03
20-Mar-18	20	281.82	6.23	11.66	30.12	18.94	85.65
21-Mar-18	21	296.15	6.61	11.55	31.57	19.90	90.01
22-Mar-18	22	310.29	6.98	11.46	29.96	20.85	94.31
24-Mar-18	24	291.6	6.6	11.39	33.62	19.60	88.63
25-Mar-18	25	308.2	7.11	11.17	31.36	20.71	93.67
26-Mar-18	26	306.12	7.09	11.13	34.92	20.57	93.04

(*Continued*)

Table 8.10 Input parameters and responses for full phase during 1 Jan to 25 June. (*Continued*)

Date	Exposure day (De)	Today's gen E_{out}	GHI (H)	Conversion efficiency (η_c)	Ambient temp. (Ta)	CUF	PR.
29-Mar-18	29	287.2	6.96	10.64	34.79	19.30	87.29
30-Mar-18	30	290.75	6.82	10.99	36.15	19.54	88.37
31-Mar-18	31	281.7	6.67	10.89	34.75	18.93	85.62
1-Apr-18	32	298.7	7.21	10.68	35.58	20.07	90.78
3-Apr-18	34	277.12	6.84	10.44	37.48	18.62	84.23
4-Apr-18	35	265.3	6.62	10.33	36.89	17.83	80.63
18-May-18	1	344.68	6.88	12.91	40.28	23.16	104.76
19-May-18	2	329.3	6.82	12.44	40.37	22.13	100.09
21-May-18	4	322.4	6.99	11.89	41.36	21.67	97.99
22-May-18	5	328.39	7.16	11.82	42.79	22.07	99.81
24-May-18	7	329.28	7.27	11.67	42.82	22.13	100.08
25-May-18	8	334.8	7.21	11.97	41.6	22.50	101.76
27-May-18	10	328.16	7.26	11.65	40.07	22.05	99.74

(*Continued*)

Table 8.10 Input parameters and responses for full phase during 1 Jan to 25 June. (*Continued*)

Date	Exposure day (De)	Today's gen E_{out}	GHI (H)	Conversion efficiency (η_c)	Ambient temp. (Ta)	CUF	PR.
28-May-18	11	342.4	7.51	11.75	41.11	23.01	104.07
29-May-18	12	337.2	7.38	11.78	41.24	22.66	102.49
31-May-18	14	329.2	7.39	11.48	41.31	22.12	100.05
1-Jun-18	15	312.5	7.31	11.02	42.46	21.00	94.98
2-Jun-18	16	325.12	7.28	11.51	40.79	21.85	98.81
4-Jun-18	18	295.24	6.98	10.90	41.87	19.84	89.73
5-Jun-18	19	304.6	7.48	10.50	42.07	20.47	92.58
7-Jun-18	21	287.2	7.18	10.31	42.34	19.30	87.29
8-Jun-18	22	286.8	7.03	10.51	42.97	19.27	87.17
15-Jun-18	29	289.7	6.79	11.00	40.35	19.47	88.05
20-Jun-18	34	270.2	6.89	10.11	40.81	18.16	82.12
21-Jun-18	35	258.3	6.56	10.15	40.34	17.36	78.51
22-Jun-18	36	261.7	6.32	10.67	39.12	17.59	79.54
25-Jun-18	39	250.5	6.39	10.10	39.44	16.83	76.14

8.4.6   Best Subsets Regression: Conversion Efficiency v/s Exposure Day, Ambient Temperature

Table 8.11 shows ANOVA table of conversion efficiency v/s exposure day, ambient temperature. The highest R^2 values are produced by the finest subsets regression models from full set of the predictors. Subset models may actually find the regression coefficients and forecast future responses with smaller variance than the full model utilizing every predictor. Otherwise, a regression model becomes underspecified and misleading. Each line of

Table 8.11 ANOVA table: conversion efficiency v/s exposure day, ambient temperature.

Source	DF	Adj SS	Adj MS	F-value	P-value
Regression	2	49.243	24.621	351.71	0.000
Exposure Day	1	21.444	21.444	306.32	0.000
Ambient Temp.	1	12.094	12.094	172.75	0.000
Error	69	4.830	0.0700		
Total	71	54.074			

Term	Coef	SE coef	T-value	P-value	VIF
Constant	13.7580	0.0871	157.93	0.000	
Exposure Day	-0.05303	0.00303	-17.50	0.000	1.12
Ambient Temp.	-0.03818	0.00290	-13.14	0.000	1.12

S	0.264588
R-sq	91.07 %
R-sq (adj)	90.81 %
R-sq (pred)	90.14 %

Table 8.12 Results of best subset regression analysis.

Vars	R-sq	R-sq (adj)	R-sq (pred)	S	De	Ta
1	68.7	68.3	67.2	0.49170	X	
1	51.4	50.7	48.7	0.61266		X
2	91.1	90.8	90.1	0.26459	X	X

the output represents a different model. The predictors are indicated by an X and values Vars is the total number of variables or predictors in the model. In addition to R^2 and adjusted R^2, S (square root of MSE) are used to identify the best model. It is concluded from Table 8.12 that when one predictor is used, R^2 and adjusted R^2 are relatively low and S is relatively high. But when both predictors are used in the model, the model has a significant improvement in R^2 (91.07%) and adjusted R^2 (90.8%) and the lowest S value (0.26459) among the three proposed models. This predicts the significance of using concurrently both the independent variables of dust effect D_e and ambient temperature T_a in the MLR model.

8.4.7   Regression Outputs Summary

R^2 = 86.26%, Adjusted R^2 = 85.16% for Phase I
R^2 = 96.93%, Adjusted R^2 = 96.62% for Phase II
R^2 = 93.03%, Adjusted R^2 = 92.26% for Phase III
R^2 = 91.07%, Adjusted R^2 = 90.81% for full Phase

Related to full-phase model, the regression model for each phase provides more accurate modeling for the third interval and slightly less accurate for the first and second. Table 8.13 shows the regression model for each of the three phases with their coefficients.

8.4.8   Comparison Between Measured Efficiency and Predicted Efficiency

The measured and predicted data for the daily conversion efficiency of the PV plant using MLR models for the observation period are plotted in Figure 8.34.

Table 8.13 Regression outputs summary.

Phase	Variables	Coefficients	p–value	VIF	R²	Adjusted R²
I	Intercept	13.704	0.000		86.26%	85.16%
	De	- 0.04020	0.000	3.63		
	Ta	- 0.0465	0.029	3.63		
II	Intercept	13.970	0.000		96.93%	96.62%
	De	- 0.05480	0.000	3.39		
	Ta	- 0.0424	0.034	3.39		
III	Intercept	24.52	0.000		93.03%	92.26%
	D	- 0.07172	0.000	1.19		
	T	- 0.2925	0.000	1.19		
Full phase	Intercept	13.7580	0.000		91.07%	90.81%
	D	- 0.05303	0.000	1.12		
	T	- 0.03818	0.000	1.12		

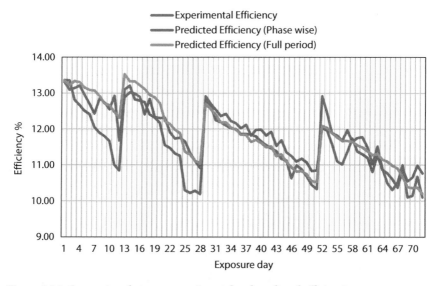

Figure 8.34 Comparison between experimental and predicted efficiencies.

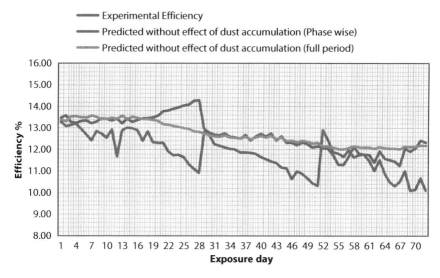

Figure 8.35 Comparison between experimental and predicted efficiencies (without dust).

8.4.9 Losses Due to Dust Accumulation

The study of the performance of a single variable based modeled system, while other variables are omitted, is possible by using an MLR model. One such way to determine the behavior of the systems under investigation is to exclude the effect of dust exposure. The response of the MLR model will be the efficiency of PV system due to all variables without the effect of dust accumulation. It is found that the average daily efficiency drops are 0.872%/day when comparing measured efficiency to predicted efficiency without dust effect using MLR models.

Figure 8.35 shows the comparison between experimental and predicted efficiencies (without dust). For the efficiency variance (with and without dust accumulation effect) and considering MLR model, the amount of average energy loss due to dust over the study period is found to be 9.935 kWh/m^2.

8.4.10 Economic Analysis

Considering that the current electricity tariff in Rajasthan for the nondomestic sector is Rs.8.80/kWh, the average loss due to dust accumulation is Rs.192.72/- per day (Rs. 13879/- for 72 study days and Rs.70342/- for one year. Assuming that the cost of cleaning is Rs. 1000 per cleaning, the estimated cost of cleaning is Rs.9000/- (assuming 9 cleanings in a year). Thus the estimated net loss per year due to dust accumulation is Rs. 61342/-.

8.5   Future Research Directions

More accurate estimations can be done for performance if other variables such as wind velocity, air mass, humidity and ambient visibility are considered. Other software packages like Ascon - Kompas 3D may be used to create both three-dimensional object models, conduct several modeling with concurrent visualization of the outcomes obtained, and form prototypes of such segments using additive technologies [43, 44]. For prediction and validation, the advance simulation, CFD modules and three-dimensional models of SPV thermal modules in CAD can be used.

8.6   Conclusion

In the present study, two independent variables, namely dust exposure (in terms of days) and ambient temperature, were considered to analyze performance of rooftop photovoltaic solar plant for a duration of 176 days. The following conclusions were derived:

(1) The average daily conversion efficiency with cleaned module predicted (using MLR model) is 12.67% and average daily conversion efficiency with dust accumulation by observation is 11.80%. The loss in average daily conversion efficiency due to dust accumulation is 0.872%.
(2) In terms of energy yield and monetary value, the loss due to dust is 9.935 kWh/m2 and Rs. 192.72 or 2.5 dollars per day for the duration of the study.
(3) For the study period, the average capacity utilization factor and average performance ratio were found to be 18.79 and 84.99 respectively. The developed model equations for calculation of PV system conversion efficiency for different phases are significant.
(4) It is concluded that periodic cleaning improves conversion efficiency andenergy yield of a solar plant significantly. The annual economic benefit estimated is Rs. 70342/- or 913.5

dollars (excluding cleaning cost) if cleaning is done within a prescribed period.

Future studies should focus on modelling the efficiency of the solar panel, and more emphasis is needed to define the optimum efficiency of the module and reducing the losses during power generation. The environmental impacts of grid-connected photovoltaic (PV) generation from solar modules may be investigated using the Life Cycle Assessment (LCA) and also find the energy payback time. Exhaustive work is needed to find out the cheap and effective ways of panel maintenance to optimize the capacity utilization factor and performance ratio.

References

1. E. M. Galán *et al.*, "Renewables Global Status Report," Vol. 4 No. 3REN21. ISBN 978-3-9815934-6-4, Paris, 2015.
2. A. Dwivedi, A. Bari, and G. Dwivedi, "Scope and Application of Solar Thermal Energy in India-A Review," *Int. J. Eng. Res. Technol.*, vol. 6, no. 3, pp. 315–322, 2013.
3. M. Goel, "Solar rooftop in India: Policies, challenges and outlook," *Green Energy Environ.*, vol. 1, no. 2, pp. 129–137, 2016.
4. N. S. Mission, "Best Practices Guide National Solar Mission Best Practices Guide," no. June, 2016.
5. D. Arvizu *et al.*, *Direct Solar Energy*, no. January. 2012.
6. Dr.Sudhanshu, "Solar Radiation Hand Book," *Sol. Energy*, pp. 1986–2000, 2008.
7. Kharchenko, V., Panchenko, V.,Tikhonov, P. V., & Vasant, P. (2018). Cogenerative PV Thermal Modules of Different Design for Autonomous Heat and Electricity Supply. In *Handbook of Research on Renewable Energy and Electric Resources for Sustainable Rural Development* (pp. 86–119). IGI Global. doi:10.4018/978-1-5225-3867-7.ch004
8. Kharchenko, V., Nikitin, B., Tikhonov, P., Panchenko, V., & Vasant, P. (2019). Evaluation of the Silicon Solar Cell Modules. In G. W. W. P. Vasant & I. Zelinka (Eds.), *Intelligent Computing & Optimization, Advances in Intelligent Systems and Computing* (pp. 328–336). Springer Nature. doi:10.1007/978-3-030-00979-3_34
9. Panchenko, V., Izmailov, A., Kharchenko, V., & Lobachevskiy, Y. (2020). Photovoltaic Solar Modules of Different Types and Designs for Energy Supply. *International Journal of Energy Optimization and Engineering*, 9(2), 74–94. doi:10.4018/IJEOE.2020040106
10. E. M. Authority, *Handbook for Solar Photovoltaic (PV) Systems Contents*, 2011.

11. Panchenko, V. (2019). Photovoltaic solar modules for autonomous heat and power supply. In *IOP Conf. Series: Earth and Environmental Science*. IOP Publishing. doi:10.1088/1755-1315/317/1/012002

12. Stuart Bowden and Christiana Honsberg, "Solar Energy-Degradation and Failure Modes." [Online]. Available: https://pveducation.org/pvcdrom/modules/degradation-and-failure-modes.

13. S. Sharma, D. K. Vishwakarma, P. Bhardwaj, and R. Mathur, "Effects of Maintenance on Performance of Grid Connected Rooftop Solar PV Module System," *Int. J. Recent Trends Eng. Res.*, vol. 4, no. 1, pp. 190–196, 2018.

14. B D Sharma, "A Report on Performance of solar power plants in India," 2011.

15. Wang, H., Meng, X., & Chen, J. (2020). Effect of air quality and dust deposition on power generation performance of photovoltaic module on building roof. *Building Services Engineering Research and Technology*, 41(1), 73–85. doi:10.1177/0143624419868806

16. Manoj, N., Prasad, R., Mathew, M., Jayakumar, A., & Kumar, N. (2019). Case Studies in Thermal Engineering Performance, energy loss, and degradation prediction of roof- integrated crystalline solar PV system installed in Northern India. *Case Studies in Thermal Engineering*, 13, 100409. doi:10.1016/j.csite.2019.100409

17. El Mouatasim, A., & Darmane, Y. (2018). Regression analysis of a photovoltaic (PV) system in FPO. *AIP Conference Proceedings*, 2056(December). Advance online publication. doi:10.1063/1.5084981

18. Guan, Y., Zhang, H., Xiao, B., Zhou, Z., & Yan, X. (2017). *In-situ* investigation of the effect of dust deposition on the performance of polycrystalline silicon photovoltaic modules. *Renewable Energy*, 101, 1273–1284. doi:10.1016/j.renene.2016.10.009

19. A. Allouhi, R. Saadani, T. Kousksou, R. Saidur, A. Jamil, and M. Rahmoune, "Grid-connected PV systems installed on institutional buildings: Technology comparison, energy analysis and economic performance," *Energy Build.*, vol. 130, pp. 188–201, 2016.

20. F. Mejia, J. Kleissl, and J. L. Bosch, "The effect of dust on solar photovoltaic systems," *Energy Procedia*, vol. 49, pp. 2370–2376, 2013.

21. D. Rajput and K. Sudhakar, "Effect of Dust on the Performance of Solar PV Panel," *Academia.Edu*, vol. 5, no. 2, pp. 1083–1086, 2013.

22. J. Tanesab, D. Parlevliet, J. Whale, and T. Urmee, "Dust Effect and its Economic Analysis on PV Modules Deployed in a Temperate Climate Zone," *Energy Procedia*, vol. 100, no. September, pp. 65–68, 2016.

23. S. A. Sulaiman, A. K. Singh, M. M. M. Mokhtar, and M. A. Bou-Rabee, "Influence of dirt accumulation on performance of PV panels," *Energy Procedia*, vol. 50, pp. 50–56, 2014.

24. M. R. Maghami, H. Hizam, C. Gomes, M. A. Radzi, M. I. Rezadad, and S. Hajighorbani, "Power loss due to soiling on solar panel: A review," *Renew. Sustain. Energy Rev.*, vol. 59, pp. 1307–1316, 2016.

25. M. Shravanth Vasisht, J. Srinivasan, and S. K. Ramasesha, "Performance of solar photovoltaic installations: Effect of seasonal variations," *Sol. Energy*, vol. 131, pp. 39–46, 2016.

26. M. Mani and R. Pillai, "Impact of dust on solar photovoltaic (PV) performance: Research status, challenges and recommendations," *Renew. Sustain. Energy Rev.*, vol. 14, no. 9, pp. 3124–3131, 2010.

27. A. Hamza, H. Ali, A. M. Serag, and S. M. Abdel-gaied, "Effect of Dust and Ambient Temperature on PV Panels Performance in Egypt," *Jordan J. Phys.*, vol. 8, no. 2, pp. 113–124, 2015.

28. T. Al Hanai, R. B. Hashim, L. El Chaar, and L. A. Lamont, "Environmental effects on a grid connected 900 W photovoltaic thin-film amorphous silicon system," *Renew. Energy*, vol. 36, no. 10, pp. 2615–2622, 2011.

29. M. Saidan, A. G. Albaali, E. Alasis, and J. K. Kaldellis, "Experimental study on the effect of dust deposition on solar photovoltaic panels in desert environment," *Renew. Energy*, vol. 92, pp. 499–505, 2016.

30. M. J. Adinoyi and S. A. M. Said, "Effect of dust accumulation on the power outputs of solar photovoltaic modules," *Renew. Energy*, vol. 60, pp. 633–636, 2013.

31. A. Bouraiou *et al.*, "Analysis and evaluation of the impact of climatic conditions on the photovoltaic modules performance in the desert environment," *Energy Convers. Manag.*, vol. 106, pp. 1345–1355, 2015.

32. F. Mani, S. Pulipaka, and R. Kumar, "Characterization of power losses of a soiled PV panel in Shekhawati region of India," *Sol. Energy*, vol. 131, pp. 96–106, 2016.

33. B. Shiva Kumar and K. Sudhakar, "Performance evaluation of 10 MW grid connected solar photovoltaic power plant in India," *Energy Reports*, vol. 1, pp. 184–192, 2015.

34. K. Sudhakar and T. Srivastava, "Energy and exergy analysis of 36 W solar photovoltaic module," *Int. J. Ambient Energy*, vol. 35, no. 1, pp. 51–57, 2014.

35. B. Hammad, M. Al-Abed, A. Al-Ghandoor, A. Al-Sardeah, and A. Al-Bashir, "Modeling and analysis of dust and temperature effects on photovoltaic systems' performance and optimal cleaning frequency: Jordan case study," *Renew. Sustain. Energy Rev.*, vol. 82, no. July 2017, pp. 2218–2234, 2018.

36. "MINITAB 17 Statistical Software 2017. Computer Software. Minitab, Inc. Available," 2017. [Online]. Available: www.minitab.com (accessed on 1 July 2018).

37. Renesola, "Virtus® II Module," 2005.

38. Hukseflux Thermal Sensors, "SR20-D2 Pyranometer."

39. http://pinetechsolutions.com/Redirect/Client#/download/87. [Accessed: 01-Jan-2018].

40. "IEC Standard 61724-1:2017, Photovoltaic System Performance—Part 1: Monitoring." [Online]. Available: https://webstore.iec.ch/publication/33622. [Accessed: 01-Jul-2018].

41. Sharma, S., Nayyar, A., & Khatri, K. K. (2021). Research on the Influence of Dust and Ambient Temperature on the Power of Photovoltaic Cells Based on the Regression Method. *International Journal of Energy Optimization and Engineering (IJEOE)*, 10(2), 24-47. doi:10.4018/IJEOE.2021040102

42. Sharma, L. K., Sharma, S., Dubey, Y., & Parwani, L. (2019). Taguchi Method Approach for Multi Factor Optimization of S1 Tool Steel in Electrochemical Machining. Academic Press.

43. Panchenko, V., Kharchenko, V., & Vasant, P. (2019). Modeling of Solar Photovoltaic Thermal Modules. In P. Vasant, I. Zelinka, & G. W. Weber (Eds.), *Intelligent Computing & Optimization* (pp. 108–116). Springer Nature. doi:10.1007/978-3-030-00979-3_11

44. Panchenko, V., & Kharchenko, V. V. P. (2018). Advances in Intelligent Systems and Computing. In G. W. Weber (Ed.), Vasant P. Zelinka I (pp. 108–116). *Intelligent Computing & Optimization*.

9

Evaluation of In-House Compact Biogas Plant Thereby Testing Four-Stroke Single-Cylinder Diesel Engine

Pradeep Kumar Meena[1]*, Sumit Sharma[2]†, Amit Pal[1] and Samsher[1]

[1]Department of Mechanical Engineering, Delhi Technological University, Delhi, India
[2]Dept. of Mech. Engg., Arya College of Engineering and IT, Jaipur, India

Abstract

In metropolitans and cities, most wastages are produced from industries, hotels, messes and households. These wastages are not properly utilized in metropolitans either because of lack of knowledge or time management. In the present study, we are investigating the usefulness of these wastages that are produced by metropolitans and cities to produce biogas. Here, an effort is made to progress a compact biogas plant which can be used to produce biogas on a small scale that can fulfill the essential requirement of common people from urban and rural areas for the purpose of cooking, operating engines, and electricity. A biogas plant requires methane-producing microorganisms to get it ongoing. Once the plant is producing biogas, the bacteria replicate and continue the ongoing process. Therefore, a comprehensive analysis of a compact biogas plant is performed in terms of its temperature, pH value, and efficiency for different kinds of wastages such as kitchen waste, fruits waste, animal dung and sugar as a catalyst, in view to increase production efficiency of biogas. Furthermore, a 4-stroke single-cylinder diesel engine is tested by using dual fuel, i.e., diesel and biogas, in terms of its brake power (BP), indicated power, brake and indicated thermal efficiency (B_{th}, I_{th}), volumetric efficiency, mechanical efficiency, BSFC and ISFC at different loads, to know the effect of biogas on performance of engine as compared with diesel as conventional fuel.

----
*Corresponding author: paru.meena@gmail.com
†Corresponding author: sumitait1111@gmail.com

Pandian Vasant, Gerhard-Wilhelm Weber, Joshua Thomas, José Antonio Marmolejo-Saucedo and Roman Rodriguez-Aguilar (eds.) *Artificial Intelligence for Renewable Energy and Climate Change*, (277–344) © 2022 Scrivener Publishing LLC

Keywords: Biogas, wastages, catalyst, conventional fuel

9.1   Introduction

Unlike other renewable sources of energy, biogas is unique because of its characteristics for use in fertilizer production, organic waste use, control and collection, as well as agricultural irrigation. The use of biogas is very simple since it has no environmental restriction nor does it need advanced technology for energy production.

9.1.1   Benefits of the Use of Biogas as a Fuel in India

Approximately 80% of India's population has access to electricity, but power cuts occur frequently. The worldwide Energy Network Institute states that cuts in several parts of the country have impacted the general economic development. Even with consistency of the electricity supply, it's vital that the population has an alternate source of power, mainly for cooking [1–3]. A biogas system offers users an appropriate method of disposing of biodegradable waste. The authorities in some major cities in Maharashtra, including Mumbai and Pune, do not have an acceptable method for waste biodegradation and it's up to individuals to seek out how to eliminate it. It should, however, be demonstrated that while it's potentially useful in urban environments to be ready to eliminate waste through biogas generators, rural areas probably utilize their biodegradable waste as fertilizer [4, 5]. The waste output slurry produced during biogas are often used as manure and may greatly increase crop yield [6]. Women are usually those delegated the job of collecting firewood for traditional cooking stoves. Gathering the weekly requirements of 30-35 kg of firewood can take up to entire day, which reduces the time that would otherwise be utilized in study or other domestic or public activities [6]. The biogas plants are often used for a source of energy and provide an answer for waste treatment in rural farms, or a source of valuable organic [7]. Biogas addresses the essential needs of rural households amongst which energy may be a priority; it supports decentralized access to household energy; its by-product – bio-slurry – enhances agricultural productivity and promotes organic farming [8]. Biogas can substitute the utilization of kerosene or LPG and also non-commercial fuels like dried trash or crop residues, and firewood, which are a commonly used source of energy for lighting and cooking in rural areas. The biogas technology is rapidly accepted in rural areas of developing countries, where there's usually a shortage of cooking fuels and within the same time a prosperous source for biogas fermentation [9].

9.1.2   Biogas Generators in India

In 1996 and 1997, Tata Energy Research Institute administered a wide-spread investigation into the utilization of biogas generators in India. They inspected over 450 biogas generators in eight states and also completed questionnaires with a variety of plant owners. They published their finding in the report "BIOGAS: The Indian NGO experience" [6]. The study suggests that 81% of the inspected biogas generators were working, and 80% of the working generators were functioning below optimal levels due to defects in equipment, improper use and lack of maintenance. It includes highlights from various studies showing that the planning of biogas generators must be improved if biogas is to become more extensively and productively utilized in India.

9.1.3   Biogas

Biogas may be a mixture of gases released from decomposition of organic matter by anaerobic bacteria within the absence of oxygen (anaerobic conditions) [10]. Major constituents of anaerobic biogas are methane and CO_2. The methane percentage can range from 40 to 85 depending on substrate quality, methanogen vitality, and reactor type [11]. An outsized fraction of the CO_2 remains in solution [12]. Table 9.1 shows the components of biogas. Biogas contains mostly methane, therefore, it is often collected and burned, like gas, for thermal or electric energy. In Denmark, the general

Table 9.1 Components of biogas [18].

Substance	Symbol	Percentage (%)
Methane	CH4	50 - 70
Carbon Dioxide	CO2	30 - 40
Hydrogen	H2	5.0 - 10
Nitrogen	N2	- 2.0
Water Vapour	H2O	0.3
Hydrogen Sulphide	H2S	Traces

public uses digesters to supply both electricity and heating potential for local farms [13]. Several companies make engines compatible with biogas, and promising technology in high-temperature fuel cells can convert and store energy from biogas [14]. The anaerobic digestion method also can be manipulated in a similar way so that it releases a higher percentage of hydrogen gas which will be useful for fuel cells [15]. Biogas often includes a little fraction of sulfide produced from sulfate-reducing bacteria which may be troublesome for various applications [16]. The precise percentage of H2S and others depends on the constituents in substrate [17]. Combustion engines are especially vulnerable to H2S impurities which may be expensive to eliminate.

9.1.3.1 Process of Biogas Production

Anaerobic digestion (AD) is defined as the biodegradation of substrate (organic materials) within the absence of oxygen. Figure 9.1 shows the path of anaerobic digestion. Biogas produced by this method contains hydrogen sulphide, methane, nitrogen, CO2 and oxygen. Normally, anaerobic digestion is administered by thermophilic and mesophilic microorganisms each varied by its temperature. Mesophilic is administered at

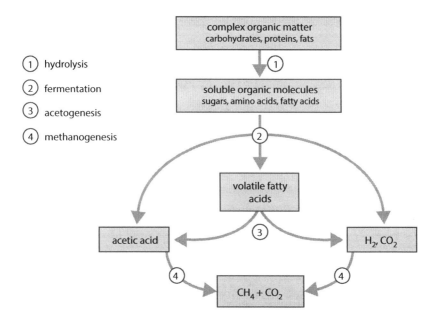

Figure 9.1 Path of anaerobic digestion.

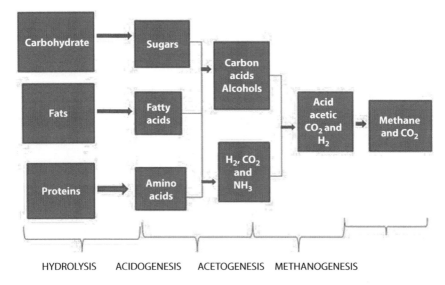

HYDROLYSIS   ACIDOGENESIS   ACETOGENESIS   METHANOGENESIS

Figure 9.2 Anaerobic process microbiology consists of four steps [18].

35°C to 40°C whereas thermophilic is administered at 53°C to 55°C. There are four stages defined in anaerobic digestion, each attributed to different trophic groups. The primary three stages are hydrolysis, acidogenesis, and acetogenesis, which are each completed by special bacterial strains. The last stage is methanogenesis, performed by specialized from of archaically as methanogens [19]. Figure 9.2 shows anaerobic process microbiology.

A. HYDROLYSIS:

This is the first phase of biogas production. In this stage, complex substance (amino acids, fatty acids and sugars) are converted into simple matters (peptidases, alcohol and cellulose) by fermentative bacteria [20]. Sometimes, the rate of biodegradation is very slow because of the complexity of substrate. Hence, a chemical compound is used along with the process to split complex into smaller. For example, polysaccharides into monosaccharides, lipid to fatty acid and protein to amino acids [22].

9.2   Literature Review

9.2.1   Wastes and Environment

According to source of origin, wastes can be divided into five groups: 1) agricultural, 2) municipal, 3) biomedical, 4) industrial, and

5) construction. The distribution of these wastes vary based on cultural background and region. Fruit and vegetable wastes (FVW) are formed by huge quantity by market and comprise a source of trouble in a municipality because of their high biodegradability. These FVW wastes are produced annually—about more than 10 million tons—and currently these are being dumped near to the outskirts of cities [23]. Sectors including agriculture and municipal are the major producers of wastes in Indian society.

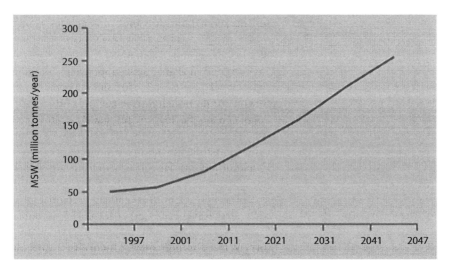

Figure 9.3 Projected trends in the generation of municipal solid waste.

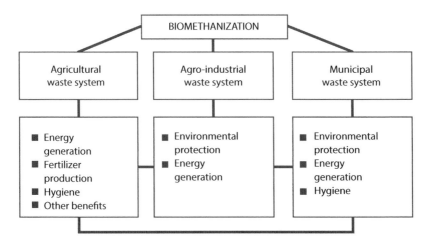

Figure 9.4 Shows the overview of the life cycle analysis of a biomethanization.

Industrial sectors have also not been able to control the emission of obnoxious gases into the atmosphere or handle and treat the wastes generated by them. In spite of strict rules and regulation by the authorities, little has been achieved in terms of minimization waste generation. Currently, waste generation is increasing at a rate of 1.33% (Figure 9.3) [24].

A succession of every energy service analyzed will begin with identification of primary energy source and advancement through the acceptable steps for energy conversion and transportation up to the ultimate devices providing energy service [25].

[26] demonstrated distribution of energy **supported** renewable energy resources like wind, solar, bio-waste and compared it with the payback time of energy. Possessing energy of building materials in India had been reported by [27] and comparisons were performed **to** estimate the energy efficiency of the walling elements and **to spot the foremost** appropriate solution [28]. Various approaches were developed **to scale back the value** and size of the biogas system [29]. The report described the history of energy consumption and building materials in transportation and manufacturing of common or alternative building materials **and therefore the** implication on the environment. Biogas plants with different plant size **are** surveyed **within the** country [30]. The report demonstrated life cycle costing technique by taking **the worth of cash to satisfy the maximum amount** as electric energy demand as possible by an optimal decentralized **mixture of** biomass gasifier generator, biogas generator and photovoltaic. Figure 9.4 shows the overview of the life cycle analysis of a biomethanization.

9.2.2   Economic and Environmental Considerations

Upon selection of anaerobic treatment, various considerations are taken. While the most concentration is on methane as an energy source, those with experience within the field have found equal or greater benefit within the stabilized sludge outcome [31]. There's also the chance to use for carbon credits through such organizations as the Chicago Climate Exchange, for actively reducing methane and CO_2 emissions [32].

Studies suggest that there's a big decrease in biogas production with a rise within the proportion of olive cake in situ of animal waste [33]. Others demonstrated a rise in biogas production when Nickel was added to some extent in anaerobic conditions. A report demonstrated that using of fish offal and brewery solids as co-digestates with cattle slurry produced a rise within the methane yield, compared thereupon of control digestion using cattle slurry alone, while the fruit, vegetable wastes and manure at a degree of 15% total solids depressed the methane yield [34].

Appropriate Rural Technology of India (ARTI), Pune (2003) has developed a compact biogas plant that uses waste food instead of any trash as feedstock, to provide biogas for cooking. This plant is satisfactorily simple and compact to be employed by urban households, and about 2,000 are presently in use both in rural and concrete households in Maharashtra. The architecture with reference to development and style may be simple; however, powerful technology for the people has won ARTI the Ashden Award for Sustainable Energy 2006 within the Food Security category. Dr Anand Karve (ARTI) developed a compact biogas system that uses starchy or sugary feedstock (leftover food, waste grain flour, green leaves, spoilt grain, fruits and rhizomes, overripe no edible seeds or misshapen fruit kitchen waste, etc.). **The sole** use **of two** kg of such feedstock produces about 500 g of methane, **and therefore the** reaction is completed within 24 hours. **The traditional** biogas systems, using sewerage, cattle dung, etc., use about 40 kg feedstock **to supply** a quantity of methane and is completed in about 40 days. Thus, from **the point** of view of the conversion of feedstock into methane, the system developed by Dr Anand Karve is 20 times as efficient **as the** conventional system, and from **the point** of view of **response time, it's** 40 times as efficient. Thus, overall, the new system is 800 times as efficient **as the** conventional biogas system [35].

The report suggests that **about** 20 times **the worldwide** warming potential of **CO2, which means** the concentration of it **within the** atmosphere, is increasing by 1 **to 2% per annum**. The article continues by highlighting that about 3 to 19% of anthropogenic sources of methane originate from landfills [36]. The experiment was conducted to increase biogas production using microbial stimulants [37]. They studied the effect of microbial stimulant aquasan and treason on biogas yield from cattle dung and combined residue of cattle dung and kitchen waste, respectively. The result shows that dual addition of aquasan to cattle dung on day 1 and day 15 increased the gas production by 55% over unimpeded cattle dung and addition of treason to cattle dung: kitchen waste (1:1) mixed residue 15% increased gas production. The report suggests that wet oxidation **within the** presence of oxygen pressure increases **the entire** amount of methane yield in digested bio-waste. Specifically, the yield, which **is generally** 50 to 60%, increased by 35 to 40%, demonstrating the increased ability to retrieve methane **to supply** economic benefits. Recently, studies by one group discussed that anaerobic digestion **may be a** suitable method for the treatment of wastewater and organic wastes, yielding biogas as a useful by-product [38]. However, **due to** instabilities in start-up and operation, **it's** often not considered.

A **standard** way of preventing instability problems and avoiding acidification in anaerobic digesters is **to stay** the organic load of the digester far below its maximum capacity. There are **an outsized** number **of things** that affect biogas production efficiency including high organic loading, inadequate alkalinity, formation of high volatile fatty acids, pH, type and quality of substrate and temperature.

9.2.3   Factor Affecting Yield and Production of Biogas

There are numerous factors involved in the digestion process inside the digester and the quantity of produced biogas: temperature, microbes balance, stirring, substrate type, total solids or moisture, grinding of organic materials, time, carbon/nitrogen ratio (C/N), presence of activators or inhibitors and acidity (pH) [19].

9.2.3.1   The Temperature

There are three ranges of temperature at which digestion process can arise and these assortments are shown in Figure 9.5 [11]:

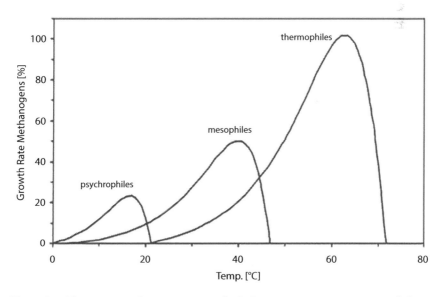

Figure 9.5 Three ranges of temperature at which digestion process can occur and these ranges are [11].

A- Low-temperature range (Psycrophilic bacteria range)
B- Medium-temperature range (Mesophilic bacteria range)
C- High-temperature range (Thermophilic bacteria range)

A. Low-temperature range (Psycrophilic bacteria range but 20°C) Psychrophilic digestion works best at ambient/room temperature and may be a newer development as an anaerobic producer of methane. Researchers in colder climates in Canada – more specifically in Manitoba and Quebec – are working to digest manure waste and produce methane at a gentle rate. The disadvantage to the present technology is that it takes much longer for the methane to be produced.

B. Medium-temperature range (Mesophilic bacteria range 20°C–40°C). It is the foremost common range of digestion due to the robust and stable nature of the bacteria involved. An extended retention time (at least 15–20 days) is required to break down the organic matter and produce biogas. This range is ordinarily most observed for agriculture-food and farming systems. Regarding garbage, several studies have shown that using mesophilic digestion can yield similar amounts of biogas under similar retention times as thermophilic systems while being more stable.

C. High-temperature range (Thermophilic bacteria range 40°C–70°C). Thermophilic digestion systems operate at the very best temperature range. The desirable aspect of this technique is the incontrovertible fact that the micro-organisms rapidly break down the organic material and produce the most important volumes of biogas. This leads to smaller digestion tanks and shorter retention times – often as short as 5-10 days. The disadvantage is that more insulation is required to take care of its temperature range, and more energy is important for heating the system. Additionally, because the method occurs so fast, it's the foremost unstable and most sensitive to small changes within the input material. It's going to be more practical in areas that are warm year-round and have a uniform waste input. It's possible to try thermophilic digestion of garbage.

For the urban environment, **the foremost** promising candidate to digest **garbage** is mesophilic digestion **due to** high organic loading, methane production rates, low retention times and overall stability.

Numerous studies have reported that at larger scales, and smaller scales, mesophilic digestion seems to be **the simplest** candidate. Thermophilic digestion allows for faster methane extraction **and thus features a** lower substrate retention time **and may** be considered in situations where size **may be a** restriction.

9.2.3.2   PH and Buffering Systems

pH is defined **as the** negative logarithm of the hydrogen-ion (H+) concentration and represents a highly important characteristic **because it** affects equilibrium between most chemical species. **So as to work out** whether a substance is acidic or basic, the pH method of expression was developed. Optimal growth **of all** the microbial groups involved in anaerobic degradation is closely connected with pH since it impacts enzyme activity in microorganisms which **may be a** prerequisite **for its** metabolism. Activity reaches a maximum at its optimal pH only within **a selected** pH range which is different **for every** group of microorganisms: for methanogenic archaea the optimal pH comprises a quite narrow interval of 5.5-8.5. For the acidogens pH ranges from 8.5 **right down to** pH 4 [39] with an optimum of around 6 **are** reported. As for the acetogens and methanogens, the optimum is around 7, **and therefore the rate of growth** of methanogens falls sharply at pH < 6.6, pH in an anaerobic one-step treatment process should be maintained **on the brink of** neutrality (6.5-8.0) since acidogenesis also functions at pH approaching neutrality and methanogenesis **is usually** the rate-limiting step [40].

A sufficient level of alkalinity is required to buffer the pH drop **due to** the formation of **acid** during the digestion process. Alkalinity is principally **due to** salts of weak acids **and powerful** bases, and such substances act as buffers to resist a **drop by** pH resulting from acid addition. It acts as a measure of the buffer capacity and is expressed in terms of **carbonate** with concentrations **within the** range of 3000 to 5000 mg/L as $CaCO3$ [41]. The pH of the system is primarily controlled by the presence of bicarbonate ions. Bicarbonate alkalinity **is made** by the destruction of matter containing nitrogen **and therefore the** reaction of the released ammonia nitrogen with the **CO2** produced **within the** reaction [42].

9.2.3.3   C/N Ratio

The relationship that exists between **the quantity** of carbon and nitrogen present in organic materials is expressed in terms of the Carbon/Nitrogen (C/N) ratio. A C/N ratio **starting from** 20 to 30 **is taken into account** optimum for anaerobic digestion. If the C/N ratio **is extremely** high, the nitrogen **are going to be** consumed rapidly by methanogens for meeting their protein requirements **and cannot** react to the leftover carbon content of **the fabric**. Therefore, gas production **is going to be** low. On **the other** hand, if the C/N ratio **is extremely** low, nitrogen **is going to be** liberated and accumulate **within the sort of** ammonia (NH4); NH4 will increase the pH value of the content **within the** digester. A pH **above** 8.5 will start exhibiting a toxic effect on the population of methanogen. Animal waste, mainly cattle dung, has **a mean** C/N ratio of about 24. Plant materials including straw and sawdust contain **a better** percentage of carbon. Human excreta have a C/N ratio as low as 8 [43, 44]. Table 9.2 C/N ratios of commonly used materials.

C/N ratio means the ratio of carbon element amount in organic **interest** its content of nitrogen element amount [19]. **The simplest** C/N ratio is 20-30 atoms of carbon **for every** atom of nitrogen (20-30 carbon atoms: 1 nitrogen atom) [11]. High or low C/N ratio will negatively affect the digestion of the substrate. Organic wastes differ in their C/N ratio, for example; C/N ratio for **trash** is 24, wheat straw is 90, chicken dung is 10 and sheep dung **is 19** [18].

Table 9.2 C/N ratios of commonly used materials.

S. N.	Raw material	C/N ratio
1	Duck dung	8
2	Human excreta	8
3	Chicken dung	10
4	Goat dung	12
5	Pig dung	18
6	Sheep dung	19
7	Cow dung/Buffalo dung	24
8	Water hyacinth	25
9	Elephant dung	43
10	Straw (maize)	60
11	Straw (rice)	70
12	Straw (wheat)	90
13	Saw dust above	200

9.2.3.4 Substrate Type

Anaerobic bacteria can digest all organic materials but they differ **within the interval** required for complete digestion. That is, some are easily digested in a **brief** time (from a few days) while others are hardly digested and take a **while** (months or years), and this is **consistent with** the compounds from which the organic matter **consists** [19]. For example, organic matter with the highest amount of lignin ("its amount increases with plant age, in plant stem **quite** in plant leaves and in horses dung **quite** in other cattle dung" [10] **is the** hardest to be digested. Also, as organic matter contents of cellulose fibers increase, its digestion becomes **harder**. The increasing of volatile solids ("the weight of organic solids burned off when heated to about 538 C°" in organic matter will increase **the quantity** of produced biogas **w**process.

9.2.3.5 Retention Time

The required time for complete digestion of the substrate inside the digester depends on the substrate particles size, substrate stirring and mainly on the temperature of the digester [10]. **Generally, the very best** digester temperature **and therefore the** finest substrate particles size is the shorter retention time. **Consistent with the foremost** reports about anaerobic digestion process the retention time of 40 to 60 days is satisfied for digesters **work on** temperature range between 20 and 35C° [10].

9.2.3.6 Total Solids

Total solids mean **the quantity** of solid particles **within the** unit volume of the slurry **and they are** usually expressed **within the** percentage form. [19] pointed out that the Report suggests that percentage of total solid should be between 5% and 12% while other sources reported that **the simplest** biogas production occur when total solid is ranged from 7% to 10% **due to** avoiding solids settling down or "impeding the flow of gas formed at the lower **part of** digester" [11].

Low solids (LS) Anaerobic digestion systems contain **but** 10% TS, medium solids (MS) about **V-J Day to twenty attempt to** high solids (HS) processes range from 22 **to** 40% [48]. **A rise** in TS **within the** reactor **leads to** a corresponding decrease in reactor volume. When the TS are relatively low, **it's referred to as** wet digestion; dry digestion is when TS is high. Therefore, dilution of organic substrate or wastes with water is required **to realize** the desirable total solids percentage.

9.2.4   Advantages of Anaerobic Digestion to Society

Even though there are many methods **to supply** biogas, anaerobic digestion **is usually** preferred. Other methods which are **related to** producing biogas include rotary drum, aerobic digestion, composting, etc. Many gains **will** be attained by applying the anaerobic digestion method [45, 46].

9.2.4.1   Electricity Generation

From statistics by Susan Reed (2011), **the bulk** of 85 anaerobic digester projects **within the US** utilize biogas produced by the anaerobic digester **to get** electricity [47]. From those projects, anaerobic digesters generate around 331 million kW of electricity annually. The generated electricity **is often** applied for electricity utility, including voltage support and power loss reduction through transmission.

9.2.4.2   Fertilizer Production

The number of fertilizers **is often** commercially produced by using anaerobic digestion. Therefore, **an outsized** amount of fertilizers **is often** produced and as a result, **the value of manufacturing** synthetic fertilizers **is often** reduced. Studies suggest that the digestion process converts organic nitrogen into a mineralized form (ammonia or nitrate-nitrogen) **which will** be **haunted** more quickly by plants than organic nitrogen [49]. **It's** also believed that the fertilizers produced have better efficiency and nutrients for the plant **to soak up** and consequently grow.

9.2.4.3   Pathogen Reduction

As already described, anaerobic digestion **is often** conducted in three temperature ranges. Using thermophilic microorganisms for **the assembly** of gases in anaerobic digestion has the potential to destruct different **sorts of** pathogens thus reducing **the probabilities** for **pollution**. Nonetheless, the high potent methane gas **is often** captured by performing anaerobic digestion. The methane which is captured will benefit by generating energy and **also hamper the speed of worldwide** warming [50]. **The advantages** of anaerobic digestion are summarized as follows.

9.3   Methodology

9.3.1   Set Up of Compact Biogas Plant and Equipments

Following is the equipments required to set up a compact biogas plant.

Table 9.3 Required equipments for a compact biogas plant.

Item	Qty.
Tank (1000 ltrs)	1
Tank (750 ltrs)	1
90 mm "T"	1
90 mm female adapter	1
90 mm male adapter	2
End cap	1
90 mm PVC pipe	15 fit
75 mm Elbow	1
63 mm check nut	1
63 mm male adapter	2
63 mm PVC pipe	15 fit
Ball valve	1
90 mm Barrel Piece	1
63 mm Barrel Piece	1
50 mm Barrel Piece	1
12.5 Barrel Piece	1
12.5 PVC male adapter	1
12.5 mm Metal Elbow	1
Epoxy hardener	30 gms
PVC solution	20 ml
Biogas stove	1
Gas pipe line	1
Gas cock	1
Mixer	1

To set up a compact biogas plant, first of all we require two main plastic tanks; one is used for digester of 1000ltrs and another one is used for gas holder of 750 ltrs. The gases can be produced conforming to the size of the plastic tank and wastage as per the necessity. The above illustrated equipments are assembled for a Compact biogas plant. Table 9.3 shows required equipments for a compact biogas plant.

9.3.2 Assembling and Fabrication of Biogas Plant

A compact biogas plant is portable, which is why it can be used anywhere in urban as well as rural areas. It requires less space because of its small size so it is called a compact biogas plant. Two tanks are required having

Figure 9.6 Assembled compact biogas plant.

volume of 1000 and 750 Ltrs, respectively. The bigger tank, i.e., 1000 Ltrs, is to be cut as per the Figure 9.6. Then two holes were created at the bottom of 90 mm and 50 mm diameter as well as two holes on the top of 63 mm and 90 mm. Then, male adapter is mounted in the hole of 90 mm having some projected part outside, over which a female adapter is attached by using adhesive. Now, a T-joint is to be attached with the female adapter with one closed end; the other end is connected to a vertical PVC pipe of length 115 cm and diameter 90 mm, over which again a T-joint is to be attached with one end open to the atmosphere in order to feed the charge through funnel and the other end is connected to the top hole of 90 mm diameter. The hole of 50 mm diameter at the bottom is used to discharge the slurry through an adapter which is regulated by ball valve, and the hole of 63 mm diameter

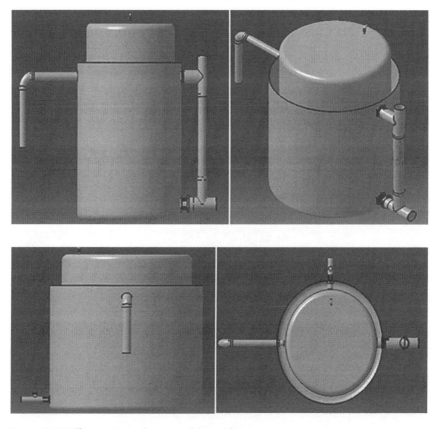

Figure 9.7 Different views of compact biogas plant.

on the top is used to check the overflow of the charge which is extruded outside through a pipe of 63 mm diameter and 45 cm long connected to a pipe of length 60 mm and diameter 63 mm with the help of an elbow. Now, another tank is also to be cut as per the Figure 9.7 and a hole is made at its bottom of 12.5 mm diameter which is extruded through the brass elbow and gas cock which is used to regulate the flow of gas. Figure 9.7 different views of compact biogas plant.

9.3.3   Design and Technology of Compact Biogas Plant

A compact Biogas system **is formed** from two cut-down standard high-density polyethene water tanks and standard plumber piping. The larger tank acts **as the** container containing the **waste** while the smaller one is inverted and telescoped into this larger one. This smaller inverted tank **is the** floating **death chamber**, whose rise is proportional to the produced gas and acts as a **space for storing** for the gas. Figures 9.8 and 9.9 shows compact biogas plant.

Space of about 2 m2 area **and a couple of** .5 m height **are required** for 1000 l as shown in Figure 9.8. The effective volume of the digester is approximately 850 Ltrs, given by the dimension of the 1000 Ltrs **cistern** (inner radius: 51.5 cm) **and therefore the** position of the overflow pipe

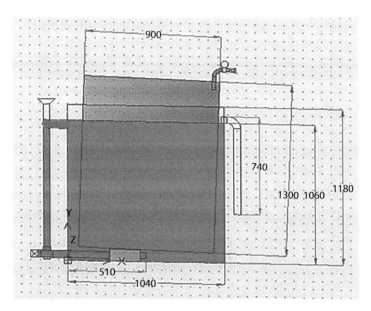

Figure 9.8 Compact biogas plant with empty gasholder at the experiment start (all dimensions in mm).

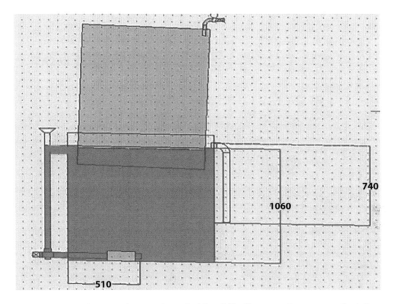

Figure 9.9 Compact biogas plant with gasholder full of biogas after 4-5 weeks (all dimensions in mm).

(1.04 m above ground level). Roughly 0.6 m2 (78%) of **the entire area** of the digester (0.83 m2) **is roofed** by the gasholder. In other words, the gas released through 22% of the digester surface is lost to the atmosphere without being utilized. The usable gas volume of the 750 l-gasholder is 400 l.

9.3.4   Gas Quantity and Quality

Figure 9.10 shows gas quantity in gas holder whereas Figure 9.11 gas quantity calculated manually.

9.3.5   Calculation of Gas Quantity in Gas Holder

Table 9.4 testing data of 50 kg animal dung along with 500 ltrs water.

Inner Radius of gas holder = 0.43 m
Area of gasholder = 3.14 x (0.43 m)^2 = 0.58 m^2
Total usable height of gas holder = 0.69 m
Usable gas volume = 0.69 m x 0.58 m^2 = 0.4m^3

First of all, marking is done from 0 to 100, 100 to 200, 200 to 300, and 300 to 400 points on the gas holder as a scale by taking of difference of 17.25 cm

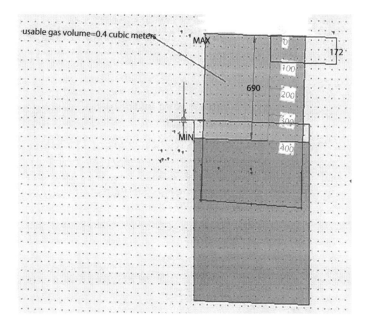

Figure 9.10 Gas quantity in gas holder (all dimensions in mm).

Figure 9.11 Gas quantity calculated manually (all dimensions in mm).

Table 9.4 Testing data of 50 kg animal dung along with 500 ltrs water.

No. of days	Temperature of digester (°C)	pH of digester	Biogas production (m³)
1	19	7	-
2	19	7	-
3	19.5	7	-
4	19.5	7	-
5	20	7	-
6	20	7	-
7	20	7	-
8	21	7	-
9	21	7	-
10	21.	6.5	-
11	22	6.5	0.0029
12	22.	6.5	0.0058
13	23	6.5	0.0116
14	23.5	6.5	0.0203
15	23.5	6.5	0.029
16	24	6.5	0.0377
17	23	6	0.0464
18	22	6	0.058
19	22	6	0.0696
20	21	6	0.0841
21	24	6	0.0986
22	24	6	0.116
23	25	6	0.1334

(*Continued*)

Table 9.4 Testing data of 50 kg animal dung along with 500 ltrs water. (*Continued*)

No. of days	Temperature of digester (°C)	pH of digester	Biogas production (m³)
24	25	6	0.1508
25	24	6	0.1682
26	25	6	0.1827
27	25.5	6	0.203
28	26.2	5.5	0.2262
29	26.2	5.5	0.2436
30	26.1	5.5	0.261
31	27	6	0.2726
32	28	6	0.2987
33	28.5	5.5	0.319
34	29	5	0.3422
35	29.2	5	0.3654
36	28.2	5	0.377
37	28	5.5	0.377
38	28	5.5	0.3828
39	28.4	5.5	0.3828
40	28.6	5.5	0.3886
41	28.8S	5.5	0.3886
42	29.2	5	0.3944
43	29	5	0.3944
44	28.4	5	0.4002

between the subsequent points. Thus, total height of gas holder for usable gas is 69 cm and volume of the gas holder occupied by the gas is calculated.

9.4   Analysis of Compact Biogas Plant

9.4.1   Experiment Result

After setup of compact biogas plant, we investigated the effect of various waste substrates (animal dung, kitchen waste, and fruit waste) and calculated the efficiency of biogas producing by these substrates. We have taken care of factor during biogas production, including temperatures, number of days and pH.

9.4.1.1   Testing on 50 Kg Animal Dung Along With 500 Ltrs Water

Interestingly, we observed temperature variation from 19 to 29.2 degree Celsius, and pH from 7.5 to 5 which took 44 days to produce 0.4 m³ of

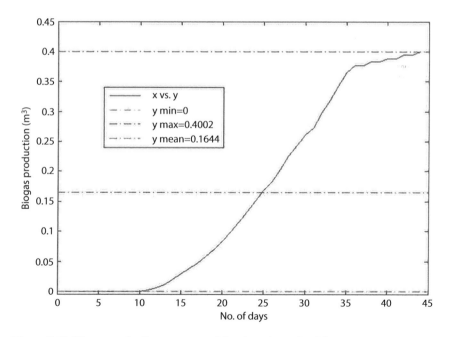

Figure 9.12 Biogas production w.r.t. no. of days by using animal dung.

biogas by using 50 kg of animal dung along with 500 ltrs of water. Figure 9.12 biogas production w.r.t. no. of days by using animal dung.

9.4.1.2   Testing on Kitchen Waste

With the use of kitchen waste for the same setup and condition, biogas production was estimated as shown below.

We observed temperature variation from 28 to 29 degrees Celsius, and pH from 6 to 6.5 which took 9 days to produce 0.4 m^3 of biogas using 3.1 kg of kitchen waste along with 11 to 12 ltrs water. Figure 9.13 shows biogas production w.r.t. no. of days by using kitchen waste. Table 9.5 testing data for kitchen waste.

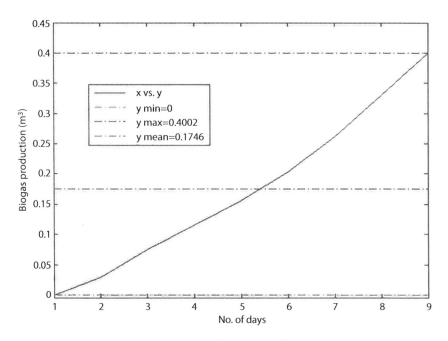

Figure 9.13 Biogas production w.r.t. no. of days by using kitchen waste.

Table 9.5 Testing data for kitchen waste.

No. of days	Content	Temp. of digester (°C)	pH of digester	Biogas production (m³)
1	500 g kitchen waste (5 Capsicum, 5 tomato, 5 brinjal, 2 onion Other) and 2.5 ltrs water	28	6	0
3	500 g kitchen waste (5 Capsicum, 5 tomato, 5 brinjal, 2 onion Other) and 2.5 ltrs water	28.2	6.2	0.0754
5.	with 700 g kitchen waste (4 edli or one potato other vegetable) with 2.8 ltrs water	28.6	6.5	0.0812
7.	1 kg kitchen waste (potato vegetable, rice) with 3 ltrs water	28	6.5	0.1044
9.	1.1 kg kitchen waste (tee or rice) total 2.9 ltrs water	27.6	6	0.1392
	Total kitchen waste = 3.1 kg			Total = 0.4002
11.	1.5 kg (tee or vegetable) total 2.5 ltrs water	29	6	0.1508

9.4.1.3   Testing on Fruits Waste

In this experiment, fruits waste was used to produce biogas instead of other wastes in the same set up.

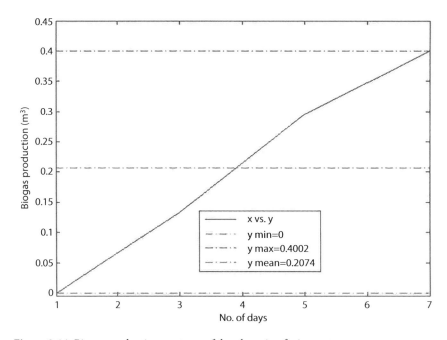

Figure 9.14 Biogas production w.r.t. no. of days by using fruits waste.

Table 9.6 Testing data of fruits waste.

No. of days	Content	Temp of digester (°C)	pH of digester	Biogas production (m³)
1.	500 gm fruits (orange, watermelon, pineapple, banana, mango) with 2.5 ltrs water	26.	6.2	0
3.	500 gm fruits (orange, watermelon, pineapple, banana, mango) with 2.5 ltrs water	27.	6.5	0.1334

(*Continued*)

Table 9.6 Testing data of fruits waste. (*Continued*)

No. of days	Content	Temp of digester (°C)	pH of digester	Biogas production (m³)
5.	700 gm fruits (orange, watermelon, pineapple, banana. mango) with 2.8 ltrs water	32.	6.5	0.1624
7.	1 kg fruits (orange, watermelon, pineapple, banana, mango) with 3 ltrs water	33	6.5	0.1798
	Total fruit waste=2.2 kg		Total biogas =	0.4756
9.	1.1 kg fruits (orange, watermelon, pineapple, banana, mango) with 2.9 ltrs water	33.	7	0.1972
11.	1.5 kg fruits (orange, watermelon, pineapple, banana, mango) with 2.5 ltrs water	32	7	0.2204

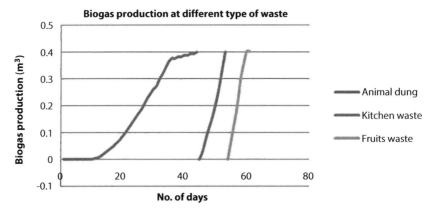

Figure 9.15 Biogas productions w.r.t. no. of days by using animal dung, kitchen waste, and fruits waste.

We observed temperature variation from 27.8 to 33.2 degree Celsius, and pH from 6.5 to 7 which took 4-5 days to produce 0.4 m³ of biogas using 2.2 kg of fruits waste along with 8 to 9 ltrs water. Figure 9.14 Biogas production w.r.t. no. of days by using fruits waste. Table 9.6 Testing data of fruits waste.

9.4.2   Comparison of Biogas by Different Substrate

Figure 9.15 shows biogas productions w.r.t. no. of days by using animal dung, kitchen waste, and fruits waste.

9.4.3   Production of Biogas Per Day at Different Waste

Figure 9.16 shows variation of biogas production per day for 34 days by using animal dung; average production per day is 0.012 m³.

Figure 9.17 shows variation of biogas production on alternate day for 9 days by using kitchen waste; average production per day is 0.044 m³.

Figure 9.18 shows variation of biogas production on alternate day for 7 days by using fruits waste; average production per day is 0.057 m³.

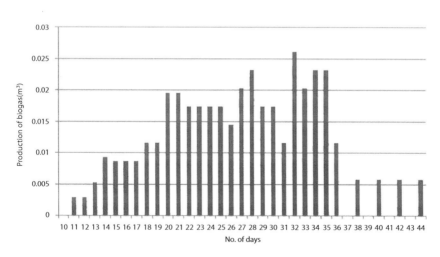

Figure 9.16 Production of biogas per day for animal dung.

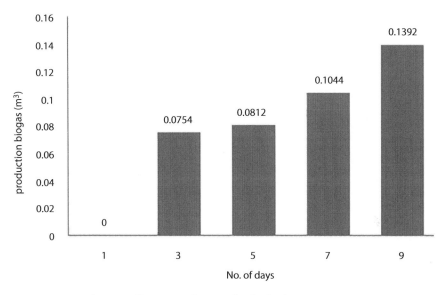

Figure 9.17 Production of biogas on alternate day for kitchen waste.

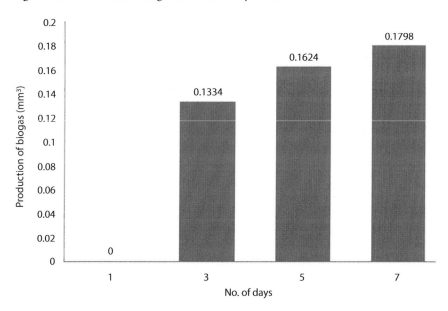

Figure 9.18 Production of biogas on alternate day for fruits waste.

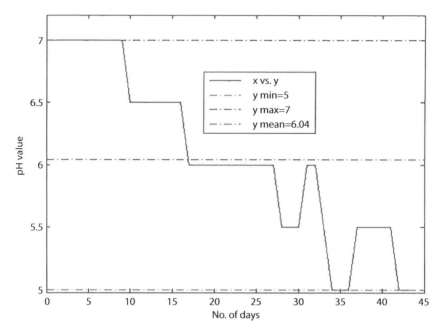

Figure 9.19 pH value variation w.r.t. no. of days by using animal dung.

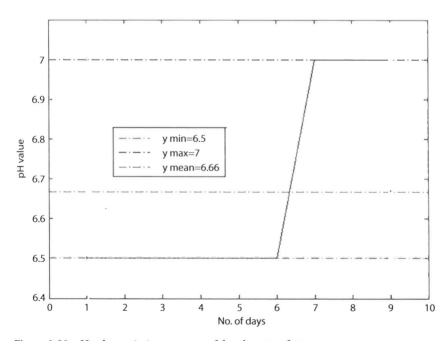

Figure 9.20 pH value variation w.r.t. no. of days by using fruits waste.

9.4.4 Variation of PH Value

Figures 9.19 and 9.20 shows variation of PH value w.r.t. no. of days for animal dung, kitchen waste and fruits waste.

9.4.5 Variation of Average pH Value

- It is observed in Figure 9.19 that minimum pH is 5, and maximum pH is 7.5 and mean pH 6.09 for animal dung during 44 days of experiment. pH value is dropping due to formation of carbonic acid.

$$CO_2 + H_2O \rightleftharpoons H_2CO_3$$

This carbonic acid is neutralized by bicarbonate which is obtained by the reaction of ammonia released from nitrogen containing waste and CO_2 with water

$$NH_3 + H_2O + CO_2 \rightarrow NH_4^+ + HCL_3^-$$
$$HCO_3^- + HA_C \rightleftharpoons H_2O + CO_2 + A_{C^-}$$

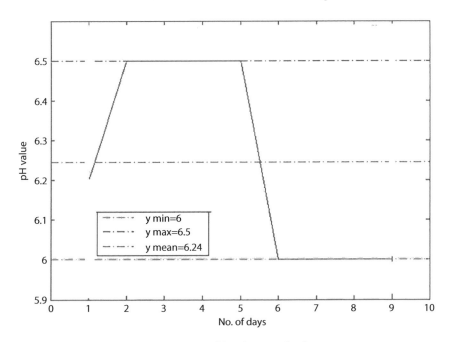

Figure 9.21 pH value variation w.r.t. no. of days by using kitchen waste.

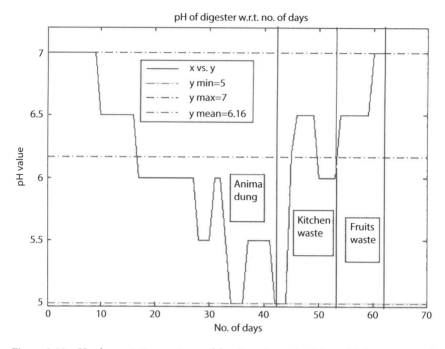

Figure 9.22 pH value variation w.r.t. no. of days by using animal dung, kitchen waste, and fruits waste.

In this case the carbonic acid is continuously forming, and because of less amount of nitrogen contents by animal dung, this results in the decrease in formation of bicarbonate, which helps in the neutralization of the acid. Therefore, the acidity of the waste is increased, which results in the decrease in the pH value. By adding strong base (calcium hydro oxide) externally, the acidity of the waste is neutralized, thereby increasing pH value. Figure 9.19 shows that minimum pH is 6.5, maximum pH is 7 and mean pH 6.66 for fruits waste during 9 days of the experiment. Figure 9.21 shows that minimum pH is 6, maximum pH is 6.5 and mean pH 6.24 for kitchen waste during 9 days of the experiment. Figure 9.22 shows that minimum pH is 5, maximum pH 7.5 and mean pH is 6.22 for animal dung, kitchen waste, and fruits waste during 62 days of the experiment.

9.4.6 Variation of Temperature

Figures 9.23, 9.24, 9.25 shows variation of temperature w.r.t. no. of days for animal dung, kitchen waste and fruits waste.

9.4.7   Variation of Average Temperature With Respect to No. of Days for Animal Dung, Kitchen Waste, Fruits Waste and Sugar

- It is observed in Figure 9.23 that minimum temperature was 19°C maximum temperature 29°C and mean temperature 24.44°C of animal dung during 44 days of experiment. Figure 9.24 shows that minimum temperature was 27.6°C, maximum temperature 29°C and mean temperature 28.28°C of kitchen waste during 9 days of the experiment. Figure 9.25 shows that minimum temperature was 27.8°C, maximum temperature 33.2°C and mean temperature 31.76°C of fruits waste during 9 days of the experiment. It is also observed in Figure 9.26 that minimum temperature was 19°C, or maximum temperature 33.2°C and mean temperature 26.38°C of animal dung, kitchen waste, and fruits waste during 62 days of the experiment.

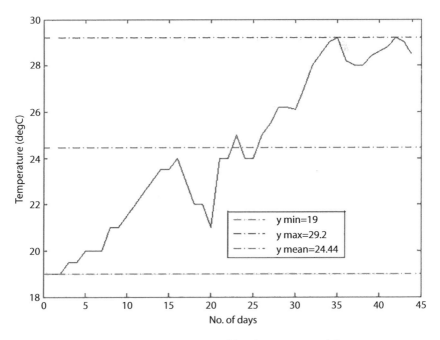

Figure 9.23 Temperature variation w.r.t. no. of days by using animal dung.

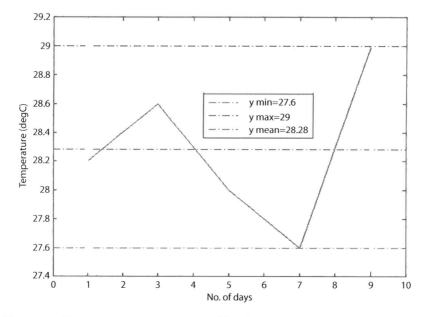

Figure 9.24 Temperature variation w.r.t no. of days by using kitchen waste.

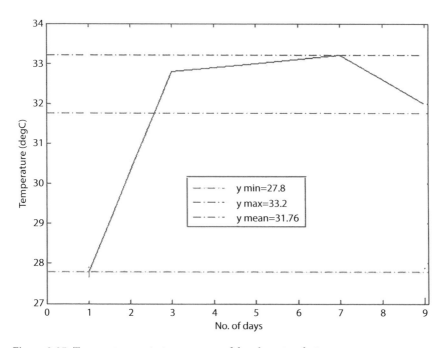

Figure 9.25 Temperature variation w.r.t. no. of days by using fruits waste.

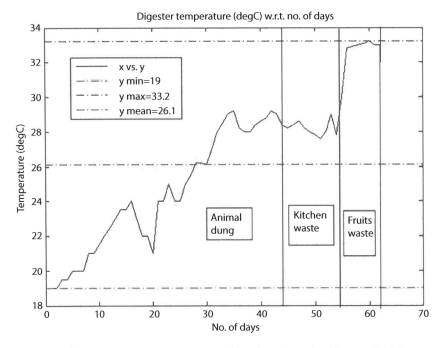

Figure 9.26 Temperature variation w.r.t. no. of days by using animal dung animal dung, kitchen waste, and fruits waste.

9.4.8   Variation of Biogas Production W.R.T. Quantity of Kitchen Waste and Fruits Waste

- Figure 9.27 shows biogas production at different quantities of kitchen waste and minimum production of biogas starts from 0 and approaches maximum production of 0.1508 m^3 with mean production of 0.09183 m^3 for different quantities of kitchen waste ranging from 0 to 1500 gm, i.e., minimum and maximum quantity of kitchen waste with mean quantity of 800 gm.

- Figure 9.28 shows biogas production at different type of quantity of kitchen waste and minimum production of biogas starts from 0 and maximum production of biogas is 0.2204 m^3 and mean biogas production is 0.1489 m^3 at minimum quantity of fruits waste which ranges from 0 to 1500 gm, i.e., maximum quantity of fruits waste or mean quantity is 800 of fruits waste. We observed that experimentally biogas production rate is increased by using fruits waste in comparison to kitchen waste.

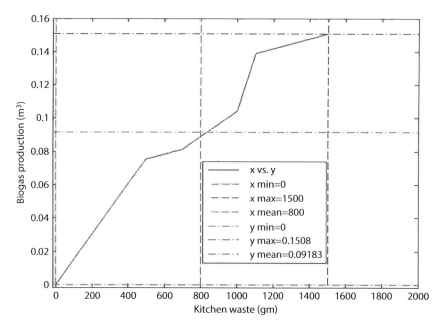

Figure 9.27 Biogas production at different quantities of kitchen waste.

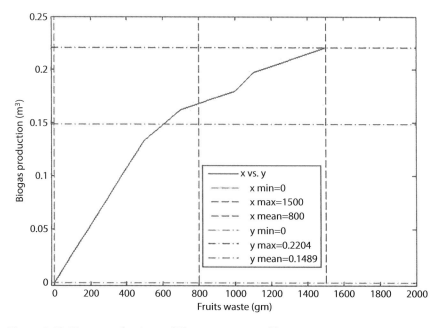

Figure 9.28 Biogas production at different quantities of fruits waste.

9.5 Analysis of Single-Cylinder Diesel Engine on Dual Fuel

Diesel oil supply is connected with burette through **an impact** valve which is further connected to the injector of the engine. Fuel consumption is measured with **reference to** time through **the size** on the burette. The air pipe is connected to the engine, and water from the pump **is employed to chill** the engine and its inlet and outlet temperature is measured at different loads; **also the** inlet and outlet temperature of the water entering the calorimeter **is additionally** measured during the experiment. Exhaust gas temperature is measured at two different points, i.e., inlet and outlet of the calorimeter. The dynamometer **is used to vary** the load on the engine. Figure 9.29 schematic diagram of 4-stroke single-cylinder diesel engine.

9.5.1 Testing on 4-Stroke Single-Cylinder Diesel Engine

After production of the biogas successfully, it's utilized to run a 4-stroke single-cylinder diesel so as to work out the performance of the engine in terms of its power and efficiency. The diesel is converted into a dual-fuel engine followed by its comparative analysis [51]. Table 9.7 shows time taken to consume 10 cc of fuel (10 ml) at different load and constant rpm.

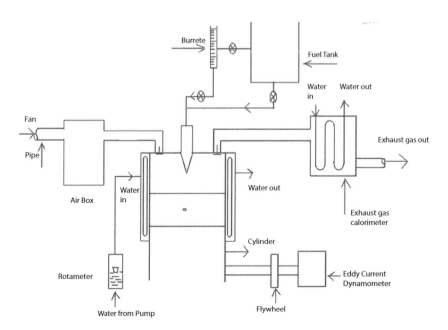

Figure 9.29 Schematic diagram of 4-stroke single-cylinder diesel engine.

Table 9.7 Time taken to consume 10 cc of fuel (10 ml) at different load and constant rpm.

S. no.	Weight (W) kg	Speed (rpm)	Time taken to consume 10 cc of fuel (10ml) i.e 't' sec
1	0	685	74
2	0	685	73
3	0	685	69
4	0	685	70
5	0	685	74
			Average time = 72
1	2	685	56
2	2	685	54
3	2	685	55
4	2	685	53
5	2	685	52
			Average time = 54
1	4	685	45
2	4	685	43
3	4	685	41
4	4	685	42
5	4	685	44
			Average time = 43
1	6	685	37
2	6	685	34
3	6	685	33
4	6	685	36
5	6	685	35

(Continued)

Table 9.7 Time taken to consume 10 cc of fuel (10 ml) at different load and constant rpm. (*Continued*)

S. no.	Weight (W) kg	Speed (rpm)	Time taken to consume 10 cc of fuel (10ml) i.e 't' sec
			Average time = 35
1	8	685	28
2	8	685	29
3	8	685	25
4	8	685	24
5	8	685	29
			Average time = 27
1	10	685	23
2	10	685	25
3	10	685	24
4	10	685	21
5	10	685	22
			Average time = 23

Table 9.8 Testing results by using diesel fuel on 4-stroke single-cylinder diesel engine.

Sr. no.	Particulars						
1	Weight (W) kg	0	2	4	6	8	10
2	Speed (N) rpm	685	685	685	685	685	685
3	Time taken to consume 10 cc of fuel (10ml) i.e. 't' sec.	72	54	43	35	27	23
4	Temperature of Cooling Water entering the jacket in °C (T_{wi})	29	29	29	29	29	29

(*Continued*)

Table 9.8 Testing results by using diesel fuel on 4-stroke single-cylinder diesel engine. (*Continued*)

Sr. no.	Particulars						
5	Temperature of Cooling Water leaving the jacket in °C (T_{wo})	38	40	43	45	48	50
6	Quantity of jacket Cooling water in lit/hr (M_{wj})	160	160	160	160	160	160
7	Exhaust gas temperature leaving cylinder and entering calorimeter in °C ($T_g = T_{gi}$)	130	165	200	260	315	380
8	Temperature of water entering in to calorimeter in °C (T_{wic})	29	29	29	29	29	29
9	Temperature of water leaving from calorimeter in °C (T_{woc})	34	34	35	36	38	39
10	Temperature of exhaust gases leaving the calorimeter in °C (t_{g2})	40	43	44	58	63	78
11.	RPM of the fan	450	450	450	475	475	465
12	Room Temperature in °C	24	24	24	24	24	24
13	Quantity of water supplied to exhaust gas calorimeter in lit/hr (M_{wc})	135	135	135	135	135	135

Table 9.8 shows testing results by using diesel fuel on 4-stroke single-cylinder diesel engine.

9.5.2   Calculation

Specification and constants

1. Sp. Gravity of fuel = .83
2. Sp. Gravity of water = 1
3. Water density, $\rho_w = 1000$ kg/m³

4. Sp. heat of water = K = 4.187 kJ/kg K
5. Gas constant for air Ra) = 0.287 kJ/kg K
6. Calorific value of fuel (C_v) = 42500 kJ/Kg
7. Bore = 0.102 m
8. Stoke = 0.111 m
9. Power = 7.5 kW at 1500 rpm
10. Speed = 1500
11. Radius of fan = 0.274 m
12. Arm length of dynamometer = 0.4 m
13. Diameter of pipe = 0.06 m
14. Compression ratio = 18.5
15. All reading is taken at constant 685 RPM

For 0 kg load

A. Mass of fuel/s =?

10 cc fuel in 72 sec

So, for $1\sec = \dfrac{10}{72}$ cc, and $\dfrac{10}{72} \times 10^{-6} \times$ sp. gravity of fuel $\times$ water density

So, for $1\sec = \dfrac{10}{72} \times 0.83 \times 10^{3} \times 10^{-6} = 0.11 \times 10^{-3}$ kg/sec

For 2 kg load,

10 cc in 54 sec
So, for

$$1\sec = \frac{10}{54} \times 0.83 \times 10^{3} \times 10^{-6} = 0.15 \times 10^{-3} \text{kg/sec} \qquad (9.1)$$

A. Brake power $= \dfrac{2\pi NT}{60}$

(Torque) T = 2x 9.81 x arm length

T = 2 x 9.81 x .4

T = 7.84 Nm

So, BP = 0.562 kW

For 4 kg load,

10 cc in 43 sec
So, for

$$1\,\sec = \frac{10}{43}\times 0.83\times 10^{3}\times 10^{-6}=0.19\times 10^{-3}\text{kg/sec} \qquad (9.2)$$

A. $BP = \dfrac{2\pi NT}{60}$

T = 4 × 9.81 × 0.4 = 15.69 Nm
BP = 1.12 kW

For 6 kg load

10 cc in 35 sec
So, for

$$1\,\sec = \frac{10}{35}\times 0.83\times 10^{3}\times 10^{-6} = 0.23\times 10^{-3}\text{kg/sec} \qquad (9.3)$$

T = 6 x 9.81 x0.4 = 23.544 Nm
A. Brake power (BP) $= \dfrac{2\pi NT}{60} = 1.68$ kW

For 8 kg load

10 cc in 27 sec
So, for

$$1\,\sec = \frac{10}{27}\times 0.83\times 10^{3}\times 10^{-6}=0.30\times 10^{-3}\text{kg/sec} \qquad (9.4)$$

T = 8 x 9.81 x 0.4
T = 31.392 Nm
A. $BP = \dfrac{2\pi NT}{60} = 2.25$ kW

For 10 kg load
Figure 9.30 shows brake power (BP) vs. Mass flow rate of diesel testing.

Mass of fuel/sec = ?
10 cc in 23 sec
So, for

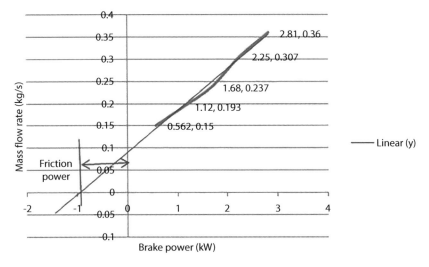

Figure 9.30 Brake power (BP) vs. Mass flow rate of diesel testing

$$1 \sec = \frac{10}{23} \times 0.83 \times 10^3 \times 0^{-6} = 0.36 \times 10^{-3} \text{kg/sec} \qquad (9.5)$$

(Torque) T = 10 x 9.81 x arm length
T = 10 x 9.81 x 0.4
T= 39.24 Nm

B. Brake Power (BP) $= \dfrac{2\pi NT}{60}$

BP = 2.81 kW

2. Find out the friction power (FP) 0.9 kW take from graph

3. Indicated power (IP)

$$IP = BP + FP$$

- Indicated power for 2 kg load = 0.562 +0.9 = 1.462 kW

4. Brake thermal efficiency (B_{th})

$$B_{th} = \frac{Brake\ power}{Mass\ flow\ rate \times calorific\ value\ of\ fuel} \times 100$$

- Brake thermal efficiency for 2 kg load

$$= \frac{0.562}{0.15 \times 10^{-3} \times 42500} = 8.81\%$$

5. Indicated thermal efficiency (I_{th})

$$I_{th} = \frac{Indicated\ power}{Mass\ flow\ rate \times calorific\ value\ of\ fuel} \times 100$$

- Indicated thermal efficiency for 0 kg load

$$= \frac{0.9}{0.11 \times 10^{-3} \times 42500} \times 100 = 19.25\%$$

- Indicated thermal efficiency for 2 kg load

$$= \frac{1.462}{0.15 \times 10^{-3} \times 42500} \times 100 = 22.93\%$$

6. Brake specific fuel consumption (BSFC)

$$BSFC = \frac{Mass\ flow\ rate}{Brake\ power}$$

- Brake specific fuel consumption for 2 kg load

$$= \frac{0.15 \times 3600 \times 10^{-3}}{0.562} = 0.96\ kg/kWh$$

7. Indicated specific fuel consumption

$$Indacated\ specific\ fuel\ consumption\ (ISFC) = \frac{Mass\ flow\ rate}{Indicated\ power}$$

- Indicated specific fuel consumption for 2 kg load

$$= \frac{0.15 \times 3600 \times 10^{-3}}{1.462} = 0.36 \text{ kg/kWh}$$

8. Mechanical efficiency

Table 9.9 shows results of diesel testing.

$$\text{Mechanical efficiency} = \frac{Brake\ power}{Indicated\ power}$$

Table 9.9 Results of diesel testing.

Sr. no.	Particulars						
1	Load W in kg	0	2	4	6	8	10
2	BP in kW	0	0.562	1.12	1.68	2.25	2.81
3	FP in kW	0.9	0.9	0.9	0.9	0.9	0.9
4	IP in kW	0.9	1.462	2.02	2.58	3.15	3.17
5	Brake thermal efficiency in %		8.81	13.65	16.67	17.24	18.36
6	Indicated thermal efficiency in %	19.25	22.93	24.62	25.61	24.14	24.24
7	Mechanical efficiency in %	0	38.44	55.44	65.11	71.42	75.74
8	BSFC in kg/kWH	-	0.96	0.62	0.5	0.49	0.46
9	ISFC in kg/kWH	0.44	0.36	0.34	0.33	0.35	0.34
10	Volumetric efficiency in %	71.36	71.36	71.36	75.25	75.24	73

- Mechanical efficiency for 2 kg load $= \dfrac{0.562}{1.462} = 38.44\%$

9. Volumetric efficiency in %

$$\text{Volumetric efficiency} = \dfrac{Actual\ volume}{Theroretical\ volume}$$

- Volumentric efficiency for 2 kg load

$$= \dfrac{\dfrac{\pi}{4} \times 0.06^2 \times 0.0275 \times \dfrac{2\pi \times 450}{60}}{\dfrac{\pi}{4} \times 0.102^2 \times 0.11 \times \dfrac{685}{2\ x\ 60}} = 71.36\%$$

9.5.3 Heat Balance Sheet

Calculation for 2 kg load,
Tables 9.10 to 9.14 shows the heat balance sheet with different loads.

Table 9.10 Heat balance sheet for 2 kg load.

Sr. no.	Heat supplied	kJ/min		% heat supplied
1	Heat Supplied by combustion of fuel	382.5		100%
2	Heat Expenditure		%	
A.	Heat equivalent of BP	33.75	8.81	
B.	Heat lost to jacket cooling water	122.76	32.09	
C.	Heat lost to exhaust gases	52.42	32.09	
D.	Heat lost due to radiation, errors of observation etc. by difference	173.6	13.7	
			Total = 100%	Total = 100%

Table 9.11 Heat balance sheet for 4 kg load.

Sr. no.	Heat supplied	kJ/min	% Heat expenditure	% Heat supplied
1	Heat Supplied by combustion of fuel	492.15		100%
2	Heat Expenditure			
A.	Heat equivalent of BP	67.2	13.65	
B.	Heat lost to jacket cooling water	156.24	31.74	
C.	Heat lost to exhaust gases	61.85	12.42	
D.	Heat lost due to radiation, errors of observation etc. by difference	207.18	42.09	
			Total = 100%	Total = 100%

Table 9.12 Heat balance sheet for 6 kg load.

Sr. no.	Heat supplied	kJ/min	% Heat expenditure	% Heat supplied
1	Heat Supplied by combustion of fuel	604.35		100%
2	Heat Expenditure			
A.	Heat equivalent of BP	100.8	16.67	
B.	Heat lost to jacket cooling water	178.56	29.54	
C.	Heat lost to exhaust gases	75.28	12.44	
D.	Heat lost due to radiation, errors of observation etc. by difference	250.13	41.38	
			Total = 100%	Total = 100%

Table 9.13 Heat balance sheet for 8 kg load.

Sr. no.	Heat supplied	kJ/min	% Heat expenditure	% Heat supplied
1	Heat Supplied by combustion of fuel	782.85		100%
2	Heat Expenditure			
A.	Heat equivalent of BP	135	17.24	
B.	Heat lost to jacket cooling water	212.05	27.08	
C.	Heat lost to exhaust gases	96.06	12.27	
D.	Heat lost due to radiation, errors of observation etc. by difference	340.77	43.47	
			Total = 100%	Total = 100%

Table 9.14 Heat balance sheet for 10 kg load.

Sr. no.	Heat supplied	kJ/min	% Heat expenditure	% Heat supplied
1	Heat Supplied by combustion of fuel	920.21		100%
2	Heat Expenditure			
A.	Heat equivalent of BP	168.6	18.32	
B.	Heat lost to jacket cooling water	234.37	18.36	
C.	Heat lost to exhaust gases	109.3	11.87	
D.	Heat lost due to radiation, errors of observation etc. by difference	407.94		
			Total = 100%	Total = 100%

1. Heat supplied = M_f x C_v

Heat supplied = 0.15 x 10^{-3} x 60 x 42500 = 382.5 kJ/min   (9.1)

Heat equivalent to BP = 0.562 x 60 = 33.72 kJ/min   (9.2)

Heat lost to jacket cooling water = $m_w Cp_w$ $(Tw_o - Tw_i)$ = 2.67 x 4.18 (40-29) = 122.76 kJ/min   (9.3)

Heat lost due to exhaust gases = $m_g Cp_g (T_g - T_a)$

$$Now, m_g Cp_g (Tg - Tg_{oc}) = m_{wc} Cp_w (Tw_{oc} - Tw_{ci})$$

$$= \frac{135}{60} \times 4.18 (34 - 29) = 47.025$$

$$m_g Cp_g = \frac{47.025}{(165 - 43)} = 0.385$$

$$m_g Cp_g (T_g - T_a) = 0.385 (165 - 29) = 52.42 \text{ kJ/min} \quad (9.4)$$

Heat unaccounted, = Eq^n (1)-(2)+(3)+(4) =173.6 kJ/min
Heat supplied = 100 %

$$\text{Heat equivalent to BP} = \frac{BP}{Heat\ supplied} = \frac{33.72}{382.5} = 8.81\%$$

$$\text{Heat lost to jacket cooling water} = \frac{122.76}{382.5} = 32.09\%$$

$$\text{Heat lost to exhaust gases} = \frac{52.42}{382.5} = 13.70\%$$

$$\text{Heat unaccounted} = \frac{173.6}{382.5} = 45.38\%$$

Similarly, Heat balance sheet can be prepared for 4 kg, 6kg, 8 kg,10 kg load.

9.5.4 Testing Result With Dual Fuel (Biogas and Diesel) on 4-Stroke Single-Cylinder Diesel Engine

Venturi pipe is connected in between air pipe which is connected to the engine and other inlet of venturi pipe is connected to the gasometer

Figure 9.31 Connection of dual fuel engine.

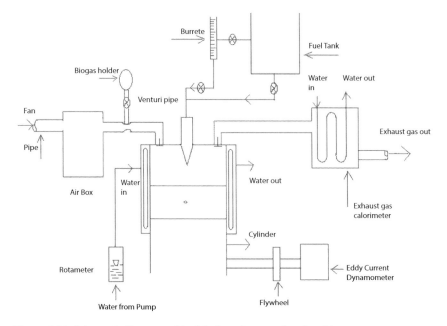

Figure 9.32 Schematic diagram of dual fuel mode using diesel and biogas.

through gas pipe. Mixing of air and biogas occurs within the reduced section of the venturi due to the pressure difference, and this mixture enters into the engine where it's compressed to boost the temperature above the auto-ignition temperature of the diesel. Since the auto-ignition temperature of the biogas is far above that of diesel the mixture doesn't pre-ignite within the engine. As soon as the mixture enters into the engine, it's compressed, and diesel is injected which further increases the general temperature of the fuel after burning for the entire combustion of dual fuel. Figure 9.31 connection of dual fuel engine whereas Figure 9.32 shows schematic diagram of dual fuel mode using diesel and biogas. Table 9.15 shows time taken to consume 10 cc of fuel (10 ml) at different loads and constant rpm. Table 9.16 shows testing results by using dual fuel on 4-stroke single-cylinder diesel engine.

Table 9.15 Time taken to consume 10 cc of fuel (10 ml) at different loads and constant rpm.

S. no.	Weight (W) kg	Speed (rpm)	Time taken to consume 10 cc of fuel (10ml) i.e. 't' sec
1	0	685	128
2	0	685	127
3	0	685	124
4	0	685	125
5	0	685	126
			Average time = 126
1	2	685	115
2	2	685	111
3	2	685	113
4	2	685	112
5	2	685	114
			Average time = 113
1	4	685	82

(*Continued*)

Table 9.15 Time taken to consume 10 cc of fuel (10 ml) at different loads and constant rpm. (*Continued*)

S. no.	Weight (W) kg	Speed (rpm)	Time taken to consume 10 cc of fuel (10ml) i.e. 't' sec
2	4	685	79
3	4	685	81
4	4	685	78
5	4	685	80
			Average time = 80
1	6	685	64
2	6	685	62
3	6	685	61
4	6	685	60
5	6	685	63
			Average time = 62
1	8	685	45
2	8	685	41
3	8	685	44
4	8	685	40
5	8	685	45
			Average time = 43
1	10	685	31
2	10	685	28
3	10	685	30
4	10	685	26
5	10	685	30
			Average time = 29

Table 9.16 Testing results by using dual fuel on 4-stroke single-cylinder diesel engine.

Sr. no.	Particulars						
1	Weight (W) kg	0	2	4	6	8	10
2	Speed (N) rpm	685	685	685	685	685	685
3	Time taken to consume 10 cc of fuel (10ml) i.e., 't' sec.	126	113	80	62	43	29
4	Temperature of Cooling Water entering the jacket in °C (T_{wi})	29	29	29	29	29	29
5	Temperature of Cooling Water leaving the jacket in °C (T_{wo})	30	35	38	42	45	48
6	Quantity of jacket Cooling water in lit/hr (M_{wj})	160	160	160	160	160	160
7	Exhaust gas temperature leaving cylinder and entering calorimeter in °C $(T_g = T_{gi})$	120	165	200	230	235	280
8	Temperature of water entering in to calorimeter in °C (T_{wic})	29	29	29	29	29	29
9	Temperature of water leaving from calorimeter in °C (T_{woc})	33	34	35	36	38	40
10	Temperature of exhaust gases leaving the calorimeter in °C (t_{g2})	40	50	52	55	60	75
11.	RPM of the fan	470	475	475	500	500	480
12	Room Temperature in °C	24	24	24	24	24	24
13	Quantity of water supplied to exhaust gas calorimeter in lit/hr (M_{wc})	135	135	135	135	135	135

9.5.5 Calculation

Specification and constants

Sp. Gravity of diesel fuel = .83 and biogas sp. Gravity = 0.94
Biogas Cv = 19744 kJ/kg

For 2 kg load

Mass of fuel/s = ?
10 cc in 113 sec
So, for

$$1 \text{ sec} = \frac{10}{113} \text{cc, and } \frac{10}{113} \times 10^{-6} \times \text{sp. gravity of diesel fuel} \times \text{water density}$$

$$\text{So, for } 1 \text{ sec} = \frac{10}{113} \times 0.83 \times 10^3 \times 10^{-6} = 7.34 \times 10^{-5} \text{kg/s}$$

Flow rate for 2 kg load at dual fuel 7.34 x 10^{-5}kg/s
Flow rate for 2 kg load at diesel fuel = 1.53 x 10^{-4}kg/s from $eq^n(1)$
Saving of diesel = 1.53 x 10^{-4}- 7.34 x 10^{-5} = 7.96 x 10^{-5} (i.e., saving diesel mean biogas used in that place.)
So, mass flow rate is replaced by biogas is = 7.96 x 10^{-5}kg/s
So. We can say that mass flow rate of biogas is 7.96 x 10^{-5}kg/s

2. Brake power (BP)

$$\text{So, } BP = \frac{2 \times 3.14 \times 685 \times 7.848}{60} = 0.562 \text{ kW}$$

3. Friction power 0.9 kW take from graph
4. IP=BP + FP =0.562+0.9 = 1.462 kW
5. Brake thermal efficiency

$$= \frac{BP}{\left(\dot{md}\right)dual \times Cv \text{ of } diesel + \left(\dot{mb}\right)biogas \times Cv \text{ of } biogas}$$

$$= \frac{0.562}{7.34 \times 10^{-5} \times 42500 + 7.96 \times 10^{-5} \times 19740}$$

6. Indicated thermal efficiency

$$^r = \frac{IP}{\left(\dot{md}\right)dual \times Cv \text{ of } diesel + \left(\dot{mb}\right)biogas \times Cv \text{ of } biogas}$$

$$= \frac{1.462}{7.34 \times 10^{-5} \times 42500 + 7.96 \times 10^{-5} \times 19740} = 31.16\%$$

7. $\text{BSFC} = \dfrac{(\dot{md})dual + (\dot{mb})}{BP}$

$$= \frac{(7.34 \times 10^{-5} + 7.96 \times 10^{-5}) \times 3600}{0.562} = 0.980 \, \text{kg} / \text{kWh}$$

Table 9.17 Result table of dual fuel testing.

Sr. no.	Particulars						
1	Load W In kg	0	2	4	6	8	10
2	BP in kW	0	0.562	1.12	1.68	2.25	2.81
3	FP in kW	0.9	0.9	0.9	0.9	0.9	0.9
4	IP in kW	0.9	1.462	2.02	2.58	3.15	3.71
5	Brake thermal efficiency in %	-	11.98	18.19	21.79	21.52	20.61
6	Indicated thermal efficiency in %	23.34	31.16	32.82	33.47	30.13	27.21
7	Mechanical efficiency in %	0	38.44	55.44	65.11	71.42	75.74
8	BSFC in kg/ kWh	-	0.98	0.62	0.508	0.491	0.4623
9	ISFC in kg/ kWh	0.461	0.376	0.343	0.33	0.35	0.35
10	Volumetric efficiency in %	74.36	75.34	75.34	79.34	79.34	76.16

8. $\text{ISFC} = \dfrac{(\dot{md})dual + (\dot{mb})}{IP}$

$= \dfrac{(7.34 \times 10^{-5} + 7.96 \times 10^{-5}) \times 3600}{1.462} = 0.3767 \text{ kg}/\text{kWh}$

9. $\text{Mecahnical efficiency} = \dfrac{0.562}{1.462} = 38.44\%$

10. Volumetric efficiency for

$2 \text{ kg load} = \dfrac{\dfrac{\pi}{4} \times 0.06^2 \times 0.0275 \times \dfrac{2\pi \times 470}{60}}{\dfrac{\pi}{4} \times 0.102^2 \times 0.11 \times \dfrac{685}{2 \times 60}} = 74.57\%$

Similarly, all the calculations for different loads can be seen in Table 9.17.

Table 9.18 Heat balance sheet for 2 kg load.

Sr. no.	Heat supplied	kJ/min		% Heat supplied
1	Heat Supplied by combustion of fuel	282.34		100%
2	Heat Expenditure		%	
A.	Heat equivalent of BP	33.72	11.94	
B.	Heat lost to jacket cooling water	56.93	23.71	
C.	Heat lost to exhaust gases	55.61	19.69	
D.	Heat lost due to radiation, errors of observation etc. by difference	136.08	48.19	
			Total = 100%	Total = 100%

Table 9.19 Heat balance sheet for 4 kg load.

Sr. no.	Heat supplied	kJ/min		% Heat supplied
1	Heat Supplied by combustion of fuel	369.24		
2	Heat Expenditure		%	
A.	Heat equivalent of BP	67.2	18.19	
B.	Heat lost to jacket cooling water	100.44	27.2	
C.	Heat lost to exhaust gases	65.19	17.65	
D.	Heat lost due to radiation, errors of observation etc. by difference	136.4	36.94	
			Total = 100%	Total = 100%

Table 9.20 Heat balance sheet for 6 kg load.

Sr. no.	Heat supplied	kJ/min		% Heat supplied
1	Heat Supplied by combustion of fuel	462.44		
2	Heat Expenditure		%	
A.	Heat equivalent of BP	100.8	21.79	
B.	Heat lost to jacket cooling water	145.08	31.37	
C.	Heat lost to exhaust gases	75.61	16.35	
D.	Heat lost due to radiation, errors of observation etc. by difference	140.95	30.47	
			Total = 100%	Total = 100%

Table 9.21 Heat balance sheet for 8 kg load.

Sr. no.	Heat supplied	kJ/min		% Heat supplied
1	Heat Supplied by combustion of fuel	627.17		100%
2	Heat Expenditure		%	
A.	Heat equivalent of BP	135	21.52	
B.	Heat lost to jacket cooling water	178.56	28.47	
C.	Heat lost to exhaust gases	99.63	15.88	
D.	Heat lost due to radiation, errors of observation etc. by difference	214	34.12	
			Total = 100%	Total = 100%

Table 9.22 Heat balance sheet for 10 kg load.

Sr. no.	Heat supplied	kJ/min		% Heat supplied
1	Heat Supplied by combustion of fuel	817.96		100%
2	Heat Expenditure		%	
A.	Heat equivalent of BP	168.8	20.61	
B.	Heat lost to jacket cooling water	212.05	25.92	
C.	Heat lost to exhaust gases	124.14	15.17	
D.	Heat lost due to radiation, errors of observation etc. by difference	313.17	38.28	
			Total = 100%	Total = 100%

9.5.6   Heat Balance Sheet

Calculation for 2 kg load,
Tables 9.18 to 9.22 shows heat balance sheets.

1.   Heat supplied $= M_f \times C_v$

$$\text{Heat supplied} = (\dot{m}_d \times c_v) + (\dot{m}_b \times c_v)$$

Where $\dot{m}_d$ = mass flow rate of diesel, $\dot{m}_b$ = mass flow rate of biogas.

Heat supplied = $\{(7.345 \times 10^{-5} \times 42500) + (8.025 \times 10^{-5} \times 19740)\}$ 60
= 282.34 kJ/min   (A)

Heat equivalent to BP = $0.562 \times 60 = 33.72$ kJ/min   (B)

Heat lost to jacket cooling water = $m_w Cp_w (Tw_o - Tw_i) = 2.67 \times 4.18$
(35-29) = 66.96 kJ/min   (C)

Heat lost due to exhaust gases = $m_g Cp_g (T_g - T_a)$

$$\text{Now, } m_g Cp_g (Tg - Tg_{oc}) = m_{wc} Cp_w (Tw_{oc} - Tw_{ci})$$

$$= \frac{135}{60} \times 4.18 \, (34 - 29) = 47.025$$

$$mgCp_g = \frac{47.025}{(165 - 50)} = 0.408 \tag{D}$$

$$mgCp_g (T_g - T_a) = 0.408(165 - 29) = 55.61 \text{ kg/min}$$

Heat unaccounted, = Eq^n (A) − (B) + (C) + (D) =136.08 kJ/min

Heat supplied = 100 %

$$\text{Heat equivalent to BP} = \frac{BP}{Heat\ supplied} = \frac{33.72}{282.34} = 11.94\%$$

$$\text{Heat lost to jacket cooling water} = \frac{66.96}{282.34} = 23.71\%$$

$$\text{Heat lost to exhaust gases} = \frac{55.61}{282.34} = 19.69\%$$

$$\text{Heat unaccounted} = \frac{136.08}{282.34.} = 48.19\%$$

9.6   General Comments

Following are the observations made after the complete analysis of compact biogas plant and dual fuel engine.

- By using animal dung during the experiment, mean pH and mean temperature of biogas were calculated 6.2 and 24.25°C respectively.
- It took 44-45 days to produce 0.4 m³biogas from 50-55 kg animal dung.
- After animal dung, we used kitchen waste and found mean pH 6.24 and mean temperature 28.28°C and it took 9 days to produce 0.4 m³biogas from 3-3.5 kg kitchen waste.

Effect of Dual fuel on single-cylinder diesel engine.

Figure 9.33 shows brake power vs brake thermal efficiency. Figure 9.34 shows indicated thermal efficiency versus indicated power. Figure 9.35 shows volumetric efficiency vs. brake power. Figure 9.36 shows brake specific fuel consumption versus brake power whereas Figure 9.37 shows indicated power vs. ISFC for dual fuel and diesel.

- Then, we used fruits waste and found mean pH 6.6 and mean temperature 31.5°C and which took 7 days to produce 0.4 m³ biogas from 2-2.5 kg fruits waste.
- Maximum amount of biogas was produced from kitchen and fruits waste with increased temperatures and pH values.
- Volumetric efficiency $I_{th},$ $B_{th},$BSFC and ISFC of 4-stroke single-cylinder diesel engine have been found increased for dual fuel engine.
- Consumption rate of diesel decreases when dual fuel (Diesel + Biogas) is used.
- Dual fuel (Diesel + Biogas) is more effective at low load, when load is increased then effectiveness of dual fuel is low.

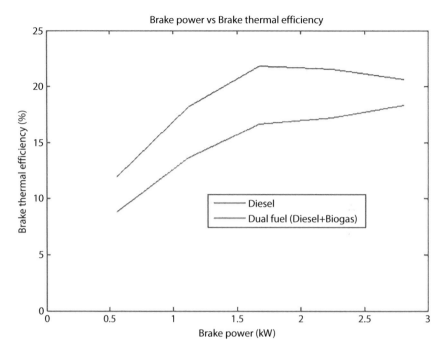

Figure 9.33 BP vs B_{th}.

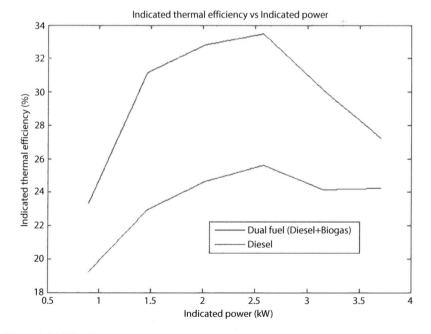

Figure 9.34 IP vs I_{th}.

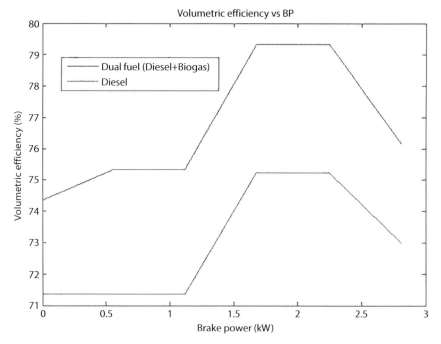

Figure 9.35 Vol^m efficiency vs. Brake power.

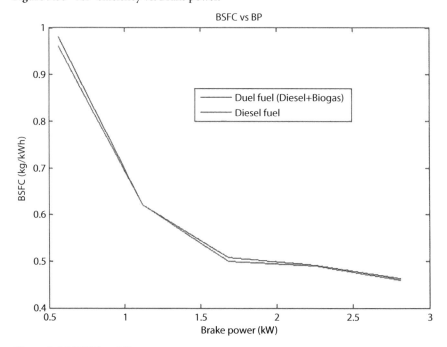

Figure 9.36 BSFC vs. BP.

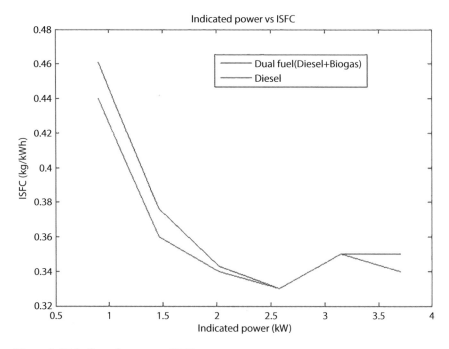

Figure 9.37 Indicated power vs. ISFC.

9.7   Conclusion

Compact biogas plant is portable, which is why it can be used anywhere. Traditionally, animal dung was used for biogas production, which is a time-consuming process. Our results suggest that using of wastages such as kitchen and fruits can increase the efficiency of biogas production as compared to using animal dung. Therefore, it can be positively concluded that the compact biogas plant can be used for household resolve in rural as well as urban areas because it is low-priced and ecological. These kitchen wastages can properly be utilized by every citizen of the society and compact biogas plant can be installed at small scale. In this way, it can be utilized for electricity generation, cooking and other purposes. It can be used with diesel as a dual fuel which results in the reduced consumption of diesel, thereby increasing the Volumetric efficiency I_{th}, B_{th}. The slurry of the biogas plant is an excellent fertilizer which can be used for agricultural purpose. The gas production is high in summer and low in winter.

9.8   Future Scope

In this project work, a comprehensive analysis of compact biogas plant is carried out thereby testing the effect of biogas on diesel engine by using dual fuel. This work is restricted to compact biogas plant which can be expanded by incorporating some more provisions such as

- ➢ A water separator can be incorporated near the gas cock. It ensures separation of water droplets.
- ➢ Calorific value of biogas can be increased by using different type of catalysts and chemicals which will result in the increase in efficiency of the engine.
- ➢ The plant of large capacity can be built in order to get high amount of gas when the waste available is in very high quantity.
- ➢ A solar water heater can be attached to ensure that hot water is provided in feed. It helps greatly during winters for bacteria production.

Similar kind of analysis can be performed on petrol (SI) engine in order to enhance the performance of the engine.

References

1. Office of the Registrar General and Census Commissioner, Distribution of Ofoefule, Akuzuo,U., Nwanko, Joseph,I., Ibeto, & Cynthia, N. (2010). Biogas production from paper waste and its blend with cow dung. Pelagia Research ed. TERI Press, New Delhi.
2. Amon, T., Amon, B., Kryvoruchko, V., Werner Zollitsch, W., Mayer, Anaerobic Digestion. *Carcass Disposal: A Comprehensive Review*, 7, 1-23.
3. Teune, B. 2007. The Biogas Programme in Vietnam; Amazing Results in Poverty Reduction and Economic Development, [online]. Available at http://www.hedon.info/docs/BP53-Teune-5.pdf Agriculture, Ecosystems and Environment 118, 173–182.
4. Dutta, S., *et al.*, *Biogas: The Indian NGO Experience*. 1997. 3rd ed.
5. NBPE, 2007. Biogas for Better Life: Brief Program Profile.
6. SNV (2011), Brief report 2010 and plan 2011 of the Working Group on Domestic Biogas under the Energy for All Partnership. Retrieved on October 26, 2011, from http://www.snvworld.org/en/Pages/Publications-item.aspx?publication=596.

7. Mattocks, Richard: Understanding Biogas Generation. VITA. Arlington, Virginia, USA. 1984. Available at website: http://www.vita.org/.Methodology for Potential Estimation, *Renewable Energy*, 26(2), 235-246.

8. Yacob, S., Y. Shirai, M. A. Hassan, M. Wakisaka, and S. Subash. 2006. Start-up Operation of Semi-commercial Closed Anaerobic Digester for Palm Oil Mill Effluent Treatment. *Process Biochemistry* 41(4): 962-964.

9. Shelton, D. R. and J. M. Tiedje. 1984. General Method for Determining Anaerobic Biodegradation Potential. *Applied and Environmental Microbiology* 47(4): 850-857.

10. Angelidaki, I., L. Ellegaard, and B. K. Ahring. 1999. A Comprehensive Model of Anaerobic Bioconversion of Complex Substrates to Biogas. Biotechnology and Bioengineering 63(3): 363-372. Available at: Census of India. 2001. [online].

11. Bove, R. and P. Lunghi. 2006. Electric Power Generation from Landfill Gas using Traditional and Innovative Technologies. *Energy Conservation and Management.*

12. Han, S.-K., S.-H. Kim, and H-S. Shin. 2005. UASB Treatment of Wastewater with VFA and Alcohol Generated during Hydrogen Fermentation of Food Waste. *Process Biochemistry* 40.

13. Speece, R. E. 1996. *Anaerobic Biotechnology for Industrial Wastewaters.* Nashville, TN: Archae Press.

14. Isa, Z., S. Grusenmeyer, and W. Verstraete. 1986. Sulfate Reduction Relative to Methane Production in High-Rate Anaerobic Digestion: Technical Aspects. *Applied and Environmental Microbiology* 51(3): 572-579.

15. FAO/CMS. A system Approach to Biogas Technology. Biogas Technology: a training manual for extension. 1996. Available at website: http://www.fao.org.

16. Bouallagui, H., O. Haouari, Y. Touhami, R. Ben Cheikh, L. Marouani, and M. Hamdi. 2004b. Effect of Temperature on the Performance of an Anaerobic Tubular Reactor Treating Fruit and Vegetable Waste. *Process Biochemistry* 39(12): 2143-2178.

17. Nayono, S.E., Gallert, C. & Winter, J. (2009). Foodwaste as a Co-Substrate in and a Fed-Batch Anaerobic Biowaste Digester for Constant Biogas Supply. *Water Science and Technology,* 59 (6), 1169–1178.

18. Sharma, S., Meena, R., Sharma, A., & Goyal, P. (2014). Biomass conversion technologies for renewable energy and fuels: a review note. *IOSR J. Mech. Civ. Eng.,* 11(2), 28-35.

19. Li, Y., Park, S.Y., & Zhu, J. (2011). Solid state anaerobic digestion for methane production from organic waste. *Renewable and Sustainable Energy,* 15, 821-826.

20. Babaee, A., & Shayegan, J. (2010). Anaerobic digestion of vegetable waste. Sharif University of Technology, 1-6. Biotechnology and Food research Centre PCSIR Laboratories Complex. *Bioresource Technology* 35 pp. 283-289.

21. A.K. Kalia, S.S. Kanwar, "Long-term evaluation of a fixed dome Janata biogas plant in hilly conditions", *Bioresource Technology*, Volume 65, Issues 1–2, 1998, Pages 61-63, ISSN 0960-8524,https://doi.org/10.1016/S0960-8524(98)00021-2.

22. Tester J.W., E.M. Drake, M.J. Driscoll, M.W. Golay and W.A. Peters, 2006, *Sustainable Energy: Choosing Among Options*, Prentice-Hall of India Pvt. Ltd. Publishing House, New Delhi.

23. Chandra A., 2007, Distributed Energy Systems: Energy Pay Back Time and Environmental Benefits, *Proceeding of 3rd International Conference on Solar Radiation and Day Lighting*, 269-277.

24. Chani, P.S., Najamuddin and Kaushik, S.K., 2003, Comparative analysis of embodied energy rates for walling elements in India, *Journal of the Institution of Engineers (India): Architectural Engineering Division* (2003), 84(2 Oct.): 47-50

25. Das A. and T.C. Kandpal, 1997, Energy Environment Implications of Cement Manufacturing in India: A scenario Analysis, *Int J of Energy Research*, 21(4), 299-308

26. Reddy A. K. N., C. R Prasad, P. Rajabapaiah and S. P. C. Sathyanarayan, 1979, *Proceeding of Indian Acad. Sci.* C 2 (3), 387.

27. TERI, 1982, Source: Punjab Agricultural University, Ludhiana, 38.

28. Tekin, A. R. and A. C. Dalgiç. 2000. Biogas Production from Olive Pomace. *Resources, Conservation and Recycling* 30(4): 301-313.

29. Jensen, J. 2006. Opportunities from Emerging Greenhouse Gas Markets. In Anaerobic Treatment of High-Strength Industrial Wastes Practical Course Proceedings. Milwaukee, WI: Marquette University.

30. Al-Masri, M.R.: Changes in biogas production due to different ratios of some animal and agricultural wastes. Elsevier Science Ltd. *Bioresource Technology* 77/2001, 97-100.

31. Callaghan, F.J., Wase, D.A.J, Thayanithy, K., and Forster, C.F.:Co-digestion of waste organic solids: batch studies. Elsevier Science Ltd. *Bioresource Technology* 67/1999, 117-122.

32. Karve, A.D. (2007), Compact biogas plant, a low cost digester for biogas from waste starch. http://www.arti-india.org. Karve of Pune A.D (2006). Compact biogas plant compact low cost digester from waste starch. www.bioenergyl-ists.org.

33. Kumar, S. Gaikwad, S.A. Shekdar, A.K., Kshirsagar, P.K., Singh, R.N. (2004). Estimation method for national methane emission from solid waste landfills. *Atmospheric Environment* 38: 3481–3487.

34. Shalini sing, sushil kumar, M.C. Jain, Dinesh kumar (2000), the increased biogas production using microbial stimulants.

35. Jantsch, T.G., Matttiason, B. (2004). An automated spectropphoyometric system for monitoring buffer capacity in anaerobic digestion processes. *Water Research* 38: 3645- 3650.

36. Hwang M. H., Jang N. J., Hyun S. H. and Kim I. S. (2004). Anaerobic bio-hydrogen production from ethanol fermentation: the role of pH. *Journal of Biotechnology*, 111 (3), 297–309.
37. Bischofsberger W., Dichtl N., Rosenwinkel K.-H., Seyfried C. F. and Böhnke B. (2005). Anae-robtechnik, 2nd Ed., ISBN 3-540-06850-3, Springer-Verlag, Heidelberg, Germany.
38. Tchobanoglous G., Burton F. L. and Stensel H. D. (2003). Wastewater Engineering: Treat-ment and Reuse. Metcalf & Eddy, Inc., Tata McGraw-Hill Publishing Company Ltd., 4th Ed.
39. Grady C. P. L., Daigger G. T. and Lim H. C. (1999). *Biological Wastewater Treatment.* 2nd Ed., Marcel Dekker Inc., New York.
40. Boe K. (2006). Online monitoring and control of the biogas process. PhD Thesis, Institute of Environment & Resources, Technical University of Denmark, Lyngby, Denmark.
41. Gray N. F. (2004). *Biology of wastewater treatment.* 2nd ed., Imperial College Press, London.
42. Eder B. and Schulz H. (2006). *Biogas Praxis* [in German], 3rd Edition, ISBN 3-936896-13-5 ökobuch Verlag, Staufen, Germany.
43. Monnet, F. (2003, November 7). An introduction to anaerobic digestion of organic wastes. Remade Scotland, 1-48. [Accessed November 2007]. [accessed 01/11/2009]
44. Khalid, A., Arshad, M., Anjum, M., Mahmood, T., & Dawson, L. (2011). The anaerobic digestion of solid organic waste. *Waste Management*, 31, 1737-1744.
45. Talyan, V., Dahiya, R.P., Anand, S., & Sreekrishnan, T.R. (2007). Quantification of methane emission from municipal solid waste disposal in Dehli. *Resource, Conservation and Recycling*, 50, 240-259.
46. Purohit P., A. Kumar, S. Rana and T.C. Kandpal, 2002,Using Renewable Energy Technologies for Domestic Cooking in India: A Methodology for Potential Estimation, *Renewable Energy*, 26(2), 235-246.
47. Susan, R., (2011, January 20). Anaerobic digesters farm opportunities and pathways. Minnesota Project, 1-24Library, 1(2), 1-8.] *Anaerobic Digestion Process. Water Science & Technology* 53(4-5): 55-61.47(11-12): 1391-1401.
48. Nelson, C., & Lamb, J. (2002, August 7). Haubenschild farms anaerobic digester. *The Minnesota Project*, 2, 1-39.
49. Erickson, L.E., Fayet, E., Kakamanu, B.K., & Davis, L.C C. (2004, August 6).
50. GTZ. "Biogas Digest Volume II. Biogas - Application and Product Development. Information and Advisory Service on Appropriate Technology." 1999. http://www.gtz.de/de/dokumente/en-biogas-volume2.pdf (accessed February 8, 2008).
51. Pradeep Kumar Meena, Amit Pal, S. (2020). Experimental Analysis of Four-Stroke Single-Cylinder Diesel Engine Using Biogas as a Dual Fuel. *Recent Advances in Mechanical Engineering*, 395–406. https://doi.org/https://doi.org/10.1007/978-981-15-9678-0_35

10

Low-Temperature Combustion Technologies for Emission Reduction in Diesel Engines

Amit Jhalani[1]*, Sumit Sharma[2], Pushpendra Kumar Sharma[3] and Digambar Singh[3]

[1]Department of Mechanical Engineering, Swami Keshvanand Institute of Technology, Management and Gramothan, Jaipur, Rajasthan, India
[2]Department of Mechanical Engineering, Arya College of Engineering and IT, Jaipur, India
[3]Department of Mechanical Engineering, Malaviya National Institute of Technology, Jaipur, Rajasthan, India

Abstract

Diesel engines are lean burn engines; hence CO and HC emissions do not occur in substantial amounts in diesel exhaust. The emissions of serious concern in compression ignition engines are particulate matter and nitrogen oxides because of elevated temperature conditions of combustion zone. Hence researchers have been striving continuously to lower the temperature of combustion in order to bring down the emissions of CI engines. This has been tried through premixed charge compression ignition, homogeneous charge compression ignition (HCCI), gasoline compression ignition and reactivity controlled compression ignition (RCCI). In this study, an attempt has been made to critically review the literature on low-temperature combustion conditions using various conventional and alternative fuels. Water-in-diesel emulsion technology has been discussed in detail. Most of the authors agree over the positive outcomes of water-diesel emulsion for both performance and emissions simultaneously. The problems and challenges augmented with the different strategies have also been described.

Keywords: Engine emissions, low-temperature combustion, HCCI engines, RCCI engines, water-diesel emulsion

**Corresponding author*: jhalaniamit@gmail.com

Pandian Vasant, Gerhard-Wilhelm Weber, Joshua Thomas, José Antonio Marmolejo-Saucedo and Roman Rodriguez-Aguilar (eds.) Artificial Intelligence for Renewable Energy and Climate Change, (345–370) © 2022 Scrivener Publishing LLC

Abbreviations

BS- bharat stage	HC- hydro-carbons
SI- spark ignition	PM- particulate matter
CI- compression ignition	IC- internal combustion
HCCI- homogeneous charged compression ignition	LTC- low-temperature combustion
RCCI- reactive controlled compression ignition	AQI- air quality index
PPCI- partially premixed compression ignition	DPF- diesel particulate filter
CO- carbon monoxide	DOC- diesel oxidation catalysts
NO_x- nitrogen oxides	EGR- exhaust gas recirculation
BTE- brake thermal efficiency	LTR- low-temperature range
CN- Cetane number	CR- compression ratio
DBTP- di-tertiary butyl peroxide	CA- crank angle
RCM- rapid combustion machine	WED- water-in-diesel emulsion

10.1 Introduction

Most of the research associated with the automotive industry is mainly focused on two aspects, i.e., first, to provide fuel-efficient technology and second, reduction of exhaust emissions. In automotive applications, CI engines are more common because of their better thermal efficiency and heavy-duty viability. But the high exhaust emissions out of diesel engines limit its use which is a matter of great concern [1]. Authorities are continuously making the emission standards more stringent to control the greenhouse emissions (Figure 10.1). In India, BS-VI is going to be implemented by 2020, surpassing BS-V to address the alarming pollution stage. It would be pretty challenging for the automotive industries [2]. These stringent emission regulations and continuous depletion of fossil fuel reserves have compelled the researchers to develop new, efficient, eco-friendly combustion technologies and arrangements which could operate on alternative

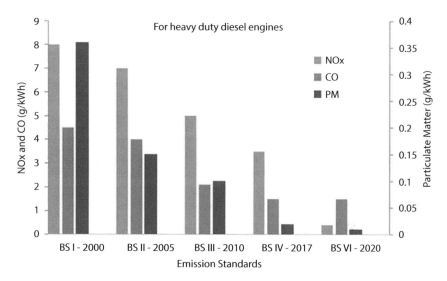

Figure 10.1 Emission standards getting more stringent year by year [12].

fuels also. Since compression ignition engines require high pressure conditions (compression ratio) and hence it develops a high temperature environment. These high temperature conditions are responsible for NO, soot, smoke and particulate matter emissions [3]. So, it has been tried in various studies to lower this temperature to achieve lower emissions. These technologies are specifically called low-temperature combustion (LTC) technologies. Review of important research related from fundamentals to recent advancements in this field has been discussed in this paper. Special focus has been given to water-emulsion diesel fuels, since this technology has been marked as fuel-efficient and low-emission without requiring any modifications in the existing conventional engines [4].

10.1.1 Global Scenario of Energy and Emissions

The current era of energy crisis, environmental imbalance and stringent emission standards stresses improvement in energy efficiency along with the reduction in harmful emissions. The high rate of increase in population, urbanization, globalization and motorization in the developing world contributes to this imbalance created by the developed world. The UN is predicting the world's population to increase by 2 billion to reach 9.7 billion in the upcoming 30 years by 2050 [5]. Moreover, the level of comfort and facilities which are being planned for the generations ahead will enhance the energy demand at an even higher rate as shown in Figure 10.2.

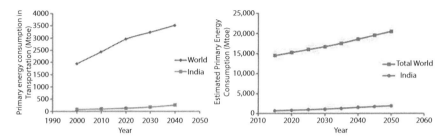

Figure 10.2 Increase in energy demand [7].

All countries are striving hard to make themselves energy sustainable as energy is the basic entity for humans to survive. Researchers over the globe are attempting to develop smart and efficient technologies for sustainable use of the available resources [6].

However, there is a good sign of shifting the energy dependency from fossil fuels to renewable fuels which also shows how rising prosperity drives an increase in global energy demand and how that demand will be met over the coming decades through a diverse range of supplies including oil, gas, coal and renewables [7]. Countries like Nigeria consume a good amount (80%) of biomass and waste for their total primary energy need [8]. In countries like Indonesia researchers are trying for synthetic fuels [9]. However, while most of the energy-dependent areas have seen a good transition from conventional to renewable energy, many sectors like transportation are still only at an introductory level in use of renewable fuels [10]. Owing to high power density, internal combustion engines are extensively used in transportation and as a stationary power source [11]. The emerging transport sector raises a big alarm for continuously depleting fossil fuels and increasing harmful emissions coming from the vehicles.

10.1.2 Diesel Engine Emissions

NO_x, CO, HC, SO_x, particulates, soot and smoke are major exhaust emissions of I.C. engines [13]. Out of these, CO and HC are common in SI engines while NO and smoke (soot) are more common in diesel engines [14]. Rich air-fuel mixture creates a situation of lesser oxygen availability, where reaction between carbon and oxygen becomes difficult and it results in excess of CO and HC emission in the exhaust gases. In advanced combustion technologies, complete combustion of fuel hydrocarbons reduces the likelihood of CO and HC emission because diesel engines are lean burn engines.

The formation of oxides of nitrogen in diesel is mostly because of the nitrogen present in air. Nitrogen exists in a stable diatomic form at low temperatures. At a temperature range of 2500-3000K, a significant amount of very reactive monoatomic nitrogen is generated [15]. The higher the combustion temperature, the more monoatomic nitrogen will be formed by the dissociation of diatomic nitrogen and hence more NO$_x$ formation will occur. Improper combustion and high temperature conditions promotes smoke. Many cities (like New Delhi in India) are gripped by heavy smoke which is a big threat to our health and complete eco-system, in fact. Seven out of the ten most polluted cities in the world are in India with an average 113.5g/m^3 concentration of PM2.5 in Delhi [8]. Figure 10.3 shows that a significant amount of this particulate matter is from the

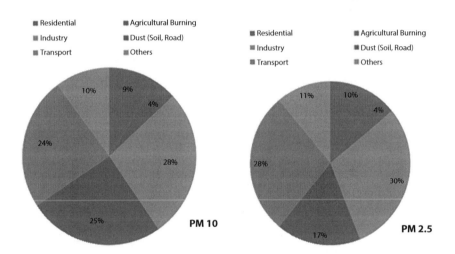

Figure 10.3 Sources of particulate matter in New Delhi sector-wise [16].

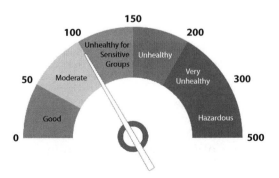

Figure 10.4 Various AQI levels and their effects [17].

transportation sector [16]. Many regions in New Delhi have recorded an Air Quality Index (AQI) up to 720 in regular days as compared to a good and satisfactory range of 0-50 and 51-100, respectively, which is a very serious concern (Figure 10.4).

10.1.3 Mitigation of NO_x and Particulate Matter

As discussed in the above paragraph, the two important diesel emissions, i.e., soot and oxides of nitrogen, could be controlled using various techniques. Mitigation of soot and NOx emissions together is not an easy task due to the process difference of their generation. By taking an example, the most common technique to reduce NOx emission is exhaust gas recirculation (EGR) but it results in increased PM emission [18]. Contrary to it, advancing the injection timing decreases the PM emissions with an increase in NO_x emission [19]. High oxygen content of biodiesel fuel blends do normally generate less amount of carbon monoxide (CO), hydrocarbon (HC) and smoke (PM) emissions but its proximity to generate NO_x emission is more. However, various appropriate after-treatment technologies like diesel particulate filter (DPF) [20], diesel oxidation catalyst (DOC) [21, 22] and catalytic converters [23] are successfully employed to curb both the emissions simultaneously with drawbacks like high cost, lower fuel economy and unnecessary maintenance. Hence, to avoid these drawbacks and expensive maintenance, certain low-temperature combustion (LTC) techniques have been developed over the years which address the problem of both NO_x and soot/particulate matter. The significant highlights of LTC involve lower temperature of combustion zone, better fuel atomization and homogenization, and lower local equivalence ratios [24]. These features of LTC increase the potential to reduce the PM and NOx emissions together. A major problem has been found which is associated with LTC engines is its higher carbon monoxide (CO) and hydrocarbon (HC) emissions. However, HC and CO emissions remain in the prescribed limits yet it has been suggested in the literature that it could be dealt with by after-treatment devices like catalytic converter [25].

10.1.4 Low-Temperature Combustion Engine Fuels

Conventionally, CI engines are fuelled with diesel fuel and sometimes with a small amount of biodiesel of low volatility, high viscosity and, moderate cetane number [26]. It does not let the air-fuel mixture become

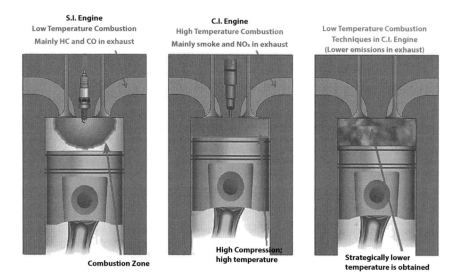

S.I. Engine
Low Temperature Combustion
Mainly HC and CO in exhaust

C.I. Engine
High Temperature Combustion
Mainly smoke and NOx in exhaust

Low Temperature Combustion
Techniques in C.I. Engine
(Lower emissions in exhaust)

Combustion Zone

High Compression;
high temperature

Strategically lower
temperature is obtained

Figure 10.5 Effect of low-temperature combustion shown graphically.

homogeneous before the beginning of combustion and hence it tends to generate locally rich regions with high-temperature conditions (Figure 10.5). It results in emission of more PM and NOx emissions [27]. Thus, in LTC, the facility of increased air-fuel mixing does not let fuel-rich regions develop, which lowers the temperature of combustion zone and hence decreases both NOx and PM emissions, respectively [28, 29]. Lower cetane number fuels were used by most of the researchers for LTC as it prolongs ignition delays and allows more time for homogeneous mixture to be developed [30, 31]. Judit *et al.* [32] explained the LTC phenomenon in depth by studying the kinetics involved in the reactions during LTC. A water emulsified diesel fuel technique also works on the same principle which improves thermal efficieny along with a decrease in emissions [33].

10.2   Scope of the Current Article

This article focuses on various LTC technologies and their effects on the performance parameters, combustion characteristics and exhaust emissions of the engine with conventional as well as non-conventional fuels. Agarwal *et al.* [34] and Pachiannan *et al.* [19] have also reviewed the LTCs but the water emulsified diesel fuel technology is missing from them. Physicochemical properties of fuel influence the combustion quality and hence the combustion characteristics [35]; hence these have also been discussed in detail for water emulsified diesel fuel. Because of the change in these properties, the effects it creates on the engine parameters have also been reviewed to understand the engine behaviour. Briefing all the important strategies of LTC, this paper provides a detailed review on the chemistry, preparation, performance, combustion and emission characteristics of water-in-diesel emulsion along with other biodiesels.

10.3   HCCI Technology

Homogeneous charge compression ignition combustion (HCCI) is a process of combustion in which a homogeneous charge of air and fuel is fed to cylinder and compressed as in a diesel engine, so that at the end of the compression stroke, fuel gets auto-ignited. This process is considerably faster than either spark ignition or compression ignition combustion [36]. A comparative analysis in HCCI, CI, and SI combustion processes has been performed based on different parameters influencing the combustion. Details are shown in Table 10.1 and Table 10.2.

HCCI combustion could improve the BTE while controlling the emissions and is applicable in both CI and SI engines after some modification.

Table 10.1 Comparison of HCCI with SI engine.

Basis of comparison	Efficiency	Throttle losses	Compression ratios	Combustion duration	HC and CO emissions
SI Engine	Less	More	Low	More	Comparatively More
HCCI Engine	More	No	High	Less	Less

Table 10.2 Comparison of HCCI with CI engine.

Basis of comparison	Efficiency	Combustion temperatures	Cost	Combustion duration	PM & NOx emissions
Diesel Engine	High	1900-2100 K	Comparatively High	More	More
HCCI Engine	Equally High	800-1100 K	Less	Less	Less

A range of alternative fuels could be used. Lean air fuel mixtures are preferred in HCCI engines. The charge ignites automatically at several locations and unlike SI engine combustion takes place without any visible flame of propagation [37]. It shows high rate of heat release because of simultaneous burning of fuel in very low combustion time [38]. Some advantages of HCCI combustion are:

(1) Along with meeting the stringent emissions standards, HCCI provides up to a 30% fuel savings [39].

(2) HCCI engines works on leaner air-fuel ratios which facilitates higher compression ratios like diesel (>15). It results in attainment of higher efficiencies as compared to conventional spark-ignited petrol engines [40].

(3) Homogeneous mixing of air and fuel emits lower emissions and hence cleaner combustion. Since peak temperatures in typical spark ignited engines are significantly lower, NO_x levels are almost negligible. Moreover, lean premixed mixtures do not produce soot and smoke. HCCI engines can be fuelled with gasoline, diesel, or any other alternative fuels such as biodiesels.

Alternatively, there are also certain drawbacks to HCCI such as high peak pressures which may harm the engine with high diesel knock. Engine-wear increases because of high rate of rise in pressure and high rate of heat release. Auto ignition control is difficult in HCCI, which is not so in the case of gasoline (SI) and diesel engines. The lower combustion duration and low in-cylinder temperatures, emissions like hydrocarbon (HC) and carbon monoxide (CO) are higher than a usual spark ignition engine [41].

10.3.1 Principle of HCCI

HCCI is a combination of the two most common combustion phenomena which utilizes principles of SI and CI engines. Likewise spark ignition, homogeneous charge of the fuel and oxidizer are fed together in mixed form [42], whereas density and temperature of the charge in diesel engine are increased by compression till the whole mixture reaches to auto-ignition. Combustion initiates at the border of air-fuel mixing at the start of injection event, to initiate combustion [43].

During combustion with HCCI, simultaneous ignition occurs at several sites. There is no automatic combustion initiator. This makes it fundamentally difficult to control the process [42]. With the continuous advancements in microprocessors, HCCI can be operated with diesel like higher efficiency and gasoline-like lower emissions. In addition, it has been shown that HCCI engines produce extremely low levels of NO_x emissions without any after-treatment process like catalytic converter. Because of lower peak temperatures, Carbon monoxide emissions and unburned hydrocarbons are still high as in petrol engines and need to be handled to comply with automobile emissions regulations [44].

10.3.2 Performance and Emissions with HCCI

Most of the researchers [45, 46] have observed that performance of HCCI engines is better in terms of thermal efficiency as compared to conventional diesel engines. Swaminathan *et al.* [47] used biogas as a fuel in their study to compare and analyze the effect of an HCCI engine with a conventional diesel engine. They used different intake temperatures and found that the thermal efficiency higher than a diesel engine at 135°C intake temperature. With hydrogen as a fuel Gomesantunes *et al.* [48] reported 45% higher thermal efficiency than diesel engines. Canacki *et al.* [49] also found similar results with gasoline as fuel. Alternatively, some researchers also got opposite trends [15, 50, 51]. This lower efficiency was attributed to improper mixture formation, quality of fuel, etc. Since HCCI engines operate on lean air-fuel ratios, the in-cylinder gas temperature remains below the range of 2000-2100 K. This low temperature does not provide atmosphere for NOx formation because NOx is formed at high temperature conditions [52]. In the literature, it is a finding of almost all the authors that NOx emissions become almost negligible in HCCI combustion as compared to normally operated CI engine [36, 47, 49, 51, 53, 54].

10.4 Partially Premixed Compression Ignition (PPCI)

Various limitations of HCCI, like high rate of pressure rise, shorter combustion duration and difficulty in controlling the initiation of combustion, led to the development of a newer concept of PPCI combustion. An important difference between HCCI and PPCI combustion is the charge distribution of PPCI which is somewhat heterogeneous compared to HCCI. EGR is employed to achieve low combustion temperatures. In conventional diesel engine fuel is injected little before the top dead-center and ignition initiates before the complete injection. Thus, less fuel entered is premixed before the start of combustion. In PPCI, premixing of complete injected fuel is facilitated, even the fuel injected at the end.

With high rate in rise of pressure in the cylinder, more knocking is observed. This imposes constraints on the required dilution and further increases in the CO and unburned HC. Zhang *et al.* (2012) used gasoline and mineral diesel (dieseline) for their investigation for the partially pre-mixed compression ignition (PPCI) system of combustion [55]. For PPCI combustion, injection timings and EGR rates were varied to get different combinations. Up to 95% reduction in NOx and smoke emissions were observed with dieseline fuel PPCI as compared to combustion in con-ventional diesel engine. Lewander *et al.* [56, 57] conducted experiments to evaluate the single-injection PPCI operating area for three different fuels, *viz.*, higher standard octane gasoline, diesel, and low-octane gaso-line fuel with characteristics similar to diesel. Fuel with high-octane num-ber was found better for PPCI combustion as it elongates ignition delay period which significantly extended the operating region of PPCI in single injection mode. Musculus *et al.* [58] developed some conceptual mod-els to explain the spray pattern, evaporation, charge formation, ignition, and combustion mechanisms which were found to be consistent with the experimental observations. It was found very useful to predict the pre-mixed charge combustion behavior. Kimura *et al.* developed a new concept to lower down NOx and smoke emissions simultaneously. They called it Modulated Kinetics combustion and employed premixed combustion as a low temperature combustion strategy.

10.5   Exhaust Gas Recirculation (EGR)

To curb the NO_x emission specially, exhaust gases recirculation (EGR) is a most common and effective technology among various strategies. Up to 50% or even more of the exhaust gas can be recirculated in CI engines but in SI engines maximum EGR is limited to 20% [59]. However, in SI engines, NO_x reduction is achieved at a cost of poor combustion stability. In EGR (exhaust gas recirculation) a part from exhaust emissions is recirculated back to the combustion chamber through externally made arrangements. Exhaust Gas Recirculation performs as a heat sink and reduces the amount of air intake (oxygen specifically) with diluents (carbon dioxide and water) to discourage the formation of NO_x. The diluents have high heat capacity which leads to lower rate of combustion resulting in low in-cylinder tem-peratures [18]. Ming *et al.* [60] employed EGR for biodiesel derived from Canola and yellow grease and observed simultaneous drop in NOx and particulate matter. It was achieved by elongation of ignition delay through more than 50% EGR at low load conditions.

Zheng *et al.* [61] comprehensively studied several ways of employing the EGR for reducing NO_x. They have aptly highlighted the importance of EGR. After analysis of EGR they proposed newer ways of EGR hydrogen reforming and EGR stream treatment. Although EGR gives lower NO_x emissions it promotes HC, CO, soot emissions and poor performance of engine [62, 63]. Ladomattos *et al.* performed a comprehensive experimental study for EGR impacts on combustion process in a CI engine. In their experiments, they have found the effect of individual diluents such as CO_2, vaporized water and their combinations [64, 65]. For this they introduced them separately along with the intake air to carry out exhaustive simulation of EGR [66]. In these experiments, it was found that the main factor that affected the variation in emission characteristics of NOx and soot was dilution effect of individual additives. The displacement of oxygen intake with the implementation of exhaust gas recirculation which leads to the reduction of the excess air proportion, which tends to increases the delay in ignition. This affects the temperature of the combustion zone and the formation of soot [67]. To overcome the dilution effect, a few researchers used a turbocharger with a turbine having a variable area of nozzle to encourage additional EGR. Through this method, exhaust gasses were pumped together and recycled with the induced air rather than replacing only a part of it. This extra charge leads to enhance the heat inlet efficiency resulting in lower temperature of combustion and NOx emission. In fact, the level of inlet oxygen remains unaffected; thus, the process of soot oxidation will not be exacerbated.

10.6   Reactivity Controlled Compression Ignition (RCCI)

With an objective to reduce EGR requirements in PPCI strategies, Inagaki *et al.* [68] investigated dual-fuel mode PCI with directly injected diesel and premixed iso-octane. They operated conveniently up to 12 bar IMEP in the PCI mode in this study. They concluded that operating conditions differ with the change in fuel blends. For example, a fuel with low cetane number performs better at higher loads and vice versa. It generates the requirement of the system to be operated with different fuels and their blends that covers a range of fuel from bare gasoline to bare diesel. It could be facilitated by injecting low cetane number (high delay period/low reactive) fuel in the intake port and early cycle direct injection of high cetane number fuel (lower ignition delay) [69]. Hence, RCCI can be defined as a dual fuel combustion technology which works on in-cylinder fuel blending of different reactivity fuels and multiple injections to control the in-cylinder rate of combustion. Optimization of combustion duration, phasing and rate is required. The process of RCCI involves addition of a low-reactive agent/fuel into the cylinder to create a proper-mixed charge with recirculated gases. Then, a fuel of high reactivity is directly injected in the combustion chamber before the ignition of premixed charge using single or multiple injections. As compared to strategies like dual fuel PCCI, dual fuel HCCI, and PPC, the RCCI technology has been found with better governing over combustion process, and this concept has demonstrated high thermal efficiencies of up to 60% [19, 70].

10.7   LTC Through Fuel Additives

The composition of fuel determines fuel combustion as it affects the duration of combustion, the delay in ignition and the auto-ignition temperature. The main effect of fuel additives is the LTR, due to which beginning of the main reaction is affected. The density, lower heating value and latent heat of evaporation are the main properties of fuel which affects the physical delay period, while the fuel's self-ignition and distillation properties affect the chemical delay [71]. Common ways of classifying fuels are based on the ease of self-ignition defined as CN or auto-ignition resistance [72]. A high number of cetane represents lesser self-ignition resistance, which includes straight chain paraffins. A high octane number includes branched chain paraffin which represents the resistance against auto-ignition. With high octane number gasoline has almost no low-temperature reactions which causes combustion to start at about 950 K [19]. Mineral diesel like fuels exhibit major reactions at low temperatures from 750 K [73].

Starck *et al.* [74] conducted experiments to determine the effect of fuel properties on HCCI combustion and found that lower CN fuels are good HCCI fuels. Exhaust gas recirculation and timing for fuel injection were optimized to control the HCCI combustion. Therefore, optimum combustion speed and the fuel having low cetane number could increase the combustion range of HCCI due to low-combustion speed which allows more duration for homogenization of charge and hence superior combustion during HCCI. Tanaka *et al.* [75] used a RCM (rapid compression machine) to analyze the influence of fuel chemistry and additives on HCCI combustion of pure HC fuels and their blend/mixtures. It was observed that saturated compound fuels show combustion in two stages while fuels with unsaturated hydrocarbon compounds exhibit single-stage combustion.

Aceves *et al.* [76] conducted a numerical analysis for fuels and additives in HCCI combustion. They carried out their work for a heavy-duty engine in which they selected a number of HCCI fuels and estimated acceptable operating range for CR, intake air temperature and equivalence ratio. The authors have experimentally investigated a large number of additives and enlisted the potential ones. In their experiments, adding a small quantity of additives (secondary fuels) could bring a significant effect over HCCI combustion characteristics which could regulate the combustion of HCCI in a better way. Through experimental work and numerical modeling, Mack *et al.* [77] studied the effect of the additive "di-tertiary butyl peroxide" (DTBP) on HCCI combustion. Small amounts of DTBP were mixed to 100% ethanol and DEE-mixed ethanol to conduct engine tests at a range of fuel injection times and load conditions. DTBP addition to the test fuel advances combustion timing in each condition. Experimental results were validated with numerical model analysis. Use of additives combustion timings for 100% ethanol and DEE-ethanol mixtures were found to be advanced. In case of DEE ethanol mixtures which confirmed the thermal and kinetic effects of the DTBP addition resulted in more advance timing.

10.8   Emulsified Fuels (Water-in-Diesel Emulsion Fuel)

Out of the various strategies, water emulsion in diesel (WED) has been found as a prominent alternative fuel which could improve efficiency along with reducing pollution [4, 78–81]. Emulsified diesel does not need any engine modification. Water-diesel emulsion has shown various advantages as fuel in the literature [82]. Along with improvement in combustion efficiency, it lowers various exhaust emissions such as CO, HC, NOx, particulate matter and soot. Since the boiling point of diesel is more than that of water, when water-in-diesel emulsion enters into the high temperature zone, the water droplets trapped inside the diesel fuel evaporate first and break the surrounding diesel layer in finer spray. This phenomenon can be called as micro-explosion [83]. The contact/surface area between air and fuel gets increased due to this dispersion which results in better combustion efficiency. Evaporated water takes away some heat which reduces peak combustion temperature in the form of latent heat of vaporization. Better combustion and the reduction in peak temperature cut down the NOx and PM emissions, respectively [84]. Aligning to this technology Jhalani *et al.* [85] investigated gomutra emulsified diesel fuel for CI engine application, which gave promising results.

10.8.1   Brake Thermal Efficiency (BTE)

To analyze the performance of an engine, BTE is a prominent parameter to study and determine the impact of the tested fuel. Most of the studies have found that thermal efficiency improves with the use of water-in-diesel emulsion fuel [80, 81]. Basha and Anand [86] found that the thermal efficiency increased up to 26.9% with emulsion fuel as compared to the bare diesel efficiency 25.2%. Jhalani et al. [87] found a noticeable 9.28% increase in BTE with 23.89% efficiency as compared to 21.86% with neat diesel. A good relationship between the delay period and the micro-explosion phenomenon with increase in the combustion efficiency was observed. The experimental results indicated that as the water in the emulsion fuel increases, both physical and chemical delay increases. Because of increase in ignition delay more diesel fuel get accumulated so sufficient time is available for preparation of combustible charge for chemical reaction. It results in a rise of the heat release rate [88]. The change in delay period is because of moisture present in the emulsion which slows down the process of physical and chemical reactions [24]. The water content of emulsion during the process of vaporization forms latent heat. Emulsification increases the density and viscosity of fuel. It results in increase of physical delay. Further, water reduces the calorific value which causes an increase in chemical delay period. Thus, the physical and chemical delay results in elongation of overall ignition delay [89]. This delay period normally increases about 4 degree CA with water-in-diesel emulsion fuel, while in terms of time it increases around 0.2 ms as compared to diesel fuel. Though it was expected that the peak in-cylinder temperature would increase because of high heat release rates, it had been observed that due to the presence of water in the emulsion, the temperature decreases [90]. Most of the studies have observed increased diesel knock with the increase in ignition delay [91].

10.8.2   Nitrogen Oxide (NO_x)

Many studies have reported that the emission of oxides of nitrogen can be reduced by using water emulsified diesel fuel [92–95]. NO_x formation has been found to reduce by up to 50% in various studies. Attia and Kulchitskiy [96] found up to 25% reduction in NO_x with use of water droplets of large size in the emulsion. Park et al. [95] observed up to 20% reduction with 20% water emulsified diesel. In addition, a strong relationship between the increases in the water percentage with the decrease in NOx emissions has also been reported. Many researchers agree that the reduction of NOx is directly related to an increase in the proportion of water. Such temperature drop is due to the heat loss of latent heat caused by water evaporation in the emulsion. As per Jazair *et al.* [97], an endothermic reaction occurs because of change in the phase of water into steam which decreases the temperature of the combustion zone. This decreases NOx formation in the combustion chamber. Further, Farfaletti *et al.* [98] explains the fall in combustion temperature because of the heat sink effect. The water content absorbs the heat from the combustion. It therefore decreases the temperature of burning gas within the cylinder and thus limits the formation of NOx.

10.8.3   Soot and Particulate Matter (PM)

Particulate matter is an outcome of a complex phenomenon that happens from the reactions in diesel exhaust. It carries carcinogenic poly aromatic hydrocarbons which are very hazardous to human health [99]. These particles are very small in size and therefore can reach the smallest cavities of the lungs, which may cause health hazards. PM consists of mainly adsorbed hydrocarbons, elemental carbon, sulphates and inorganic compounds, etc. [100].

In CI engines, the measurement of emissions of particulate matter is a tedious task which requires much facilities and resources. From the experimental results, it has been shown that PM emissions are proportional to the smoke emissions [101, 102]. Therefore, for simplicity, smoke emissions are generally measured to estimate the particulate matter and soot emissions in the engine exhaust. At low loads, the fuel-air combination remains lean. So, significant smoke is not emitted. On the other hand, higher emissions of smoke are prominent at top loads because the fuel-air ratio is more. Good air-fuel mixing conditions support lower smoke emissions. Hence due to the micro-explosion phenomenon, enhanced break-up of diesel occurs with water addition. It lowers smoke [4]. Moreover, due to water part mixture becomes somewhat leaner, which also affects smoke emission. Addition of water enhances the proximity of presence of OH radicals [33, 103]. High OH radicals help the soot to get oxidized. As a result, smoke emission is reduced [104]. Particulate matter in the exhaust is mostly soot and ash which is the outcome of condensed unburned HC. This ash is formed due to the burning of lubricating oil. Instead, generation of soot is caused in the regions where fuel is rich inside cylinder when the fuel injection time is finished [3]. Again the observed reduction in the formation of particulate is due to the micro-explosion process which happens because of the volatility difference in diesel and water and then, by a secondary break-up of fuel [105]. This violent disintegration encourages the mixture of fuel and air, improving the efficiency of combustion and eliminating soot and unburned HC formation. Hence, the combustion becomes better and homogeneous, which reduces the particulate emission [106]. Honnery *et al.* [107] attributes the reduction in formation of soot particles to high latent heat escaped out with the vaporized water. Hasannuddin *et al.* [108] estimated a trend of an average reduction in particulate matter which is equal to double the mass fraction of water in the fuel emulsion.

10.9   Conclusion and Future Scope

In this review paper, various low-combustion strategies have been reviewed to address the exhaust emission problems of diesel engines. It is clear from the above studies that if the temperature of the combustion can be controlled by any means, it results in lower NO_x emissions and in some cases also lower soot and particulate matter, depending on the technology used. Out of the above strategies, water in diesel emulsion method is found to be a prominent one which does not require any special arrangements and modifications. However, the issue of emulsion stability is a big drawback associated with emulsified fuel which limits its usage for stationary engines. If this issue is addressed properly, this technique may give better results for improved performance and lower emissions simultaneously. On the basis of the present literature review it is found that various research opportunities are available in the area of the low-temperature combustion process. Future research should focus on the identification of different techniques to lower the combustion chamber temperature without affecting the efficiency.

Acknowledgement

The authors would like to thank all the researchers who performed experiments and explored various possible ways to lower the temperature of combustion chamber, which provide the basis of this review article.

References

1. Nayyar A, Sharma D, Soni SL, Gautam V, Kumar C, Augustine M. Study of performance and emissions of a stationary DI variable compression ratio CI engine fueled with n-butanol/diesel blends using Taguchi technique:

analytical and experimental analysis. *Energy Sources, Part A Recover Util Environ Eff* 2019. https://doi.org/10.1080/15567036.2019.1666937.

2. UITP India. India Will Implement Euro-Vi Emission Standard For Vehicles By 2020 2018. http://www.india.uitp.org/articles/euro-vi-emission-standards-by-2020 (accessed January 1, 2018).

3 .Kumar Sharma P, Sharma D, Lal Soni S, Jhalani A. Characterization of the Nonroad Modified Diesel Engine Using a Novel Entropy-VIKOR Approach: Experimental Investigation and Numerical Simulation. *J Energy Resour Technol* 2019;141. https://doi.org/10.1115/1.4042717.

4. Mondal PK, Mandal BK. A comprehensive review on the feasibility of using water emulsified diesel as a CI engine fuel. *Fuel* 2019;237:937–60. https://doi.org/10.1016/j.fuel.2018.10.076.

5. United Nations. World population prospects 2019. *United Nations Dep Econ Soc Aff* 2019.

6. Nižetić S, Djilali N, Papadopoulos A, Rodrigues JJPC. Smart technologies for promotion of energy efficiency, utilization of sustainable resources and waste management. *J Clean Prod* 2019;231:565–91. https://doi.org/10.1016/j.jclepro.2019.04.397.

7. Centre for Energy Economics Research and Policy. *BP Statistical Review of World Energy Statistical Review of World.* 2019.

8. Ben-Iwo J, Manovic V, Longhurst P. Biomass resources and biofuels potential for the production of transportation fuels in Nigeria. *Renew Sustain Energy Rev* 2016;63:172–92. https://doi.org/10.1016/j.rser.2016.05.050.

9. Amrullah A. Gasoline and Synthetic Fuel from Plastic Waste. *Int J Manuf Mater Mech Eng* 2016;6:41–50. https://doi.org/10.4018/IJMMME.2016040103.

10. EIA. International Energy Outlook 2017. US Energy Inf Adm 2017;IEO2017. https://doi.org/www.eia.gov/forecasts/ieo/pdf/0484(2016).pdf.

11. Kumar Sharma P, Sharma D, Lal Soni S, Jhalani A, Singh D, Sharma S. Energy, exergy, and emission analysis of a hydroxyl fueled compression ignition engine under dual fuel mode. *Fuel* 2020;265:116923. https://doi.org/10.1016/j.fuel.2019.116923.

12. Sharma PK, Sharma D, Soni SL, Jhalani A, Singh D, Sharma S. Characterization of the hydroxy fueled compression ignition engine under dual fuel mode: Experimental and numerical simulation. *Int J Hydrogen Energy* 2020;45:8067–81. https://doi.org/10.1016/j.ijhydene.2020.01.061.

13. Kancherla PR, Basava VAR. Experimental Investigation on Cylinder Vibration Analysis, Combustion, Emission and Performance of An IDI Engine. *Int J Manuf Mater Mech Eng* 2017;7:18–36. https://doi.org/10.4018/IJMMME.2017010102.

14. Sharma S, Sharma D, Soni SL, Singh D, Jhalani A. Performance, combustion and emission analysis of internal combustion engines fuelled with acetylene – a review. *Int J Ambient Energy* 2019:1–19. https://doi.org/10.1080/01430750.2019.1663369.

15. Singh G, Singh AP, Agarwal AK. Experimental investigations of combustion, performance and emission characterization of biodiesel fuelled HCCI engine using external mixture formation technique. *Sustain Energy Technol Assessments* 2014;6:116–28. https://doi.org/10.1016/j.seta.2014.01.002.

16. Mackintosh E. The perfect storm fueling New Delhi's deadly pollution. CNN 2019. https://doi.org/https://edition.cnn.com/2019/11/04/india/delhi-smog-pollution-explainer-intl/index.html.

17. Standard B. What is air quality index (AQI). Bus Stand 2020. https://www.business-standard.com/about/what-is-air-quality-index (accessed May 30, 2020).

18. Thangaraja J, Kannan C. Effect of exhaust gas recirculation on advanced diesel combustion and alternate fuels - A review. *Appl Energy* 2016. https://doi.org/10.1016/j.apenergy.2016.07.096.

19. Pachiannan T, Zhong W, Rajkumar S, He Z, Leng X, Wang Q. A literature review of fuel effects on performance and emission characteristics of low-temperature combustion strategies. *Appl Energy* 2019;251:113380. https://doi.org/10.1016/j.apenergy.2019.113380.

20. Gupta PK, Sharma D, Soni SL, Goyal R, Johar DK. Experimental investigation of impact of diesel particulate filter on smoke and NOx emissions of a Euro-I compression ignition engine with active and off-board regeneration. *Clean Technol Environ Policy* 2017;19:883–95. https://doi.org/10.1007/s10098-016-1279-8.

21. Laddha P, Yadav K, Sharma D, Jhalani A. Study of the Effects of Diesel Oxidation Catalyst (DOC) on Emission Control in Diesel Engine - A Review. *J Mater Sci Mech Eng* 2019;6:103–8.

22. K. S. N, Banapurmath NR, D M, Yunus Khan TM. Pre- and post-combustion emission reduction techniques for engine fuelled with diesel/DEE blends by three approaches. *Energy Sources, Part A Recover Util Environ Eff* 2019:1–18. https://doi.org/10.1080/15567036.2019.1663304.

23. Spassova I, Tsontcheva T, Velichkova N, Khristova M, Nihtianova D. Catalytic reduction of NO with decomposed methanol on alumina-supported Mn-Ce catalysts. *J Colloid Interface Sci* 2012;374:267–77. https://doi.org/10.1016/j.jcis.2012.01.042.

24. Subramanian KA, Ramesh A. A study on the use of water–diesel emulsions in a DI diesel engine. *2nd Int. SAE-India Mobil. Conf., IIT Madras: 2001*, p. SAE paper no. 2001-28-0005; 2001.

25. Lee Y, Huh KY. Analysis of different modes of low temperature combustion by ultra-high EGR and modulated kinetics in a heavy duty diesel engine. *Appl Therm Eng* 2014. https://doi.org/10.1016/j.applthermaleng.2014.05.090.

26. Singh D, Sharma D, Soni SL, Sharma S, Kumari D. Chemical compositions, properties, and standards for different generation biodiesels: A review. *Fuel* 2019;253:60–71. https://doi.org/10.1016/j.fuel.2019.04.174.

27. Yang B, Yao M, Cheng WK, Zheng Z, Yue L. Regulated and unregulated emissions from a compression ignition engine under low temperature combustion

fuelled with gasoline and n-butanol/gasoline blends. *Fuel* 2014;120:163–70. https://doi.org/10.1016/j.fuel.2013.11.058.

28. Benajes J, García-Oliver JM, Novella R, Kolodziej C. Increased particle emissions from early fuel injection timing Diesel low temperature combustion. *Fuel* 2012;94:184–90. https://doi.org/10.1016/j.fuel.2011.09.014.

29. Kukkadapu G, Kumar K, Sung CJ, Mehl M, Pitz WJ. Autoignition of gasoline surrogates at low temperature combustion conditions. *Combust Flame* 2015. https://doi.org/10.1016/j.combustflame.2015.01.025.

30. Ciatti S, Subramanian SN. An Experimental Investigation of Low Octane Gasoline in Diesel Engines. *ASME 2010 Intern. Combust. Engine Div. Fall Tech. Conf., ASME*; 2010, p. 329–39. https://doi.org/10.1115/ICEF2010-35056.

31. Wang H, Zheng Z, Yao M, Reitz RD. An Experimental and Numerical Study on the Effects of Fuel Properties on the Combustion and Emissions of Low-Temperature Combustion Diesel Engines. *Combust Sci Technol* 2014;186:1795–815. https://doi.org/10.1080/00102202.2014.920836.

32. Zádor J, Taatjes CA, Fernandes RX. Kinetics of elementary reactions in low-temperature autoignition chemistry. *Prog Energy Combust Sci* 2011;37:371–421. https://doi.org/10.1016/j.pecs.2010.06.006.

33. Liang Y, Shu G, Wei H, Zhang W. Effect of oxygen enriched combustion and water-diesel emulsion on the performance and emissions of turbocharged diesel engine. *Energy Convers Manag* 2013;73:69–77. https://doi.org/10.1016/j.enconman.2013.04.023.

34. Agarwal AK, Singh AP, Maurya RK. Evolution, challenges and path forward for low temperature combustion engines. *Prog Energy Combust Sci* 2017;61:1–56. https://doi.org/10.1016/j.pecs.2017.02.001.

35. Singh D, Sharma D, Soni SL, Sharma S, Kumar Sharma P, Jhalani A. A review on feedstocks, production processes, and yield for different generations of biodiesel. *Fuel* 2020;262:116553. https://doi.org/10.1016/j.fuel.2019.116553.

36. Gan S, Ng HK, Pang KM. Homogeneous Charge Compression Ignition (HCCI) combustion: Implementation and effects on pollutants in direct injection diesel engines. *Appl Energy* 2011. https://doi.org/10.1016/j.apenergy.2010.09.005.

37. Kong SC, Marriott CD, Reitz RD, Christensen M. Modeling and experiments of HCCI engine combustion using detailed chemical kinetics with multidimensional CFD. *SAE Tech. Pap.*, 2001. https://doi.org/10.4271/2001-01-1026.

38. Soylu S. Examination of combustion characteristics and phasing strategies of a natural gas HCCI engine. *Energy Convers Manag* 2005. https://doi.org/10.1016/j.enconman.2004.02.013.

39. Mack JH, Aceves SM, Dibble RW. Demonstrating direct use of wet ethanol in a homogeneous charge compression ignition (HCCI) engine. *Energy* 2009. https://doi.org/10.1016/j.energy.2009.02.010.

40. Warnatz J, Maas U, Dibble RW. Combustion: Physical and chemical fundamentals, modeling and simulation, experiments, pollutant formation. 2006. https://doi.org/10.1007/978-3-540-45363-5.

41. Hairuddin AA, Wandel AP, Yusaf T. An introduction to a homogeneous charge compression ignition engine. *J Mech Eng Sci* 2014. https://doi.org/10.15282/jmes.7.2014.3.0101.

42. Bendu H, Murugan S. Homogeneous charge compression ignition (HCCI) combustion: Mixture preparation and control strategies in diesel engines. *Renew Sustain Energy Rev 2014*. https://doi.org/10.1016/j.rser.2014.07.019.

43. Bogin GE, Mack JH, Dibble RW. Homogeneous charge compression ignition (HCCI) engine. *SAE Int J Fuels Lubr* 2009. https://doi.org/10.4271/2009-01-1805.

44. Yao M, Zheng Z, Liu H. Progress and recent trends in homogeneous charge compression ignition (HCCI) engines. *Prog Energy Combust Sci* 2009. https://doi.org/10.1016/j.pecs.2009.05.001.

45. Stanglmaier RH, Dingle PJ, Stewart DW. Cycle-Controlled Water Injection for Steady-State and Transient Emissions Reduction from a Heavy-Duty Diesel Engine. *J Eng Gas Turbines Power* 2008;130:032801. https://doi.org/10.1115/1.2830856.

46. Venkataramana P. Homogeneous Charge Compression Ignition. *Int J Eng Res Technol* 2013.

47. Swami Nathan S, Mallikarjuna JM, Ramesh A. An experimental study of the biogas-diesel HCCI mode of engine operation. *Energy Convers Manag* 2010. https://doi.org/10.1016/j.enconman.2009.09.008.

48. Gomesantunes S J, Mikalsen R, Roskilly A. An investigation of hydrogen-fuelled HCCI engine performance and operation. *Int J Hydrogen Energy* 2008;33:5823–8. https://doi.org/10.1016/j.ijhydene.2008.07.121.

49. Canakci M. An experimental study for the effects of boost pressure on the performance and exhaust emissions of a DI-HCCI gasoline engine. *Fuel* 2008;87:1503–14. https://doi.org/10.1016/j.fuel.2007.08.002.

50. Ganesh D, Nagarajan G. Homogeneous charge compression ignition (HCCI) combustion of diesel fuel with external mixture formation. *Energy* 2010;35:148–57. https://doi.org/10.1016/j.energy.2009.09.005.

51. Ma J, Lü X, Ji L, Huang Z. An experimental study of HCCI-DI combustion and emissions in a diesel engine with dual fuel. *Int J Therm Sci* 2008;47:1235–42. https://doi.org/10.1016/j.ijthermalsci.2007.10.007.

52. Guo H, Hosseini V, Neill WS, Chippior WL, Dumitrescu CE. An experimental study on the effect of hydrogen enrichment on diesel fueled HCCI combustion. *Int J Hydrogen Energy* 2011. https://doi.org/10.1016/j.ijhydene.2011.07.143.

53. Thangaraja J, Kannan C. Effect of exhaust gas recirculation on advanced diesel combustion and alternate fuels - A review. *Appl Energy* 2016;180:169–84. https://doi.org/10.1016/j.apenergy.2016.07.096.

54. Hasan AO, Abu-Jrai A, Al-Muhtaseb AH, Tsolakis A, Xu H. HC, CO and NOx emissions reduction efficiency of a prototype catalyst in gasoline bi-mode SI/HCCI engine. *J Environ Chem Eng* 2016;4:2410–6. https://doi.org/10.1016/j.jece.2016.04.015.

55. Zhang F, Xu H, Zeraati Rezaei S, Kalghatgi G, Shuai S-J. Combustion and Emission Characteristics of a PPCI Engine Fuelled with Dieseline. *SAE Tech. Pap.*, 2012. https://doi.org/10.4271/2012-01-1138.

56. Lewander M, Ekholm K, Johansson B, Tunestål P, Milovanovic N, Keeler N, *et al.* Investigation of the combustion characteristics with focus on partially premixed combustion in a heavy duty engine. *SAE Int J Fuels Lubr* 2009. https://doi.org/10.4271/2008-01-1658.

57. Lewander CM, Johansson B, Tunestal P. Extending the operating region of multi-cylinder partially premixed combustion using high octane number fuel. *SAE Tech. Pap.*, 2011.

58. Musculus MPB, Miles PC, Pickett LM. Conceptual models for partially premixed low-temperature diesel combustion. *Prog Energy Combust Sci* 2013;39:246–83. https://doi.org/10.1016/j.pecs.2012.09.001.

59. Sher E. Environmental Aspects of Air Pollution. *Handb. Air Pollut. from Intern. Combust. Engines*, Elsevier; 1998, p. 27–41. https://doi.org/10.1016/B978-012639855-7/50041-7.

60. Zheng M, Mulenga MC, Reader GT, Wang M, Ting DSK, Tjong J. Biodiesel engine performance and emissions in low temperature combustion. *Fuel* 2008. https://doi.org/10.1016/j.fuel.2007.05.039.

61. Zheng M, Reader GT, Hawley JG. Diesel engine exhaust gas recirculation - A review on advanced and novel concepts. *Energy Convers Manag* 2004. https://doi.org/10.1016/S0196-8904(03)00194-8.

62. *Handbook of Air Pollution From Internal Combustion Engines*. Elsevier; 1998. https://doi.org/10.1016/B978-0-12-639855-7.X5038-8.

63. Ladommatos N, Abdelhalim S, Zhao H. The effects of exhaust gas recirculation on diesel combustion and emissions. *Int J Engine Res* 2000. https://doi.org/10.1243/1468087001545290.

64. Ladommatos N, Abdelhalim SM, Zhao H, Hu Z. The dilution, chemical, and thermal effects of exhaust gas recirculation on diesel engine emissions - Part 3: Effects of water vapour. *SAE Tech. Pap.*, 1997. https://doi.org/10.4271/971659.

65. Ladommatos N, Abdelhalim SM, Zhao H, Hu Z. The effects of carbon dioxide in exhaust gas recirculation on diesel engine emissions. *Proc Inst Mech Eng Part D J Automob Eng* 1998. https://doi.org/10.1243/0954407981525777.

66. Ladommatos N, Abdelhalim S, Zhao H. Control of oxides of nitrogen from diesel engines using diluents while minimising the impact on particulate pollutants. *Appl Therm Eng* 1998;18:963–80. https://doi.org/10.1016/S1359-4311(98)00031-3.

67. Ladommatos N, Abdelhalim SM, Zhao H, Hu Z. The Dilution, Chemical, and Thermal Effects of Exhaust Gas Recirculation on Diesel Engine Emissions - Part 4: Effects of Carbon Dioxide and Water Vapour. *SAE Tech. Pap.*, 1997. https://doi.org/10.4271/971660.

68. Inagaki K, Fuyuto T, Nishikawa K, Nakakita K, Sakata I. Dual-Fuel PCI Combustion Controlled by In-Cylinder Stratification of Ignitability. *SAE Tech. Pap.*, 2006. https://doi.org/10.4271/2006-01-0028.

69. Kokjohn S, Hanson R, Splitter D, Kaddatz J, Reitz RD. Fuel Reactivity Controlled Compression Ignition (RCCI) Combustion in Light- and Heavy-Duty Engines. *SAE Int J Engines* 2011;4:2011-01–0357. https://doi.org/10.4271/2011-01-0357.

70. Wissink ML, Lim JH, Splitter DA, Hanson RM, Reitz RD. Investigation of injection strategies to improve high efficiency rcci combustion with diesel and gasoline direct injection. *ASME 2012 Intern. Combust. Engine Div. Fall Tech. Conf. ICEF 2012*, 2012. https://doi.org/10.1115/ICEF2012-92107.

71. Sharma N, Agarwal RA, Agarwal AK. Particulate Bound Trace Metals and Soot Morphology of Gasohol Fueled Gasoline Direct Injection Engine. *J Energy Resour Technol* 2018;141:022201. https://doi.org/10.1115/1.4040580.

72. Niemeyer KE, Daly SR, Cannella WJ, Hagen CL. A Novel Fuel Performance Index for Low-Temperature Combustion Engines Based on Operating Envelopes in Light-Duty Driving Cycle Simulations. *J Eng Gas Turbines Power* 2015;137. https://doi.org/10.1115/1.4029948.

73. Agarwal AK, Agarwal RA, Gupta T, Gurjar BR. Introduction to Biofuels. *Green Energy Technol.*, 2017, p. 3–6. https://doi.org/10.1007/978-981-10-3791-7_1.

74. Starck L, Lecointe B, Forti L, Jeuland N. Impact of fuel characteristics on HCCI combustion: Performances and emissions. *Fuel* 2010. https://doi.org/10.1016/j.fuel.2010.05.028.

75. Tanaka S, Ayala F, Keck JC. A reduced chemical kinetic model for HCCI combustion of primary reference fuels in a rapid compression machine. *Combust Flame* 2003. https://doi.org/10.1016/S0010-2180(03)00057-9.

76. Aceves SM, Flowers DL, Martinez-Frias J, Smith JR, Westbrook CK, Pitz WJ, *et al.* A Sequential Fluid-Mechanic Chemical-Kinetic Model of Propane HCCI Combustion. *SAE Tech. Pap.*, 2001. https://doi.org/10.4271/2001-01-1027.

77. Mack JH, Dibble RW, Buchholz BA, Flowers DL. The Effect of the Di-Tertiary Butyl Peroxide (DTBP) additive on HCCI Combustion of Fuel Blends of Ethanol and Diethyl Ether. *SAE Tech. Pap.*, 2005. https://doi.org/10.4271/2005-01-2135.

78. Ithnin AM, Noge H, Kadir HA, Jazair W. An overview of utilizing water-in-diesel emulsion fuel in diesel engine and its potential research study. *J Energy Inst* 2014;87:273–88. https://doi.org/10.1016/j.joei.2014.04.002.

79. Debnath BK, Saha UK, Sahoo N. A comprehensive review on the application of emulsions as an alternative fuel for diesel engines. *Renew Sustain Energy Rev* 2015;42:196–211. https://doi.org/10.1016/j.rser.2014.10.023.

80. Jhalani A, Sharma D, Soni SL, Sharma PK, Sharma S. A comprehensive review on water-emulsified diesel fuel: chemistry, engine performance and exhaust emissions. *Environ Sci Pollut Res* 2019. https://doi.org/10.1007/s11356-018-3958-y.

81. Vellaiyan S, Amirthagadeswaran KS. The role of water-in-diesel emulsion and its additives on diesel engine performance and emission levels: A retrospective review. *Alexandria Eng J* 2016;55:2463–72. https://doi.org/10.1016/j.aej.2016.07.021.

82. M. MM. Reduction of NOx on a Single Cylinder CI Engine Running on Diesel-Biodiesel Blends by New Approach, 2020, p. 159–72. https://doi.org/10.4018/978-1-7998-2539-5.ch008.

83. Saravanan M, Anbarasu A, Gnanasekaran BM. Study of performance and emission characteristics of IC engines by using diesel-water emulsion. *Int J Adv Manuf Technol* 2013;69:2531–44. https://doi.org/10.1007/s00170-013-5132-5.

84. Bedford F, Rutland C, Dittrich P, Raab A, Wirbeleit F. Effects of Direct Water Injection on DI Diesel Engine Combustion. *SAE Pap* 2000;2000-01-29:1–10. https://doi.org/2000-01-29.

85. Jhalani A, Sharma D, Soni S, Sharma PK, Singh D. Feasibility assessment of a newly prepared cow-urine emulsified diesel fuel for CI engine application. *Fuel* 2020;288:119713. https://doi.org/10.1016/j.fuel.2020.119713.

86. Basha JS, Anand RB. Effects of nanoparticle additive in the water-diesel emulsion fuel on the performance, emission and combustion characteristics of a diesel engine. *Int J Veh Des* 2012;59:164. https://doi.org/10.1504/IJVD.2012.048692.

87. Jhalani A, Sharma D, Soni SL, Sharma PK. Effects of process parameters on performance and emissions of a water-emulsified diesel-fueled compression ignition engine. *Energy Sources, Part A Recover Util Environ Eff* 2019. https://doi.org/10.1080/15567036.2019.1669739.

88. Dhole AE, Yarasu RB, Lata DB. Investigations on the combustion duration and ignition delay period of a dual fuel diesel engine with hydrogen and producer gas as secondary fuels. *Appl Therm Eng* 2016;107:524–32. https://doi.org/10.1016/j.applthermaleng.2016.06.151.

89. Reyes JGT, Quiros EN. Determination of the Start and End of Combustion in a Direct Injection Diesel Engine Using the Apparent Heat Release Rate. *Proc. ASME 2017 Power Conf. Jt. with ICOPE-17, North Carolina*: ASME; 2017, p. 1–6.

90. Seifi MR, Hassan-Beygi SR, Ghobadian B, Desideri U, Antonelli M. Experimental investigation of a diesel engine power, torque and noise emission using water-diesel emulsions. *Fuel* 2016;166:392–9. https://doi.org/10.1016/j.fuel.2015.10.122.

91. Nour M, Kosaka H, Abdel-Rahman AK, Bady M. Effect of Water Injection into Exhaust Manifold on Diesel Engine Combustion and Emissions. *Energy Procedia* 2016;100:178–87. https://doi.org/10.1016/j.egypro.2016.10.162.

92. Baskar P, Senthil Kumar A. Experimental investigation on performance characteristics of a diesel engine using diesel-water emulsion with oxygen enriched air. *Alexandria Eng J* 2017;56:137–46. https://doi.org/10.1016/j.aej.2016.09.014.

93. Suresh, V., Amirthagadeswaran KS. Combustion and Performance Characteristics of Water-in-diesel Emulsion Fuel. *Energy Sources, Part A Recover Util Environ Eff* 2015;37:2020–8. https://doi.org/10.1080/15567036.2015.1072605.

94. Kumar PS, Venkatesh B, Khan SPS. Emission control by using water emulsified diesel in single cylinder diesel engine. *Int J Adv Eng Technol* 2013;5:263–73.

95. Park JW, Huh KY, Lee JH. Reduction of NOx, smoke and brake specific fuel consumption with optimal injection timing and emulsion ratio of water-emulsified diesel. *Proc Inst Mech Eng Part D-Journal Automob Eng* 2001;215:83–93. https://doi.org/10.1243/0954407011525476.

96. Attia AMA, Kulchitskiy AR. Influence of the structure of water-in-fuel emulsion on diesel engine performance. *Fuel* 2014;116:703–8. https://doi.org/10.1016/j.fuel.2013.08.057.

97. Jazair W, Azrin M. Combustion performance and exhaust emission of DI diesel engine using various sources of waste cooking oil. *Combust. Altern. Fuel, Malaysia: 2010.*

98. Farfaletti A, Astorga C, Martini G, Manfredi U, Mueller A, Rey M, *et al.* Effect of water/fuel emulsions and a cerium-based combustion improver additive on HD and LD diesel exhaust emissions. *Environ Sci Technol* 2005;39:6792–9. https://doi.org/10.1021/es048345v.

99. Wang Y, Liu H, Lee CFF. Particulate matter emission characteristics of diesel engines with biodiesel or biodiesel blending: A review. *Renew Sustain Energy Rev* 2016;64:569–81. https://doi.org/10.1016/j.rser.2016.06.062.

100. Stein R, Boucsein B, Fahl K, Garcia de Oteyza T, Knies J, Niessen F. Accumulation of particulate organic carbon at the Eurasian continental margin during late Quaternary times: controlling mechanisms and paleo-environmental significance. *Glob Planet Change* 2001;31:87–104. https://doi.org/10.1016/S0921-8181(01)00114-X.

101. Merkisz J, Pielecha J. Analysis of Particle Concentrations and Smoke in Common-Rail Diesel Engine. *Sae Tech. Pap.*, 2008. https://doi.org/10.4271/2008-01-1743.

102. Sung Y, Jung G, Park J, Choi B, Lim MT. Relation between particulate emissions and exhaust smoke level in premixed charge compression ignition engine. *J Mech Sci Technol* 2014;28:783–7. https://doi.org/10.1007/s12206-013-1144-1.

103. Samec N, Kegl B, Dibble RW. Numerical and experimental study of water/oil emulsified fuel combustion in a diesel engine. *Fuel* 2002;81:2035–44. https://doi.org/10.1016/S0016-2361(02)00135-7.

104. Roth P, Brandt O, Gersum SVON. High Temperature Oxidation of Suspended Soot Particles Verified by CO and CO2 Measurements. *Symp Combust* 1990;23:1485–91. https://doi.org/https://10.0.3.248/S0082-0784(06)80417-0.

105. Kadota T, Yamasaki H. Recent advances in the combustion of water fuel emulsion. *Prog Energy Combust Sci* 2002;28:385–404.

106. Lif A, Holmberg K. Water-in-diesel emulsions and related systems. *Adv Colloid Interface Sci* 2006;123–126:231–9. https://doi.org/10.1016/j.cis.2006.05.004.
107. Honnery, DR, Tappe M, Kent, JH. Two Parametric Models of Soot Growth Rates in Laminar Ethylene Diffusion Flames. *Combust Sci Technol* 1992;83:305–21. https://doi.org/10.1080/00102209208951838.
108. Hasannuddin AK, Wira JY, Sarah S, Ahmad MI, Aizam SA, Aiman MAB, *et al.* Durability studies of single cylinder diesel engine running on emulsion fuel. *Energy* 2016;94:557–68. https://doi.org/10.1016/j.energy.2015.10.144.

11

Efficiency Optimization of Indoor Air Disinfection by Radiation Exposure for Poultry Breeding Rational for Microclimate Systems Modernization for Livestock Premises

Dovlatov Igor Mamedjarevich* and Yurochka Sergey Sergeevich

*Federal Scientific Agroengineering Center VIM (FGBNU FNAC VIM),
Russian Federation, Moscow, Russia*

Abstract

In I, II and III climatic zones of Russia, where the winter temperature reaches -18°C and the average wind velocity makes up to 3.6 m/s, the majority of farmers use no means of forced ventilation in cowsheds because they are energy-consuming. This leads to the fact that in winter, the air exchange rate in cowsheds tends to 0 times/hour); due to the gas composition, both the cows' productivity and the milk quality fall. In the framework of this study, the publications search and analysis was carried out. It showed that the gas making the heaviest impact on the cows' productivity is ammonia; and a non-compliance with its maximum admissible concentration (MAC) in the gas composition leads to a productivity loss up to 20%. In the course of both theoretical and experimental researches on a dairy farm in the Moscow region, the following results were obtained. The error of convergence between the theoretical modeling results and the natural measurements made 11.4% for NH_3, 29.8% for the air velocity, and 0% for H_2S. The air exchange rate in the premises was no more than 0.22 times per hour. During day and night, MAC exceeding on H_2S was increased from 0.23 mg/m³ up to 2.62 mg/m³, while the same on NH_3 from 5.15 mg/m³ to 28.11 mg/m³. By way of increase of the computational grid, increase of a number of theoretical modeling iterations and setting of greater number of boundary conditions, it is possible to reduce the convergence error of the theoretical and the practical results down to 5%. In order

*Corresponding author: Dovlatovim@mail.ru

Pandian Vasant, Gerhard-Wilhelm Weber, Joshua Thomas, José Antonio Marmolejo-Saucedo
and Roman Rodriguez-Aguilar (eds.) *Artificial Intelligence for Renewable Energy and Climate Change,*
(371–388) © 2022 Scrivener Publishing LLC

to automate the microclimate monitoring process, it is proposed to install sensors of the gas composition in livestock premises. The sensors installation should be done at the height of 1.5 – 2 m.

Keywords: Microclimate, air cleanliness, livestock premise, air exchange

11.1   Introduction

In modern dairy farming, an urgent problem is the optimal conditions control for animal keeping [1–4]. In the case of a high concentration of livestock on the premises, the air quality gets deteriorated and the maximum admissible concentrations (MAC) are exceeded for a number of gases including carbon dioxide, hydrogen sulfide and ammonia, the dust content and the pathogenic micro-flora concentration in the air. Additionally, for effective microclimate monitoring, it is necessary to control such air parameters as its temperature, humidity and flow velocity. The results of numerous studies indicate that the non-compliance with the standards reduces the animals' productivity, which leads to significant financial losses.

In the modern publications, the natural ventilation use in cowsheds is proposed [5, 6]. Based on the analysis of the study [7] results, it is possible to assert that regardless of the cattle's keeping methods, whether tethered or loose type, in cowsheds with the natural ventilation system, the microclimate parameters are changed depending on the season of the year and a sector inside of the premise. An insufficient number of air-shafts (both of supply and exhaust types) create unfavorable microclimate conditions throughout the year.

Also, in favor of the natural ventilation, the statistics speak. In the paper [8], it is described that in livestock premises, about 2 billion kWh of electricity per year is spent on ventilation in order to remove the formed harmful substances from the air. Along with that, additionally, the premises heating appliances take 1.8 billion kWh of electricity, 0.6 million meters of natural gas, 1.3 million tons of liquid fuel and 1.7 million tons of solid fuel.

A deviation of the microclimate parameters in livestock buildings from standard limits leads to the following consequences:

- the decrease in cow milk yield by 10-20%;
- the decrease in cows' live weight gain by 20-30%;
- the increase in the death rate of young animals by 5-40%;
- the decrease in productivity by 30-35%;
- the reduction in equipment service life by 15-20%;
- an increase in feed and labor costs per unit of production;
- the threefold reduction in the livestock buildings service life; and
- an increase in repairing costs of technological equipment [9, 10].

For the dairy cows bred in free stalls, the foreign authors [11] propose to solve the heat stress problem with aid of forced ventilation in combination with an automatic irrigation system installed on a network of water pipes, where water flows constantly.

The paper [12] describes the studying of the Holstein dairy herd keeping. A correlation is found between the environmental factors (including temperature, humidity and wind velocity outside cowsheds) and the cows' productivity. The studies were conducted from May 1 to August 31, 2017; this number of days makes 98.6% of the year's warm period. During this period, the clear weather days amounted to 77.4%, the days with moderate clouds 18.1%, the days with precipitation 3.3%, and the days with black clouds 1.2%.

In the study [13], the influence was found of the changes in the ambient temperature and the relative humidity (THI) on the daily cow milk productivity. The research shows that every increase by a unit in THI (temperature-humidity index) causes a decrease of 0.05344 kg in the milk yield per day.

Also, the authors of the paper [14] produced similar results. From January 2005 to April 2010, in Croatia, the effect of THI was studied on the cow milk yield. It was found that with an increase in THI above the critical value (72 units), the daily milk loss made >0.9 kg/day.

In the study [15], the microclimate was analyzed in a cowshed with natural ventilation. The study was conducted according to the principle of analogues; this means that the animals were studied in three zones of the premise: two groups of animals were located close to the cowshed entrances and exits and one group stayed in the center of the premise. The following parameters were studied: the cow milk yield, THI, the ammonia content and the carbon dioxide content in the air. According to the results of the research, it was found that during the stall period of the year, the animals in the control groups located at the ends of the buildings (near the exits) had a higher milk yield per a cow by 90 liters, as compared to the animals placed in the center of the cowshed (Figure 11.1). This is due to the negative effect of MAC exceeding, specifically, of exceeding the admissible concentration of ammonia and carbon dioxide in the air in the center of the cowshed, where the air exchange rate is lower than that close to the ends of the building.

In the studies [16], it was found that in cowsheds, the MAC excess for a number of microclimate parameters (ammonia, carbon dioxide, THI) results in the milk yield reduction by 10-20%, the decrease in live weight gain by 20% and the increase in the young animals' mortality by 5 to 40%.

So, this study is aimed at conducting of both a theoretical simulation of air movement and levels of H_2S and NH_3 getting formed inside a livestock

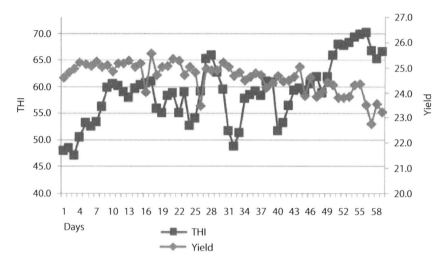

Figure 11.1 Impact of average temperature and humidity index (THI) on daily cow milk yield [15].

premise and a practical measurement of the air velocity, the air humidity and the levels of H_2S and NH_3 in the same livestock premises. Based on the results of the both theoretical and practical researches, it is planned to compare the convergence of the results obtained and to assess the current state of the gas contamination inside the premises.

In I, II and III climatic zones of Russia, where the winter temperature reaches -18°C and the average wind velocity makes up to 3.6 m/s, the majority of farmers do not use the forced ventilation means in cowsheds because they are energy-consuming. Instead, natural ventilation is used. In winter, all the air supply openings (ventilation shafts, windows) are closed and the air exchange rate tends to 0 times/hour. So based on the obtained results, it is planned to assess the current state of the microclimate inside livestock premises in the I, II, III climatic zones of Russia in winter in the conditions of the closed supply valves.

11.2   Materials and Methods

The study was conducted in 2020 on the farm called "K. A. Timiryazev RGAU-MSKhA", the coordinates of which are 55°49'39.2"N 37°32'48.4"E (Figure 11.2). As for the period of year, January was chosen. The average air temperature during the two days of the data collection made -13°C;

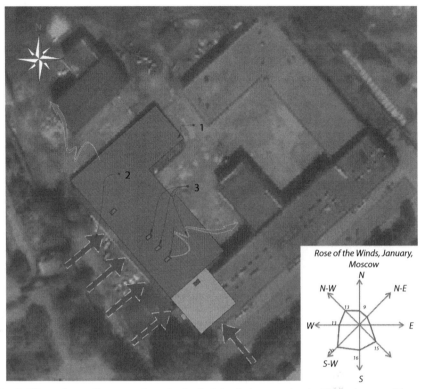

Rose of the Winds, January, Moscow

1 – Building, where milk cows are kept; 2 – Fresh air intake into premise; 3 – Waste air removal from premise.

Figure 11.2 Layout of the farm "K. A. Timiryazev RGAU-MSKhA" used the natural ventilation with the wind rose in winter period.

the weather was clear; the outdoor air movement velocity during the two days was no more than 1 m/s.

Figure 11.2 shows the farm layout with the wind rose [17, 18].

In two premises No. 1 and No. 2 (Figure 11.3), the analysis of the air gas composition was carried out. In the premise No. 1, there were kept the full-aged healthy cows of the black-and-white breed with lactation during 1-4 years and the average live weight 550 kg. In the premise No. 2, calves were kept. The animals' keeping system was tethered in 2 rows. The method of the manure removal is based on use of scraper conveyors (Figure 11.3) b). The sizes of the premise No.1 are 27x15x3.45 (LxWxH); the volume is 1397.25 m³. The sizes of the premise No. 2 are 15x15x3.45 m; the volume is 776.25 m³. The fresh air intake into the premises was carried out by windows opening (natural ventilation). The premise No. 1 has 9 windows with

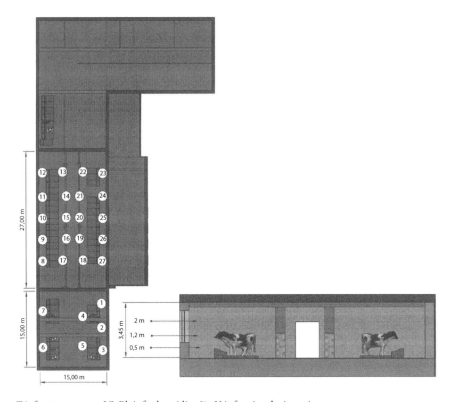

T is for temperature, °C; Rh is for humidity, %.; V is for air velocity, m/s.

Figure 11.3 Farm layout. Measurement points of air gas composition.

vents; the total area of the openings is 5.52 m². The premise No. 2 has 8 windows with a total area of openings of 4.91 m².

There are three ventilation shafts here, 6 holes in each shaft, the area of 1 hole is S=0,0416 m²; the area (S) of the exhaust vents is equal to 0.74m². The premises, where the animals are kept, are not heated.

The data collection took place over two days on January 21 and 22, 2020. On the first day, the measurements were carried out from 8:00 am to 4:00 pm. The gas composition of the indoor air was determined. It was done at 3 different heights (0.5 m; 1.2 m; 2 m) at 27 points of the cowshed. On the second day, the measurements were carried out from 6:00 a.m. to 6:00 p.m. The indoor air gas composition measurement was carried out in order to determine the change in the gas composition during a day. The distance was measured using SNDWAY SW-T60, the laser rangefinder of 2nd class. The measurements of the gas composition were carried out at 27 points of the premise at three heights of 0.5 m, 1.2 m,

2 m at each point. There was determined the amount of hydrogen sulfide H_2S mg/m³ and the amount of ammonia NH_3 mg/m³ in the air. The determination of the gas composition of the air was carried out with use of the portable device "Geolan-1P". This appliance has the functions of forced gas sample taking and of percentage determination of the following substances: NH_3, H_2, SF_6, NO_2 and NO, SO_2, O_2 and O_3, CO_2 and CO, H_2CO, CH_4, C_3H_8, C_2H_4, C_6, H_{14}. At 12 points in the premise, the following measurements were carried out: the air velocity V, ??/??, the humidity level and the indoor temperature. Two measurement points were located in the center of the premises No. 1 and No. 2 at the height of 1.5 m. The location of the remaining 10 points is shown in Figure 11.3. With the device "Meteoscope-M", the temperature, the relative humidity, the air flow velocity and the atmospheric pressure were measured. During the two days of measurement making, the wind direction was northeast. Figure 11.3 shows the layout of the farm, where the points are marked of the measurements of the gas composition of the air and the air velocity on the first and second days of the research.

In the course of the research, in the software packages SketchUp 2020 and SolidWorks 2020m, the simplified model of the farm was developed with full compliance with the overall dimensions of the premises as well as the air supply and exhaust openings layout. The modeling of air movement was carried out in the software package SolidWorks 2020.

For the theoretical modeling of the indoor air movement in the SolidWorks 2020 software package, the following boundary conditions were set. A cross-section of the building was taken, displaying the following elements: a window acting as an air supply channel; a stall (a cow's place); an air exhaust shaft. The calculations were based on the assumption that the average weight of a cow is 550 kg. The day before the theoretical studies in the premises, the "Meteoscope-M" device measured the velocity of the air supply through the window; it made 1 m/s. (As the speed of the outside air on the street was 1 m/s and in accordance with Bernoulli's law, the air entering a window increases its velocity in the window opening just slightly, the assumption for the theoretical modeling was made to establish the boundary condition for the air velocity to be 1 m/s.) Also, on the day before the theoretical studies, the velocity of the exhaust air passing through the ventilation shafts was measured; it made 0.067m/s. The supply air temperature was -13°C, the internal air temperature was -13°C, the pressure was 101325 Pa, and the external air velocity along the X axis was 1 m/s. The outdoor air temperature, the air velocity and the direction of air movement were identical during the two days of the research. The temperature of the inner walls was set to +5°C.

In the SolidWorks 2020 software package, for the theoretical modeling of indoor air filling with ammonia and hydrogen sulfide, the following boundary conditions were set. The average indoor ammonia concentration was 0.00409% part by volume, which was equal to 57.96 mg/m³. The average indoor hydrogen sulfide concentration was 05% part by volume, which was equal to 0.98 mg/m³. The data on the average concentrations were obtained by the measurements conducted on the first day in the middle of the premises (Figure 11.3, point 12) at the height of 1.5 m with aid of the device "Geolan-1P". The average values were determined by the following appropriate settings on this device: every 20 minutes, the device collected the data and, based on the results, gave the average value. The set average humidity made 35%. Due to the complexity of the modeling, neglected was such a boundary condition as the hierarchical movement of air caused by the working staff members.

It was found that over time, the content of the detected gases tends to disappearance exponentially [19]. Having developed a natural logarithm for calculation of the air exchange rate per time unit for the two gases under study, we determined that the negative values obtained indicate the negative air exchange, i.e., describe the situation when the gases release during the vital activity of animals occurs more actively than the natural ventilation. On the contrary, positive values speak for the positive air exchange. The calculation of the values of the air exchange was carried out according to the formula 11.1:

$$N = \frac{lnC(t_1) - lnC(t_0)}{t_1}, \tag{11.1}$$

where N is air changes per hour; $C(t^0)$ is concentration of certain gas at a time; $C(t^1)$ is average concentration of gas per hour; and t^1 is 1 hour of time. In this article, we assume that a decrease in a concentration of a certain gas was not always correctly recorded due to the fluctuating air flows. The latter were caused, firstly, by the unstable velocity of external flows, and, secondly, by the difference in pressure caused by the movements of doors and gates. It was not possible to prevent the opening and closing of the farm gates by the staff members due to the mandatory execution of the working processes. Originally, the formula was described by the authors Alaa Kiwan [Kiwan et al.]. In this article, the formula was changed and the calculation method of our own was proposed. This was done as in this study, the results obtaining based on this formula were impossible due to the fact that when calculating $ln\ x$ in this context, x could not be less than zero.

11.3   Results

As the result of the theoretical studies conducted in the SolidWorks 2020 software package based on the conditions described above for the air velocity calculating in the 0YX plane (Figure 11.4), it was found that the average air velocity in the zone 2 (the cow breathing zone) made 0.468 m/s. The average air velocity in the zone 4 and throughout the premise was 0.124 m/s, which does not correspond to the MAC for closed rooms [20]. Also, the obtained air velocity around a cow (2 m/s) does not correspond to the norm [21]. The maximum air velocity (1 m/s) was observed in the zone 1, i.e., directly in the window. The air velocity in the zone 6 was 0.067 m/s, and in the zone 5 it was even lower.

Figure 11.5 shows the results of the theoretical study of the indoor air gas composition change per unit of time. The fresh air with a minimum amount of both ammonia and hydrogen sulfide enters the room from the point 1. At the point 2 (the cow's breathing zone) at the height of +0.5m from the floor level, the hydrogen sulfide level is 0.35 mg/m^3, and the ammonia

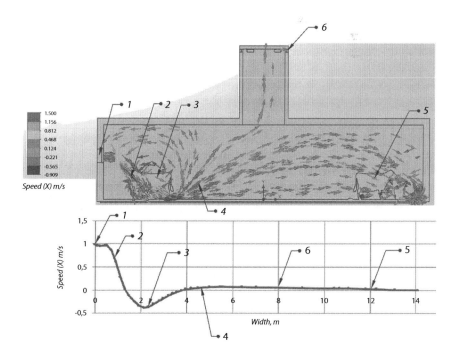

Figure 11.4 Theoretical study of air velocity in plane 0YX.

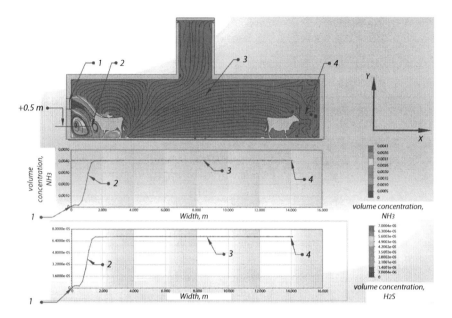

Figure 11.5 Theoretical study of volume concentration of ammonia and hydrogen sulfide in plane 0YX.

concentration is 18.38 mg/m³. In the remaining zones (the point 3), the concentrations are equal to the established norms. In the point 4, vortices are observed associated with the air flows movements. Here, for H_2S/m^3, the MAC value is not more than 3 and for NH_3/m^3, it is not more than 20 [21].

Figure 11.6 shows the results of the practical measurements of the ammonia and the hydrogen sulfide at the points 10, 15, 20, 25 at three heights: 0.5 m, 1.2 m, 2 m. In the zone of the cows' respiration at the point 10 at the height of 0.5 m, the H_2S concentration is equal to 0.35 mg/m³ and the same of NH_3 is 18.38 mg/m³.

Figure 11.7 shows the changes in the concentrations of H_2S and NH_3 during day and night. The change in the gas contamination is well explained by the following fact: from 6:00 p.m. to 6:00 a.m. (at nights), the doors and windows in the premise where the cows are kept are closed. At this time, the animal waste products are accumulated in the premise. At 6:00 a.m., the staff starts cleaning the premise. From 7:00 to 8:00 a.m., the scraper conveyor is working actively. The concentrations of H_2S and NH_3 reach values 48.11 mg/m³ and 5.62 mg/m³ respectively. The manure movement causes an active release of the gases. Then the staff members clean the premises; at that time, the windows and doors are open. By 2:00 p.m.,

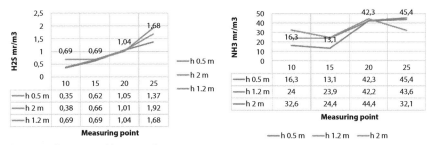

a)– H2S milligram/m3; b) NH3 milligram/m3

Рисунок 6 – Результаты практического замера аммиака и сероводорода в точках 10, 15, 20, 25 (см.рис.3)

Figure 11.6 Results of practical measurement of ammonia and hydrogen sulfide contents at points 10, 15, 20, 25 (see Figure 11.3).

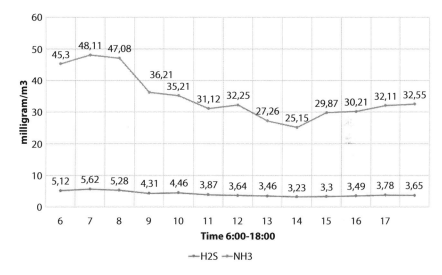

Figure 11.7 Results of practical measurement of H2S and NH3 contents from 6:00 a.m. to 6:00 p.m.

when the premise cleaning is finished up, the values H_2S and NH_3 fall to the minimum values 25.15 mg/m³ and 3.23 mg/m³ respectively. By 6:00 p.m., when the active cleaning is finished, all sources of the fresh air intake (the windows and the doors) are shut up and the animals stay for night.

Table 11.1 shows measurement results in the period from 12:00 a.m. to 2:00 p.m. on the parameters T, Rh, V.

Table 11.1 Measurement of temperature, air velocity, humidity.

Point	Parameters		
	T, °C	Rh, %	V, м/с
1	17,3	39,6	1,02
2	17,3	33	0,33
3	16,6	36,2	0,22
4	16,3	40	0,2
5	16,3	40,6	0,2
6	15,1	35,5	0,31
7	14,5	35,5	0,31
8	14	31,2	0,61
9	13,6	34,2	0,1
10	13,4	34,4	0,43
11	13,2	35,4	0,16
12	12,5	12,5	0,18
13	15,8	37,3	0,21
Average	15,1	34,3	0,33

11.4   Discussion

At conducting of the theoretical studies in the SolidWorks 2020 software package on the above-described boundary conditions for the air velocity in the 0YX plane (Figure 11.4), it was found that at the point 2 (the cow's breathing zone), there is a decrease in the average air velocity; meanwhile at the point 3, a swirl of the air flow forms, which causes a significant decrease in the velocity pressure. On the remaining way part, the steady uniform flow rate is formed. Thus, the average air velocity in the zone 4 and throughout the premise is 0.124 m/s.

The results of the theoretical studying of the changes of the H_2S and NH_3 concentrations and the air velocity show a good coincidence with the natural measurements. The results are represented in Table 11.2.

Table 11.2 Comparison between results of theoretical studying and natural measurements.

Parameters	Theoretical studying in cow breathing zone (Figure 11.5, point 20)	Natural measurements
H_2S	0.35 mg/m³	0.35 mg/m³
NH_3	18.4 mg/m³	16.3 mg/m³
Air velocity	0.47 m/s	0.33 m/s

The comparison between the practical and theoretical results was conducted based on the comparison between the natural measurement results at the point 10 at the height of 0.5 m (Figure 11.3) and the theoretical study results at the point 2 (Figure 11.5). The comparison of the results for these points is expedient for the reason that the pressure of the external air exceeds the pressure caused by the hierarchical air flows associated with the staff activities (doors opening/closing). Within this study, it would be incorrect to compare the convergence of the results at other points as otherwise a maximum set of conditions should be taken into account in the simulation, which was not the purpose of this study. This point is chosen because it is a cow's breathing zone, and we needed to find out the real quality of air received by cows standing near the natural supply ventilation system. It is obvious that due to the lack of ventilation of the air supply type in the cowshed, the animals breathe air in which the concentrations of H_2S and NH_3 exceed MAC.

The small holes in the cutoff shown in Figure 11.3 have their total area of 0.24 m². Previously in this cowshed, the forced ventilation system was used, where both the air supply and air exhaust systems were present. Now the system is out of order and does not function any longer. The low air velocity in the exhaust shaft is explained by the fact that the exhaust air leaves the premise in hierarchical manner; and the available pressure difference, the temperature difference and the height of the pipes do not allow reaching the exhaust air velocity equal to the velocity of the air inflow.

The present state of the turned off ventilation system and the exhaust shafts is shown in Figure 11.8.

With use of the formula (11.1) and the data given in Figure 11.7, the air exchange coefficient was determined on H_2S and NH_3. Figure 11.9 shows the calculation results.

For calculating of the air exchange rate on NH_3 and H_2S, the time was taken from 9:00 a.m. to 11:00 a.m. for the reason that it was not possible to

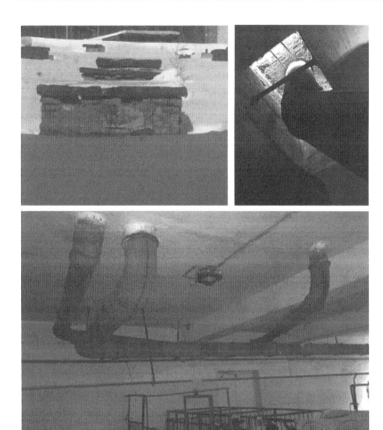

Figure 11.8 State of ventilation system.

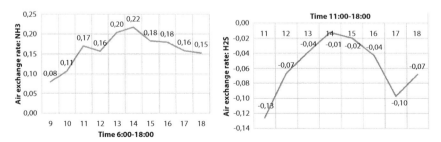

a)– NH3 milligram/m3; b)– H2S milligram/m3

Figure 11.9 Air exchange rate on NH3 and H2S.

calculate the logarithm with a negative value. The minimum air exchange rate on NH_3 is observed at 9:00 a.m. and it is equal to 0.08 times per hour. This is due to the fact that at this time, the premise undergoes cleaning; neither windows nor doors are open in full; the supply of fresh air is minimal. The maximal air exchange rate on both diagrams is observed at 2:00 p.m. and it is equal to 0.22 times. As for the hydrogen sulfide, its air exchange rate during the day is always negative and varies from -0.13 times to -0.1 times. This is due to the fact that in the air intake places (windows), outside of the building, there is a walking area for animals, where the manure is accumulated at the time of the cows' walking. In the case of a wind blowing from north to south, the air entering the cowshed is a mixture of the fresh air with the hydrogen sulfide and the ammonia.

Of all the gases existing on the farm, ammonia is the most harmful; its presence has a serious effect on the cows' productivity reduction. The ammonia affects the animals' liver and ketone bodies in their urine; so the ammonia not only lowers the cows' productivity but also deteriorates the milk quality [22–24]. During this study, it was found that in a cowshed, it is necessary to place sensors-analyzers of ammonia, hydrogen sulfide and carbon dioxide. If the ammonia sensors are activated, the gas removal system should be turned on. The ammonia is heavier than the air; however, the maximum concentrations of the ammonia are recorded at the height of 1.5-2 m, in the breathing zones of cows and above. This is due to the ascending air flows; the air rises to the extraction spots. That is why the ammonia, hydrogen sulfide and carbon dioxide sensors should be installed at the height of 1.5-2 m. A specific height and installation location is selected depending on the type of agricultural farm and the design features of the cowshed.

11.5   Conclusions

The study was conducted in the farm "K. A. Timiryazev RGAU-MSKhA" located in the Moscow region and keeping the milking herd. Based on the analysis of the microclimate of the livestock premises and results of the theoretical modeling conducted for determination of the air velocity and the levels of the ammonia and the hydrogen sulfide contents in the air, the following conclusions were made:

1) When comparing the results of the theoretical modeling and the natural measurements, the accuracy was as follows: 88.6% on NH_3; 71.2 % on air velocity, and 100% on

H_2S. With an increase in the calculated grid, an increase in the number of iterations of the theoretical modeling, as well as with setting a higher number of boundary conditions, it is possible to reduce the error to 5%.

2) The air exchange rate in the premises made no more than 0.22 times per hour. This is due to two parameters: the insufficient area of the window openings and the insufficient area of the exhaust opening. The height of the exhaust pipe does not create sufficient traction so that to increase the air exchange rate.

3) The MAC exceeding on H_2S during day and night varies from 0.23 mg/m^3 up to 2.62 mg/m^3.

4) The MAC exceeding on NH_3 during day & night varies from 5.15 mg/m^3 up to 28.11 mg/m^3.

References

1. Dovlatov I.M., Yuferev L.Yu., Mikaeva S.A., Mikaeva A.S., Zheleznikova O.E. Development and testing of combined germicidal recirculator. *Light & Engineering*, 2021. Vol. 29. No. 3. pp. 43-49.

2. Tomasello, Nicoletta; Valenti, Francesca; Cascone, Giovanni. Development of a CFD Model to Simulate Natural Ventilation in a Semi-Open Free-Stall Barn for Dairy Cows, *BUILDINGS* Volume: 9 Issue: 8 Article Number: 183, Aug. 2019.

3. Dovlatov I.M., Rudzik E.S. Improvement of microclimate in agricultural premises by air disinfecting with ultraviolet radiation. *Innovations in Agriculture*. 2018. No. 3 (28) pp. 47-52.

4. Tikhomirov, Dmitry; Izmailov, Andrey; Lobachevsky, Yakov; Tikhomirov, Anatoly V. Energy Consumption Optimization in Agriculture and Development Perspectives. *International Journal of Energy Optimization and Engineering* (2020) Vol. 9. Issue 4, pp. 1-19. DOI: 10.4018/IJEOE.2020100101

5. Natural Ventilation for Freestall Dairy Barns https://vtechworks.lib.vt.edu/bitstream/handle/10919/56809/442-763.pdf?sequence=1

6. Tomasello, Nicoletta; Valenti, Francesca; Cascone, Giovanni. Development of a CFD Model to Simulate Natural Ventilation in a Semi-Open Free-Stall Barn for Dairy Cows. *BUILDINGS* Volume: 9 Issue: 8 Article Number: 183, Aug. 2019.

7. Martynova E.N., Yastrebova E.A. Features of microclimate in cowsheds with natural ventilation system. *Veterinary Medicine, Animal Science and Biotechnology*. 2015. No. 6. pp. 52-56.

8. Nalivayko A.P. Microclimate regulation system on cattle farms and com-plexes. *Scientific and educational potential of young people in solving urgent problems of XXI century.* 2017. No. 6. pp. 177-180.

9. Martynova E.N., Yastrebova E.A. Physiological state of cows depending on microclimate in premises. *Achievements of Science and Technology in Agro-Industrial Complex.* 2013, No. 8. pp. 53-56.

10. Dovlatov, I., Yuferev, L., Pavkin, D. Efficiency Optimization of Indoor Air Disinfection by Radiation Exposure for Poultry Breeding. *Advances in Intelligent Systems and Computing,* 2020. 1072, pp. 177-189.

11. Alessandro D'Emilio, Simona M.C. Porto, Giovanni Cascone, Marco Bella, Marco Gulino. Mitigating heat stress of dairy cows bred in a free-stall barn by sprinkler systems coupled with forced ventilation. *Journal of Agricultural Engineering,* Volume 48, Issue 4, pp. 190-195. Article Number: 691, 2017.

12. Mylostyvyi, Roman; Chernenko, Olexandr. Correlations between Environmental Factors and Milk Production of Holstein Cows DATA Volume: 4 Issue: 3 Article Number: 103, Sep 2019.

13. Kučević D. *et al.* Influence of microclimatic conditions on the daily produc-tion of dairy cow. *Biotechnology in Animal Husbandry,* 2013. Vol. 29. No. 1. pp. 45-51.

14. Gantner V. *et al.* Temperature-humidity index values and their significance on the daily production of dairy cattle. *Mljekarstvo: časopis za unaprjeđenje proizvodnje i prerade mlijeka.* 2011. Vol. 61. No. 1. pp. 56-63.

15. Sofronov V. G. *et al.* Microclimate influence on body and milk productivity of dairy cows. *Scientific Notes of Kazan State Academy of Veterinary Medicine Named After N. E. Bauman,* 2016. Vol. 227. No. 3.

16. Lantsova E. O. Changes in ammonia concentration during cleaning of cattle manure with scraper conveyor. *Proceedings of St. Petersburg State Agrarian University,* 2017. No. 4 (49).

17. URL: https://maps.google.ru/ (Application date: 06.07.2021).

18. URL: http://stroydocs.com/info/e_veter (Application date: 06.07.2021).

19. Kiwan A. K. *et al.* Tracer gas technique, air velocity measurement and natural ventilation method for estimating ventilation rates through naturally venti-lated barns. *Agricultural Engineering International: CIGR Journal,* 2012. Vol. 14. No. 4. pp. 22-36.

20. Order of Ministry of Agriculture on December 13, 2016. No. 551 "On approval of Veterinary rules of keeping cattle for purpose of its reproduction, cultivation and sale".

21 Order of Ministry of Agriculture on December 13, 2016. No, 551 "On approval of Veterinary rules of keeping cattle for purpose of its reproduction, cultivation and sale".

22. Lee C. *et al.* Effects of metabolizable protein supply and amino acid supple-mentation on nitrogen utilization, milk production, and ammonia emissions

from manure in dairy cows *Journal of Dairy Science*, 2012. Vol. 95. No. 9. pp. 5253-5268.

23. Vtoryi V. F., Vtoryi S. V., Ilyin R. M. Ammonia concentration in cow barn under limited air exchange. *Proc. 18th Int. Sc. Conf. Engineering for Rural Development*, 2019. pp. 1593-159.

24. Moorby J. M., Theobald V. J. The effect of duodenal ammonia infusions on milk production and nitrogen balance of the dairy cow. *Journal of Dairy Science*, 1999, Vol. 82, No. 11, pp. 2440-2442.

12

Improving the Efficiency of Photovoltaic Installations for Sustainable Development of the Urban Environment

Pavel Kuznetsov[1]*, Leonid Yuferev[2] and Dmitry Voronin[3]

[1]Department of Renewable Energy Sources, Sevastopol State University, Sevastopol, Russian Federation
[2]Federal Scientific Agroengineering Center VIM, Moscow, Russian Federation
[3]Department of Software Engineering of Intelligent Systems, Sevastopol State University, Sevastopol, Russian Federation

Abstract

This work is devoted to an important scientific and practical task aimed at improving the energy efficiency of photovoltaic installations with parallel and mixed connection of modules. This problem is solved by equalizing the voltages of parallel arrays of modules operating in conditions of partial shading. The proposed method for increasing the energy efficiency of photovoltaic installations operating in conditions of partial shading has extreme practical importance for solving the problems of smart urban environment development. It allows to minimize the detrimental effect of existing urban objects (buildings, trees, communications, etc.) on the efficiency of photovoltaic installations introduction, which are an excellent alternative to using existing urban electrical grids, which sometimes require destructive interference in urban processes and lead to significant financial costs, in some cases exceeding the cost of the installed equipment. In addition, meeting the increased energy needs only through the use of traditional electricity generation will lead to a deterioration of the environmental situation. Thus, the authors see the creation of a methodology for parametric optimization of power plants operating from renewable energy sources that contribute to the sustainable development of the urban environment in the context of digital transformation as an extremely important area of further research.

Keywords: Photovoltaic, PV, shading, parallel, mixed, connection, efficiency, sustainable development

*Corresponding author: pavelnik2@gmail.com

Pandian Vasant, Gerhard-Wilhelm Weber, Joshua Thomas, José Antonio Marmolejo-Saucedo and Roman Rodriguez-Aguilar (eds.) *Artificial Intelligence for Renewable Energy and Climate Change*, (389–422) © 2022 Scrivener Publishing LLC

12.1   Introduction

The use of modern technologies to improve the efficiency of organizing the functioning of urban processes and the provision of innovative services forms the basis of the concept of a smart sustainable city (SSC) [1–5]. Its main provisions, the proposed criteria and models for assessing its effectiveness [4, 5] are a kind of response to emerging environmental problems and other risks associated with an increase in the proportion of the population living in cities [1, 2]. Special attention should be paid to the set of strategies for the conceptual development of urban areas, which are called "smart" cities in the literature, proposed by many studies [6–8]. The concept of a "smart" city is aimed at finding new ways to counter these challenges based on the integration of information and communication technologies, the introduction of modern advances in artificial intelligence, big data processing, decision support technologies and IoT [7–10]. Thus, the implementation of the concept of a smart sustainable city in practice allows us to meet the growing needs of the present and future generations while minimizing the negative impact of the implemented technical solutions on the economic, social and environmental components of the city [6–10]. The technological base for ensuring sustainable development of SSC cities is the so-called "smart" solutions in the field of digital transformation of urbanized territories [9–11]. Examples of such solutions are: smart power grids, effective video surveillance systems, intelligent traffic management and housing and communal services. However, the general systemic limitation of the widespread implementation of such solutions is the difficulty of providing them with electricity using city power supply networks. This is due to the need for significant, sometimes destructive interference in urban processes and leads to significant financial costs, in some cases many times higher than the cost of the installed equipment. In addition, meeting the increased energy needs only through the use of traditional types of energy will lead to a deterioration of the environmental situation.

Global development of power plants running on renewable energy sources shows that one of the most dynamically developing branches of the energy direction is solar photovoltaics. Over the past ten years, the world's annual increase in electricity generation due to these resources reached 20-30% of the expected output by 2040 to the level of 6.2% of global electricity production [7–10]. The advantages of this energy source are environmental friendliness, which makes it possible to use it practically at any scale without causing damage to the environment, as well as availability in almost every point of our planet, differing by radiation density by no more than two times [11]. In addition, the modular design of photovoltaic systems allows them to be designed for almost any power, which makes these installations a universal and reliable solution, widely used both in industrial power generation and in small power supply systems [12, 13].

Often, in the design of solar installations, variants of the layout of PV modules are used, suggesting their operation under conditions of uneven illumination, or partial shading for a sufficiently long period of time [13, 14]. The use of such schemes is associated with the limited space of the proposed installation, the desire to save space, or the properties of the terrain. This often does not take into account some of the features of the photovoltaic modules, which leads to a significant decrease in their already low efficiency [15]. Also, uneven lighting of photovoltaic modules can arise due to factors not depending on the design [2]. Examples of such cases can be a shadow from buildings, trees, clouds, etc.

To achieve the required electrical power, solar power plants use serial, parallel and mixed switching of photoelectric cells. In each version of connection, the reduction in efficiency from uneven lighting occurs for various reasons, which requires various technical, economically feasible solutions to increase their energy production when operating under such conditions. This article is devoted to this urgent problem, which needs to be solved considering the significant increase in the number of solar power plants in recent years, about 70% of which has a design with a multi-row arrangement of solar modules with the inherent problem of shading the lower rows with low sun height values [12–15].

Currently, there are a number of ways to partially level out the problem of uneven illumination of photovoltaic systems, consisting of the use of shunt diodes, individual matching DC-DC converters, micro-inverters, tunable switching systems and differentiated maximum power selection systems [16–23]. However, their use often does not allow to significantly increase the energy efficiency of installations, because the solution of this problem requires an integrated approach. For example, the use of only shunt diodes leads to the shunting of shaded photovoltaic modules, which, with mixed switching, significantly reduces the energy production of the group including these modules, due to its voltage mismatch at the points of maximum power with other parallel-connected groups. A similar effect will be manifested when using individual matching converters. The solution of the problem of voltage matching in the parallel array of modules is given special attention in this article, because at the present time there are no economically justified technical solutions on the market capable of solving this problem in ground-based solar stations, as evidenced by their use only in special space installations [25, 26].

Section 12.1 presents the results of the analysis of existing technical solutions for increasing the energy efficiency of photovoltaic installations. Their main advantages and disadvantages are considered. Section 12.2 describes the proposed innovative method for increasing the power generation of photovoltaic installations operating in conditions of partial shading. Mathematical models are presented that make it possible to evaluate the effectiveness of options for the implementation of photovoltaic installations operating in conditions of uneven illumination. Section 12.3 presents the competitive advantages of the proposed solution for ensuring the sustainable development of a smart urban environment.

12.2   Background

The main reasons hindering the widespread use of photovoltaic installations are: low conversion efficiency, high cost, and lack of available energy storage technologies. This subject area is being studied by a large number of leading scientists and specialists, including J.I. Alferov, A.F. Ioffe, G. Rauschenbach, A.P. Landsman, J. Loferensky, V.V. Elistratov, V.A. Mayorov, V.V. Kharchenko and others [27].

The main directions for the development of research in this subject area are increasing energy efficiency and reducing the cost of photovoltaic converters. To begin with, at the beginning of the twentieth century, the efficiency of photovoltaic converters did not exceed 1%. Today, the efficiency of silicon solar cells is from 14 to 18%; the best sample of gallium arsenide (GaAs) is 47% [28].

According to data published by the International Renewable Energy Agency (IRENA), the total cost of photovoltaic systems is significantly (up to times) the cost of photoelectric modules. Thus, it is advisable to focus the attention of researchers on the optimization of the remaining elements of the photovoltaic system (inverters, support structures, batteries, etc.) [29, 30].

The improvement of additional elements of photovoltaic plants, in addition to reducing costs, should be aimed at improving the reliability and stability of energy output in the face of changing environmental parameters, or the effects of external factors (shading, pollution, etc.), and achieving maximum energy efficiency. To this end, in recent years a number of new devices and technologies have been created, the main of which are [31–33]:

- application of solar concentrators;
- the use of active systems for tracking the sun;
- the use of multi-row designs.

Solar concentrators allow increasing the intensity of radiation coming to photoelectric converters and increasing the amount of electric energy received from them. In addition, concentrated radiation increases the efficiency of conversion of solar radiation.

At present, a large number of variants of the designs of solar concentrators have been created [34–37], which can be divided into two main groups: low-potential (Figure 12.1 a, b, c) - with a rectilinear or curvilinear generatrix of the reflecting surface and high potential (Figure 12.1 d, e) - lens, or with a reflecting surface close to the form of surfaces of revolution of the second order: an ellipsoid, a paraboloid, a hemisphere, a hyperboloid.

Low-potential concentrators allow obtaining low values of concentration coefficients in comparison with high-temperature ones. At the same time, their use may not require the presence of active cooling systems, which positively affects the weight and size characteristics and price. In addition, they do not require high accuracy of manufacturing a mirror surface of the reflector and high accuracy of positioning on the sun.

With all the advantages of hubs, they have significant disadvantages. The main ones are: the increase in cost and maintenance costs, the need for heat removal, and the need for trackers for automatic orientation to the sun. Due to the above disadvantages, these solutions do not find industrial application.

Active systems of orientation to the sun deserve special attention. These solutions can significantly increase the power generation of photovoltaic systems (up to 40%) and align the daily schedule of energy generation.

All tracking systems used in solar power plants can be divided into two main categories according to the degree of spatial orientation – with a partial (azimuthal or zenithal) orientation and full (azimuth and zenith) orientation.

Systems with partial orientation cannot ensure the perpendicularity of the sun's rays to the surface of solar cells during the entire daylight,

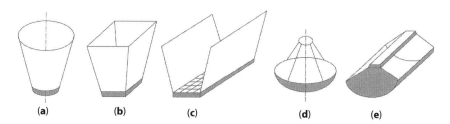

(a)   (b)   (c)   (d)   (e)

Figure 12.1 Examples of solar concentrators. (low-potential: (a) - phocon, (b) - foclin, (c) - focline with two reflecting facets; high-potential: (d) - paraboloid of rotation, (e) - parabolic cylinder).

in contrast to systems with full orientation, but they are cheaper and more reliable than the latter. At the same time, full-switching tracking systems allow not only to provide more solar energy but also to use solar modules with cheaper coating materials by reducing the reflection and refraction coefficients to the minimum values.

On average, the use of systems with partial orientation, allows to increase the daily energy production of photovoltaic installations by 20-25%, and from full to 32% [38, 39]. Also, the advantages of such systems include the possibility of an additional increase in energy output, due to their use in conjunction with certain types of solar concentrators. This is made possible by providing uniform illumination of the reflected radiation of all the solar cells of the installation.

The main disadvantages of using tracking systems are their high cost (in most cases, two or more times the cost of modules), the need for regular, expensive service (usually at least every two years), and a decrease in reliability. Also, the wide use of these systems, in the industrial generation of electrical energy by photoelectric converters, is hindered by the fact that their use leads to mutual shading, with relatively close transverse placement of installations. A consequence of this is a significant reduction in the output of the entire solar power plant, as will be shown in the following sections. Examples of such cases are shown in Figure 12.2. Rare station location is also an inefficient solution due to reduced specific power, which leads to increased area and additional electrical losses.

To increase the energy efficiency of photovoltaic plants multi-row structures are used. The use of such solutions reduces the cost and material consumption of installations. All multi-row structures used in stationary photovoltaic power plants, according to the arrangement of photoelectric modules, can be divided into two types: horizontal and vertical location [40]. Analysis of the world's industrial solar power plants showed that, with the use of the first type of structure, there are usually no more than seven rows of modules (for example, the Abakan solar power station) and, if using the second type, no more than three (for example, the Sevastopol solar power station).

The main factor hindering the effective use of such systems is the mutual shading (Figure 12.3) of the rows of photovoltaic modules at low values of the sun's height [24]. Losses include options for modules on support structures (horizontal or vertical), as well as options for switching modules (block or row). For example, using the horizontal orientation of the modules (Figure 12.4a), compared with the vertical (Figure 12.4b), allows you

Figure 12.2 Cases of shading of photovoltaic systems with a sun tracking system.

to significantly increase the energy efficiency of the photovoltaic system when partial shading occurs [41].

Various options for switching photovoltaic modules also significantly affect the amount of energy loss. The main switching options used in industrial solar power plants are "block" and "linear" (Figure 12.5). With block switching, fewer wires are used than with linear switching, which has a positive effect on the efficiency of electricity transmission from modules to inverters. However, in the case of shading, all arrays of modules (except the first row) work in partial shading conditions. Moreover, the range of input voltages of the inverter may be higher than the voltage range

Figure 12.3 Partial mutual shading of modules in solar power plants with a multi-row structure.

near the maximum power point of such arrays, as a result of which energy extraction from them will be carried out in a non-optimal mode. An example of such a case is a decrease in the output power of the Sevastopol solar power plant, where changing the switching of modules from block vertical to linear allowed increasing the daily power generation of the station in winter more than 2 times [24]. The use of linear switching avoids the operation of the upper array of modules in partial shading conditions,

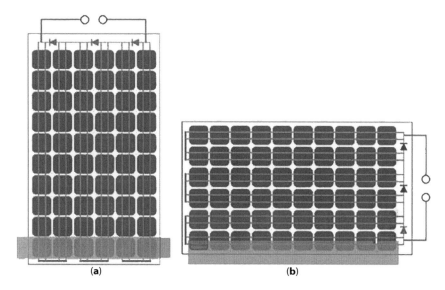

Figure 12.4 Shunting by diodes of solar cells with partial shading (a) - block switching, (b) - line switching.

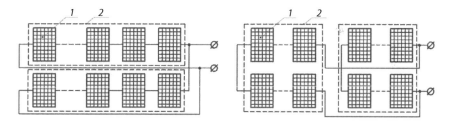

Figure 12.5 Options for switching photovoltaic modules a - row; b - block (1 - photoelectric module; 2 - array of modules).

increasing the efficiency of the entire station, while the lower (darkened) arrays are significantly limited in energy transmission.

The analysis of solutions for improving the energy efficiency of photovoltaic systems shows that the main problem of their use is partial shading. It follows from this that the solution of this problem is important for the development of solar energy.

Currently, there are a number of ways to select electrical energy, which allows to partially level the problem of uneven illumination of photovoltaic installations. Such methods include the use of shunting diodes, individual matching DC-DC converters (ICP), micro-inverters, tunable switching systems and differentiated systems for selecting maximum power.

The use of shunt diodes makes it possible to exclude the influence of shaded modules, on the energy production of other (unprotected) modules in a single serial circuit. Without their use, the current of the entire array of serially connected modules does not exceed the current of the least illuminated photocell [42]. At the same time, energy is dissipated on the shaded element (the so-called "hot spot effect"), followed by its damage [43]. In this connection, the shunt diodes also perform the protective function of the module, protecting it from damage.

The shunt diodes are located directly on the output terminals of the modules. They are connected in such a way that they conduct current in the forward direction (I_{D1}, I_{D2}) when applying the reverse bias voltage (U_{D1}, U_{D2}) to the shaded panels (Figure 12.6). The reverse bias voltage arises if the current flowing through the successive chain (I_{bat}) creates a voltage drop across the shaded area greater than the voltage generated by the shaded panel group itself. In this case, the losses are only the power dissipated in the diodes themselves, due to the voltage drop on them.

The use of shunt diodes is a prerequisite for the reliable operation of photovoltaic installations, but they are not able to solve all the problems arising in conditions of uneven illumination. To such problems, it is possible to carry:

1. disabling a sufficiently large group of solar cells (having partial or total shading), even though they are almost always capable of producing electrical energy;
2. reduce the voltage at the point of maximum power of the entire array of solar cells, which leads to a significant

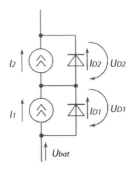

Figure 12.6 The inclusion of a shunt diode to the photovoltaic modules.

reduction in its energy efficiency when parallel arrays are connected, or using an inverter with a value of the input voltage range exceeding this value.

In order to solve the first and partly the second problem, recently, individual matching converters and micro-inverters installed on each (in some cases up to 2) photoelectric modules have become widely used [43, 44]. These devices set the selection of electrical energy to the maximum power point for each module individually, which allows receiving more energy from solar installations operating in conditions of uneven illumination. Their use makes it possible to install modules practically on any plane or site, making maximum use of all available space. The merits of such devices can also be attributed to the fact that most of them have the function of remote monitoring, which allows you to monitor the performance of each module, as well as carry out an analysis of the main electrical parameters.

Outputs of individual matching transducers are connected in series (Figure 12.7a), which makes it possible to easily introduce them on already built solar power plants. Switching micro-inverters is done through their parallel connection (Figure 12.7b), which makes it difficult to implement them on the constructed stations.

The world leader in production and implementation of individual matching converters is the American private company Tigo Energy [45]. The principle of its operation is based on the use of DC/DC SEPIC converters with an automatic control system that sets the mode of electric power extraction from the module at the maximum power point with a current equal to the current of the entire battery at the maximum power point. This means that in case of shading of one of the modules, the converter lowers the value of the output voltage, increasing the output current. Thus, the module does not go off by shunt diodes, and it continues

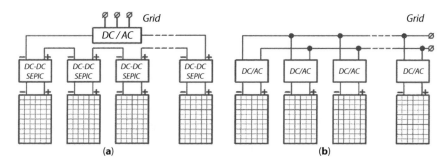

Figure 12.7 Switching of individual matching converters (a) and micro-inverters (b).

to generate electrical energy, albeit at a reduced power compared to other series-connected non-shaded modules.

The main disadvantages of individual matching converters (IMC) are:

1. significant increase in the cost of the installation (the cost of the IMC is about 15-20% of the module cost);
2. decrease in the voltage value of the entire array of photovoltaic modules at the point of maximum power, which, like in the case of shunt diodes, significantly affects the energy efficiency when parallel switching of arrays;
3. decrease of the voltage in all the array of PV modules at the point of maximum power, as is the case with shunt diodes greatly affects the energy efficiency in the parallel switching arrays.

The introduction of micro-inverters in photovoltaics is considered one of the biggest technological advances in the industry to date [46]. Manufacturers guarantee an increase in the energy production of solar installations by 5-25% due to their use [47]. The leader in the introduction and promotion of these devices is the US company Enphase Energy, which created the first successful commercial micro-inverter. At present, many companies have evaluated the advantages of this development; as a result, they began to develop and produce micro-inverters on their own [48].

The principle of operation of the micro-inverter is similar to the central inverter, the main difference is only power. The positive effect of their work is achieved due to the fact that they also, like ICP, optimize the operation of each module separately, allowing under any conditions to work at the maximum power point. The absence of a central inverter also positively affects the reliability of the installation and makes it more flexible in the possibilities of subsequent expansion, simplifies installation work and extends the service life due to the lack of active cooling systems.

Despite all the advantages of using micro-inverters, they have a number of drawbacks. The main ones are:

1. High cost. The use of micro-inverters instead of the central one in industrial power plants is on average more expensive by 50-85%.
2. Reduced energy efficiency with uniform illumination of solar cells. Because the efficiency of micro-inverters is less than the central one by an average of 2.5-4%, and also

because the voltage in the connecting wires has lower values of the voltages.

3. Lack of the possibility of implementation at existing power plants with a central inverter to solve problems of uneven illumination.

Another way to increase the energy efficiency of solar installations operating in conditions of uneven illumination is the use of tunable switching systems. Practical implementation in industrial solar power plants this method has not yet received. However, now scientists and researchers of many countries of the world are actively working in this direction [48–50].

The principle of the operation of tunable switching systems is that with the help of the switching matrix, such switching is performed, in which the shaded modules located in different arrays are included in one array, and their places are replaced by normally illuminated modules.

The use of such a method makes it possible to partially solve simultaneously the problem of switching off the shaded modules by shunt diodes, and the problem of voltage mismatch in parallel-connected array of modules operating under conditions of uneven illumination. The drawbacks of the method are:

1. Practical complexity of realization of the method in industrial solar power plants.
2. High cost, based on the use of expensive commutation matrices and a large number of connecting wires designed for a current of at least 10 A.
3. Inefficiency with a small number of shaded solar modules.

Voltage align parallel arrays of modules also enables the use of differentiated systems of maximum power selection, the structural diagram of which is shown in [48]. The principle of operation of such systems is that a parallel array of modules transmits electric energy through active voltage regulators, which determine their output voltage to one nominal value. In this case, the converters tracking for the maximum power point (MPPT) and optimize it. This allows the maximum selection of electrical energy from each array at different illumination, temperature, or the use of photovoltaic panels in arrays with different characteristics.

The main disadvantages of using such systems are:

1. The high cost and material intensity associated with the fact that the stabilizers used are designed for power with a value

not lower than the nominal power of the array of modules in which they are installed.

2. Decrease in energy efficiency due to the fact that for the voltage matching, all the energy produced by the array is converted. Thus, the output power is reduced by the value of the efficiency of the stabilizers.

The analysis shows that there are currently a large number of technical solutions that can partially reduce the effect of shading on the power generation of photovoltaic systems. Moreover, each of them has its own characteristics that prevent their widespread use in industrial solar power plants. The use of various options for supporting structures, differential power take-off systems, tracker, etc. From this it follows that in order to assess the efficiency of using various solutions, it is necessary to develop mathematical models, the result of which is the determination of the values of energy losses of solar installations with various options for switching solar cells and methods of choosing electrical energy. At the same time, some of the methods are initially not promising for implementation at industrial solar power plants due to the technical complexity or high cost of implementation at existing power plants. Such solutions include methods of matching the voltages of photovoltaic arrays with parallel switching-reconfigurable switching systems, differentiated systems and micro-inverters. It follows from this that the creation of an economically sound method that allows to take electrical energy from parallel groups of photovoltaic modules is an urgent task.

12.3   Main Focus of the Chapter

The analysis of existing solutions showed that currently there are no effective technologies that allow matching the voltage of parallel-connected photovoltaic modules. This fact is confirmed by the fact that such solutions are used only in space installations [51–59].

To match the parallel connected arrays of photovoltaic modules, the author has developed "Method of taking electrical energy from batteries of photovoltaic converters" [60]. Based on this method, a device named "Array matching device" (DCA) was manufactured. The use of the developed device allows the selection of electrical energy from the mismatched array of photovoltaic modules in the MPP. This is due to the fact that the load at the output of such an array corresponds to the MPP mode. In this case, the voltage at its output is equal to the voltage of other parallel arrays. The positive technical result of the implementation of the method is to increase the efficiency of obtaining electrical energy from partially or completely shaded arrays of photovoltaic modules, as well as in the case of uneven degradation of the modules, or other damage. During the development of the device, attention was paid to its cost and payback, since these characteristics are very important for industrial solar power plants. At the same time, the design optimization was carried out through the use of technological, modern engineering and scientific and technical solutions.

To understand the principle of the method, it is necessary to consider two current-voltage characteristics of arrays of photovoltaic modules (Figure 12.8): with normal illumination (all modules generate energy) and partial shading (some of the modules are shunted by diodes). It can be seen from the characteristics that the voltages of the arrays at the points of maximum power are not the same ($U_2 < U_1$). Due to the fact that these arrays of photovoltaic converters are connected in parallel, the output power of the array having a lower output voltage will be significantly limited. In other words, the voltage mismatch by the value of ΔU will lead to a change in the operating mode of the array from point P_3 to point P_2, which will significantly reduce the current from I_1 to I_2.

To increase the energy efficiency of a partially shaded array of photovoltaic modules (setting the operating mode from point P_2 to P_3), it is necessary to install an additional battery with a voltage equal to ΔU and a current of at least I1. Thus, the power of the additional battery can be calculated from Eq. (12.1).

$$P' = \Delta U \cdot I_1, \qquad (12.1)$$

The main positive effect of the implementation of the proposed method is that the electrical power consumed by the additional battery is much less

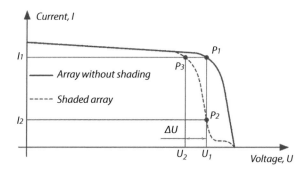

Figure 12.8 Current-voltage characteristics of the PV module arrays.

than the additional power received from its introduction into the shaded module. This can be clearly demonstrated by analyzing the characteristics presented in Figure 12.8. It can be seen from the figure that the area of the rectangle U_1, U_2, P_3, P_1 is less than the area of the rectangle P_1, P_2, I_2, I_1.

The principle of the method is explained in Figure 12.9; it consists of the following: to increase the energy efficiency of arrays of photovoltaic modules: (1) they are coordinated by sequentially switching on additional batteries, (2) in this case, the voltage values of each additional power element are set by the microcontroller device (5), up to the maximum value of the total power of the photovoltaic installation. Electric energy is supplied to the additional power cell from the same arrays of photovoltaic modules, providing galvanic isolation. (It is possible to supply electrical energy from an external source, in this case, galvanic isolation is not required.) At the same time, in order to set the optimal operating mode of all arrays of PV modules, it is necessary to set the load to the maximum power point using the MPPT controller (3). From the MPPT controller, electrical energy can be transferred directly to the load (4) or battery, or transferred to the electrical grid via a voltage inverter.

To assess the energy characteristics of photovoltaic installations operating in various conditions, based on the sources [54, 55], a mathematical model of a solar cell was compiled (2). Comparison of the experimental results with the results obtained as a result of mathematical modeling showed that the accuracy of such a model is sufficient for engineering calculations and does not go beyond the design tolerance.

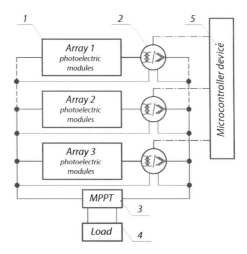

Figure 12.9 Block diagram of a method for matching arrays of PV modules.

$$\begin{cases} I = I_{ph} - I_0 \left[\exp\left(\frac{q(U + IR_s)}{AkT} \right) - 1 \right], \\[2ex] I_\Phi = [I_{sc(stc)} + K_i(T - T_{stc})] \frac{\beta}{\beta_{stc}}, \\[2ex] I_\Phi = [I_{sc(stc)} + K_i(T - T_{stc})] \frac{\beta}{\beta_{stc}}, \\[2ex] I_0 = \dfrac{I_\Phi}{\exp\left[\dfrac{q[U_{oc} + K_u(T - T_{stc})]}{AkT} \right] - 1}, \\[3ex] T = T_{at} + K_t\beta. \end{cases}$$

$$(12.2)$$

where: I – load current, (A); I_{ph} – photocurrent, (A); I_0 – reverse saturation current, (A); q – electron charge, (C); U – output voltage, (V); I_d – current flowing through the diode, (A); T – the absolute temperature of the solar cell, (K); k – Boltzmann constant, (J/K); R_s – series resistance of the solar cell, (Ohm); $I_{sc(stc)}$ – short-circuit current in standard test conditions (STC); K_u – temperature coefficient of open circuit voltage, (V/K); T_{at} – ambient temperature, (K); A – coefficient of ideality of the solar cell; U_{oc} – open circuit voltage, (V); K_t – temperature coefficient of temperature increase, ((K·m2)/W); β – intensity of solar radiation, (W/m²); β_{stc} – intensity of solar radiation at STC, (W/m²).

In the event of partial shading of a photovoltaic installation with mixed switching of solar cells, energy losses are of different magnitude depending on the nature of partial shading: uniform (Figure 12.10a), or uneven (Figure 12.10b).

With a uniform shading of the array of a photovoltaic installation, the total power losses (P_{los}) will consist of a decrease in power losses as a result of disconnection (shunting) of partially shaded photovoltaic modules by diodes (P_{sh}) and losses arising from different voltages of the arrays in terms of voltage at the point of maximum power ($P_{\Delta U}$).

$$P_{los} = P_{sh} + P_{\Delta U} = n_{p\,sh}(P_{mpp1} - P_{mpp2}) + P_{\Delta U}, \qquad (12.3)$$

where P_{mpp1} is the maximum photovoltaic power of normally illuminated array modules, (W); P_{mpp2} - maximum power of uniformly shaded array of photovoltaic modules, (W).

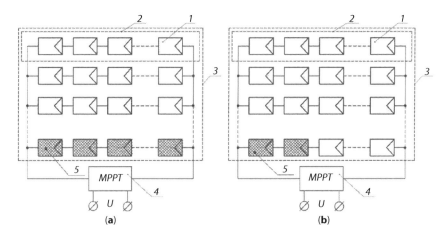

Figure 12.10 Options for partial shading of a photovoltaic installation: (a) - uniform shading; (b) - uneven shading (1 - illuminated solar cell; 2 - array of photovoltaic installation; 3 - solar photovoltaic installation; 4 - MPPT controller; 5 - shaded solar cell).

Meaning photovoltaic power loss due to the voltage difference at the points of maximum power can be calculated from the relation:

$$P_{\Delta U} = U_{1max} \sum_{i=1}^{n_p} I_{1max\,i} - U_{2max} \sum_{i=1}^{n_p} I_{2max\,i}, \qquad (12.4)$$

where n_p is the number of parallel connected arrays of photovoltaic modules; U_{1max}, U_{2max} - voltage values of parallel connected arrays of photovoltaic modules operating without shading and with shading at the points of maximum power, (V); $I_{1max\,i}$, $I_{2max\,i}$ - values of currents of arrays of photovoltaic modules without shading and with shading at the points of maximum power, (A).

The total current value of the PV array arrays can be calculated by substituting the voltage value corresponding to the maximum power point of the entire PV installation (U_{1max}). The voltage value at the point of maximum power U_{1max} can be computed according to eq. (12.5).

The voltage value of the array of photovoltaic modules with a uniform partial shading pattern when the mode of electric energy extraction is set to the global maximum point can be calculated in accordance with equation (12.7), and when the MPPT controller sets the selection mode to the local maximum point by equation (12.6).

$$\frac{dP_{1max}}{dU_{1max}} = I_{1max} + U_{1max} \frac{dI_{1max}}{dU_{1max}} = n_p \left[I_{ph} - I_0 \left[\exp \left(\frac{q(U_{1max} + I_{1max}R_s)}{n_s(AkT)} \right) - 1 \right] \right]$$

$$- \frac{n_p q(U_{1max} + I_{1max}R_s) I_0 \exp \left(\frac{q(U_{1max} + I_{1max}R_s)}{n_s(AkT)} \right)}{n_s(AkT)} = 0,$$

(12.5)

$$\frac{q(U_{1max} + I_{1max}R_s)}{n_s(AkT)} - \ln \frac{I_0 + I_{ph}}{I_0 \left(1 + \frac{q(U_{1max} + I_{1max}R_s)}{n_s(AkT)} \right)} = 0.$$

(12.6)

where: U_{1max} - voltage at the points of maximum power of the parallel-connected arrays, partially shaded and without shading, (V); I_{1max} - current at the points of maximum power of parallel-connected arrays, partially shaded and without shading, (A).

$$\frac{dP}{dU_{2max}} = n_{p\,sh} \left[I_{ph\,sh} - I_{0\,il} \left[\exp \left(\frac{q(U_{2max} + I_{2max}R_s)}{n_s(AkT)} \right) - 1 \right] \right] - U_{2max}$$

$$\left[n_{p\,sh}I_{0\,sh} \frac{q(U_{2max} + I_{2max}R_s)}{n_s(AkT)} \exp \left(\frac{q(U_{2max} + I_{2max}R_s)}{n_s(AkT)} \right) \right.$$

$$+ n_{p\,il}I_{0\,il} \frac{q(U_{2max} + I_{1max}R_s)}{n_s(AkT)} \exp \left(\frac{q(U_{2max} + I_{1max}R_s)}{n_s(AkT)} \right) \right]$$

$$+ n_{p\,il} \left[I_{il} - I_{0\,il} \left[\exp \left(\frac{q(U_{2max} + I_{1max}R_s)}{n_s(AkT)} \right) - 1 \right] \right] \approx n_{p\,sh}I_{ph\,sh}$$

$$+ n_{p\,il}I_{0\,il} - \exp \left(\frac{q(U_{2max} + I_{1max}R_s)}{n_s(AkT)} \right)$$

$$\times \left(\frac{q}{n_s(AkT)} (n_{p\,sh}I_{0\,sh}(U_{2max} + I_{2max}R_s) + n_{p\,il}I_{0\,il}(U_{2max} + I_{1max}R_s)) \right) = 0,$$

(12.7)

where: $n_{p\,sh}$ and $n_{p\,il}$ - the number of arrays of photovoltaic modules with partial shading and normal illumination; n_p is the number of arrays of photovoltaic modules; $I_{ph\ sh}$ and $I_{ph\ il}$ - value of photocurrents of arrays with partial shading and normal illumination, (A).

As a result, the total power losses of the photovoltaic installation with uniform partial shading of the groups of solar cells and the setting of the mode of taking electrical energy to the point of the global maximum are determined by the system of equations 12.8:

$$P_{los} = F_1 U_{1max} n_p - U_{2max}(F_2 n_{p\ sh} + F_1 n_{p\ il}),$$

$$F_1 = I_{ph\ il} - I_0\left[\exp\left(\frac{q(U_{1max} + I_{1max} R_s)}{n_s(AkT)}\right) - 1\right],$$

$$F_2 = I_{ph\ sh} - I_0\left[\exp\left(\frac{q(U_{2max} + I_{2max} R_s)}{n_s(AkT)}\right) - 1\right],$$

$$\frac{q(U_{1max} + I_{1max} R_s)}{n_s(AkT)} - \ln\frac{I_0 + I_{ph}}{I_0\left(1 + \frac{q(U_{1max} + I_{1max} R_s)}{n_s(AkT)}\right)} = 0,$$

$$n_{p\ sh} I_{ph\ sh} + n_{p\ il} I_{0\ il} - \exp\left(\frac{q(U_{2max} + I_{1max} R_s)}{n_s(AkT)}\right)$$

$$\times\left(\frac{q}{n_d(AkT)}(n_{p\ sh} I_{0\ sh}(U_{2max} + I_{2max} R_s) + n_{p\ il} I_{0\ il}(U_{2max} + I_{1max} R_s))\right) = 0.$$

(12.8)

The value of the voltage mismatch at the points of maximum power, leading to additional power losses of the photovoltaic installation, can be calculated:

$$\Delta U = U_{1max} - U_{2max}, \tag{12.9}$$

and the value of the losses themselves, arising from the voltage inconsistency, according to the transformed equation (12.10):

$$P_{\Delta U} = P_{loss} - n_{p\,sh}\left(P_{mpp1} - P_{mpp2}\right), \qquad (12.10)$$

where:

$$P_{mpp1} = U_{1max}I_{1max}, \qquad (12.11)$$

$$P_{mpp2} = U_{2max}I_{2max} \qquad (12.12)$$

Figure 12.11 shows the results of calculating the value of the power loss of a photovoltaic installation formed from three serial PV-250 photovoltaic modules. One of the installation modules is partially shaded. Figure 12.12 shows the results of calculating the value of the power loss of the same installation and the value of the voltage mismatch; however, in this case, the power take-off mode of the MPPT controller is set to the point of the local maximum.

With an uneven shading pattern of PV array arrays, total power loss (P_{los}) will occur due to shunting of the shaded modules by diodes. In this case, the losses will be the sum of the losses caused by the voltage

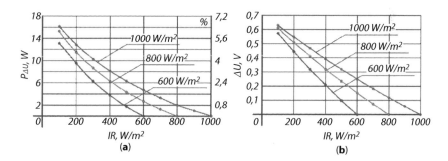

Figure 12.11 Results of modeling power losses of a photovoltaic installation depending on the intensity of solar radiation in the shade with a uniform shading pattern: (a) - losses caused by voltage mismatch; (b) - the value of the voltage mismatch.

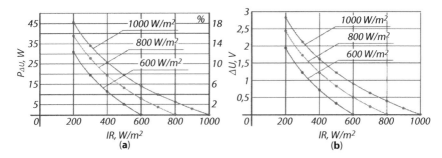

Figure 12.12 Results of modeling power losses of a photovoltaic installation depending on the intensity of solar radiation in the shade with an uneven shading pattern: (a) - losses caused by voltage mismatch; (b) - the value of the voltage mismatch.

mismatch ($P_{\Delta U}$), as shown earlier, and the losses caused by the voltage drop across the shunt diodes (P_{sh}). It should be noted that with this type of shading, the value of the mismatch voltage will be significantly higher in comparison with the uniform nature of shading. The value of the mismatch voltage for this nature of partial shading will be determined in accordance with eq. (12.13).

$$\Delta U = U_{1max} - U'_{2max} = p(U_n + U_D) \qquad (12.13)$$

where: p is the number of groups of solar cells shunted by diodes; U_n - voltage value of photovoltaic converters in the shunt diode circuit, (V); U_D is the voltage drop value of the shunt diode, (V).

As a result, a mathematical model was obtained that allows calculating the power parameters of arrays of photovoltaic modules with an uneven shading of photovoltaic converters and setting the controller of the power take-off mode to the maximum power point (global extremum point):

$$P_{loss} = U_{1max} n_p I_{1max} - U'_{2max} \left(n_{p\,il} I'_1 + n_{p\,sh} I'_2 \right),$$

$$P_{\Delta U} = P_{loss} - pP,$$

$$P = U_n I_{1max},$$

$$I_{1max} = I_{ph} - I_0 \left[\exp\left(\frac{q(U_{1max} + I_{1max} R_s)}{n_{s\,il}(AkT)} \right) - 1 \right],$$

$$I_{ph}(n_{p\,sh} + n_{p\,il}) - \frac{U'_{2max} q I_0}{AkT}(F_1 + F_2) = 0, \text{ at } U'_2 < U_{2max},$$

$$F_1 = \frac{n_{p\,sh} \exp\left(\frac{q(U' + I'_2 R_s + U_D)}{n_{ssh}(AkT)} \right)}{n_{ssh}},$$

$$F_2 = \frac{n_{p\,il} \exp\left(\frac{q(U'_{2max} + I'_1 R_s)}{n_s(AkT)} \right)}{n_s},$$

$$U'_{2max} = U_{1max}, \text{ at } U'_2 \geq U_{2max},$$

$$\frac{q(U_{1max} + I_{1max} R_s)}{n_s(AkT)} - \ln \frac{I_0 + I_{ph}}{I_0\left(1 + \frac{q(U_{1max} + I_{1max} R_s)}{n_s(AkT)}\right)} = 0,$$

$$I'_1 = I_{ph} - I_0 \exp\left(\frac{q(U'_{2max} + I'_1 R_s)}{n_{s\,il}(AkT)} \right),$$

$$I'_2 = \begin{cases} n_{p\,sh}\left(I_{ph} - I_0 \exp\left(\dfrac{q(U'_{2max} + I'_2 R_s + U_D)}{n_{s\,sh}(AkT)} \right) \right), \text{at } U'_2 < U_{2max}, \\[4mm] n_{p\,sh}\left(I'_{ph} - I'_0 \exp\left(\dfrac{q(U'_{2max} + I'_2 R_s + U_D)}{n_{s\,il}(AkT)} \right) \right), \text{at } U'_2 \geq U_{2max}. \end{cases}$$

$$(12.14)$$

Where I'_{ph} – photocurrent of a group of solar cells with illumination equal to the illumination in the region of partial shading, (A); I'_1 и I'_2 – value of currents in parallel array without shading and with shading under voltage U'_{2max}, (A); I'_o – value inverse saturation current of a group of solar cells with an illumination equal to the illumination in the region of partial shading, (A).

Figure 12.13 shows power loss graphs for an installation consisting of parallel-connected arrays consisting of 10 PS-250 photovoltaic modules connected in series when MPPT is set in the first local maximum point. The presented graph shows the value of the battery power loss consisting of any number of parallel connected solar cell arrays, since the voltage at the output of all arrays will be equal to the voltage of the MPP arrays that do not have shading. It can be seen from the modeling results that when one module is shaded, the power of the group is reduced by half, and the more significant shading practically does not allow to generate energy to the array.

Due to the stated value of the losses of the power array of photovoltaic modules can be calculated from equations 12.15 with an uneven shading and setting the controller of the power take-off mode to a local maximum point.

The installation of devices DCA, into the mismatched arrays of solar cells, makes it possible to increase their output power. At the same time, the mathematical description of the battery operation of solar cells with the DCA will differ slightly, depending on the version of their inclusion in the battery – "in-line", or "battery" (Figure 12.14).

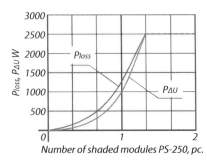

Figure 12.13 Results of calculating the values of power losses of arrays of photovoltaic modules depending on the number of shaded groups of modules.

$$\left\{ \begin{aligned}
& P_{loss} = U_{1max} n_p I_{1max} - U_{1max}(n_{p\,il} I_1' + n_{p\,sh} I_2'), \\
& \qquad P_{\Delta U} = P_{loss} - pP, \\
& \qquad\quad P = U_n I_{1max}, \\
& I_{1max} = I_{ph} - I_0 \left[\exp\left(\frac{q(U_{1max} + I_{1max} R_s)}{n_{s\,il}(AkT)} \right) - 1 \right] \\
& \frac{q(U_{1max} + I_{1max} R_s)}{n_s(AkT)} - \ln \frac{I_0 + I_{ph}}{I_0\left(1 + \dfrac{q(U_{1max} + I_{1max} R_s)}{n_s(AkT)}\right)} = 0, \\
& \qquad I_1' = I_{ph} - I_0 \exp\left(\frac{q(U_{2max}' + I_1' R_s)}{n_{s\,il}(AkT)} \right), \\
& I_2' = \begin{cases} n_{p\,sh}\left(I_{ph} - I_0 \exp\left(\dfrac{q(U_{2max}' + I_2' R_s + U_D)}{n_{p\,sh}(AkT)} \right) \right), & \text{at } U_2' < U_{2max} \\[2em] n_{p\,sh}\left(I_{ph} - I_0 \exp\left(\dfrac{q(U' + I_2' R_s + U_D)}{n_{p\,sh}(AkT)} \right) \right), & \text{at } U_2' < U_{2max} \end{cases}
\end{aligned} \right.$$

$$(12.15)$$

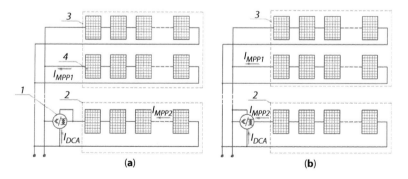

Figure 12.14 Incorporating DCA into an array of solar cells ((a) - in-line, (b) – battery)
1 - DCA, 2 - mismatched array of solar cells, 3 - normally illuminated arrays of solar cells,
4 - photoelectric module.

The inclusion of DCA in partially shaded arrays allows you to increase the value of its output voltage, while setting the load corresponding to the mode of taking electrical energy to the point of maximum power. This makes it possible to eliminate power losses caused by voltage mismatch and to increase the energy efficiency of the photovoltaic installation. The power loss value when using DCA can be calculated according to the following system of equations 12.16.

$$P_{loss} = n_p \ P - (n_{p \ il}P_{il} + n_{p \ sh}P_{sh}) = n_{p \ sh}(P_{il} - P_{sh}),$$

$$P_{il} = \ I_{mpp1}U_1,$$

$$P_{sh} = I_{mpp1}U_2 - \frac{\Delta U I_{mpp1}}{U_1}U_2(1 - \eta_{dca}),$$

$$I_{mpp1} = I_{ph} - I_0\left[\exp\left(\frac{q(U_1 + I_{mpp1}R_s)}{n_{s \ il}(AkT)}\right) - 1\right],$$

$$\frac{q(U_1 + I_{mpp1}R_s)}{n_s(AkT)} - \ln\frac{I_0 + I_{ph}}{I_0\left(1 + \frac{q(U_1 + I_{mpp1}R_s)}{n_s(AkT)}\right)} = 0,$$

$$\frac{q(U_2 + I_{mpp1}R_s + U_D)}{(n_{s \ sh}(AkT)} - \ln\frac{I_0 + I_{ph}}{I_0\left(1 + \frac{q(U_2 + I_{mpp1}R_s + U_D)}{n_{s \ sh}(AkT)}\right)} = 0$$

(12.16)

where η_{dcs} – efficiency DCA.

Figure 12.15 presents summary power loss graphs of a photovoltaic system consisting of parallel connected arrays formed from 10 PS-250 photovoltaic modules connected in series with partial sequential shading of the modules of one of the arrays, obtained as a result of mathematical modeling:

It can be seen from the graphs presented that when installed in shaded arrays of photovoltaic modules, DCA can significantly increase the energy efficiency of partially shaded photovoltaic modules by reducing losses resulting from the voltage mismatch between the shaded array and the array without shading. At the same time, the greatest positive effect from the use of this device is achieved when it is used in photovoltaic installations made up of a large number of parallel-connected arrays of modules, as well as when using MPPT controllers that use algorithms for finding

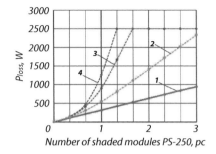

Figure 12.15 Plots of power loss of a photoelectric installation against partial shading of photovoltaic modules of one of the arrays of solar cells 1 - with DCA; 2 - consisting of 3 arrays of solar cells and set MPPT in global maximum point; 3 - consisting of 10 arrays of solar cells a and set MPPT in global maximum point; 4 - with and set MPPT in local maximum point.

the maximum power point that are not able to accurately set the mode of taking electrical energy into the point of the global maximum. Figure 12.15 shows that partial shading of more than one module in ten makes the array virtually unable to transmit electrical power without using DCA.

Figure 12.16 shows the experimental volt-ampere and power characteristics of arrays of photovoltaic modules obtained at an industrial solar power plant. From these characteristics, it can be seen that the DCA device allows you to change the mode of electric energy output by increasing the output voltage of the array of photovoltaic modules and reducing it. In this case, the output power of the array corresponds to the maximum power

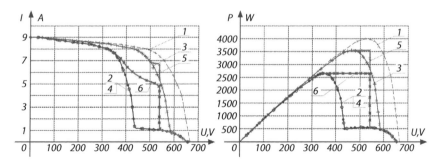

Figure 12.16 Volt-ampere and power characteristics of an array of photovoltaic modules (1-without shading; 2 - with partial shading and block vertical connection of modules; 3 - with partial shading and block horizontal connection of modules; 4 - with partial shading and horizontal arrangement of modules; 5 - with partial shading, horizontal block connection and installed DCA; 6 - with partial shading, horizontal or block vertical connection and installed DCA).

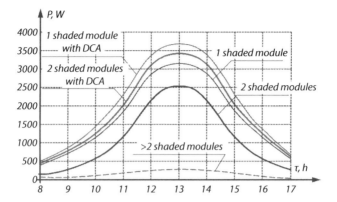

Figure 12.17 Diagram of the daily energy output of arrays of photovoltaic modules operating under different types of shading.

point. As a result, when uniform partial shading occurs (10-30%), the output power of the array increases by 78% (2092 W) with a block vertical or horizontal switching of photovoltaic modules and by 22.2% (787 W) with a block horizontal switching of photovoltaic modules in the array.

From the presented experimental graphs, it can be seen that when shading two photovoltaic modules out of eighteen, the DCA installation allows to reduce the power loss value by 2.6 (from 34% to 13%). At the same time, in the case of greater shading, the array without DCA practically does not generate electrical power (the output power parameter corresponds to the value generated by the array when the value of solar radiation is equal to the value in the shadow). With partial shading of one module in an array consisting of 10 photovoltaic modules, the DCA installation allows to reduce power losses by 3.4 (from 34% to 10%), and with partial shading of two or more photovoltaic modules, energy generation by the array, as in the previous case, is practically not performed.

In order to obtain experimental data on the daily energy production of a photovoltaic array operating under various shading modes and the DCA installation, a study was carried out, during which, in the daytime, artificial shading of the modules of one array of an industrial solar power plant was performed in turn. During the study, after each shading, its output power was measured. The results of the study are shown in Figure 12.17, from which it follows that in the case of partial shading of two photovoltaic modules out of eighteen, the DCA installation allows increasing the daily energy production of the sodul array by 43.7%, and with shading of one - by 19.7%.

12.4   Solutions and Recommendations

The results obtained are an important scientific and practical basis for the development of the concept of introducing smart technologies in the urban space. Modern technical solutions in the field of digital urbanism require autonomous power supply sources. The solutions proposed in this chapter minimize the risks associated with the negative impact of shading from urban facilities on the energy efficiency of solar photovoltaic installations. This will allow the development of the urban environment in order to improve the comfort of residents, taking into account the requirements for the sustainable development of urban areas. Renewable energy sources make it possible to minimize anthropogenic impact on the environment and thus improve the overall ecological state of the region. The economic feasibility of the solution proposed in the chapter is beyond doubt, since it implements innovative technical solutions that make it possible to increase the average annual energy efficiency of photovoltaic converters operating in uneven lighting conditions by up to 25%. At the same time, the financial costs for the implementation of the proposed approach do not exceed 1.2% of the cost of the entire solar installation.

The mathematical models presented by the authors make it possible to calculate the energy efficiency of photovoltaic installations with various options for switching solar cells. These models make it possible to effectively organize in an automated mode the implementation of procedures for the structural and parametric synthesis of photovoltaic installations, taking into account the specific conditions of the installation and subsequent operation. In addition, the results carried out at industrial power plants showed that the use of the solutions proposed in the chapter can significantly increase the output power of arrays of photoelectric converters by matching them in voltage. With partial shading of two photovoltaic modules in an array of eighteen modules, the output power of the array increases by more than 40%, and when more than two modules are shaded, the generation of electrical energy by the shaded array without voltage equalization is practically not carried out. The described method also makes it possible to increase the output power of the array with a uniform shading pattern up to 22%, and the daily power generation by 8.7%.

Acknowledgements

The reported study was funded by RFBR and Sevastopol Government (project № 20-47 - 920006), as well as the Sevastopol State University in the framework of the internal grant № 27/06-31 under the project "Development of competitive technologies for creating components of a mobile photovoltaic installation of high efficiency".

References

1. Höjer, M., & Wangel, J. (2015). Smart sustainable cities: definition and challenges. In *ICT Innovations for Sustainability* (pp. 333-349). Springer, Cham.
2. Martin, C. J., Evans, J., & Karvonen, A. (2018). Smart and sustainable? Five tensions in the visions and practices of the smart-sustainable city in Europe and North America. *Technological Forecasting and Social Change, 133,* 269-278.
3. Hara, M., Nagao, T., Hannoe, S., & Nakamura, J. (2016). New key performance indicators for a smart sustainable city. *Sustainability, 8*(3), 206.
4. Bibri, S. E. (2018). A foundational framework for smart sustainable city development: Theoretical, disciplinary, and discursive dimensions and their synergies. *Sustainable Cities and Society, 38,* 758-794.
5. Al-Nasrawi, S., Adams, C., & El-Zaart, A. (2015). A conceptual multidimensional model for assessing smart sustainable cities. *JISTEM-Journal of Information Systems and Technology Management, 12*(3), 541-558.
6. Albino, V., Berardi, U., & Dangelico, R. M. (2015). Smart cities: Definitions, dimensions, performance, and initiatives. *Journal of Urban Technology, 22*(1), 3-21.
7. Kummitha, R. K. R., & Crutzen, N. (2017). How do we understand smart cities? An evolutionary perspective. *Cities, 67,* 43-52.
8. Batty, M., Axhausen, K. W., Giannotti, F., Pozdnoukhov, A., Bazzani, A., Wachowicz, M., ... & Portugali, Y. (2012). Smart cities of the future. *European Physical Journal Special Topics, 214*(1), 481-518.
9. Al-Hader, M., & Rodzi, A. (2009). The smart city infrastructure development & monitoring. *Theoretical and Empirical Researches in Urban Management, 4*(2 (11), 87-94.
10. Al-Nasrawi, S., Adams, C., & El-Zaart, A. (2015). A conceptual multidimensional model for assessing smart sustainable cities. *JISTEM-Journal of Information Systems and Technology Management, 12*(3), 541-558.
11. Ghosal, A., & Halder, S. (2018). Building intelligent systems for smart cities: issues, challenges and approaches. In *Smart Cities* (pp. 107-125). Springer, Cham.
12. Woyte, A., Nijs, J., & Belmans, R. (2003). Partial shadowing of photovoltaic arrays with different system configurations: literature review and field test results. *Solar Energy, 74*(3), 217-233.

13. Dereli, Z., Yücedağ, C., & Pearce, J. M. (2013). Simple and low-cost method of planning for tree growth and lifetime effects on solar photovoltaic systems performance. *Solar Energy, 95*, 300-307.
14. Badescu, V. (2014). *Modeling Solar Radiation at the Earth's Surface* (Vol. 1). Berlin Heidelberg: Springer.
15. Rauschenbach, H. S. (2012). *Solar Cell Array Design Handbook: The Principles and Technology of Photovoltaic Energy Conversion*. Springer Science & Business Media.
16. Liu, T., Liu, Z., Ren, J., Zhao, Q., He, H., Wang, N., ... & Huang, X. (2018). Operating temperature and temperature gradient effects on the photovoltaic properties of dye sensitized solar cells assembled with thermoelectric–photoelectric coaxial nanofibers. *Electrochimica Acta, 279*, 177-185.
17. Balato, M., Costanzo, L., & Vitelli, M. (2015). Series–Parallel PV array re-configuration: Maximization of the extraction of energy and much more. *Applied Energy, 159*, 145-160.
18. Gao, W. X., Wang, M. Y., Wang, L. J., & Liu, Y. (2012). Review of research on photovoltaic micro-inverter. *Power System Protection and Control, 40*(21), 147-155.
19. Carrington, G., & Stephenson, J. (2018). The politics of energy scenarios: Are International Energy Agency and other conservative projections hampering the renewable energy transition?. *Energy Research & Social Science, 46*, 103-113.
20. Yang, C. (2015). Renewable Energy for a Sustainable Future. *Trends in Renewable Energy, 1*(1), 3.
21. Dudley, B. (2018). BP statistical review of world energy. *BP Statistical Review*, London, UK, accessed Aug, 6(2018), 00116.
22. Bogachkova, L. Y., Guryanova, L. S., Usacheva, N. Y., & Usacheva, I. V. (2020, March). Conditions and Trends of Green Energy Development in the Largest Economies of the Post-soviet Space. In *Institute of Scientific Communications Conference* (pp. 152-163). Springer, Cham.
23. Kannan, N., & Vakeesan, D. (2016). Solar energy for future world:-A review. *Renewable and Sustainable Energy Reviews, 62*, 1092-1105.
24. Kuznetsov, P. N., Abd, A. L. M., Kuvshinov, V. V., Issa, H. A., Mohammed, H. J., & Al-bairmani, A. G. (2020). Investigation of the losses of photovoltaic solar systems during operation under partial shading. *Journal of Applied Engineering Science, 18*(3), 313-320.
25. Kuznetsov P.N. (2017). Development of a device for increasing the efficiency of photovoltaic plants. *Collected articles of the scientific and practical conference with international participation «Environmental, Industrial and Energy Security" – 2017*, 728-731.
26. Kuznetsov, P. N., Lyamina, N. V., & Yuferev, L. Y. (2019). A device for remote monitoring of solar power plant parameters. *Applied Solar Energy, 55*(4), 247-251.

27. Jennings, C. E., Margolis, R. M., & Bartlett, J. E. (2008). *Historical Analysis of Investment in Solar Energy Technologies (2000-2007)* (No. NREL/TP-6A2-43602). National Renewable Energy Lab. (NREL), Golden, CO (United States).

28. Alferov Zh.I., Andreev V.M., & Rumyantsev V.D. (2004) Tendencies and prospects for the development of solar photovoltaics. *Physics and Technology of Semiconductors* 38/8. 937-948.

29. Kitaeva M.V. (2015) Solar tracking systems for solar energy. Collection XV International *Scientific and Practical Conference «Modern technology and technology»*. 54-55.

30. Gevorkian P. (2016) *Solar Power Generation Problems, Solutions, and Monitoring*. USA: Cambridge University Press.

31. Strebkov D.S., Tver'yanovich E.V. (2007). *Concentrators of solar radiation*. Moscow. 316p.

32. Andreev V.M., Davidyuk N.Yu., Ionova E.A. (2010) Optimization of the parameters of solar modules on the basis of lens radiation concentrators and cascade photoelectric converters. *Journal of Technical Physics 80*. Issue 2. 118-125.

33. Akhmetshin, A.T., Galimardanov I.I. (2010). Solar installations with fixed concentrator and mobile mobile system with photoelectric converter. *Materials of the XLIX International Scientific and Technical Conference «Scientific achievements - agro-industrial production»*. Chelyabinsk, 278-282.

34. Griliches V.A. (1986) *Solar space power plants*. Leningrad. Nauka, 182 p.

35. Kuvshinov V.V., Morozova N.V., Kuznetsov P.N. (2017) *Installations for solar energy*. Publishing house "Sputnik +", Moscow, 177 p.

36. Petrusev, A. S., Rulevskiy, V. M., Sarsikeyev, Y. Z., & Lyapunov, D. Y. (2016, May). Solar tracker with active orientation. In *2016 2nd International Conference on Industrial Engineering, Applications and Manufacturing (ICIEAM)* (pp. 1-4). IEEE.

37. Kalogirou, S. A. (1996). Design and construction of a one-axis sun-tracking system. *Solar Energy, 57*(6), 465-469.

38. Barsoum, N. (2011). Fabrication of dual-axis solar tracking controller project. *Intelligent Control and Automation, 2*(02), 57.

39. Solar panels. Installation manual. Solar energy. from http://instructions.sannycom.ru/manual_solar_pannels.pdf

40. Golomazov Ye.G. (2012) The concept of the development of an electronic module of autonomous power supply based on solar batteries. *Izvestiya KSTU. I. Razzakova 26*. 6-8.

41. Martins, P., (2012). MPPT for a Photovoltaic Micro-Inverter. *Faculdade de Engenharia da Universidade do Porto.*

42. Malathy, S., & Ramaprabha, R. (2018). Reconfiguration strategies to extract maximum power from photovoltaic array under partially shaded conditions. *Renewable and Sustainable Energy Reviews, 81*, 2922-2934.

43. Yuan, J., Blaabjerg, F., Yang, Y., Sangwongwanich, A., & Shen, Y. (2019, April). An Overview of Photovoltaic Microinverters: Topology, Efficiency, and Reliability. In *2019 IEEE 13th International Conference on Compatibility, Power Electronics and Power Engineering (CPE-POWERENG)* (pp. 1-6).
44. Zhang, Z., He, X. F., & Liu, Y. F. (2013). An optimal control method for photovoltaic grid-tied-interleaved flyback microinverters to achieve high efficiency in wide load range. *IEEE Transactions on Power Electronics*, *28*(11), 5074-5087.
45. Annsmol, J. and E.G. Stany. (2016). Reconfiguration of Solar Array under Partial Shaded Condition for Maximum Energy Harvesting. *International Journal of Advanced Research in Electrical, Electronics and Instrumentation Engineering*, Vol. 5, Issue 9: 7397-7402.
46. Christabel, S.C., Winston D.P. and Kumar B.P. (2016). Reconfiguration solution for extracting maximum power in the aged solar PV systems. *Journal of Electrical Engineering* 16. 440-446.
47. Shubhankar, N.D. and Sumedh B.D. (2015). Solar PV array reconfiguration under partial shading conditions for maximum power extraction using genetic algorithm. *Renewable and Sustainable Energy Reviews,* Vol. 43. 102-110.
48. Chernyshev, Yu.A., Shinyakov A.I., Gordeev K.G. (1991) Autonomous power supply system. Patent of the Russian Federation 2035109 IPC H02J 7/35.
49. Kudryashov V.S., Elman V.O., Nesterishin M.V. (2009). The power supply system of the spacecraft. Patent of the Russian Federation 2396666 H02J7/35.
50. Kuznetsov P.N., Borisov A.A. (2017) A method for selecting electric energy from photovoltaic converter batteries. Patent of the Russian Federation 2634590.
51. Tian, H., Mancilla-david, F., Ellis, K., Jenkins, P., & Muljadi, E. (2012). A Detailed Performance Model for Photovoltaic Systems Preprint. *Solar Energy Journal*.
52. Petreuş, D., Fărcaş, C., & Ciocan, I. (2008). Modelling and simulation of photovoltaic cells. *Electronics*, *49*(1), 42–47.
53. Krasovsky G.I., Filaretov G.F. (1982). Planning an experiment. *BSU V.I. Lenina,* Moscow. 302 p.
54. Novikov A.M. (1998). *Scientific and experimental work in an educational institution*. Business Councils, Moscow. 134 p.
55. Guba A. (2006) Digital sensors of illumination MAX44007 and MAX44009 of Maxim Company. *Electronic Components 6.* 11-13.
56. Russkin V.A., Semenov S.M., Dickson R.K. (2016) Investigation of the search algorithms for the point of maximum power for the boost converter of the solar inverter voltage. *Izvestiya Tomsk Polytechnic University. Engineering of Geo-Resources 4.* 78-87.
57. Sridhar, T. and J. Anish kumar. (2012). Development of Solar MPPT System Using Boost Converter with Microcontroller. *International Journal of*

Advanced Research in Electrical, Electronics and Instrumentation Engineering, Vol. 1, Issue 4: 334-340.

58. Badis, A., Boujmil, M. H., & Mansouri, M. N. (2018). A comparative study on maximum power point tracking techniques of photovoltaic systems. *International Journal of Energy Optimization and Engineering (IJEOE), 7*(1), 66-85.

59. Mäki, A., & Valkealahti, S. (2011). Power losses in long string and parallel-connected short strings of series-connected silicon-based photovoltaic modules due to partial shading conditions. *IEEE Transactions on Energy Conversion, 27*(1), 173-183.

60. Kuznetsov, P.N., Borisov, A.A. (2017). Method of taking electrical energy from batteries of photovoltaic converters. Patent RF, no RU2634590C.

13

Monitoring System Based Micro-Controller for Biogas Digester

Ahmed Abdelouareth* and Mohamed Tamali

ENERAGRID, Laboratory of Energetic in Arid Zones, SimulIA Research Team, Faculty of Technology, Electrical Engineering Department, TAHRI Mohamed Bechar University, Bechar, Algeria

Abstract

We all know that the only way to control a process is to measure its state parameters, and that its supervision becomes more difficult if its composition is complex. For this purpose, Telemetry provides an additional ability to the measurement system by taking advantage of the transmission of the measured values through the local network or the internet. In this work, we have proposed to control the process by measuring the state parameters of an anaerobic digester (methane is generated by the fermentation of waste deposited in the reactor). The system that we have proposed for online monitoring is all open-source hardware and software; on top of which the Raspberry Pi (RPi) is well known for its compactness, size, cost and ability to host data processing algorithms.

Keywords: Raspberry Pi, open source, node-RED, monitoring, anaerobic digester

13.1 Introduction

Anaerobic digestion (AD) or bio-methanation is the transformation of organic matter in the absence of oxygen by microbial fermentation into a combustible gas called biogas composed mainly of methane CH_4 and carbon dioxide CO_2 [1, 2]. The available knowledge about the process,

---

*Corresponding author: Abdelouareth.ahmed@gmail.com

Pandian Vasant, Gerhard-Wilhelm Weber, Joshua Thomas, José Antonio Marmolejo-Saucedo and Roman Rodriguez-Aguilar (eds.) *Artificial Intelligence for Renewable Energy and Climate Change*, (423–434) © 2022 Scrivener Publishing LLC

digestion technologies in use and the industrial sensors available on the market are all factors of extreme importance that will help select the parameters for supervision and control of the AD process [3].

The proper functioning of the anaerobic digestion process—particularly its energetic potential (maximum of methane production)—is conditioned mainly by the physicochemical conditions of the treated substrate in which the temperatures (i.e., mesophilic between 30 and 45° C, thermophilic between 50 and 65° C), pH nature, pressure, agitation, and gaseous quantitative productivity are experimentally tracked throughout the production cycle [4].

To obtain this vital data remotely and on a continuous basis, there are large-scale remote monitoring and data transmission systems, but their relatively high cost and complexity makes it impractical and inappropriate for small implementations and applications [5].

To overcome this constraint and to contribute to the establishment of a system characterized by a motivating quality-price relationship, we have proposed an online monitoring system for anaerobic digesters (ADOLMS) that will allow permanent monitoring and supervision of the parameters. The anaerobic digester data can easily be accessed via the web page. The proposed system was designed on all hardware and open-source software, mainly the Raspberry Pi card.

With wide availability of single-panel computers and their affordable price, the RPi is considered as one of the best and most popular systems in the scientific community; the evidence is the many scientific articles and the increasing reliance on the RPi in scientific challenges because of the low-cost device and its small size, in addition to its distinctive and flexible software, not to mention the active support of both creators and society [6].

13.2   Related Work

A monitoring system within the wastewater treatment plant was proposed and implemented in [7]. Many tools were utilized. For communication and graphic interface (Visual Basic 5.0), for database management (Access 7.0) and for scientific calculation (Matlab 5.0) were the software chosen for their powerful and adaptable applications. As for hardware equipment, a programmable logic controller (PLC) (Siemens 95-U) for acquisition and for the actuation of the final control element was selected. The PLC sends the information to the computer through a RS-232 series port, which makes the development of a standard interactive information exchange possible.

Control and supervision concepts for micro biogas plant in [8] are based on a compact programmable logic controller (PLC controller– Astraada One ECC2250) and an operator panel with integrated HMI SCADA (Astraada AS43TFT1525) for production process management and archiving data measured by the following sensors: temperature sensors, biomass level sensors, gas pressure sensors, gas flow meters, and gas detectors (explosion protection).

In another related study, L. Matindife & Z. Wang [9] proposed an integrated fault detection and control strategy for biogas systems. In this strategy adopted to measure methane gas, detection gas pressure, biomass level, and oxygen trace, the following sensors were used, respectively the Flying Fish MH MQ2, the model RC 300 Liyuan Electronic 1MPa 4-20mA 24V gas pressure sensor, two stainless steel sealed vertical float switches, and a "galvanic fuel cell" oxygen analyzer. The software was written in the C high level language. This was simulated in the MPLAB X programming environment. After simulation and fine-tuning, using the same programming environment as described previously, the software was burnt into the PIC18F4550I/P microcontroller with the assistance of the Pickit3 programmer/debugger.

13.3   Methods and Material

13.3.1   Identification of Needs

We have several conditions that control the process of anaerobic digestion and the quantity and quality of biogas produced. The underlying conditions to be monitored are physiochemical factors such as temperature, the pressure inside a digester, the neutral pH which is a highly influential agent in the process, and the presence of biogas (mostly methane).

The proposed system allows the acquisition of the previous data with the possibility of online supervision using sensors and RPi as a platform where we can develop our project. All processing and control of the acquired data is RPi's responsibility. In it, the data is treated, converted, filtered and stored in a local database [10].

13.3.2   ADOLMS Software Setup

The RPi as a telemetry system computer runs with the current version of Rasbian, the Debian-based GNU-Linux operating system. To achieve better recommendations, the practice must satisfy system requirements, and some configurations need to be made; for instance, SPI interface is enabled for communication with the analogue digital converter (ADC) chip. The connection with other computers in the field without the need for a DHCP server, SSH server is enabled, and a static IP address is assigned to the onboard Ethernet adapter [6, 11].

In this system, we have adopted Node-RED as a programming tool that allows us to visualize and store our data. Node-RED is a tool that allows interesting ways to connect devices with online services [12]. Flows are programs edited using Nod-RED. They are similar to the visual flow systems that connect the nodes through wires and allow the program to drop the node templates that represent the various units of input and output and data processing on the board and then finally connected. These nodes are drawn on the user interfaces from the flow editor [12, 13]. We have used the Dashboard module, which allows us to add a beautiful graphic interface to our project quickly. With this module, displays can be added to visualize measurements in different forms: gauges, graphs, text, notifications, or free HTML code. We can also add fields for interactions: buttons, switches, sliders (linear potentiometers), the input fields (text or numeric), choice lists, and forms.

There are several ways of data storage for after-acquisition use, such as text files in .csv formats for direct processing in spreadsheets, as well as in relational or non-relational databases. This choice must be considered according to the needs of the developed application. The database management system (DBMS) is software that supports the structuring, storage, updating, and maintenance of a database. It is the only interface between computer scientists and data (definition of schemas, programming of applications), as well as between users and data.

In our application we have used MySQL as an open-source DBMS; it is a free tool which is characterized by quality, durability, and security, making it the most famous DBMS in the world and it is widely used in web applications thanks to its speed and efficiency [10].

13.3.3   ADOLMS Sensors

Sensors are the first element of the data acquisition chain, and one of the top development priorities is to minimize the cost of the measurement system [2]. For that reason we chose sensors specially designed for open-source boards.

Digital Temperature and Humidity Sensor DHT-22

We used a DHT-22 sensor with a digital signal via single-bus output to measure the temperature and humidity of the digester; its sensing elements are connected with an 8-bit single-chip computer with typical power supply 5V DC, operating range temperature between -40°C to +80°C and humidity between 0 to 100 %RH with 2 seconds Sensing period [14].

Analog Pressure Sensor MPX5010DP

The analogue value of pressure sensor MPX5010DP is used to measure the difference between internal and external digester pressure. This piezoresistive transducer is ideally compatible with applications that use a microcontroller or microprocessor with A/D inputs which is the case of our project; the sensor output signal relative to pressure input is shown in Figure 13.1. Typical minimum and maximum output curves are shown for operation over a temperature range of 0° to 85°C, and the output will saturate outside of the specified pressure range. According to this curve [15], the Linear equation of the transfer function is described below in (13.1).

$$V_{OUT} = V_S (0.09\ P + 0.04) \pm 5.0\%\ V_{FSS} \qquad (13.1)$$

The unknown of this equation is the pressure to calculate P, V_{FSS} Full Scale Span is defined as the algebraic difference between the output voltage at full rated pressure and the output voltage at the minimum rated pressure.

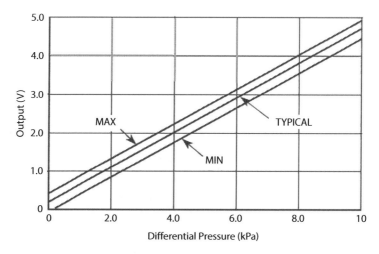

Figure 13.1 Output vs. pressure differential [12].

The MPX5010DP operated with power supply $V_S = 5.0$ Vdc; it measures the pressure between 0 to 10 Kpa with 5% accuracy.

Analogue pH Sensor

To read the pH values, we used an analogue pH sensor kit from Logoele composed of a pH probe and a Module V1.1 with BNC connector based on the AVR/51 controller. The sensor performs pH readings from 0 to 14 with stability time of around 60 seconds. It functions with input voltage of 5 Vdc with an average consumption of 0.995 mA and Component consumption less than 0.6 W [16].

The operating principle of this sensor is based on Nernst equation shown in (13.2), in which R is the ideal gas constant, T is the temperature in Kelvin, F is the Faraday constant and E° is the reference potential constant.

$$E = E° - (2.303RT/F) \text{ pH} \qquad (13.2)$$

The total potential difference E measured in mV.

MQ-4 Gas Sensor

To detect the presence of methane gas concentration, we used the MQ-4; it is a semiconductor gas sensor used in domestic and industrial gas leakage detecting equipment to detect CH4, natural gas and other gas such as cigarette smoke noise and cooking fumes.

The methane gas sensor MQ-4 detects the concentration of methane in the air and outputs the result as an analogue voltage. The detection concentration ranges between 200 ppm and 10000 ppm; its sensor can operate at temperatures from -10 to 50° C and consumes less than 150 mA at 5 V [17].

13.3.4 ADOLMS Hardware Architecture

We have used a Raspberry Pi 2 model B SOC system-on-a-chip computer as a central part of the measurement computer [2]; this minicomputer is shown in Figure 13.2 and is characterized by a dimension of 85x56x17 mm, a 900 MHz CPU, a Quad-core ARM Cortex-A7 architecture, 1 GB LPDDR2 of RAM, onboard peripherals including Ethernet, 4 USB ports controller and SPI bus beside 40 pins of general-purpose input output (GPIO) header which represents the physical interface between the RPi and the outside world. This latter needs the power supply of 5 V-1.8 Amp. In this paper, a micro SD card of 16 GB in memory card slot is used and to connect with the internet we use a wireless USB Wi-Fi [11, 18].

Figure 13.2 Raspberry Pi 2 Model B 1G.

The digital sensors connected directly to GPIO pins. Due to the lack of direct analog inputs in the Raspberry Pi, the use of the MCP3008 is a solution for direct connection without the need for other board; this chip provides 8 10-bit A/D converters with values from 0 to 1023 and communicates with the host over SPI serial interface. The digital output code calculation is explained in the equation (13.3), where V_{IN} is the analog input voltage, and V_{REF} is analog reference voltage [19].

$$\text{Digital Output Code} = 1024 \times V_{IN} / V_{REF} \qquad (13.3)$$

The various hardware and software components of the system are illustrated in Figure 13.3, attached to Table 13.1, showing the approximate price of the used instruments.

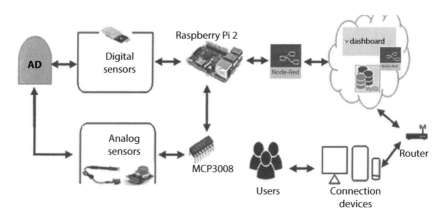

Figure 13.3 ADONMS general diagram.

Table 13.1 System cost.

Component	Price
Raspberry Pi 2	39.95 $
DHT-22	4.94 $
pH Probe	24.00 $
MQ-4	1.69 $
MPX5010DP	8.53 $
WLAN 802.11n	2.00 $
Total	81.11 $

13.4 Results

After the implementation of all the equipment of the proposed model, as is shown in Figure 13.4, and the calibration of the different sensors, the results of the acquired data are displayed in the interface created with the

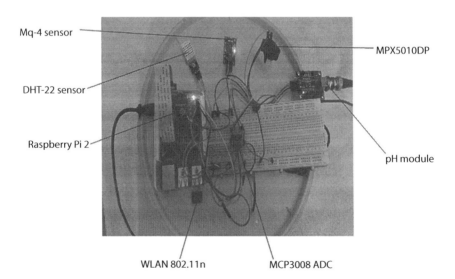

Figure 13.4 System implementation.

help of the dashboard module on Node-RED. For the supervision in real time of the anaerobic digester with *ADONMS*, merely enter the IP address of the Raspberry Pi followed by the port 1880 (@IP_Raspberry_Pi:1880/ ui) on the web browser-either by computer as is indicated in Figure 13.5 or by smartphone in Figure 13.6. The interface is protected by username and password. The results are presented by gauges attached by graphical curves which represent the evolution of these parameters over time. We note that all the data acquired and presented are stored in a MySQL database.

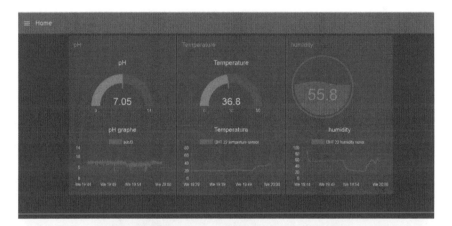

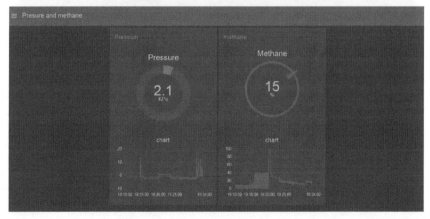

Figure 13.5 The graphical interface that represents the evolution of different parameters.

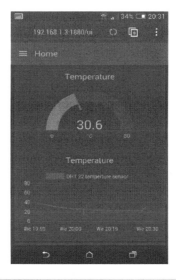

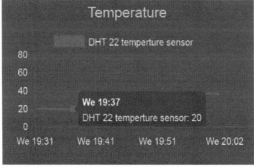

Figure 13.6 Interface accessed by phone with temperature evolution graph.

13.5 Conclusion

In this work, we have proposed a real-time telemetry system, with commercial open-source devices and cost-free software for Linux Embedded. Among the microcontrollers, we have chosen the Raspberry Pi as a platform to create and develop this system due to its performance and its low cost.

In this project, ADOLMS provides online monitoring, collection and preservation of parameters affecting the anaerobic digester for biogas production, such as temperature and pH, as well as the concentration of biogas produced.

ADOLMS is currently being implemented on a physical site with an extension, and the results of this installation will be described in the next article.

Acknowledgements

This work was financially supported by the ENERGARID laboratory, SimulIA team and Tahri Mohammed University Bechar 08000 ALGERIA, under the scientific Programme Project Electro-energetique Industrial Option Smart Home

References

1. Saidi, A., Abada, B.: La biométhanisation: une solution pour un développement durable. *Revue des Energies Renouvelables* CER'07 Oujda, 31-35 (2007).
2. Steyer, J.P., Buffiere, P., Rolland, D., Moletta, R.: Advanced Control of Anaerobic Digestion Process through Disturbances Monitoring, *Wat. Res.* Vol. 33, No. 9, pp. 2059-2068, ELSEVIER, Great Britain (1999).
3. Motta, R.: Anaerobic Digestion Monitoring and Control, France.
4. M'sadak, Y., Ben M'barek, A. Baraket, S.: Suivis physico-chimique et énergétique de la biométhanisation expérimentale appliquée à la biomasse bovine, *Nature et Technologie* (2011).
5. Pereira, R.I.S., Dupont, I.M., Carvalho, P.C.M., Jucá, S.C.S.: IoT Embedded Linux System based on Raspberry Pi applied to Real-Time Cloud Monitoring of a decentralised Photovoltaic plant, *Measurement* (2017).
6. Ambrož, M.: Raspberry Pi as a low-cost data acquisition system for human-powered vehicles, *Measurement* (2016).
7. Puñal, A., Roca, E., & Lema, J.: An expert system for monitoring and diagnosis of anaerobic wastewater treatment plants. *Water Research*, 36(10), 2656-2666 (2002).
8. Budnik, K., Szymenderski, J., & Walowski, G.: Control and Supervision System for Micro Biogas Plant. *19th International Conference Computational Problems of Electrical Engineering* (2018).
9. Matindife, L., & Wang, Z.: Biogas system fault detection and control. *2016 International Conference on Advances in Computing and Communication Engineering (ICACCE)* (2016).
10. Teixeira, P.F.S., Moura, L.F., Lima, S.W.S., Albiero, D., Gondim, F.A. and de Alexandria, A.R. Development of a Low-Cost Data Acquisition System for Biodigester. *Journal of Sustainable Bioenergy Systems.* 7, 117-137 (2017).
11. Dhavani, S., Vinayak, S.: IoT based Biometrics Implementation on Raspberry Pi. *Procedia Computer Science.* 79, 328-336 (2016).

12. Node-RED dashboard User Manual Getting started https://nodered.org/.

13. Blackstock, M., Lea, R.: FRED: A Hosted Data Flow Platform for the IoT built using Node-RED. The Mashup of things and APIs (MOTA) part of the ACM Middleware workshop in Trento, Italy (2016).

14. Digital relative humidity and temperature sensor AM2302/DHT22, https://cdn-shop.adafruit.com.

15. Integrated Silicon Pressure Sensor On-Chip Signal Conditioned, Temperature Compensated and Calibrated, https://www.nxp.com.

16. Utilisation d'un module chinois de mesure de PH, https://matdomotique.wordpress.com.

17. Technical data mq-4 gas sensor, https://www.sparkfun.com.

18. Sachdeva, P., Katchi, S.: A Review Paper on Raspberry Pi, *International Journal of Current Engineering and Technology*, E-ISSN 2277-4106, P-SSN 2347-5161 (2014).

19. 2.7V 4-Channel/8-Channel 10-Bit A/D Converters with SPI Serial Interface, http://www.alldatasheet.com).

14

Greenhouse Gas Statistics and Methods of Combating Climate Change

Tatyana G. Krotova

*Department of Economic Policy and Public-Private Partnership,
MGIMO University, Moscow, Vernadsky Avenue, Russia*

Abstract

The fight against climate change is urgent as never before. Man inflicts irreparable damage to nature through economic, industrial, and transport activities. National economies have long developed to the detriment of nature. Thus, economic growth in China has caused an unprecedented surge in carbon dioxide emissions. Tackling environmental problems is a primary task for the world community [1]. Six of the seventeen Sustainable Development Goals (SDGs) on the 2030 Agenda relate to environmental problems in one way or another. The thirteenth SDG addresses climate change [2]. The authors of this article endeavor to find out the sources of environmental pollution entailing climate warming and simulate an econometric model to calculate the values of statistical indicators required for the leveling-down of environmental pollution.

Keywords: Climate change, SDG13, the sustainable development
Q5, C150, O44

Introduction

Economic growth has long been at the political forefront of all countries. But the history of the last two centuries shows that economic growth results in the depletion of natural resources, air pollution, and climate warming. The influence of these processes is obvious, but the implications and their scale are still unpredictable. The deterioration of the environment in a

---

Email: tatyana.krotova.mgimo@gmail.com

Pandian Vasant, Gerhard-Wilhelm Weber, Joshua Thomas, José Antonio Marmolejo-Saucedo and Roman Rodriguez-Aguilar (eds.) *Artificial Intelligence for Renewable Energy and Climate Change,* (435–456) © 2022 Scrivener Publishing LLC

country impairs the population's health, diminishes life expectancy, and standard of living. Changing these indicators for the better is the underlying factor of the Sustainable Development concept. As national economies grow, the harm to the environment should be reduced. Therefore, we need a transition to other sources of energy to make the mining and processing industries environmentally friendly, as well as take care of waste disposal and wastewater treatment [3].

Several international organizations intend to solve this problem, conclude international agreements, and develop strategies and plans (Paris Agreement, Kyoto Protocol, etc.).

In our paper, we attempt to find statistical benchmarks to which governments should lean when fighting against climate change and not infringe on the economic interests of their population.

Methodology
The authors employed statistical research methods, including regression analysis.

Findings
Let's scrutinize the indicators of the main emitters and sources of greenhouse gas emissions as of now.

The bulk of greenhouse gases accrue due to carbon (CO_2) emissions. Greenhouse gases also include methane (CH_4), nitrous oxide (N_2O), and fluorinated gases (F-gases) (see Chart 14.1) [4].

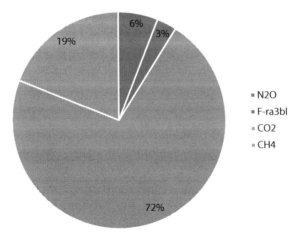

Source: drawn up by the author based on data of Trends in global CO2 and total greenhouse gas emissions report.

Chart 14.1 Percentage distribution of greenhouse gases.

The main emitters of greenhouse gases (62 percent of emissions) are six countries (we take the EU as a single source of greenhouse gases): China, USA, EU (28), India, Russia, and Japan (see Figure 14.1).

As can be seen in Figure 14.2, greenhouse gas emissions are steadily increasing in China and India. The increase is mainly explained by the

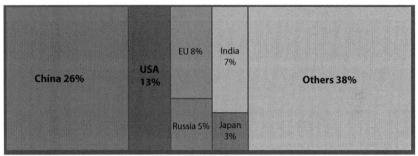

Source: drawn up by the author based on data of Trends in global CO2 and total greenhouse gas emissions report.

Figure 14.1 Countries as emitters of greenhouse gases.

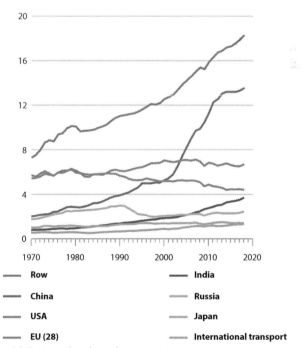

Source: Trends in global CO2 and total greenhouse gas emissions.

Figure 14.2 The behavior pattern of greenhouse gas emissions in CO2 equivalent, Gt.

growing demand for energy resources. Emissions in China have risen since the start of the millennium due to the explosive growth of the economy.

Chart group 14.2 illustrates the main sources of greenhouse gases.

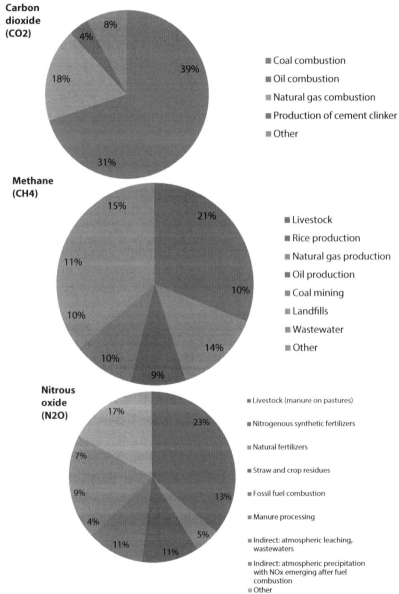

Source: drawn up by the author based on Trends in global CO2 and total greenhouse gas emissions report.

Charts 14.2 Main sources of gas emissions.   (*Continued*)

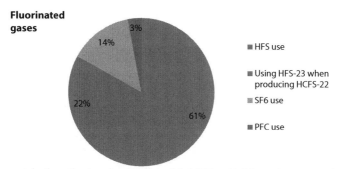

Fluorinated gases

- HFS use
- Using HFS-23 when producing HCFS-22
- SF6 use
- PFC use

Source: drawn up by the author based on Trends in global CO2 and total greenhouse gas emissions report.

Charts 14.2 (Continued) Main sources of gas emissions.

Greenhouse gas emissions around the world grew by 2 percent (37.5 Gt) in 2018 against the previous year. This was caused by increased CO2 emissions. Of course, the indicator is lower compared to the figure at the start of the millennium (2.8 percent), but after average annual growth of 1.2 percent over six years it looks discouraging[1].

CO2 emissions go up because the consumption of coal as an energy source increases (annual growth of 1.4 percent). India, China and Russia demonstrate especially high growth rates (+ 8.7 percent, + 0.9 percent, + 4.9 percent, respectively). Changes in coal consumption in China are of primary importance as this energy source accounts for half of the world's consumption.

At the same time, coal consumption is steadily declining in the USA, the EU, and Japan, (-4.3 percent, -5.1 percent, -2.1 percent, respectively). This decline largely depends on the transition to renewable energy sources, reconstruction of coal-fired power stations, and their conversion to natural gas.

Global consumption of oil and natural gas also keeps rising (+ 1.2 percent and + 5.3 percent in 2018, respectively). Leading consumers of petroleum products are China, the USA, and India (+ 5.0 percent, + 2.1 percent, + 5.1 percent, respectively). Gas consumption has considerably grown in the USA, China, and the Russian Federation (+ 10.5 percent, + 17.7 percent + 5.4 percent, respectively).

---

[1] Available at: https://data.worldbank.org/indicator/EN.ATM.CO2E.PC (published on 26 July 2020)

As of now, the global energy demand is supported by fossils (64 percent) and renewable energy and nuclear power (36 percent) [4].

Methane emissions also contributed to greenhouse gas emissions in 2018. Their rate for two years in a row has been 1.8 percent (the absolute indicator of CH4 emissions amounted to 9.7 Gt in CO2 equivalent).

The main sources of methane emissions are coal and natural gas mining, livestock, and wastewaters. Net growth in global methane emissions by one-fifth is contributed by China (then follow Indonesia, USA, India, Russia).

Emissions of nitrogen oxide and fluorinated gases in 2018 equaled 2.8 Gt in CO2 equivalent (0.8 percent increase against 2017).

Higher N2O emissions are associated with more frequent use of synthetic nitrogenous and natural fertilizers, growing livestock, and the cultivation of nitrogen-containing crops. Brazil, India, the USA, and China are the main emitters of this gas.

Governments are unable to determine whether the measures introduced to change the indicators of greenhouse gas emissions work properly. Besides, there is a time lag between the introduction of a specific measure to reduce gas emission and its effect on the atmosphere. Therefore, reputable world agencies use the index method and ranking of countries indicators (0-100 points) in addition to absolute indicators.

When approaching the task, the authors used data publicly provided by the Institute of Scientific Communications (INC) in Russian. INC Dataset contains statistics on government control practices in the field of sustainable development and combating climate change [5].

We will explore the impact of government policies on environmental pollution. For this purpose, we chose the Index of Environmental Pollution, which shows the scale of environmental pollution, as a dependent variable.

As independent variables, we utilized the indicators taken from the INK dataset:

- Energy trilemma index[2] (the balance between energy security, energy balance, and environmental sustainability of countries);
- Industrial profile of the economy (the share of the mining and manufacturing industries in the GDP breakdown) (calculated by INC);

---

[2]Available at: https://www.visualcapitalist.com/countries-most-sustainable-energy-policies/ (accessed 10 August 2020)

- Natural rent as a percentage of GDP (the share of the mining industry in the GDP breakdown);
- Adjustment of energy efficiency (index of adequacy of state measures for entrepreneurs in pursuing energy policy);
- Adjustment of renewable energy (index of government requirements for the utilization of renewable energy by businesses);
- Environmental requirements (the number of environmental standards operating in the country)[3,4].

The authors arranged indicators and took the latest data across all countries with an entire set of statistics (see Table 14.1).

Let's carry out a correlation analysis (Table 14.2).

After correlation analysis was completed, we found that there is multicollinearity between the Energy Trilemma Index and adjustment of energy efficiency and renewable energy.

For the following analysis, we take the energy trilemma index, natural rent as a percentage of GDP, and environmental requirements.

Finally, we carry out regression analysis (Table 14.3).

The analysis of regression statistics showed that we managed to get a model of the dependent variable behavior (the index of environmental pollution), which by 70 percent depends on the changes in the independent parameters of the model.

Verification of the regression significance in general:
We put forward a hypothesis:
H0: $\beta 1 = \beta 2 = \beta 3 = 0$, i.e., the regression is insignificant in general since the combined factors do not affect the dependent variable in the population;
H1: $\beta 1^2 + \beta 2^2 + \beta 3^2 > 0$, i.e., at least one factor affects the dependent variable;
Let's make verification by Fisher's criterion:
Fkr = 2.73;
F = 51, hence F>Fkr hypothesis H1 is true, and the regression is significant in general.

---

[3] Available at: https://www.weforum.org/reports/how-to-end-a-decade-of-lost-productivity-growth (accessed 11 August 2020)

[4] Available at: https://www.archilab.online/data2/861-dataset-korporativnaya-sotsialnaya-otvetstvennost-ustojchivoe-razvitie-i-borba-s-izmeneniem-klimata-imitatsionnoe-modelirovanie-i-nejrosetevoj-analiz-v-regionakh-mira-2020 (accessed 11 August 2020)

Table 14.1 Initial data.

Country	Environmental pollution index, 1-100 points	Energy trilemma index	Industrial pattern of the economy	Resouce rent in GDP, percent	Adjustment of energy efficiency, 1-100 points	Adjustment of renewable energy, 1-100 points	Environmental requirements, 1-100 points
Argentina	50,67	72,40	36,00	1,32	34,10	59,00	79,00
Australia	23,46	74,70	30,00	7,21	84,30	76,90	83,00
Austria	22,19	80,70	43,00	0,14	73,00	65,60	83,00
Bangladesh	86,21	47,10	47,00	0,66	28,90	42,30	69,00
Belgium	52,94	75,20	31,00	0,02	72,80	68,70	90,00
Brazil	54,98	71,60	28,00	3,53	51,80	70,90	86,00
Bulgaria	65,33	71,30	38,00	1,43	71,70	82,60	93,00
Chile	65,78	69,40	41,00	11,48	59,40	72,70	83,00
China	80,77	63,70	70,00	1,50	73,50	66,40	83,00
Columbia	62,83	69,30	38,00	4,32	37,50	43,60	66,00
Croatia	30,46	74,90	32,00	0,67	64,50	56,00	90,00

(Continued)

Table 14.1 Initial data. (*Continued*)

Country	Environmental pollution index, 1-100 points	Energy trilemma index	Industrial pattern of the economy	Resouce rent in GDP, percent	Adjustment of energy efficiency, 1-100 points	Adjustment of renewable energy, 1-100 points	Environmental requirements, 1-100 points
Cyprus	53,55	67,90	17,00	0,02	75,10	76,50	79,00
Czech Republic	40,23	77,40	55,00	0,31	74,80	71,10	86,00
Denmark	21,33	84,70	34,00	0,51	78,20	79,30	100,00
Ecuador	57	69,60	47,00	5,51	47,90	35,60	90,00
Egypt	85,65	59,90	51,00	5,40	61,00	68,30	72,00
Estonia	19,81	73,80	37,00	1,05	75,10	76,50	93,00
Finland	11,55	81,10	39,00	0,58	73,20	70,60	100,00
France	43,56	80,80	27,00	0,04	72,40	86,30	97,00
Georgia	71,09	63,10	29,00	1,08	50,70	52,70	66,00
Germany	29,03	79,40	47,00	0,07	84,50	96,60	100,00

(*Continued*)

Table 14.1 Initial data. (*Continued*)

Country	Environmental pollution index, 1-100 points	Energy trilemma index	Industrial pattern of the economy	Resouce rent in GDP, percent	Adjustment of energy efficiency, 1-100 points	Adjustment of renewable energy, 1-100 points	Environmental requirements, 1-100 points
Greece	52,55	69,50	25,00	0,13	60,70	81,70	86,00
Hungary	48,29	76,80	44,00	0,29	81,80	79,90	93,00
Iceland	16,21	76,20	29,00	0,00	75,10	76,50	72,00
India	78,87	50,30	42,00	2,14	66,40	87,30	90,00
Indonesia	66,56	64,10	60,00	3,48	25,70	53,70	76,00
Iran, Islamic republic	77,45	63,60	47,00	17,78	75,70	59,00	72,00
Ireland	33,99	75,20	69,00	0,14	85,30	81,40	90,00
Israel	57,25	73,30	31,00	0,14	50,20	68,30	55,00
Italy	55,63	76,80	36,00	0,07	89,20	84,10	83,00
Japan	39,59	73,80	50,00	0,03	68,50	77,40	90,00

(*Continued*)

Table 14.1 Initial data. (*Continued*)

Country	Environmental pollution index, 1-100 points	Energy trilemma index	Industrial pattern of the economy	Resouce rent in GDP, percent	Adjustment of energy efficiency, 1-100 points	Adjustment of renewable energy, 1-100 points	Environmental requirements, 1-100 points
Jordan	77,78	58,50	47,00	0,73	56,80	63,00	83,00
Kazakhstan	75,15	66,60	44,00	16,19	48,80	60,00	59,00
Kenia	76,6	51,30	24,00	2,48	50,50	56,00	83,00
Kuwait	68,69	65,20	67,00	37,14	28,40	13,10	69,00
Latvia	33,73	76,10	29,00	0,86	75,10	76,50	83,00
Lebanon	88,37	61,60	22,00	0,00	51,50	56,00	72,00
Lithuania	28,8	72,40	43,00	0,33	75,10	76,50	86,00
Republic of Madedonia	80,23	63,70	37,00	1,91	71,40	69,60	59,00
Malaysia	63,18	68,50	60,00	6,31	57,80	57,70	72,00
Mexico	66,1	71,30	48,00	2,88	68,60	68,70	83,00

(*Continued*)

Table 14.1 Initial data. (*Continued*)

Country	Environmental pollution index, 1-100 points	Energy trilemma index	Industrial pattern of the economy	Resouce rent in GDP, percent	Adjustment of energy efficiency, 1-100 points	Adjustment of renewable energy, 1-100 points	Environmental requirements, 1-100 points
Morocco	70,64	61,10	42,00	1,63	55,50	66,60	83,00
Netherlands	27,41	77,80	29,00	0,36	83,50	82,30	100,00
New Zealand	23,4	79,40	29,00	1,04	46,80	53,60	79,00
Nigeria	87,63	40,70	36,00	8,67	18,50	30,40	79,00
Norway	20,35	79,30	38,00	5,92	75,60	74,00	100,00
Oman	37,74	65,50	85,00	23,49	34,60	13,90	72,00
Pakistan	74,25	49,60	30,00	1,05	34,60	55,00	76,00
Panama	63,09	69,50	35,00	0,19	52,20	55,00	86,00
Peru	84,13	66,80	44,00	8,91	32,20	51,90	79,00
Philippines	74,28	58,60	50,00	1,21	61,40	62,40	83,00
Poland	54,46	68,30	46,00	0,96	49,70	44,90	83,00

(*Continued*)

Table 14.1 Initial data. (*Continued*)

Country	Environmental pollution index, 1-100 points	Energy trilemma index	Industrial pattern of the economy	Resouce rent in GDP, percent	Adjustment of energy efficiency, 1-100 points	Adjustment of renewable energy, 1-100 points	Environmental requirements, 1-100 points
Portugal	30,89	74,00	31,00	0,35	83,50	78,40	97,00
Qatar	61,06	67,90	70,00	17,95	39,90	27,90	69,00
Rumania	58,42	75,10	49,00	0,85	85,40	68,30	86,00
Russia	62,79	71,20	44,00	10,70	59,20	59,90	66,00
Saudi Arabia	65,09	62,80	63,00	23,76	58,80	31,00	66,00
Serbia	60,32	63,80	40,00	1,31	66,10	52,90	72,00
Singapore	33,48	71,20	46,00	0,00	74,60	53,90	62,00
Slovakia	39,66	75,60	50,00	0,29	82,90	82,60	86,00
Slovenia	24,06	79,20	48,00	0,21	75,10	76,50	93,00
South Africa	57,3	58,90	38,00	5,14	76,20	76,10	83,00

(*Continued*)

Table 14.1 Initial data. (*Continued*)

Country	Environmental pollution index, 1-100 points	Energy trilemma index	Industrial pattern of the economy	Resouce rent in GDP, percent	Adjustment of energy efficiency, 1-100 points	Adjustment of renewable energy, 1-100 points	Environmental requirements, 1-100 points
Republic of Korea (South Korea)	62,48	71,70	62,00	0,03	87,20	83,10	86,00
Spain	39,99	77,00	31,00	0,10	70,60	66,10	97,00
Sri-Lanka	59,14	60,10	43,00	0,14	47,50	55,10	72,00
Sweden	18,09	85,20	36,00	0,54	67,60	80,40	100,00
Switzerland	22,39	85,80	43,00	0,01	68,80	86,70	90,00
Thailand	75,07	64,60	62,00	1,67	59,50	47,00	72,00
Turkey	67,35	64,90	48,00	0,36	62,50	74,70	59,00
Ukraine	65,08	66,00	35,00	4,00	50,70	62,70	69,00

(*Continued*)

Table 14.1 Initial data. (*Continued*)

Country	Environmental pollution index, 1-100 points	Energy trilemma index	Industrial pattern of the economy	Resouce rent in GDP, percent	Adjustment of energy efficiency, 1-100 points	Adjustment of renewable energy, 1-100 points	Environmental requirements, 1-100 points
UAE	51,15	68,30	56,00	13,69	65,20	72,30	72,00
Great Britain	40,56	81,50	27,00	0,44	84,20	90,60	97,00
USA	36,88	77,50	29,00	0,47	82,00	58,40	55,00
Uruguay	44,84	77,2	36	1,6491	62,7	56	86
Vietnam	86,47	58,9	50	2,8614	72	66,7	79

Source: compiled by the author based on the INK dataset, available at: https: //www.archilab.online/data2/861-dataset-korporativnaya-sotsialnaya-otvetstvennost-ustojchivoe-razvitie-i-borba-s-izmeneniem-klimata-imitatrosionnoe- i-nejrosetevoj-analiz-vr.

Table 14.2 Correlation analysis.

	Environmental pollution index, 1-100 points	Energy trilemma index	Industrial pattern of the economy	Resource rent in GDP, percent	Adjust of energy efficiency, 1-100 points	Adjustment of renewable energy, 1-100 points	Environmental requirements, 1-100 points
Environmental pollution index, 1-100 points	1.0						
Energy trilemma index	-0.8	1.0					
Industrial pattern of the economy	0.2	-0.2	1.0				

(Continued)

Table 14.2 Correlation analysis. (*Continued*)

	Environmental pollution index, 1-100 points	Energy trilemma index	Industrial pattern of the economy	Resource rent in GDP, percent	Adjust of energy efficiency, 1-100 points	Adjustment of renewable energy, 1-100 points	Environmental requirements, 1-100 points
Resource rent in GDP, percent	0.2	-0.2	0.5	1.0			
Adjustment of energy efficiency, 1-100 points	-0.5	0.6	-0.1	-0.4	1.0		
Adjustment of renewable energy, 1-100 points	-0.4	0.5	-0.4	-0.6	0.8	1.0	
Environmental requirement, 1-100 points	-0.5	0.5	-0.2	-0.4	0.4	0.5	1.0

Source: drawn by the author.

Table 14.3 Regression analysis of the data.

Regression statistics									
Multiple R	0.8								
R-square	0.7								
Standardized R-square	0.7								
Standard error	12.06								
Observations	75								
Analysis of variance									
	df	SS	MS	F	Significance F				
Regression	3	22,385.36	7,461.79	51,30	0.00				
Residual	71	10,327.82	145.46						
Total	74	32,713.17							

(*Continued*)

Table 14.3 Regression analysis of the data. (*Continued*)

Regression statistics

	Factors	Standard error	t-statistics	P-Value	Lower 95 percent	Upper 95 percent	Lower 95.0 percent	Upper 95.0 percent
Y-intersection	196.14	13.24	14.81	0.00	169.74	222.54	169.74	222.54
Variable X 1	-1.72	0.17	-9.85	0.00	-2.07	-1.37	-2.07	-1.37
Variable X 2	0.04	0.23	0.16	0.88	-0.42	0.49	-0.42	0.49
Variable X 3	-0.29	0.14	-2.05	0.04	-0.57	-0.01	-0.57	-0.01

Source: compiled by the author.

Verification by Fznach gives the same result, since Fznach = 0.000, which is much less than α = 0.05.

Let's check out whether our coefficients are in the confidence intervals:

- 2.07< β1<-1.37, therefore, β1 insignificantly differ from -1.72;
- 0.42< β2<0.49, therefore, β2 insignificantly differ from 0.04;
- 0.57< β3<-0.01, therefore, β3 insignificantly differ from 0.29;

Statistical tests prove the high quality of the ultimate model.

Let's write the final multiple regression equation:

EnvPollution= 196.14-1.72EnTr+0.04NatRent-0.29NatCare+ε,

where **EnvPollution** is the value of the environmental pollution index;

EnTr is the value of the energy trilemma index;

NatRent is the value of resource rent in percent of GDP;

NatCare is the importance of environmental requirements;

ε is an error.

Thus, if the value of the energy trilemma index rises by 1 point, the value of the environmental pollution index decreases by 1.72 points (while other factors remain unchanged).

As the value of environmental protection requirements multiplies by one point, the value of the environmental pollution index drops by 0.29 points on average (while other factors remain unchanged).

With an increase in resource rent, the index of environmental pollution gains 0.04 points on average (while other factors remain unchanged).

Conclusion

The paper proposed a model connecting the index of environmental pollution with the index of the energy trilemma, the share of resource rent in the country's GDP, and the number of environmental requirements.

Changing the model parameters, we can calculate approximate values of the energy trilemma index, the share of resource rent in the country's GDP, and environmental requirements to reach a desired level of the environmental pollution index.

The resulting model makes obvious that changes in the value of the energy trilemma index, i.e., maintaining a balance between environmental protection, energy security, and the availability of energy sources) can greatly reduce the environmental pollution index. Thus, if we make this parameter go up, we will help the country's economy to grow (which is directly related to energy security and the availability of energy) and at the same time will reduce the harm to the environment.

References

1. Guillaume L. *et al.*, 2019. The Sustainable Development Report. Available at: https://www.sustainabledevelopment.report/ (accessed 1 September 2020).
2. Nilsson, M, Griggs, D, Visbeck, M, 2016: "A guide to SDG interactions: from science to implementation." Available at: https://pure.iiasa.ac.at/id/eprint/14591/1/SDGs-Guide-to-Interactions.pdf (accessed 30 September 2020).
3. Electronic resource, available at: https://neftegaz.ru/tech-library/ekologiya-pozharnaya-bezopasnost-tekhnika-bezopasnosti/521106-dekarbonizatsiya-ekonomiki-i-energeticheskikh-sistem/ (published 21 January 2020).
4. J.G.J. Olivier and J.A.H.W. Peters, 2019. Trends in global CO2 and total greenhouse gas emissions: 2019 Report. Available at: https://www.pbl.nl/sites/default/files/downloads/pbl-2020-trends-in-global-CO2-and-total-greenhouse -gas-emissions-2019-report_4068.pdf
5. Dataset "Korporativnaja social'naja otvetstvennost', ustojchivoe razvitie i bor'ba s izmeneniem klimata: imitacionnoe modelirovanie i nejrosetevoj analiz v regionah mira – 2020" [Dataset "Corporate social responsibility, sustainable development and the fight against climate change: simulation and neural network analysis in world regions – 2020"], available at: https://www.archilab.online/data2/861-dataset-korporativnaya-sotsialnaya-otvetstvennost-ustojchivoe-razvitie-i-borba-s-izmeneniem-klimata-imitatsionnoe-modelirovanie-i-nejrosetevoj-analiz-v-regionakh-mira-2020. (accessed 10 August 2020).

About the Editors

Pandian Vasant, PhD, is Editor-in-Chief of the *International Journal of Energy Optimization and Engineering* and senior research associate at MERLIN Research Centre of Ton Duc Thang University, HCMC, Vietnam. He holds a PhD in computational intelligence from UNEM, Costa Rica, and he has co-authored over 300 publications, including research articles in journals, conference proceedings, presentations and book chapters. He has also been a guest editor for various scientific and technical journals, and, in 2009 and 2015, he was awarded top reviewer and outstanding reviewer for one journal. He has 31 years of teaching experience, as well.

Gerhard-Wilhelm Weber, PhD, is a professor at Poznan University of Technology, Poznan, Poland. He received his PhD in mathematics, and economics/business administration, from RWTH Aachen. He held professorships by proxy at University of Cologne, and TU Chemnitz, Germany. At IAM, METU, Ankara, Turkey, he was a professor in the programs of financial mathematics and scientific computing.

J. Joshua Thomas, PhD, has been a senior lecturer at KDU Penang University College, Malaysia since 2008. He obtained his PhD in intelligent systems techniques in 2015 from University Sains Malaysia, Penang, and is an editorial board member for the *International Journal of Energy Optimization and Engineering.* He has also published more than 30 papers in leading international conference proceedings and peer reviewed journals.

Jose A. Marmolejo Saucedo, PhD, is a professor at Pan-American University, Mexico. He received his PhD in operations research at the National Autonomous University of Mexico. He is also an SNI Fellow, Level 2, the second highest country-wide distinction granted by the Mexican National System of Research Scientists for scientific merit. He has co-authored research articles in scientific and scholarly journals, conference proceedings, presentations, books, and book chapters.

Roman Rodriguez-Aguilar, PhD, is a professor in the School of Economic and Business Sciences of the "Universidad Panamericana" in Mexico. He received his PhD at the School of Economics at the National Polytechnic Institute, Mexico. Prior to joining Pan-Americana University, he has worked as a specialist in economics, statistics, simulation, finance, and optimization, occupying different management positions in various public entities such as the Ministry of Energy, Ministry of Finance, and Ministry of Health. H is also an SNI Fellow, Level 2, the second-highest country-wide distinction granted by the Mexican National System of Research Scientists for scientific merit. He has co-authored research articles in scientific and scholarly journals, conference proceedings, presentations, and book chapters.

Index

Also of Interest

Check out these other related titles from Scrivener Publishing

Encyclopedia of Renewable Energy, by James G. Speight, ISBN 9781119363675. Written by a highly respected engineer and prolific author in the energy sector, this is the single most comprehensive, thorough, and up to date reference work on renewable energy. *NOW AVAILABLE!*

ARTIFICIAL INTELLIGENCE AND DATA ANALYTICS FOR EXPLORATION AND PRODUCTION, By Fred Aminzadeh, Cenk Temizel, and Yasin Hajizadeh, ISBN: 9781119879695. The groundbreaking new book is written by some of the foremost authorities on the application of data science and artificial intelligence techniques in exploration and production industry. This volume presents the most comprehensive and updated new processes, concepts, and practical applications in the field. *COMING IN SUMMER 2022!*

RENEWABLE ENERGY FOR SUSTAINABLE GROWTH ASSESSMENT, Edited by Nayan Kumar and Prabhansu, ISBN: 9781119785361. Written and edited by a team of experts in the field, this collection of papers reflects the most up-to-date and comprehensive current state of renewable energy for sustainable growth assessment and provides practical solutions for engineers and scientists. *COMING IN SUMMER 2022!*

SMART GRIDS AND MICROGRIDS: Concepts and Applications, Edited by P. Prajof, S. Mohan Krishna, J. L. Febin Daya, Umashankar Subramaniam, and P. V. Brijesh, ISBN: 9781119760559. Written and edited by a team of experts in the field, this is the most comprehensive and up to date study of smart grids and microgrids for engineers, scientists, students, and other professionals. *NOW AVAILABLE!*

MICROGRID TECHNOLOGIES, Edited by C. Sharmeela, P. Sivaraman, P. Sanjeevikumar, and Jens Bo Holm-Nielsen, ISBN 9781119710790. Covering the concepts and fundamentals of microgrid technologies, this volume, written and edited by a global team of experts, also goes into the practical applications that can be utilized across multiple industries, for both the engineer and the student. *NOW AVAILABLE!*

INTEGRATION OF RENEWABLE ENERGY SOURCES WITH SMART GRIDS, Edited by A. Mahaboob Subahani, M. Kathiresh and G. R. Kanagachidambaresan, ISBN: 9781119750420. Provides comprehensive coverage of renewable energy and its integration with smart grid technologies. *NOW AVAILABLE!*

Green Energy: *Solar Energy, Photovoltaics, and Smart Cities*, edited by Suman Lata Tripathi and Sanjeevikumar Padmanaban, ISBN 9781119760764. Covering the concepts and fundamentals of green energy, this volume, written and edited by a global team of experts, also goes into the practical applications that can be utilized across multiple industries, for both the engineer and the student. *NOW AVAILABLE!*

Energy Storage, edited by Umakanta Sahoo, ISBN 9781119555513. Written and edited by a team of well-known and respected experts in the field, this new volume on energy storage presents the state-of-the-art developments and challenges in the field of renewable energy systems for sustainability and scalability for engineers, researchers, academicians, and other energy professionals. *NOW AVAILABLE!*

Energy Storage 2nd Edition, by Ralph Zito and Haleh Ardibili, ISBN 9781119083597. A revision of the groundbreaking study of methods for storing energy on a massive scale to be used in wind, solar, and other renewable energy systems. *NOW AVAILABLE!*

Hybrid Renewable Energy Systems, edited by Umakanta Sahoo, ISBN 9781119555575. Edited and written by some of the world's top experts in renewable energy, this is the most comprehensive and in-depth volume on hybrid renewable energy systems available, a must-have for any engineer, scientist, or student. *NOW AVAILABLE!*

Progress in Solar Energy Technology and Applications, edited by Umakanta Sahoo, ISBN 9781119555605. This first volume in the new groundbreaking series, Advances in Renewable Energy, covers the latest concepts, trends, techniques, processes, and materials in solar energy, focusing on the state-of-the-art for the field and written by a group of world-renowned experts. *NOW AVAILABLE!*

A Polygeneration Process Concept for Hybrid Solar and Biomass Power Plants: Simulation, Modeling, and Optimization, by Umakanta Sahoo, ISBN 9781119536093. This is the most comprehensive and in-depth study of the theory and practical applications of a new and groundbreaking method for the energy industry to "go green" with renewable and alternative energy sources. *NOW AVAILABLE!*